Praise for Jacqueline Wilson:

Her characters are entirely credible: real
people living difficult lives . . . Wilson is a
natural storyteller . . . compulsive reading
Guardian

A brilliant writer of wit and subtlety
The Times

Literary Superstar
Independent

The triumph of Jacqueline Wilson is her ability
to enter the often multi-layered world of young
women with humour and subtlety yet she succeeds
in never patronising her audience
Liverpool Echo

Has a rare gift for writing lightly and
amusingly about emotional issues
Bookseller

www.kidsatrandomhouse.co.uk

Also available by Jacqueline Wilson

Published in Corgi Pups, for beginner readers:
THE DINOSAUR'S PACKED LUNCH
THE MONSTER STORY-TELLER

Published in Young Corgi, for newly confident readers:
LIZZIE ZIPMOUTH
SLEEPOVERS

Available from Doubleday/Corgi Yearling Books:
BAD GIRLS
THE BED & BREAKFAST STAR
BEST FRIENDS
BURIED ALIVE!
THE CAT MUMMY
CANDYFLOSS
CLEAN BREAK
CLIFFHANGER
THE DARE GAME
THE DIAMOND GIRLS
DOUBLE ACT
GLUBBSLYME
THE ILLUSTRATED MUM
JACKY DAYDREAM
LOLA ROSE
THE LOTTIE PROJECT
MIDNIGHT
THE MUM-MINDER
SECRETS
STARRING TRACY BEAKER
THE STORY OF TRACY BEAKER
THE SUITCASE KID
VICKY ANGEL
THE WORRY WEBSITE

Collections:
THE JACQUELINE WILSON COLLECTION
includes THE STORY OF TRACY BEAKER and
THE BED AND BREAKFAST STAR
JACQUELINE WILSON'S DOUBLE-DECKER
includes BAD GIRLS and DOUBLE ACT
JACQUELINE WILSON'S SUPERSTARS
includes THE SUITCASE KID and THE LOTTIE PROJECT
THE JACQUELINE WILSON BISCUIT BARREL
includes BURIED ALIVE and CLIFFHANGER

Available from Doubleday/Corgi books, for older readers:
DUSTBIN BABY
GIRLS IN LOVE
GIRLS UNDER PRESSURE
GIRLS OUT LATE
GIRLS IN TEARS
LOLA ROSE
LOVE LESSONS
KISS

Jacqueline Wilson

Lola Rose and The Diamond Girls

Illustrated by Nick Sharratt

CORGI BOOKS

JACQUELINE WILSON: LOLA ROSE and THE DIAMOND GIRLS 2-in-1
A CORGI BOOK 978 0 552 55819 8

This collection first published exclusively for Waterstone's in Great Britain
by Corgi Books, an imprint of Random House Children's Books
A Random House Group Company

Collection copyright © Jacqueline Wilson, 2007
Illustration copyright © Nick Sharratt, 2007

1 3 5 7 9 10 8 6 4 2

LOLA ROSE
First published in Great Britain by Doubleday, 2003
Corgi edition published 2004
Corgi edition reissued 2007

Copyright © Jacqueline Wilson, 2003
Illustrations copyright © Nick Sharratt, 2003

THE DIAMOND GIRLS
First published in Great Britain by Doubleday, 2004
Corgi edition published 2005
Corgi edition reissued 2007

Copyright © Jacqueline Wilson, 2004
Illustrations copyright © Nick Sharratt, 2004

The Random House Group Limited makes every effort to ensure that the papers
used in its books are made from trees that have been legally sourced from well-managed
and credibly certified forests. Our paper procurement policy can be found at:
www.randomhouse.co.uk/paper.htm

Set in Garamond
Corgi Books are published by Random House Children's Books,
61–63 Uxbridge Road, London W5 5SA

www.kidsatrandomhouse.co.uk
www.rbooks.co.uk

Addresses for companies within The Random House Group Limited can be found at:
www.randomhouse.co.uk/offices.htm

THE RANDOM HOUSE GROUP Limited Reg. No. 954009

A CIP catalogue record for this book is available from the British Library.

Printed and bound in Great Britain by
Cox & Wyman Ltd, Reading, Berkshire

Lola Rose

Jacqueline Wilson

In memory of Zoe Biller
a very special girl

One

Have you ever wondered what you'd do if you won the lottery?

My mum won. She did, really. OK, she didn't win the jackpot. We don't live in a great big mansion. I wouldn't want to even if Mum had won mega-millions. I'd hate to live in a big house with heaps of rooms. You'd never be able to keep track of everyone. Someone could be creeping along the corridor ready to get you and you'd never know.

I'd like a really small house. A caravan would be even better. It could be ultra-luxurious, with purple velvet fitted sofas and matching purple curtains

7

and purple satin sheets on the bunk beds. We could even have a huge purple glass plate piled high with big purple bars of Cadbury's milk chocolate for us to nibble on any time we fancy. But it would have this never-fail alarm system if anyone approached. Then I'd strap Kenny and me to the sofa and Mum would jump in the purple Ferrari permanently hooked to the caravan and whizz us off to safety at hundreds of miles an hour.

Mum didn't win the lottery on the television. She won with a scratch card. I'm not talking ten pounds though. *Ten thousand!*

She looked at the card in the street and she gave this great whoop. She picked my little brother Kenny up and whirled him round and round until he squealed. She couldn't pick me up too because my mum's quite little and I'm big for my age, but she gave me a huge hug and kissed me on both cheeks and then on the tip of my nose too, which made me giggle.

'Right, let's get back inside the shop,' she said. 'We're going to spend spend spend! Only don't tell old Sid behind the counter. He's such a gossip he'll tell everyone on the whole estate and then the next time we're down the pub we'll be buying drinks all round for people we haven't met before.'

'Right, Mum,' I said. I gave Kenny a little nudge. 'Are you taking this in, chum? Keep that little lip zipped.'

Kenny giggled and acted out zipping his lip. Then we went back in the shop.

'Come for another scratch card, Nikki?' said old

Sid, shaking his head. 'You mums and your lottery cards!'

'Yeah, right, tragic, isn't it?' said Mum. 'And no one round here ever wins, do they?'

She caught my eye and grinned. Kenny grinned too. He opened his mouth.

'*Zip!*' I hissed, and hustled him over to the ice-cream cabinet.

'I've decided to pack in buying scratch cards altogether,' said Mum. 'So I'm going to spend my lottery money on treats for the kids. OK, Jayni, Kenny, what are you having?'

I chose a white Magnum and a tube of Rolos and a packet of marshmallows and a giant bar of Cadbury's fruit and nut and a bottle of Coke and a *Girltalk* and a *Doll Collector* and a *Puppies and Kittens* because they all have good pictures for my scrapbook.

Kenny chose a small red ice lolly and a *Thomas the Tank Engine* comic.

'You can have more than that, Kenny. Anything. Sweets, chocolate, more comics, whatever you want.'

'I don't want whatever. I want my lolly and my comic, like always,' said Kenny.

'But you can choose *more*, Kenny.'

'I can't choose,' said Kenny, starting to sound upset.

'Oh, leave him be, Jayni,' said Mum.

She had no problem choosing a *Hello!* and an *OK!* and a *Cosmo* and a big fat *Vogue* and a bottle of diet Coke and a large pack of posh ciggies.

'I thought you were buying treats for the kids,' said Sid.

'Yeah, well, I'm a kid at heart too,' said Mum, paying him.

She used up nearly all the money in her purse but she'd get the £10,000 soon and then we'd be laughing.

'I should be so lucky, lucky, lucky, lucky,' Mum sang, to the old Kylie song. She did a little dance, shaking her hips and sticking her chest out, twirling Sid's carrier bag full of goodies. She took Kenny's hand and mine and made us dance too, even though it was hard for us to hang onto our ice creams. Kenny nearly stuck his lolly up his nose every time he tried to take a lick.

A lorry driver hooted when he saw Mum dancing. He yelled something and Mum laughed and waggled her bum at him.

I just love it when Mum laughs. She tosses her soft blonde hair and opens her mouth and shows all her lovely white teeth. They're little and even and pearly white even though she smokes lots of fags. She doesn't have any fillings. I've got five already.

Mum turns heaps of heads even when she's not dancing around. She did a bit of modelling when she was younger. She's got her own scrapbook with pages cut out of newspapers and magazines. We're not supposed to look, Kenny and me, because Mum isn't wearing a lot and some of the poses are quite sexy.

I've tried locking the bathroom door and

stripping down to my knickers and trying out some of those poses myself. I look *ridiculous*. I'm as tall as my mum but I haven't got a proper figure. It doesn't go in and out in the right places. My hair's wrong too, even though I've grown it past my shoulders at long last. It's boring old mouse and Mum says I can't have it highlighted her colour blonde until I'm a teenager. It costs a fortune to have it done properly.

Up until the day Mum won the lottery we were always strapped for cash. Mum had to stop modelling when she got married because Dad didn't like it.

'I'm not having other guys ogling my wife,' he said. 'You're giving it up, Nikki, understand?'

Mum understood. You don't argue with my dad.

I wondered if Mum was going to tell Dad about the lottery money. I knew we should keep our mouths zipped with him too. But Mum was so so so stupid when it came to dealing with Dad. She'd do anything for him, give him anything, do exactly what he said. It was partly because she was scared of him. But it was also because she was still crazy about him. He's so good-looking, my dad, lean and tall, with deep blue eyes and a great tangle of black, wavy hair. Everyone thinks he looks incredible, it's not just us. Lots of the women on our estate were nuts about him. Even some of the girls at school acted like he was a rock star.

He was once. Well, he used to sing in this band, the Mad Beggars. They didn't make any actual albums but they sold their own tapes at all their gigs. They played in pubs and clubs all over the city.

Mum went along one night with her mates and stood at the front, right underneath my dad on the stage.

'And I fell in love, *whoomph*, just like that,' Mum said, snapping her fingers.

Dad was the one who snapped his fingers. She went off with him that night. She's been with him ever since.

Dad's band broke up after a year or so. Dad had a fight with the lead guitarist. It looked like Dad and Mum might break up too because Dad didn't really want to be tied down with a steady girlfriend. But Mum told him I was on the way.

'You brought us together again, Jayni,' she said.

That's why my name's spelt in such a weird way. They called me after both of them. My dad's called Jay and Mum's Nikki.

I might have brought them together but I cried a lot as a kid and it got on my dad's nerves so he cleared off once or twice. Then Mum cried a lot too. She loved him so much even though he'd started hitting her by this time. She hit back at first but then he hit harder.

He hit other people too. He ended up doing time in prison for GBH. We went to see him once a month, Mum and me. I remember he was very sweet to us then. He made a big fuss of me, telling me I was his pretty little princess, though I was this plain, podgy kid with no front teeth at that stage. That's the really scary thing about my dad. He can make you feel so special – but he can also smash your face in.

I knew it was wicked but I wished he could stay in prison for ever. He was safe behind bars and we were safe at home. But he got out eventually, even though he had to serve his full term because he kept getting into fights.

For a week or so it was like Mum and Dad were on their second honeymoon. Dad made a big fuss of me too. He bought Mum a huge bouquet of red roses and he bought me a big bunch of purple freesias. He bought Mum a bottle of pink champagne with a pink ribbon round it and he bought me a bottle of Ribena with a purple ribbon. He bought Mum a huge box of white cream chocolates and he bought me a giant bar of Cadbury's, so big I could hardly hold it in my two hands. But it all started to go wrong when I was only halfway through the chocolate.

Dad thought Mum was flaunting herself when they went out to this club and he hit her when they got home. He started to hit her if a man so much as looked at her. He was convinced she'd had all these boyfriends when he was in prison.

He'd ask me about it, over and over. He shouted with his face up really close so his spit sprayed all over me. I told him that Mum only had eyes for him but he wouldn't believe me. He went on hitting Mum even though she was now pregnant with Kenny.

Mum called him Kenneth, after her dad. This was a bit weird of her, because we never ever went to visit my grandad or grandma or Mum's older sister, Auntie Barbara. Grandad told Mum he never wanted to see her again when she went off with Dad. He said she was throwing herself away. He insisted my dad was Trouble with a capital T.

I suppose my grandad was right. But he was wrong the way he treated Mum. And us. He didn't want to see Kenny even though he was named after him. He didn't even say much to Mum and Kenny and me when we went to see Grandma in hospital when she was dying of cancer.

It was worse at the funeral. Mum tried to hug Grandad afterwards but he pushed her away. He said it was all her fault Grandma got ill. It was the shame of having her daughter living with a vicious criminal.

We haven't seen him since. It was a waste of time lumbering Kenny with such a duff name. It will be much worse when he's old enough to watch *South Park*.

Dad was OK for a bit after Kenny was born. We've got a photo taken on a day at the seaside and Dad's got baby Kenny on his shoulders, a little skinny knee either side of his cheeks. Kenny looks scared stiff but he's clinging grimly to Dad's long hair. Mum is laughing up at him, holding a beach ball. She's wearing a bikini top and a tiny skirt, showing off her pierced belly button. Her tummy is as flat as a pancake even after having Kenny and me.

I'm standing by her side. I'm wearing a bikini top and a tiny skirt too. This is a BIG mistake. My tummy isn't like a pancake. I look as if I've *swallowed* a beach ball.

Dad loved having a son. As soon as Kenny could toddle he was kicking a ball to him and taking him down the pub. Kenny struggled so hard to kick the ball back he usually fell over, and he drank so many Cokes and lemonades down at the pub trying to drink pint for pint with Dad that he often wet himself on the way home.

Dad was surprisingly gentle with him. He didn't even get cross when Kenny cried. He refused to acknowledge that our Kenny was the wimpiest little kid on the whole estate.

'He's a holy terror, my lad Kenny,' Dad would boast, holding Kenny high above his head until he squealed. 'Growing up into a regular little bruiser, scrapping all over the place. He'll be banned from his nursery school if we don't watch out.'

Kenny did get into fights at nursery, but it was with the little girls. He wanted to squeeze into the playhouse with thcm. They weren't having any so they hit him with the plastic teapot and gave him a black eye.

Dad even boasted to the teachers when Kenny started in reception that they'd have their work cut out coping with *his* little lad.

I'm the one who had her work cut out coping with Kenny. I'd sneak over to the babies' playground to find Kenny trailing around by himself, head drooping. The other little kids would push him over just for the fun of it, leaving him snivelling, rubbing his eyes with his grazed hands, blood trickling down into his socks. He'd scream if the teachers or dinner ladies went near him. I was the one who had to pick him up and mop him.

I do all the mopping up. I remember when Mum really was playing around with this guy she met up the park. He was running, training because he was in some reserve football team. He looked a *bit* like David Beckham.

I caught him with Mum when I came home early from school because I'd been sick. Mum made out he'd just popped in for a coffee, but they looked all hot and rumpled.

I was sick again because I was so scared. I didn't see how she could take such a crazy risk. I knew Dad was up north for a couple of weeks on some dodgy-sounding business trip but he had lots of mates spying for him and telling him if his missus was playing around.

'Are you *crazy*, Mum?' I said.

'I can't help it, Jayni. He made me feel like a girl again,' said Mum, her cheeks bright pink. 'It's not been right between me and your dad, not for a long time.'

'But Dad'll kill you if he finds out,' I said.

'He *won't* find out. Well. Not yet.'

'You can't tell him!'

My stomach churned. Mum could be so stupid. I knew that look in her eyes. She was telling herself a little fairy tale. The footballer would clasp her to his six-pack chest and tell her he'd been picked to play for Manchester United and would she be his bride in the million-pound mansion that he'd just bought. Plus he'd take Kenny and me too. Mum drifted into Dreamworld and went shopping with Victoria Beckham every day while Kenny and I asked Brooklyn and Romeo round to play with all our new toys . . .

'Mum!' I wanted to shake her. I knew her footballer. He had a different girl every week. He'd never stick with Mum. And he wouldn't want Kenny and me tagging along. Anyway, even if it all came true, even the Man U part, Mum couldn't possibly live happily ever after. Dad would smash his way through the big picture window and tear the footballer's head off his shoulders and then he'd beat her until the fluffy white carpets turned red.

I hated saying this to Mum but I had to make her see sense. Then Dad heard some rumour anyway and came straight back home. You could tell by the way he banged the front door that this was it. Big trouble.

He didn't start straight away. He asked Mum questions, his voice very quiet, very soft. 'Come on, Nikki, don't look so scared. I just want you to tell me I've got it all wrong. If I have, then fine, I'll drop it straight away. I'm a reasonable guy, aren't I?' Then, suddenly yelling, *'Aren't I?'*

Mum panicked. She gabbled that he'd got it all wrong, she'd never so much as looked at another man, though of course she couldn't help being lonely while Dad was away, but even so she'd never dream of talking to any other guy, let alone ask them in for a coffee . . .' Any minute now she'd be letting it all out, telling him everything.

I wished I were as little as Kenny. He always hid under his bed, clamping his hands over his ears so he couldn't hear. I had to listen, even though I couldn't bear it.

Dad took much longer than usual. He said he was teaching her a lesson she'd never forget.

When he'd finished he stormed off out again. I ran to Mum. I wondered if I should call an ambulance. She couldn't speak because her mouth was all bloody and swollen but she shook her head when she saw me pick up the phone. She'd been up to the hospital several times in the past. She never told on Dad, she always said she'd tripped or walked into a lamppost, but Dad got even madder if he found out.

I mopped her up as best I could, holding a cold flannel to her poor face. I cried all over her. I felt so bad that I hadn't been able to protect her.

She couldn't go out for a week because of the bruises. Not just on her face. I saw her in the bath. Her breasts and stomach were black.

I looked at my mum then and knew I hated my dad.

'Don't tell Dad about the lottery money,' I begged Mum.

'Don't worry, I'm keeping quiet. Lips zipped, like I said.'

She asked for it in five-pound notes so it looked as impressive as possible.

'We're in the money!' she sang, tossing handfuls of fivers in the air. They fluttered like big blue butterflies, sticking in her hair, catching on her clothes, landing all over the carpet.

'Mum, stop it, you'll lose some!' I said, trying to gather them up.

'You win some, you lose some,' Mum laughed, tossing more.

Kenny laughed too, kicking his way through a pile of notes as if they were autumn leaves.

'Leave *off*, Kenny,' I said.

But I started to get carried away too, scooping the money up and then scattering it again. These crisp new notes didn't seem real. I thought of the picture of the denim jacket lined with soft pink fur I'd cut out and stuck in my scrapbook. I knew if I could only own such a garment I might have a chance of looking as little and cute and blonde as the girl model.

'What are you dreaming of buying, Jayni, eh?' said Mum, putting her arm round me. She rubbed her soft cheek against mine.

'Well, there's this jacket—' I started. Then I swallowed. 'No, it's your money, Mum. You already treated us in Sid's.'

'Don't be so daft. What's mine is yours. And yours too, Kenny. What do you want, my little pal?' Mum asked.

'A comic and a red ice lolly,' said Kenny.

We groaned at him.

'Something else, Kenny. Something big. Like a denim jacket with fur.'

'I'd like a jacket like Dad's. Leather!' said Kenny, his eyes shining. 'Then I'd look a big boy. Big and tough.'

'You, big and tough, matie?' I said, picking him up and blowing a raspberry on his tummy.

'What about Dad?' said Kenny, squealing. 'What's he getting?'

I looked at Mum. She sighed and started gathering up the money. I set Kenny down and started helping her.

'We're not telling Dad, Kenny,' I said, smoothing the five-pound notes, assembling them into neat rectangles.

'*Why?*'

I looked at Mum.

'Why aren't we telling him, Jayni?' she said.

'Because we know what he's *like*. He could take it all for himself and waste it on some business deal that goes wrong. Or he could take it down the betting shop, or go away on a bender with his mates – and it's your money, Mum.'

'Yeah, but maybe it's not fair, if we're all having presents,' said Mum. 'Here, I could kid on I just won a bit, right, and then hide the rest.'

'He'll find out and then he'll be furious. And then he'll start.'

'Yeah, OK,' said Mum flatly. 'Right. Well, we'll be sensible. I'll put the money in a building society and save it for a rainy day. And you won't get your new jackets, kids, but we can't make your dad suspicious – isn't that right, Jayni?'

'Yes,' I said, putting the money in her bag.

I hated it that I had to be the one to be sensible. And I ached for that denim jacket.

'Can't I have my leather jacket like Dad's?' said Kenny.

'No, love. Jayni says we can't,' said Mum.

It wasn't fair. I hate the way Mum twists things sometimes. She tries to turn *me* into the mum. Then she blames me for spoiling things.

I threw the rest of the money at her and went off to my bedroom to work on my scrapbook. I started cutting up my new magazines, though Kenny had been at my scissors and they were all gummed up with sellotape. I picked all the mucky little sticky bits off the blades, my teeth clenched. Then I carefully cut out a Victorian doll with a purple crinoline. I snipped my way round every little twist and turn of her full frock and steered very slowly around her tiny button boots and cut in and out of her fiddly little fingers. I pretended I was a Victorian girl in a big purple dress and this was my matching doll. I had a little brother who was very obedient and adored his elder sister. We didn't have a papa.

Then I cut out a tiny, toffee-brown cocker spaniel puppy with very floppy ears and a Siamese kitten with a delicate heart-shaped face and big blue eyes. These were our pets, Toffee and Bluebell. I cut some flowers from my birthday card box and a blue sky background and then I tried to draw a big Victorian house because I couldn't find a proper picture of one anywhere. I'm not very good at drawing so I just did a rough outline of a big house. I cut out girls' faces from *Girltalk* and stuck them looking out of all the windows, bordered by wax crayon purple velvet curtains. These were all my very best friends, Charlotte, Victoria, Emily, Evangeline and Jemima. It took me ages to think up special Victorian names.

I was so lost in my scrapbook world that I didn't hear the front door bang. I didn't know my dad was home until I heard him call, 'Where's my princess then?'

I shut my scrapbook up quick and shot into the living room. It's never a good idea to keep my dad waiting. But he'd called me princess, which was a promising sign. He might be in a good mood.

He smiled as I rushed into the room. 'There's my girl!' he said, beckoning me over to his armchair. Kenny was already on his knee. Mum was snapping open a can of beer and pouring it for him.

'Great, isn't it, Dad's home early,' she said.

I breathed in. 'Hi, Daddy,' I said in this false small-girly voice.

'Hi, Princess,' Dad said, and he patted the arm of his chair.

I perched there obediently. I stretched a smile across my face while my eyes swivelled all round the room, looking for a forgotten fiver on the rug, under the coffee table, tucked in the telly mags. I couldn't see any but I still couldn't breathe out comfortably. Dad was in a good mood, but he could turn in seconds. You never knew what might set him off. Some silly little thing you said – sometimes just a look, sometimes it seemed like no reason at all. It was as if Dad's head was wired up weirdly and every so often he was programmed to explode.

But today he seemed mellow, even though he said he'd had a row at work so he'd walked out. 'And about time too. Who wants their poxy job?' he said.

Three months ago, when he'd started working there, he'd had us all reciting that it was the best job ever, his Fresh Start.

He was making another Fresh Start now. He'd met an old mate down the pub at lunch time who was setting up his own minicab firm. He wanted Dad to join his team of drivers.

'Will he provide the car, like?' Mum asked.

'No, I've got to get the wheels, babe.'

Mum always softened when Dad called her babe. She forgot that he could also call her a dozy cow or worse.

'Still, that shouldn't present too many problems. There's a mate of mine wants rid of a very nice little Escort, two years old, not much mileage to speak of. He'll let me have it dirt cheap too. I've just got to raise a few thousand. I'll get a loan off someone, just you wait and see, babe. My luck's changed. I can feel it.' He reached out and patted Mum on her bum.

'Jay!' She laughed at him – and I felt my stomach screw up in a knot. She was looking at him like he'd suddenly turned into a handsome prince. 'It *is* our lucky day,' she said.

She was going to blow it. She was going to tell him.

Don't! I mouthed at her. She just blinked at me, pretending she hadn't seen.

'You'll never ever guess what, Jay,' she said. She went to her handbag and fanned out a great handful of fivers. 'Here's your car money, darling. I won it on a scratch card! There'll be enough for treats for all of us. Our Kenny wants a little leather jacket just like his dad. Jayni wants one of them denim jackets lined with fur – *pink* fur, isn't that right, pet?'

I had to smile and say yes and act all excited.

I was scared it was going to go horribly wrong. Dad paused, staring at the money in Mum's handbag. You could see his brain going tick, tick, tick. But then he threw Kenny right up in the air and caught him and whirled him round. He pulled me up too and we danced round and round and then he danced with Mum, giving her a great big movie-star kiss, telling her she was his Lady Luck.

We went out for our tea to T.G.I. Friday's to celebrate. Mum and Dad had fancy cocktails and then we ordered this h-u-g-e meal. I started to wonder if it was going to be all right after all. Dad was larking about and cracking jokes and flirting with the waitress. I wanted to believe in fairy tales and have fun too. I ate all my giant burger and chips and then an entire Death by Chocolate.

These women on an office outing came over to Dad, as giggly as girls, and asked if he was Jay Fenton who used to sing with the Mad Beggars. When Dad said he was they all squealed. The prettiest one with the lowest-cut top stuck her head up close and asked if he'd give them a little song now. They were having a great night out but this would be the icing on the cake.

'I'll be the cherry on top of the icing, darling,' said Dad, and he went over to their table and sang to them all.

Mum drained her glass of wine and then ordered another bottle. '*What?*' she snapped when she saw me looking at her. 'Those women are buying your dad drinks, look.'

I didn't want to look. I hated it when Mum and Dad drank lots because it always ended up in a fight. I buried my head in the menu instead, though I was so full up I had to undo the top button of my jeans. I read each meal description very carefully. I wished I could cut out some of the pictures for my scrapbook.

I used to play this game with Kenny – I'd find a picture in a magazine of a big chocolate cake with layers of thick cream and I'd reach out my finger and touch the paper cake and pretend to lick the cream off my finger, going, 'Yum yum yum'. Sometimes it seemed like I could taste the cake, feel the smooth cream and the sponge crumbs on my tongue.

Kenny would beg me for a piece of cake. I'd hold the page out to him. He'd stab his fingers all over the slippery paper, trying to reach through into the soft cake. He'd suck hard at his fingers but he could never imagine it for himself. 'I want the *cake*!' he'd wail.

'God, you're not still hungry?' Mum said, pouring the new bottle of wine.

'God, you're not still *thirsty*?' I said.

'Don't you go all snippy with me, miss,' said Mum, giving me a kick under the table. She was wearing her best black high heels with very pointy toes.

'That *hurt*, Mum!'

'Rubbish,' said Mum, but she reached under the table and rubbed my shin. 'There, that better?' She was leaning so far forward she overbalanced and ended up *under* the table.

'Whoops!' She tried to get up and banged her head. She started half laughing, half crying.

'Mum!' I hissed, trying to hook her out.

'Mum!' said Kenny, giggling, thinking it was a big joke. He slid off his chair and squatted beside her, going, 'Shh!' as if it were a game of hide and seek.

'Oh please, get *up*, Kenny. Mum, Dad will see. Quick!'

She couldn't be quick to save her life. She just crouched there, clutching Kenny, tickling him now. Dad was looking our way. I gave him a sickly grin, waving like everything was all right. Dad stopped singing and came over to us.

'What the hell . . . ?'

'Kenny fell under the table. Mum's just trying to pick him up,' I gabbled.

'Dad! Dad, we're hiding!' Kenny squealed.

'Well, now I've found you, and you're coming up out of there, my lad,' said Dad. He seized him under the arms and pulled. Kenny came up laughing and kicking.

'Mind your drink, Kenny!' I said, grabbing it just in time.

'What about *my* drink?' Mum said, trying to crawl out on her hands and knees.

'What are you playing at, Nikki? Are you drunk?' said Dad.

'No – but what a good idea! Let's all get drunk to celebrate. I'm Lady Luck, that's what I am,' Mum said, hauling herself up. Her hair was all tousled and her mascara was smudged.

'You look a right mess,' said Dad. 'Come on, let's go home. Jump to it.'

We jumped. I was scared all the way home, wondering what was coming. There was this awful Voice of Doom in my head. *He's going to beat her up.*

Maybe Mum could hear the voice too. She started singing to shut it up, all her favourite old pop songs. Then Kenny started whimpering and Mum picked him up, balancing him on her hip, singing 'Mr Sandman'. She used to sing it to me when I was little, very softly, very slowly, and whenever she came to the 'lend me your ear' bit she'd nuzzle it, pretending she was going to nibble it right off. It always soothed me and made me go to sleep. But Mum's voice was too high and wobbly now. Dad didn't join in the singing. He didn't say a word all the way home.

The first thing he did when he got in was pour himself a large glass of whisky. He drank it back like tap water.

'Right! Here we are. Our happy little family. Lucky us, won the lottery. Only it just suddenly occurs to me, Nikki, you've been acting a bit odd about all this. Why didn't you tell me right away, eh? Why didn't you yell it out the minute I got in? Were you going to keep it a secret? Were you going to keep quiet about the cash, keep it all for yourself, eh? Or maybe you were going to spend it on lover boy? Your little footballing chum. Still in touch, are we?'

'Of course not, Jay. You're the only guy for me, you know that,' Mum said. She was still clutching Kenny. 'Look, let me tuck Kenny up, OK? And you get to bed too, Jayni.'

'Oh yes, to give you time to make up a few excuses,' said Dad. 'I wouldn't bother, Nikki. I'll get the truth out of you one way or another.'

Mum carried Kenny out of the room. She called to me to come too.

'Are you deaf, Jayni?' said Dad. 'Get to bed.'

I wanted to go to bed and pull the covers right up over my head. But I didn't go. 'I'm staying up, Dad,' I said.

'You what?' said Dad. Nobody ever spoke back to him. Especially not me.

'You heard me, Dad,' I said. My mouth was so dry the words were whispers. My chocolate pudding stirred round and round in my stomach.

'Get to bed this instant, you cheeky little cow,' said Dad. He got out of his chair and raised his hand.

I wanted to be brave but I couldn't help squealing then. I didn't make much noise but Mum came running. She saw us, Dad's hand in the air, me ducking, like we were both stuck playing a grim game of statues.

'Get to *bed*, Jayni!' Mum said.

'I'm staying here,' I cried.

'What's got into you?' Dad said.

'It's you! You spoil everything! Even a lovely thing like Mum winning the lottery. It's all spoilt because of you and your moods and your shouting and your hitting. I *knew* you'd be like this. Why can't you be like a real dad?' I yelled.

Dad's head jerked as if *I'd* hit *him*. He stood still, shaking his head, as if he couldn't quite work it out. I think that's why he hit me. He didn't know what else to do.

It was a slap across my face that lifted me right off my feet. I ended up flat on my back on the carpet. Mum leapt at Dad, scratching his face with her long nails. He punched her and then when she was on the ground beside me he kicked her. Then he spat at both of us and walked out. The door slammed behind him.

'Oh, Jayni, let's look at you,' said Mum, kneeling beside me.

'I'm ... OK. He hit you more, much more.'

'Can you get up, darling? We've got to be quick,' Mum said, pulling at me. Her nose was bleeding and she wiped it impatiently with the back of her hand. 'Come on, sweetheart! I need you to help me pack.'

'What?' I stared at Mum. I didn't know what she was talking about.

She cupped my burning face with her hands. 'We're not staying. Now he's started on you he won't stop. I'm not having that. We're running away!'

Three

Running Away

I stared at Mum.

'*How* can we run away?'

'Easy. I've still got the ten thousand pounds in my handbag. Well, we're about fifty quid down because of the meal, but never mind. Thank God I didn't give it to him for that stupid car. OK, OK, *I'm* the big stupid. He said he'd knock some sense into me – and he has, he has. I'm not having him using you as a punchbag, kiddo. Come *on*, then. You are up for it, aren't you?'

'Yes! Yes, of course I am. But he'll go berserk when he finds us.'

'He won't. We'll get right away, you and me and Kenny. A completely fresh start. So come on. Pack a bag, just a little one you can carry. And do one for Kenny too while I go through all my stuff.'

'Mum . . . this isn't a game, is it?'

'Do I look like I'm playing a blooming game?' said Mum, wiping her nose again. 'He'll be down the pub till closing time but we want to be well away then. So come on, Jayni, jump to it.'

So I jumped. I ran into our bedroom and snapped on the light. I looked weird in the mirror, one side of my face bright red where Dad had hit me, one side chalk-white. Kenny blinked in the sudden bright light and tried to pull the duvet over his head.

'No, Kenny, we're getting up. Come on, you've got to get dressed.'

'But it's night time.'

'Yes, but we're going out again.'

'With Dad?'

'No, just you and me and Mum.' I hauled him out of bed and hugged his little squirmy body hard. 'And you're going to be a big big boy and help.'

Kenny reached out and touched my red cheek. 'Ouch!'

'Will it get right again?' said Kenny.

'Of course it will. Now!' I stood him on the floor and looked at him. He was still wearing his T-shirt and pants and socks. I had a brainwave. I rummaged in his drawer. 'Put these on then, OK?' I said, thrusting more pants and socks at him. '*Over* the other ones. And another T-shirt. And then there's your red jumper, you like that, and the blue Thomas the Tank Engine one, and your jeans . . . We'll have to pack a spare pair, we'll never get another lot on over the top.'

Kenny started giggling hysterically as I shoved as many clothes on him as I could. He waddled about so comically I couldn't help laughing too, though my heart was going thump thump because I was so scared Dad might come back and catch us.

'What are you kids *laughing* at? Come *on*,' Mum called urgently.

I set Kenny to packing his favourite toys in his school bag and started on my own clothes. It was easier for me. All my stuff was getting too small and tight and made me look far too fat. I hated nearly everything. I was already wearing my favourite outfit, my purple velvet skirt and my black grown-up top. I shoved a big black cardie on over the top and then my horrible padded white jacket, which made me look like a snowman – but never mind, I could get the denim jacket now we had lots of money.

I packed my underwear and my jeans and my pink top with the hearts and my suede boots which rubbed a lot but I still loved them. Then I remembered my pyjamas, and my old bear Pinkie was tangled up inside them. All her fur's worn smooth and shiny and she's lost an eye which gives her a lopsided expression. She's really tatty now and I'm too old for teddies anyway but I still crammed her into my bag.

Kenny was making even sillier choices, shoving

a yoyo without any string and broken crayons and a jigsaw set with half the pieces missing into his school bag, but forgetting his new wax crayons and little Bob, the blue bear he's had since he was born. I repacked for him, and then jiggled my own stuff around, packing a big carrier bag with my scrapbook and my new magazines and scissors and sellotape and Pritt.

'We're done, Mum,' I said, going into her bedroom.

She looked as if she was in fast forward, rushing round like crazy, ransacking her wardrobe and her chest of drawers. Her nose still wouldn't stop bleeding. It made a garish trail past her lips, down her chin, dripping onto her blue top.

'Your best blue top, Mum!'

'It'll wash out. I'll leave it on. Though it looks a mess. Should I just dump it?' Mum stood still, suddenly freeze-framed.

'Put a sweater over it. I've got Kenny wearing half his clothes,' I said.

'You're a clever kid,' said Mum.

She didn't think me so clever when she saw my carrier bag. 'You can't drag that along too, Jayni!'

It was one of those big strong fifteen-pence supermarket carriers but my scrapbook only just fitted inside. It's a huge, old-fashioned accounts book with hundreds of pages. I bought it for a pound two years ago at a car boot fair. It is my most valued possession. Mum knew this, but she still argued.

'You can't take that great big thing, not when

you've got your own bag, and you'll probably have to carry Kenny's too.'

'I'll carry it all, I promise. I *have* to have my scrapbook.'

'You could start a new one.'

'I need this one. It's got all my best ever pictures. I *have* to take it, Mum.'

'Oh, for God's sake, do as you're *told*!' Mum shouted. Then she stopped, her hand over her mouth.

We heard footsteps walking along the balcony towards our flat.

'He's back!' Mum hissed, and we clutched each other.

But the footsteps went past our front door and on down the balcony. Mum breathed out and tapped her hand over her heart. Then she gave me a quick pat on the shoulders. 'OK, OK, take the bloody scrapbook. Let's just get *out* of here, quick.'

She got her suitcase and her handbag, still wadded tight with five-pound notes. We hung Kenny's heavy satchel over his small shoulders. I grabbed my own school bag and the scrapbook carrier. We looked round the flat one quick last time.

Kenny suddenly wailed that he wanted to take Bubble, our goldfish. I promised him he could have a whole tank of tropical fish in our new place but Kenny wouldn't be diverted. He started howling, his arms round Bubble's bowl.

'Oh God, what next?' said Mum. She poured some water into a polythene bag and tipped Bubble

into it. 'OK, he's coming too,' she said. 'Now, let's
go.'

So we went, staggering along the balcony and
down in the lift. I was terrified we'd walk out
and bump straight into Dad but there was no sign
of him, or any of his mates.

'They'll still be in the pub, with any luck,' said
Mum. 'Still, the sooner we scarper the better.'

A taxi drew up down the road and three old
ladies got out, back from their bingo.

'Hey! Hey, taxi!' Mum yelled.

She nodded at me proudly, as if she'd summoned
it up herself out of thin air. The taxi driver shook
his head at us as we hobbled towards him. He
shook his head again when he saw Mum's bloody
nose.

'Do you want the hospital, love?'

'No, the railway station, please,' Mum said
briskly. She wiped her nose. 'Walked straight into a
lamppost, didn't I?'

The taxi driver raised his eyebrows but didn't
comment. My cheek had calmed down now,
though it still hurt. My teeth felt funny too. I hoped
they weren't going to fall out. Still, it might make
my cheeks look hollow. I hated my fat face.

The taxi driver was peering at Kenny and his
bag. 'What you got there, son? Is it a baby shark?'

'No, it's a goldfish,' said Kenny.

'It's never!' said the taxi driver. 'Well, I'm not
supposed to carry no livestock. That's what a gold-
fish is, livestock. So he'll have to swim his own way
through the puddles to the railway station, right?'

Kenny's face crumpled.

'He's joking, Kenny,' I said, pushing him into the taxi.

'I didn't mean to set him off. It's just my funny way,' said the taxi driver.

'That's OK, mate,' said Mum, getting in after us. 'But can you kind of step on it?'

'Sure. What time's your train, then?' he said.

Mum hesitated. 'Not quite sure. But we're running late, I know that.'

We set off, round the estate, down the road, right past The Albert, Dad's pub. Mum and I looked at each other. Mum slid down in her seat. I did too, pushing Kenny's head down.

'You're hurting me, Jayni,' he complained.

'Well, scrunch down, Kenny. Go on, right down,' I urged.

'*Why?*'

The taxi driver was staring at us in the mirror, sucking his teeth, sussing out the situation. We sat up properly when we were past the pub. Mum peered in her powder compact, wiping her nose and rubbing all the smudged mascara off her eyes.

'Look, love, I know it's none of my business . . .' the taxi driver started.

'Yeah, that's right,' said Mum, powdering her swelling face.

'It's obvious your old man's given you a right going over. Why not go to the police?'

'Them!' Mum said a very rude word. 'They're useless when there's a domestic. Oh yeah, they might arrest him, but they're not going to keep him banged up down the station, are they? And he's not going to be in a very nice mood when he gets back home, is he?'

'Yeah, well, I suppose you've got a point. So, you're doing a runner, are you, you and the kids?'

'I don't want to talk about it,' said Mum. She started biting the skin around her thumb. 'Not in front of the kids, eh?'

I knew this was just a ploy to get him to shut up, but I resented it all the same. I wasn't a *kid*, not like Kenny. I knew what was going on all right. I knew as much as Mum anyway.

We got to the station and Mum paid the driver. She struggled to hide the contents of her handbag but he spotted some of the fivers. He raised his eyebrows.

'Strewth, have you just robbed a bank, girl?'

'Wouldn't you like to know,' said Mum, standing on the pavement while I hauled Kenny out and then all our bags.

'Thelma and Louise all rolled into one, that's me.' She put two fingers together and cocked her thumb. 'Bang!' she said, aiming at the taxi driver's head.

He laughed and ducked. 'I'm not arguing with you, then. Still, best of luck.'

Mum gave him extra as a tip. 'You won't say where you dropped us off if anyone asks?' she said, serious now.

The driver ran his finger over his lips to show they were sealed. Mum stared after him as he drove off.

'Nice guy, that,' she muttered wistfully.

I could see the story going on in her head. The taxi driver would suddenly turn back, tell us to hop in and take us wherever we wanted – London, New York, Disneyland. He'd look after us and earn money for us and never ever hit us.

That was the story version. In real life he drove off to join the other taxis at the rank and didn't even give us a wave.

'Come on, then,' said Mum, sniffing.

She was still wearing her best high heels, twisting her ankles because her heavy suitcase made her walk lopsided. Kenny and I staggered after her.

The station was almost empty. My heart started thumping again. What if there weren't any more trains? The station would be one of the first places Dad would come looking for us.

Mum was standing at the information board, running her finger down the train timetable, looking worried. Then she stabbed a line with her finger, suddenly smiling. 'It's OK! It's leaving in ten minutes.'

'Where are we going, Mum?'

'London!'

I swallowed. 'Yeah, but where in London? We don't know anyone there.'

'That's right. That's good! Fresh start and all that. Let's get straight on the train. We can always pay if the ticket man comes round. That way there's no record of any transaction at the main ticket office.' Mum giggled. 'I feel like I'm in some cops and robbers film. It's kind of fun, isn't it?'

She didn't look like it was fun. Her face looked worse in the bright light of the station. Her giggling sounded weird, too much like crying. But she wanted us to agree with her so I nodded determinedly.

'Yes, it's like an adventure, Mum. Isn't it, Kenny?'

Kenny was almost out of it, practically sleep-walking, though he managed to concentrate enough to clutch Bubble's bag. As soon as I'd lifted him onto the train his head lolled and he fell fast asleep. I had a peep at Bubble. He didn't look too happy but there was nothing I could do about it.

'We can get Bubble a proper fish tank, can't we, Mum?'

'Yeah, sure. And we'll get lots more goldfish. And what do you call those massive ones that cost a fortune?'

'Koi carp. But they'll be much too big, won't they?'

'So? We'll have a gigantic aquarium. With dolphins!'

'No, *sharks*,' I said, baring my teeth.

It was mad. We were discussing a proper home for Bubble when we still had no idea where we were going to live ourselves.

'Mum? When we get to London where exactly are we going to go?'

'We'll stay in a hotel just until we get ourselves sorted.'

'Yes, but it'll be very late when we get there. What if all the hotels are closed for the night? What if we can't find anywhere? What if—?'

'Oh give it a rest, Jayni, you're doing my head in.'
'But—'
'Shut up, will you?'

I curled up against Kenny and tried to go to sleep. I couldn't manage it. Everything kept going round and round in my head. Every time I looked over at Mum I could see they were going round and round in her head too. She was gnawing her thumb. It looked like she wouldn't have any skin left by the time we got to London.

Four

It was easy after all. When we got to the station the Upper Crust food stall was still open. Mum bought us all a sandwich and asked the woman serving us if she knew if there were any hotels nearby. She drew us a little map on a paper napkin. It turned out there was a whole street of hotels only five minutes away.

'Though they look a bit seedy,' said Mum, when we got there. 'We're in the money now. We could stay at the blooming Ritz if we wanted.'

But Kenny was so out of it Mum had to carry him on her hip, lugging her case as best she could. It was obvious we couldn't go any further.

The first hotel said they were full. No one came to the door of the second hotel, though the hall light was on and we rang and rang. I started to panic then, thinking we were going to stagger round half the hotels in London.

Mum said brightly, 'Third time lucky' – and it was. A man came to the door and said he had a double room for the night, £45 to be paid now, and a fiver each if we wanted a continental breakfast.

Mum handed over the money and then signed the register. She's got very big, sprawly writing. She swirls every loop and puts little hearts instead of dots over her 'i's. But she made her writing little and squiggly in his greasy register, so that it was very hard to read. It didn't look anything like Mum's name, Nikki Fenton.

Still, the hotel man didn't seem bothered. He didn't even give Mum's sore face a second glance. Her nose was all crusty now. She dabbed at it self-consciously and started some spiel about falling flat on her face because of her silly high heels, but the man didn't seem to be listening. It was like he'd heard it all before a hundred times over. He just handed Mum the keys, pointed up the stairs and went back to watching Channel Five in his office.

'Charming,' Mum muttered. 'Well, we won't be stopping *here* for long.'

We hauled Kenny and our bags up three narrow flights of stairs and found our room down a dingy corridor. It had hardly any furniture, just a double bed with cigarette burns on the duvet, a wardrobe with only one hanger and a wash basin with a sliver of soap and just one towel. Mum sniffed contemptuously. She gingerly pulled back the duvet but the sheets were reassuringly white and smelt freshly laundered.

'Come on, then, let's get into bed,' she said. 'You get Kenny out of all them clothes while I go and find the toilet.'

Mum came back with her nose wrinkled. 'It's not very nice,' she said. 'Watch Kenny when you take him, Jayni. Don't let him touch anything.'

Kenny was half asleep so he did as he was told, dopily. I found it hard to go myself, not daring to sit on the filthy seat. I just sort of hung in mid-air, hoping for the best. I distracted myself reading all the rude messages scribbled on the wall.

When we got back Mum was already in bed, her mohair cardie on over her black nightie. 'Come on kids, it's freezing in here.'

We jumped in with her. It was like sliding into snow, but Mum put her arms tight round us and we all huddled up. It gradually got cosier. We heard some couple arguing along the corridor but Mum pulled the covers right up over our heads so we were in our own cave where no one could get us.

I fell asleep eventually but woke with a start in the middle of the night. I'd been dreaming of Dad. He was chasing after me. I woke up with my heart pounding as if I'd really been running. I reached out for Mum but she wasn't there. I could only feel Kenny, huddled into a little ball, breathing heavily.

I sat up, panicking. It was dark in the poky little

bedroom but I could just make out a shape over by the window.

'Mum?' I slipped out of bed and pattered across the worn carpet. 'What you doing, Mum?' I put my hand on her arm. She was shivering in spite of her mohair cardigan.

'Shh, love. Don't wake Kenny.'

'It's OK, he's dead to the world. Mum? Can't you sleep?'

'Nope. And I've run out of fags, which is a bit of a bummer. I was wondering about going out looking for a machine somewhere—'

'Don't, Mum!'

'OK. I wasn't very thrilled about the idea myself. Oh Jayni, what the hell are we *doing* here? Maybe I went a little bit nuts. Your dad wouldn't *really* start on you. He thinks the world of you, darling.'

'He thinks the world of you too, Mum, but he hits you. *Why* does he?'

'Search me. I just seem to set him off. I'm pretty useless really. Not much cop as a wife – or a mum.' She started to cry.

'You're a *lovely* mum,' I said. I put my arms round her. 'You're not useless at all. You're *lucky*. You're the only person who's ever won the lottery round our way.'

'Lady Luck,' Mum sniffed. 'That's what I signed in the register downstairs. L. Luck. Just in case your dad came snooping. Maybe it's not such a good idea to be so close to the station. This could be the first place he'll look if he comes after us. We'll leave right after breakfast, OK?'

'Is that going to be your new name then, Mum? Lady Luck?'

'Well, "Lady" sounds a bit daft, doesn't it? I could be Nikki Luck now, though. Or maybe I'll change my first name too. I'll be . . . Victoria. I always liked Posh best of all the Spice Girls. Victoria Luck. Yeah, sounds great, doesn't it?'

'Shall we change our names too, Kenny and me?'

'Yes, I think you'd better. Who do you want to be then, darling?'

I thought of all the women in my scrapbook, Britney and Charlotte and Kate and Kylie, but that didn't work because I wasn't remotely like any of them. I'd edged each picture with lots of cut-out presents for each woman – flowers and glasses of champagne and boxes of chocolates and bottles of perfume. One of the pictures had the model's name, Lola Rose.

I tried the name out inside my head. I liked it.

'I'll be Lola Rose.' I stood up straight, tossed my hair, smoothed my nightie. Lola Rose sounded a seriously cool girl. She had long, thick, curly hair (my fine, straight hair seemed thicker and curlier already). Lola Rose had a perfect model figure. I sucked in my tummy and stuck out my chest. Lola Rose wasn't scared of anyone. Not even her dad.

I breathed out slowly, a little smile on my face.

'Lola Rose Luck,' said Mum. 'OK. New name, new start.' She rubbed her watery eyes, smearing her mascara. 'Oh Gawd, look at me. Bum, I didn't pack my cleansing cream – or my make-up!'

'We can go shopping, get you heaps more. And I could have some too,' I said hopefully.

'OK, Lola Rose,' said Mum, going to the sink to wash her face. She scooped up some water – and then shrieked. 'My God!'

I'd filled the basin with cold water for Bubble. Mum had fished him out by mistake. He wriggled free and plopped back into the water while Mum and I giggled hysterically.

'Shut *up* in there, I'm trying to sleep,' someone called, banging on our wall.

Mum and I spluttered some more, hands over our mouths. Kenny woke up too.

'Where am I?' he said, starting to cry. *'Mum? Jayni?'*

'Shh, Kenny, we're here,' I said, going to him.

'And you can shut that kid up too!' the voice shouted from the other side of the wall.

'You're the one making all the noise, matie,' Mum yelled. *'You* shut up.'

'Mum! Don't! Please don't start a row,' I hissed. I had my arms round Kenny, trying to stop him wailing.

The voice yelled back something very rude, *so* rude that Mum and I got the giggles again. Mum got back into bed beside us.

'We're out of here first thing, kids,' she whispered. 'We're dossing down amongst some right nutters.'

'You're squashing me, Jayni!' Kenny complained.

'Sorry, sorry. But don't call me Jayni. I'm Lola Rose now.'

'And I'm Victoria,' said Mum.

'Is this a game?' Kenny said uncertainly. 'I don't like it. I want to go *home*.'

'No you don't,' I said quickly. 'This is much more fun. We're going shopping later on. We'll buy you all sorts, Kenny. But we're being new people now, so we've got new names. I'm Lola Rose Luck. Cool name, isn't it! And Mum's Victoria Luck. So what name are you going to choose?'

'I'm Kenny,' said Kenny.

'Yeah, but now you can be anybody. Shall I help you? What about . . . Jamie? Robbie? David?'

'Which? I won't remember,' Kenny said, looking worried.

'Yes, you will. How about something like your own name, so it doesn't sound too different. Lenny? Benny?'

'Could I be Kendall?' said Kenny.

'Kendal mint cake!' Mum spluttered.

I felt Kenny stiffen, humiliated.

'I think Kendall's a cool name,' I said.

'Yeah, right, it's totally cool. Victoria Luck has two cool kids, Kendall and Lola Rose,' said Mum, snuggling down between us. 'Shall we all try and have a little kip now?'

She cuddled us close. Kenny – *Kendall* – was quiet. I thought he'd gone to sleep. But then he piped up again. 'What's Dad going to be called?'

I waited for Mum to answer. She didn't. Maybe *she* was asleep.

'Dad isn't part of our family now, Kendall,' I whispered.

'Why not?' Kendall sounded astonished.

I couldn't see how he could be so thick. 'You *know* why!' I hissed. 'Because Dad's horrible and keeps hitting Mum. He hit me too. It still hurts whenever I move my jaw.'

'He doesn't hit me,' said Kendall.

'Don't you feel sorry he hits Mum?'

'But she deserves it,' said Kendall.

I took hold of his bony little shoulders through his T-shirt and shook him hard. 'How *dare* you say such a wicked, stupid thing!'

'But she *does* deserve it. Dad says so,' Kendall said, starting to whimper. 'Don't, Jayni, you're hurting.'

'I'm not Jayni any more, I'm Lola, Lola Rose. And you're not to say another word about Dad or I'll get really cross. We hate Dad.'

'No, we don't,' Kendall mumbled. 'We love him.'

I turned my back on him. I elbowed him away when he tried to cuddle up. I hated *him* – even though he was right.

I hated Dad. He scared me silly. But I still loved him.

I thought of him wandering round our flat all by himself, calling our names, looking in every room, pulling down bedcovers, peering in wardrobes. He'd get mad later. Fighting mad. But he'd be so hurt too. He'd cry. Our dad was the toughest man on the estate but I'd often seen him cry. He always cried after he'd hit Mum. He'd hold her hands and tell her he was sorry, tears trickling down his cheeks. He'd kiss all her bruises. He'd go down on his knees and beg her to forgive him. And she did.

It wasn't just Mum. Dad has a way of getting round anyone. When Kenny had a temper tantrum, flat on his back, drumming his heels and yelling fit to burst, Dad would pick him up, laughing. 'Let's switch off this silly noise,' he'd say, pressing Kenny's nose like a button. Kenny would stop mid-scream and laugh like it had been a joke all along.

Dad could get round me too. He'd come and sit beside me and pick up my hand and play with my fingers, calling them funny names. Once he painted each of my little bitten nails the seven colours of the rainbow and my thumbs and one pinky finger gold, silver and sparkly white. He bought me this little pack of rainbow beads and threaded them onto my plaits while he fed me rainbow-dotted chocolate buttons.

On my last birthday he gave me a great silver box tied with rainbow ribbon. There were layers of tissue inside so I knew it was a dress. I guessed it would be a rainbow dress and I felt anxious because I'm too big for that kind of party frock. It was beautiful, with smocking on the front and rainbow stripes, little puff sleeves and a big flouncy skirt. It was the sort of dress I'd have died for when I was about five. It looked *awful* on me now. It was much too tight, too bright, too babyish. But I had to smile and hold out my skirts and prance around as if I was thrilled to bits.

I had to wear it to the school disco. All the other kids laughed at me. No one wanted to dance with me so I danced by myself, leaping around wildly, pretending to be having fun. I leapt a little too wildly and split my seams. Mum tried to sew them up for me but the material was ripped and frayed. We hid the dress at the back of the wardrobe so Dad wouldn't see.

I thought about him finding it now.

I felt as if I were splitting apart just like my dress.

We checked out of that hotel straight after our continental breakfast.

'Though what's continental about cornflakes and toast and watered-down orange juice?' said Mum. 'What a rip-off! Let's splash out and stay somewhere decent.'

We chose a big new hotel overlooking the river Thames.

'Dead classy,' said Mum. 'Don't you let me down, kids.'

We were given a big bedroom with a huge bed with a pink silky cover that matched the ruffled curtains. 'And Pinkie matches too,' I said, but when I tucked her under the covers she looked horribly grey and grubby. We had our own bathroom and a television and a phone and a fridge.

'Look, we can have lots of drinks! And there's peanuts and chocolates. Wow!' said Kendall, rifling through them.

'Hang on, I don't think they're free, are they, Mum?' I said, grabbing his wrists.

'Yeah, but we're in the money, babe. Let him help himself.'

Kendall drank a can of Coke and nibbled peanuts while Mum and I had a bath together. There were dinky little bottles of shampoo and bath foam so we had the bath brimming with bubbles. We felt just like film stars.

'You come and jump in too, Kenny – *Kendall*,' Mum called.

We could hear him mumbling away to himself – or to someone else.

'Kendall?' I clambered out of the bath, wrapped one of the wonderful big fluffy towels right round me and padded into the bedroom. Kendall was leaning against the dressing table, chatting into the phone.

'Yes, Dad, it's great in London,' he said.

I froze. 'Kenny!'

He looked startled, then turned his back on me. 'Only Jayni keeps nagging at me, Dad. And I have to sleep in a big bed with her and Mum and I want my *own* bed because I'm a big boy, aren't I?' he gabbled.

Then I grabbed the phone, wrenching it out of his hand so fiercely I bent his fingers back.

'Ow!' Kenny screamed. He tried to hit me with his hand and hurt his fingers more.

'You told Dad where we are!' I said.

Then I heard the dialling tone on the phone. Kenny hadn't really been talking to Dad. He'd just been pretending.

Unless Dad had put the phone down his end . . .

'Were you *really* talking to Dad, Kenny?'

'Yes! And he said you're very mean to me and he's going to come and get you, see!' Kenny shrieked. 'And anyway, I'm not Kenny any more. I'm Kendall.'

'For God's sake!' Mum called from the bathroom. 'Stop yelling, both of you. They'll be banging on the walls here.'

'But he was trying to phone Dad!'

'Don't be so daft. He doesn't know how to. He doesn't even know the number properly.'

'I do, I do! I know our number. It's one two three four sixteen ten twenty, *see!*' said Kenny.

I did see. I picked him up and gave him a hug, saying I was really sorry I'd hurt his poor hand. Mum got out of her bath, all pink and pretty in spite of the new bruises and her sore nose. I dunked Kendall in the water and blew bubbles with him until he'd cheered up.

'Now let's go out on the razzle,' said Mum.

We started off with a second breakfast – pancakes and maple syrup and ice cream. I ate all mine and half of Kendall's, and then ran my fingers round and round the plate to get every scrap of maple syrup.

'Tut tut, your manners, Lola Rose,' said Mum. Then she stuck out her finger and did exactly the same.

I picked my plate up to lick it.

'Uh-uh! You're going a bit too far now,' said Mum. 'Come on then. Big treat time. We're going on the London Eye.'

'Big treat, big treat, big treat!' Kendall sang over and over again, until it became meaningless gabble.

He whooped with excitement when we pointed out the huge wheel with its glass pods. We watched it revolving very very slowly.

'Big treat, big treat, big treat,' Kendall gabbled all the time we queued. Everyone smiled at first and said, 'Bless him,' but eventually you could see it was getting on their nerves. It was getting on *our* nerves too, but there's no way you can shut him up when he starts. He 'big treated' right until the moment we went to step into the glass pod. Then he screamed.

'Kenny? What's up?' said Mum.

'Kendall!' I hissed. 'Come on, it's OK. Step on quick.'

'Noooo!' Kenny roared. 'It's too scary!'

I had to pick him up and lug him on, carrying him over my shoulder. He kicked and screamed, his square-toed shoes kicking me in the tummy.

'Cut it *out*, Kendall. It's lovely. Not a bit scary.'

'We'll *fall*!'

'No we won't. We're in our glass pod. We're

going right up high, just like we're flying. Look!'

Kendall wouldn't look. He stopped screaming but he stuck his head right inside my jacket and clung tightly. I wanted to get up off my seat and have a proper look, but he moaned whenever I moved.

'You are a wimp, Kendall,' said Mum. 'Here, Lola Rose, I'll take him for a bit.'

'Thanks, Victoria,' I said.

It felt as if we were actors because we hadn't quite got used to using our new names. I loved being called Lola Rose. I unhooked Kendall, parking him with Mum. I stood with my face pressed against the glass. It wasn't quite scary *enough* for me. I wanted to whizz round and round with all of London blurring. I wished our glass pod would fly off by itself, whirling us further and further away from Dad. It felt so much safer up here in the bright blue sky.

I didn't like it when we were back on the ground again. I kept thinking about Dad, looking over my shoulder.

'Don't act so twitchy, Lola Rose, it's getting on my nerves,' said Mum.

'Where are we going now?' said Kendall.

Mum didn't reply. I looked at her. She didn't *know*.

'Let's go shopping,' I said.

We couldn't see any shops, just river and walkways and big buildings. 'Where are the shops, Mum?'

'Well, kind of over there,' said Mum, gesturing

vaguely across the river. 'I suppose we'd better get up on the bridge. So what are you after, Lola Rose? That denim jacket with fur? And shall we get you your little leather jacket, Kendall?'

Kendall didn't react. He was breathing deeply, still a bit snuffly after all that screaming. He was staring up at the building beside us.

'Kendall? Have you forgotten that's your name?' I hissed.

'I know,' he said, not looking at me. He was staring at the sign on the building. 'That's the fish word.'

'Aquarium! Yeah, you're right, my lovely,' said Mum. 'Clever little lad! Imagine a little boy like you knowing a big word like aquarium!'

'Can we buy some fish to be Bubble's friends?'

'Yes, we could maybe buy a new goldfish, and some food and a proper bowl,' I said.

Bubble hadn't looked too clever this morning. We'd cleared the bath of bubbles and left him swimming in this big big pool but Bubble seemed very tired. I had a feeling he wasn't going to last much longer. It would be great if Kendall could be distracted with a whole new fishy family.

But when we went in we saw it wasn't the kind of aquarium where you buy fish. It was like a big fish zoo.

'You just look at these fish, Kendall, you can't buy them. Come on, let's go.'

'I want to look,' said Kendall.

'At a load of old fish?' said Mum. 'Give us a break, Kenny. Kendall. It'll be boring. No, we're going to the shops and we'll get you a little leather jacket.'

'*Please* let me see the fish. Will they have sharks?' said Kendall.

'Sharks!' I said, laughing.

But they did have sharks.

I was dawdling along in the dark, peering in at the tanks without much interest, thinking about denim jackets lined with fur. I wished there were some seats somewhere as I was feeling really tired now. Mum was holding Kendall up so he could see some slithery creature at the top of the tank.

I felt that if you'd seen one fish you'd seen them all. These ones weren't much more interesting than Bubble. I wandered round a corner and came to a huge tank that took up the whole wall. I leant against the glass, imagining what it would be like to be a mermaid. I remembered a mermaid cartoon video I watched with Dad ages ago – and then a huge shark swam right past me, jaw open, showing three rows of terrifying teeth an inch away from my nose.

I screamed.

Mum and Kendall came running.

I couldn't stop screaming, though I covered my mouth with both hands.

'What is it, Jayni? Is it Dad? Did you see him?' said Mum, grabbing me.

'There's a shark!' I gasped.

'Oh for God's *sake*,' said Mum, giving me a little shake. 'You gave me such a scare!'

All these Japanese tourists were pointing at me and laughing.

'You're not scared of *fish*, are you?' said Mum, laughing too.

'It's a *shark*,' I said. 'It was so big and so *close*. It was like it was touching me.'

'*I'm* not scared,' said Kendall. 'I want to see the shark! Where is it?'

'It looks like Lola Rose has frightened it away with all that screaming. Honestly, you're worse than Kendall!'

Then another huge shark – and another and another – came swimming past, with baleful eyes and huge sneery mouths. Mum stepped back smartly.

'Bloody hell!' she said, holding my hand. 'I take it all back. They're *whoppers*!'

'I like them. Sharkie, sharkie, sharkie! Good boys! Come and see me. Open your big mouths. I want to see your teeth,' Kendall begged, standing so close his nose was squashed sideways by the glass.

'Watch out!' I called, clinging to Mum.

'I *am* watching,' said Kendall. 'They're so lovely! Can I have one, Mum, please please please?'

All the tourists collapsed with laughter. I laughed too, but I was still shaking. I *hated* those sharks. I couldn't go near the glass even though I knew they couldn't swim through it. I wanted to rush past to the next room but Kenny stuck to the glass like he had little suckers on his hands and nose. When Mum tried to pull him away he started yelling.

'You kids are driving me nuts!' said Mum. 'Look, you go to the next bit, Lola Rose. We'll catch up when His Lordship has had his fill of the sharks.'

So I hurried on, round the corner and up the ramp. Then I stopped. I was up at the top of the shark tank now. There was no escape. There they were, swimming straight towards me.

I was scared I was going to start screaming again. I ran and ran, blundering down dark tunnels and through twilight rooms, fish flickering all around me. I shot straight through the aquarium to the gift shop at the end. Even the turquoise toy sharks seemed sinister.

I lurked in a far corner for ages and ages. I thought Mum and Kendall would never come. When they eventually came through they were hand in hand, and Kendall was bright pink in the face and beaming.

'Lola Rose, where did you *get* to?' Mum said.

'You were so *silly*, Jayni – sorry, Lola Rose. This man came and told me all about the sharks. There's this big big *big* one called George. He's the best. George can see ten times better than me and he smells heaps better too.'

'Yeah, they can smell one drop of blood *miles* away when they're in the ocean,' said Mum, snapping her teeth in a shark imitation.

'Shut up, Mum.'

'You're not really scared, are you, you big softie? The sharks in these tanks don't eat people. They get fed like fish *paella*, octopus and squid and stuff.

We'll have to come back and see them fed, won't we, Kendall?'

'Yeah! I want to feed George.'

'I don't think *you* can feed them, sweetheart. We'll have to watch the man. You should have stayed, Lola Rose, it was fascinating.' Mum stared at me and then came up close. 'Jayni. What's all this twitching? What's up with you, you're always so sensible?'

'I *am* sensible. Sensible people hate sharks because they look so ugly and they can rip you apart. You can take Kendall back if you like but I'm never setting foot in this place ever again,' I said. 'Not for anything.'

I walked out of the shop and stood by myself on the embankment. I stared at the river. I knew perfectly well there were no sharks in the Thames but I kept expecting a deadly dorsal fin to streak through the water.

When Mum and Kendall came out at last Kendall was clutching a big fluffy turquoise toy shark. 'Look, look, I've got my very own George!' he cried, racing up to me. 'Attack!' he yelled, whirling George by the tail and then bashing me in the face with him.

It didn't hurt. I knew George was a fluffy toy and his teeth were made of felt – but I still screamed.

'Oh, do stop it, Jayni, you're just acting soft to get attention,' Mum snapped.

I was so hurt I went into a sulk. I wouldn't talk to either of them as we crossed the bridge over the river and walked round Covent Garden. Then

Mum stopped outside this immensely posh French cake and coffee shop. 'Let's live dangerously,' she said, and went inside.

I had to talk to say which cake I wanted. It took me ages to choose because they were all so ultra-yummy and special. I eventually decided on a cream mousse gâteau with strawberries and a swirl of chocolate icing on top. Mum had an elegant almond croissant. Kendall chose a chestnut cream meringue, but he licked it half-heartedly and didn't finish it. So I did. *And* I had a hot chocolate to die for, all whippy with a big peak of cream.

Mum laughed at me. 'You've cheered up now, haven't you, Lola Rose!'

'You bet,' I said.

Then we got started on some serious shopping. We found this posh kids' shop and there was this perfect little black leather jacket that fitted Kendall perfectly. He looked so cute in it. Even the shop assistant clapped her hands and called him a pet. It cost a fortune. 'But I've *got* a fortune,' said Mum, and she handed over a fistful of notes as if they were pennies.

We looked at the girls' jackets too. They had a denim jacket with fur and my heart started beating fast but when I tried it on it was much too small. I could hardly get my arms in and it wouldn't meet across my front.

'I'm too fat,' I said, feeling awful.

'Don't be so daft. You're just getting a big girl, too big for little kids' clothes. We'll find you a proper furry denim jacket, just you wait and see,' said Mum.

We went into shop after shop after shop. Kendall stopped playing swim-through-the-air games with George and started whining. But then, in the *thirteenth* shop, my lucky number, we found a whole row of ladies' denim jackets lined with fake fur. Cream fur, blue fur, *pink* fur. I tried the pink furry one on, trembling. It fitted perfectly. Well, it was a little too long in the arms, but Mum rolled the sleeves up for me, saying it was the only cool way to wear such jackets anyway.

Mum bought it for me and I went out of the shop wearing it. It felt as if I was being cuddled by the softest teddy bear. I looked great in it, I really did. I kept peering at myself in shop windows. A new cool blue denim pink furry-collared Lola Rose stared back, smiling all over her face.

Mum was quite tempted by the denim jackets too, but then she spotted a white leather jacket, short and sexy. When she tried it on she looked so glamorous, just like a rock star, especially with her dark glasses.

We sashayed out the shop, Lola Rose in her furry blue denim, Victoria in her rock-star white leather, two absolute babes – with a baby, our Kendall, whining for England, dragging George shark by the tail.

We decided to buy him one of his favourite red lollies to shut him up. They'd proved very good dummies in the past. We could see any number of posh places selling Häagen Dazs and Ben &

Jerry's but there weren't any ordinary little corner shops with cheapo ice lollies.

'Perhaps there's one down a side street,' said Mum.

We found a little newsagent eventually. He didn't stock Kendall's strawberry shockers but Mum bought him a fistful of other flavours – orange, mango, blackcurrant, milk.

'There, kiddo, suck on that little lot and shut *up*,' said Mum.

She bought me a white Magnum. I was extra careful eating ice cream in my new denim jacket. I was concentrating so hard on licking cautiously that I almost walked straight past the special shop. It was a bookshop, but these were wonderful books – colouring books, cut-out books, sticker books, hundreds of them.

'Boring!' said Kendall, ice lolly all round his mouth like lipstick. Then he saw a colouring book of fishes of the world. He started clamouring for it, even though he goes horribly over the lines when he uses his own wax crayons and he presses too hard and makes the points furry if I let him near my felt-tip pens.

'OK OK, spoilt brat number two,' said Mum, opening up her magic handbag again. 'What about you, spoilt brat number one? Would you like a fancy colouring book too?'

I found the book I wanted most of all right at the back of this fairyland shop. It was a fat book of reproduction Victorian scraps, all ready to peel off and stick in a scrapbook. There were hundreds of children in bright pinks and purples playing with cats and dogs, flowers, birds, seaside scenes, Father Christmas, babies, butterflies, angels . . .

'Oh, Mum. Victoria. Please!' I whispered.

We spent that evening sitting up in the double bed together watching television. Mum click-flicked through channel after channel. Kendall cuddled up between us, making George swim across the bed and attack poor little Bob the bear again and again. I sat up cross-legged with my scrapbook balanced on both knees, sticking in my new scraps.

My absolute favourites were four enormous angels. They had long golden hair and flowing white robes and great grey wings springing from their shoulder blades. I stuck them in carefully, having to edge them in really close together to fit on the page. When I fell asleep I dreamt the angels were standing at each corner of our bed, wings spread out like feathery curtains protecting us.

Six

'Let's go on the razzle again,' said Mum, the minute I woke up.

She was already up and dressed. It didn't look as if she'd slept a lot – but she didn't act tired. We razzled till we dazzled. We bought new tops, new trousers, new night things and new shoes. Oh, those new shoes – wonderful, strappy sling-back stilettos for Mum and *my* first pair of proper grown-up heels too. They were only *little* heels but I still couldn't cross the room six them without twisting my ankles.

'Who cares?' said Mum. 'You'll be fine with a

little bit of practice. All set to go dancing, eh?'

She bought a little CD player and a stack of her favourite CDs. We had our own private disco in the hotel bedroom during the day when the vacuums were roaring and it didn't matter how much noise we made. Mum especially liked 'I Will Survive'. She danced to it, punching her arms in the air, and Kendall and I copied her.

The maid came in to clean our bedroom and saw us dancing. She roared with laughter and imitated us, punching her own arms. 'That's it, you tell them, girl!' she said.

She was a very very *large* lady but she was surprisingly good at dancing, jiggling her hips and strutting her stuff.

'Wasn't that lady *fat*!' Kendall whispered when she'd gone. 'She went wibble wobble, wibble wobble.'

'If you think she was fat you should see your Auntie Barbara,' said Mum.

'Your sister?' I said. I poked Mum gently in her flat-as-a-pancake tummy. 'But you're skinny!'

'Yep,' said Mum. 'We're complete opposites in every way. I always used to wonder if we had different dads. Our dad couldn't stick me right from the start.'

'Did you ask him?'

'No fear! He'd have given me a clump around the head for cheek,' said Mum. She bit her thumb again. 'What is it about me, eh? Why do all the men in my life want to thump me? What am I doing wrong?'

'You're not doing *anything* wrong, Mum! It's them, not you. But you're not you now anyway. You're Victoria and I'm Lola Rose and he's Kendall and we're the Luck Luck Lucky family.'

I put the music on again and whirled Mum round and round, while Kendal did his little jiggle-stomp with George. It was just as well he was so keen on George. Poor Bubble had died in the night. Kendall wanted to bury him properly in a shoebox but Mum said she wasn't mucking about with dead goldfish and tipped Bubble down the toilet.

We had to go back to that awful aquarium every day to keep Kendall happy, visiting the real George and his horrific fishy friends. I stayed outside on the embankment. People kept stopping to talk to me, asking if I was all right. I was scared they might fetch a policeman. And any time a tall guy with long hair and a leather jacket came loping along my heart would thump even though I could see they were all strangers.

'Come in with us, you daft banana,' said Mum.

But I couldn't. I was far too scared of those sharks. I dreamt about those gaping jaws every night. I kept waking up, shaking. Mum was often sitting up smoking, curled in a chair in the dark. I'd squash up beside her and we'd cling together while Kendall snored softly, cuddled under the covers with George.

One night I woke with a start and reached for Mum. She wasn't in the bed, she wasn't in her chair. I found her kneeling in the bathroom, handbag in her lap, five-pound notes all round her in unsteady piles.

'Show me the money!' I whispered, to try to make her laugh.

But she wasn't in a jokey mood. Her face was screwed up, a big vein standing out on her forehead. 'Somebody's stolen some of it!' she said, sniffing furiously.

'They can't have done. You carry it round everywhere with you,' I said.

Mum always clutched the handbag tightly in case someone made a snatch at her bag. She wouldn't even hide it in the hotel room when we went down to breakfast.

'*How* can someone have stolen it?'

'Don't ask me. I just know they bloody have. There's hundreds and hundreds gone missing!'

'We've spent a lot,' I said, kneeling down beside Mum and starting to count the notes.

'Not that much!'

I got a piece of paper and wrote down all the clothes we'd bought, all the meals and treats and rides, all the ordinary everyday stuff like ice creams and Mum's ciggies and bus fares.

It started to add up to hundreds and hundreds.

'And we had the night out with Dad, and the taxi and the train fare to London and the first hotel—'

'And we've still got to pay this one too,' said Mum. 'Oh God.'

'I don't think anyone's stolen any, Mum. We've just spent it.'

'Right. OK. You've made your point. We've spent it.' Mum snapped, as if it was all my fault. 'So, Miss

Clever Clogs, what are we going to do when the money runs out altogether?'

I tried to think. My brain wouldn't work. I never knew what to do when Mum turned on me. 'Maybe it won't run out for ages if we're careful,' I said. 'We could move to a smaller hotel. And eat sandwiches. And not go to the aquarium.'

'Yes, but *then* what? Are we going to sit in doorways and beg? What happens if the police catch us? They'll want you and Kenny back in school, won't they? They'll send you home to your dad . . .'

I started crying. Mum started crying too. She put her arms round me.

'I'm sorry, sweetheart. I didn't mean it. Of course you won't get sent home.'

'We won't any of us have to go home, will we, Mum?'

'No way, darling. We can't go back. Your dad was always quite clear what he'd do if I ever tried to leave him.' Mum was shivering in her thin nightie. 'I'm scared.'

'Me too, sweetheart.' Then Mum took a deep breath. 'No, sod it, I'm not *going* to be scared. I'm Lady Luck now, right? And my luck's changed. Hey, maybe I'd better buy some more scratch cards? That's what we'll do, buy a whole load of scratch cards every day and eventually we'll get lucky again.'

I didn't know if Mum meant it. It seemed a crazy idea but I couldn't come up with anything better.

We went back to bed and it took me ages to get to sleep. Then I swam among sharks – but when I awoke Mum was already up, dressed in a new blouse and skirt and her white leather jacket. She was pacing the floor in her new high heels.

I wished I could walk properly in mine. I'd tried to wear them out and turned my ankle so badly the heel snapped straight off the shoe. Mum said we could take them back and get a replacement.

'Can we see about my shoes today, Mum?'

'Maybe. If we've got time.'

'We're not going boring old shopping again, are we?' Kendall said, sitting up in bed. His hair stuck up like dandelion fluff. 'Can we go and see Big George being fed, Mum?'

'Perhaps, pet. But we've got a lot else to do today. We're going to start getting organized, right? I'm going to get a job. And find us a place to live. And get you two into schools. Simple!' said Mum, laughing.

Kendall thought it really was simple and laughed too.

I knew it wasn't simple at all. I was so worried I couldn't eat much breakfast, though Mum told us to tuck in. Mum didn't eat anything at all. She just had cup after cup of tea, going sip sip sip. Her voice still sounded dry and croaky when she asked for our bill at the reception desk. She went white when she saw how much it was, but she counted out the five-pound notes as nonchalantly as she could.

Then we went upstairs to pack. We had to nip out to the shops for another suitcase because we'd bought so much.

The nice fat maid was hoovering the corridor when we came back. Mum told her we were going, and tucked a couple of five-pound notes in her pocket. 'Thanks for looking after us so well,' she said.

'It's been a pleasure. I shall miss you lot ever so,' she said, stooping with difficulty to give Kendall a big hug. She put her arm round me too and cuddled me close. 'You're a lovely girl, Lola Rose,' she said. 'Have you enjoyed your holiday?'

I looked at Mum.

'We're not exactly on holiday,' said Mum. She raised her eyebrows significantly.

'Aha,' said the maid. 'I get you.'

'We're going to make a new life for ourselves,' said Mum. 'I'm going to need to find some work. There aren't any maids' jobs going here, are there?'

'Well, I could find out,' she said. 'But it's a rubbish job, dear, especially for a pretty little thing like you. The money's lousy, and very few people give a handsome tip like you did. You could get a good office job somewhere really smart. What are you trained for?'

'I'm not trained for anything. I used to do a bit of modelling—'

'There! I *said* you were pretty,' said the maid.

'But I've gone off a bit. I couldn't get that sort of work now, not after having the two kids. And I'm not that great at computers or figures or stuff. I don't think I could work in an office, I'd just get in a muddle.' Mum nibbled at her thumbnail.

'Well, it strikes me office work would get boring,' she said comfortingly. 'You seem like a *people* person. Maybe shop work might be more in your line? Showing off pretty clothes?'

'Well maybe,' said Mum, still biting her thumb. 'There's the tills though. I don't know how you work them. Honestly, I'm just so thick.'

'No, you're not, Mum,' I said, patting her.

It wasn't her fault. Dad never let her do anything. He kept on telling her she was thick thick thick as a brick and she believed him.

'Don't worry, pet, they'll teach you,' said the maid. 'They give you training. They even trained me how to make a bed, though I've been making six a day all my adult life.'

'Six?'

'My family. Well, there's eight now, because my Junie's here with my little grandson Marvin, bless him, though his little cot don't count.'

'So you don't live in the hotel?' said Mum. 'I thought if I got a job as a maid then they'd let me have a room for me and the kids.'

'You're not much more than a kid yourself,' she said. 'The staff don't live in here. They'd never let you keep the children here anyway. Look, maybe you should go down the social?'

'No fear! I'm not having them poking their noses into my past.'

'They won't. They'll help. Still, maybe you know best. Are you going to put yourself down on the housing list?'

'I don't see how we can. I mean, I lived in a council flat back home. I had to walk out, see. But they'll say I deliberately made myself homeless. And I'm scared they'd take the kids into care.'

'Well, try one of the special housing associations. They found my sister Elise a lovely place when she left her husband. Well, she's made it lovely now, her and her kids. Shall I give her a quick ring, find out the association address for you? It's a charity but they don't make you feel bad. And they'd never try to take your kids away. Anyone can see you're a brilliant mum.'

She was so kind Mum tried to give her more money but she wouldn't take it. She stowed our bags away when we got packed up and kissed us all and wished us luck. 'You're going to be lucky in life from now on, I can tell,' she said.

Mum's face lit up. 'Yeah, that's me, Lady Luck,' she said.

She took me by one hand and Kendall by the other and we set off. Mum sang all the lucky songs she could think of while we got the tube to the housing association place.

We were on the tube so long it was like we'd made a journey into the centre of the earth. When we emerged at last I pretended to Kendall that we were in Australia now and told him to watch out for koalas and kangaroos.

'And sharks!' said Kendall. 'They have sharks in the sea in Australia. Let's go to the seaside.'

'Will you quit winding him up, Lola Rose,' Mum snapped.

She was looking at the tacky parade of shops and the scattered French fries on the pavement and the boys goofing around outside the video shop.

'It's a bit of a dump, isn't it? Maybe it's a bit daft

wanting to live here. There must be heaps of housing associations.'

'Yeah, but it's so out the way, Mum, it feels kind of safe. Dad wouldn't ever come looking for us here, would he? And yet all the time we're wandering around the West End you feel there's a chance he might come barging round the corner.'

'I *want* Dad to come round the corner,' said Kendall. 'I want Dad. I want to go home. I don't like Australia.'

'It's not Australia, you nut,' I said, laughing at him. 'It was just a *joke*.'

'*Don't* joke, Jayni!' said Kendall, and he started hitting me with his fists, with George, with his hard little head.

'Hey, hey! Ouch! Stop it, Kendall!' I said, scooping him up and whirling him round and round.

I could usually cheer him out of a tantrum that way. It didn't work this time. He just sobbed dismally.

'Don't, Kendall,' I said, shifting him onto my hip.

'I'm Kenny!' he wept.

'Poor little kid, he doesn't know who he is or where's he going,' said Mum. 'You shouldn't have got him all wound up with that Australia lark.'

'I know. I'm sorry. I'm sorry, Kendall.'

'Kenny!'

'No. Not any more,' said Mum, cupping his damp face and looking straight into his eyes. 'This bit isn't a joke, darling. You and me and Jayni, we've all run away. Run away for good. We've run away from your dad because he kept hitting me.'

'Because you were bad,' said Kenny.

'Mum's *not* bad, you stupid little boy!' I said, giving him a shake.

'Leave him be, Jayni. He's only parrotting your dad. He doesn't really mean it,' said Mum. 'Now listen, sweetheart. No one ever deserves to get hit. *You* shouldn't ever hit anyone. You're a good boy. And Jayni's a good girl and I'm not going to risk either of you getting hurt. So we're starting our new life and we're going to make it work, right?'

'Right!' I said. I nudged Kendall. 'Say right!'

'Wrong,' Kendall mumbled into the pink fur of my denim jacket, but now he was joking.

He behaved like a little lamb in the housing association office. 'I'm Kendall Luck and I'm five years old,' he announced to everyone. His eyelashes were still wet and his little peaky face looked very earnest.

Everyone smiled and said, 'Bless him!'

It was Kenny who got us a home. We waited for ages and then a lady with glasses took down all our details. Mum was fine at first, making up all sorts of stuff, sounding so convincing, even though she was going nibble nibble on her thumbnail. But then we were led into another big room full of waiting people. It took another age before it was our turn to see anyone and then Mum had to start all over again saying the same stuff to a man with a beard while he filled in another form.

I knew Mum wouldn't be able to remember every little detail of her story. She'd been making it up as she went along. She had a stab at it, gabbling quicker and quicker to get it over with, but she got stuck when they asked about our schools. She'd made up a name before and they'd written it down. Mum tried to remember it, a vein standing out on her forehead. She looked at me desperately.

'Tell them the name of your school, Jayni,' she said.

Jayni.

I started saying something quick but the man wasn't listening. He put down his pen. 'Jayni?' he said. He looked at me. 'I though you were called Lola?'

'She is; Lola Rose. Jayni's just a silly nickname – Jayni-Payni, we've called her that for fun since she was little,' Mum said.

It was clear the man with the beard didn't believe a word she was saying. 'Mrs Luck, I get the feeling you've been a little economical with the truth,' he said. 'Some of your details don't quite add up. You need to be completely frank with us about your previous domestic circumstances. Now I'm sure you've got your reasons—'

'Yes, I've got my bloody reasons,' said Mum, going red. She yanked at her blouse and showed the man the bruises, still as purple as pansies. 'We're running away from the guy who did this to me, right? He's started on his daughter too – there'll be no stopping him now. I'm trying to make a fresh start and do my best for my kids. There's no going back. He'll kill us.'

'Have you been to the police?'

Mum snorted. 'What are they going to do?'

'Lock him up?'

'For how long? And what about his mates? And what happens when he's let out? What happens to us then?'

'I take your point, Mrs Luck. I do understand.'

'No you don't. You can take my point and shove it straight up your bottom,' said Mum, standing up. 'I suppose you're not going to find us somewhere to live now?'

'That sort of abuse isn't helpful, certainly. I will still try to help you but I can't work miracles. I'll put your family on our waiting list.'

'And what are we supposed to do meanwhile? Sit in the gutter for six months?'

Mum called him a very very rude name and then stood up. 'Come on, kids, we're going. This is a waste of time.'

Kenny looked at his hands. He looked at the chair he'd been sitting on. He looked under it. His mouth went into a letter-box shape and he started howling.

He howled and howled and howled. He wouldn't stop when I picked him up. He wouldn't stop when Mum picked him up. He wouldn't stop when the lady with glasses brought him a biscuit.

'What's the *matter* with him?' said the bearded man.

'He can't take any more,' Mum bellowed above the wails. 'It's all too much for him. We've been on the run for weeks now. I promised him I'd get him a home today. He just wants to feel *safe*.'

Everyone fussed over Kendall and looked at the

bearded man as if he were deliberately torturing my little brother. Luckily Kendall was crying too hard to draw breath and say what it was he wanted.

'Well, I suppose we might be able to put you in the emergency category. There *is* a property available – it's not ideal, and it's not in good decorative order, but if it'll act as a stop-gap . . . ?'

We were given the key to our new home just like that. We had to whizz Kenny away sharpish before he started going on about George.

We hunted for him all the way down the road back to the station but we didn't catch a glimpse of furry fin. He must have been left on the tube.

Mum took Kenny into the hotel to thank the lovely fat maid and collect our suitcases. She furtively pressed three fivers into my hand. She didn't have to tell me what to do. I ran all the way to the aquarium, begged to be let straight into the gift shop, and bought George the Second.

Seven

Our New Home

Our new home was the middle flat of a small, damp
Edwardian house with a tarpaulin over the roof and
nettles rioting in the garden. The front door was
warped so we had to put our shoulders against it
before it would budge. The hallway was littered
with freebie papers and advertising circulars so we
had to kick our way through them.

Our flat was up one flight of stairs. We had a
living room with a kitchen area in one corner, a tiny
bedroom and a toilet with a shower and basin. The
walls were a dirty cream like sour milk, with black
mould in the corners. The windowsills were wet

with condensation, the wood soft and rotten. The curtains hung limply against the damp glass. There was a stained carpet covering most of the living-room floor and a greasy cooker and a fridge – but no proper furniture.

Mum and Kendall and I walked round the flat. We walked round it again.

'Where *is* everything?' Kendall asked.

'You may well ask,' said Mum. She looked like she was going to start crying any minute.

'Where *is* everything?' I said quickly, copying Kendall.

She frowned at me – and then cottoned on. 'You may well ask,' she said.

'Where *is* everything?' Kendall and I chorused.

'You may well ask,' said Mum.

We went through this crazy routine over and over again, rushing round the room, gabbling it faster and faster until the words became gobbledegook. We ended up in a giggly heap on the carpet.

'Oh, quick, get up, kids, it's so dirty!' said Mum, pulling a face. 'We'll have to get carpet shampoo and lots of Flash. And three scrubbing brushes. And we'll buy some paint, brighten the place up. What colour, Lola Rose?'

'Purple!'

'*Purple?* OK, blow it, purple it is. We can have a purple bedroom, bed, carpet, rug, curtains. We can even paint *you* purple and all, if that's what you want.'

'And a purple living room?'

'No, it's my turn. I rather fancy a black and white theme, dead stylish, white walls, black leather furniture – with a zebra-striped rug on the floor. And I'll recline on it in a black negligée, yeah?'

'Eating black and white humbugs! Kendall, are you going to choose the bathroom colours? You could have turquoise like your horrible aquarium. We'll have a big glass tank for a bath and you can swim around inside it with George.'

'Don't start him off!' said Mum. 'She's just joking, Kendall.'

'What about my purple bedroom, Mum? Is that a joke too?'

'No, we're going to do a total *Changing Rooms* on this old dump, I promise you, darling. Money no object. Well, within reason.'

We were told about this special charity stores place where you got given all kinds of furniture if you were in need. Mum still had wads and wads of lottery money left but she'd started to worry about it now. We did go into town to look at furniture but one big squashy leather three-piece suite was three thousand pounds!

'Blow that for a lark. We'll see what these stores have got. If it's all a lot of flea-infested old rubbish then we'll just say no thanks, right?' said Mum.

But we said yes please, yes please. We even got a black leather sofa! It was old and cracked, but it still looked lovely. We found two black velvet chairs that almost matched and a fluffy rug that came up white after a good scrubbing. We got a double bed too, though Mum bought a brand-new mattress because she said she felt funny about sleeping in someone else's bedding. She bought a deep purple duvet cover just to please me, and spent a whole day painting the walls lilac.

I made her a special card with some of my best Victorian scraps, a big bright heart and bunches of lilies and roses and a host of angels swooping up and down like bungee jumpers. I wrote inside, 'You are an angel, Mum. X X X from Lola Rose', and I stuck a big red rose beside my name. Kendall added a wobbly K and his own kisses.

I put it in a proper envelope and then pretended it had been delivered by the postman. We didn't get any real post because no one knew where we were. No one knew us at all. This wasn't like a holiday any more. This was our new life.

I kept thinking about my old life and my old friends. They'd think it so weird that I'd vanished into thin air. *Thick* air. Mum was smoking more and more to steady her nerves. Our flat was grey with smoke haze. It made me cough but Mum said I was putting it on. Maybe I was, just a little bit.

Kendall coughed a lot too, but that was because he cried a lot. I suppose he was missing Dad. He often called out for him when he woke up in the night. Sometimes he didn't wake up quite quick enough and wet the bed. Mum threatened to put Kendall back in nappies if he did it again. He did, so Mum tucked a towel into his pants. Kendall howled with humiliation.

'You shouldn't get so cross with him, Mum. He can't help it. He's just upset.'

'Yeah, well, *I* shall be upset if he ruins that brand-new mattress. And you can stop being so mealy-mouthed, Miss Goody-Goody Two-Shoes,' said Mum. 'You don't half get on my nerves sometimes, Jayni.'

'Lola Rose.'

'OK, Lola Flipping Fancy-Pants Rose, just you remember I'm your *mum*. Stop acting like you're my big sister, for God's sake. You're not meant to tell me what to do. I'll do what I like, see.'

Mum looked in her handbag for her cigarettes. The packet was empty. 'Oh, bum. Run down the road to the corner shop, Jay— Lola Rose.'

'It's gone ten, Mum. It'll be shut.'

It had taken hours to settle Kendall. He'd had one of his crying fits. He was still snuffling in his sleep.

Mum bit her thumbnail agitatedly. 'For God's sake, I'm not going all night without a fag, I'm gasping. Look, there must be a pub somewhere. I'll nip out and buy myself some cigarettes from the machine. You go to bed, OK?'

'OK,' I said uncertainly. I didn't want her to go out in the dark by herself just in case something happened to her.

'You'll be fine, silly,' Mum said, not understanding. 'If there's any emergency then go and get someone in the house to help. Maybe not the old lady, she's a bit gone in the head, but the lads up above seem fine.'

We'd got to the stage of nodding at our new neighbours. Miss Parker, the old lady, proved a real nosy parker and asked all kinds of questions. We got worried, but she asked the exact same questions the next day and the next. It was obvious she didn't remember a word we told her.

Steve and Andy, the two men who lived in the flat above us, looked a bit peeved the first time we met them. We were coming up the stairs loaded with shopping bags from Tesco. Kendall was howling because he'd fallen over, Mum was shouting at him for being a big baby, I was moaning because there had been a special offer on Sara Lee chocolate cake and she wouldn't buy it. We were probably making quite a lot of noise.

Mum stopped shouting and smiled at Steve, the tall handsome one. Andy, the smaller guy with glasses, said hi to Kendall and me and helped us haul the shopping bags through to our kitchen. He told us their names. I said I was Lola Rose. Steve raised his eyebrows but Andy said he thought it was a beautiful name.

Steve acted like he was too grand to talk to us. He *did* seem too grand for this dump of a house. Andy was much more matey and told us how their old flat had been repossessed and so they'd had to come here.

'On a temporary basis,' said Steve.

'But we've still made it into our little home,' said Andy. 'And I love the way you've done up your flat, Lola Rose. It looks really great, especially the purple bedroom. Very artistic.'

I liked Andy *much* more than Steve. I still didn't think I could rush to him in an emergency though.

I hated that word. The moment Mum left our flat EMERGENCY flashed in my mind like neon lighting. Phantom alarms clanged in my head. My heart went thud thud thud inside my chest.

It was very quiet in the flat. We didn't have a television yet so I couldn't switch it on to make things sound normal. Miss Parker's telly buzzed down below, as if people were whispering bad things about me beneath my feet. Steve and Andy walked round upstairs and every time their floorboards creaked I jumped.

I kept going to check the door to make sure it was locked. I imagined someone was outside, listening, ready to shove his shoulder to the door and come bursting in. I peered out into the garden to make sure no one was creeping up on us. I could only see my own face reflected in the glass. It reminded me of the aquarium. I shut the curtains quick.

I wanted to huddle into a ball on the old leather sofa. No, I wanted to hide behind it like a really little kid. But Kendall was in the bedroom and I had to keep an eye on him. I considered climbing into bed beside him but I didn't want to take my clothes off and lie down in the dark. I needed to be fully dressed and on my toes.

I patrolled the flat. It still seemed horribly empty even now we had the stuff from the stores. It only took a few seconds to check each room. It didn't really help.

When I was in the bedroom I was sure someone was lurking in the living room, slyly cracking open a can of beer, sitting there on the sofa, *waiting*. When I was in the living room I felt someone might have got behind the door in the bathroom, ready to pounce. When I dared go into the bathroom, pushing the door inch by inch, I was sure someone had climbed through the bedroom window and was pulling Kendall out of bed, hand over his mouth to stop him screaming.

I knew Dad didn't know where we were. How could he possibly track us down? But I was still so scared I had to put on my new furry denim jacket to stop myself shivering. 'Come *back*, Mum!' I whispered, over and over.

She wasn't back by half past ten. Maybe she'd had to walk a long way to find a pub with a cigarette machine – though she was wearing her strappy sandals with high stiletto heels so she couldn't walk *that* far.

I waited and waited, staring at the clock. I started nodding my head in time to the tick and tock until I went dizzy. I tried to read one of Mum's magazines but the words jiggled about on the page and wouldn't make sense.

I got my scrapbook out and started cutting out a lovely picture of a girl rock star with long blonde hair and a jewelled navel and shiny brown legs in white leather boots. The floorboards gave a sudden creak and I cut off one of the boots by mistake. I tried to sellotape it back but it made her leg look wonky.

My own legs felt wonky as I paced the flat. It was gone eleven now. The pubs closed then. So where was Mum?

Something's happened to her, said the Voice of Doom.

Quarter past eleven.

Half past eleven.

I didn't know what to do. Maybe Dad had stalked her. I imagined him laying into her and she went as limp as my paper scrap. I wanted to rush out and find her but I couldn't leave Kendall on his own.

I started to cry, knuckling my eyes. I pressed harder until it hurt. I told myself to stop the silly snivelling. I wasn't a baby. I mustn't panic. Of course Dad hadn't found her. Maybe she'd simply got lost coming back from the pub? Mum had a hopeless sense of direction at the best of times, and now it was way after dark in a strange neighbourhood. Knowing Mum, she'd maybe even forgotten our address. She'd be stumbling round and round in her strappy sandals, cursing herself for being such a fool. She'd find us eventually, she'd be knocking at the door any minute, she'd rush in laughing . . .

But she didn't rush in.

I listened for her footsteps. I opened the curtains and stared out at the street. I even left the door on the latch and rushed down to the corner just to see if there was any sign of her.

Then I worried that someone might have slipped in and be after Kendall. I ran back and slammed the door shut and rushed into the bedroom. Kendall was still sleeping soundly in the middle of the bed, his arms and legs splayed out so he took up nearly all the space. There was no one hovering over him. I checked behind the door, the wardrobe, even under the bed. I knew I was acting crazy. I couldn't help it.

I went back into the kitchen and tried to make a cup of tea to calm myself. I was so jumpy I splashed cold water all down my front as I filled the kettle.

It was midnight.

Something *must* have happened to Mum.

So what would happen to Kendall and me?

I started crying again as the kettle boiled. I was making such a noise that I didn't hear the door. I didn't hear footsteps. Then Mum was in the kitchen, right in front of me.

'Mum!' I gasped, pouring water everywhere.

'Watch out, you'll scald yourself, you silly girl,' said Mum. 'Here, let me. I could do with a cuppa too.'

'Where have you *been*? It's gone midnight!'

'So? Who am I, flipping Cinderella?' said Mum, peering down at her sandals. 'Are these glass slippers I see before me?' She didn't exactly slur her words but she was acting silly.

'You've been down the pub drinking while I've been worrying myself sick wondering where you are!'

Mum started laughing. 'You sound so funny, Jayni, like you're *my* mum!'

'It's not funny! I was so scared Dad had got you,' I cried. I started trying to hit her, like Kendall in a tantrum.

'Hey, hey, hey,' said Mum. She caught hold of my wrists and pulled me close. She wrapped her arms round me. 'I'm so sorry, babe. I didn't realize. You always act so grown up. But there's no need to be scared about your dad, not any more. We're never ever going to see him again. We're new people now, remember, Lola Rose. I'm Lady Luck – and guess what, we're *in* luck, darling. I've got a job!'

'A job?' What kind of a job could Mum have got at midnight, for goodness' sake? For *badness*' sake?

'That's why I was such ages, darling. I thought you'd be fast asleep, cuddled up with Kendall. I don't want my girl worried – my lovely Lola Rose.' Mum stroked my hair and gave me a big kiss. She was a little bit drunk but it didn't matter. She never got really scary like Dad.

'Tell me about this job, Mum,' I said.

'I'm going to be a bar girl, plus help out with meals at lunch time.'

I relaxed against her. 'You've got a job in the pub?'

'Yeah, it's only five minutes away, it'll be brilliant. I walked in to buy my fags and I got talking to one of the guys behind the bar. He told me the manager needed more staff so I thought, OK, go for it, girl, so I did. I saw the manager, Barry – he's ever so nice. He put me through my paces after he'd closed for the night. He says I'm a natural at pulling a good pint and I can remember any number of orders and I know all the different drinks. Well, I ought to, seeing as I grew up in a pub. I told Barry I didn't have a clue how to work the till so he showed me and of course I cocked it up at first, went all panicky, but he didn't shout, he just went over it again and again until I got it. He's a lovely guy, Barry, so gentle and yet manly with it.'

I went tense again. 'You're not going to start a thing with this Barry, are you?'

'Don't be so daft, darling. He's got a wife, a nice woman, Lynn – she was kind too,' Mum said, but with less enthusiasm. 'Anyway, isn't it great? Job sorted, just like that, when I only nipped out for a packet of fags.' Mum lit up a cigarette triumphantly.

'Will it mean you working evenings, Mum?'

'You won't really mind, will you? You've babysat for Kendall heaps of times before, no bother. And it won't be every evening; my hours will vary. I don't have to start till midday though, which will be great. I'll be here to give you guys breakfast and get you off to school. Well, when you *get* a school. That's next on the agenda!'

Eight

I wished we didn't have to go to *any* school. I hadn't always got on at my old school. The lessons were OK. It just took me ages to find a friend. When my dad was in prison some of the other kids kept picking on me. Then when he came out Dad got into fights with *their* dads and then they started fighting me.

If it was hard for me it would be hopeless for Kendall. He got trampled on in his reception class.

'I've *been* to school, Mum,' he said. 'I don't need to go again.'

'Yeah, right, I've been to school too, Mum,' I said. 'Do we really have to go?'

'Oh come on, Lola Rose, don't be so daft. You've got to go to school, it's the law. Now, there's a nice primary down by the church. The kids wear a very smart uniform. We'll nip down there tomorrow morning and get you both registered,' said Mum.

It wasn't that simple. We didn't even get to see the headteacher because we didn't have a proper appointment. They told us we didn't have a hope of getting into the school as all the classes were full. They had a long waiting list of children desperate to go there. You had to have a sibling already registered and live in the right catchment area and be a regular worshipper at the church.

'Well, that's that then,' said Mum, as we walked out.

'Hurray!' said Kendall, skipping. 'No school!'

'Not *that* school, sweetheart. I wouldn't want to send you there anyway, all those poncy rules and regulations. We'll find you another better school, no bother.'

It was a lot of bother. Mum got a list of the local schools from the public library and started phoning round. They were nearly all full up. One said they could take Kendall but not me. Another said their reception class was too big already but they had room for me. The schools were miles apart so that was no good. I'd have to collect Kendall after school now Mum was working down the pub.

Larkrise Primary was right at the bottom of the

list. Mum got straight through to the headteacher, Ms Balsam.

'Yes, we've got places, Mrs Luck. Bring Lola Rose and Kendall along as soon as you like,' she said.

'There!' said Mum triumphantly. 'I knew our luck would last. Larkrise! Doesn't that sound pretty, like a little country village school?'

She walked us to Larkrise, holding our hands, singing, *'Follow, follow, follow, follow, follow the Larkrise Road'*. She even started doing that little *Wizard of Oz* dance, pointing her feet and sashaying left and right. She tried to get us to do the dance too but I felt a fool and wouldn't and Kendall tried hard but couldn't.

Even Mum stopped dancing when we turned into Larkrise Road. There were no larks rising. Only the scabbiest one-legged pigeons pecked at pizza crusts in the gutter. Big council flats towered above us in every direction, grey and bleak, water stains running down the brick as if every window eye was weeping.

We hadn't noticed the wind before but now it blew coldly in our faces and whirled the litter round our ankles. We had to pick our way carefully through sprinklings of chips and crumpled cans and dog mess. Mum gripped Kendall's hand firmly, steering him this way and that. My throat went dry. I hugged myself tight inside my furry denim jacket. It looked like I was going to have to keep it on all day or else it would get nicked.

The school looked exactly like a prison. It was an

ugly, squat, yellow-brick building with barbed wire hooked along the top of the wall and two padlocks on the iron bars of the gates.

'Is that to keep people out or the kids in?' Mum said, wavering. She gave the gates a little rattle. 'How do *we* get in, for God's sake? Maybe this isn't such a good idea.'

Kendall jumped up and pressed a button on the wall. The intercom crackled into action. We all took a step backwards.

'Quick, let's go,' I said.

Mum dithered.

A mystery voice said, 'Yes, can I help you?'

Mum cleared her throat and spoke to the brick wall. 'My name's Victoria Luck. I'm here with my two children, Lola Rose and Kendall.'

I couldn't hear our new names enough times. It made us all feel better. Mum swept her hair out of her white leather collar. I folded my arms and stuck my fingers up inside my sleeves, stroking the fur lining. Kendall squared his tiny shoulders in his hip jacket.

'Kendal *mint cake*!' he said. He looked at us expectantly. He'd made the same joke a thousand and one times but we smiled all the same.

'Do come in,' said the voice. There was a little buzzing sound and a side gate opened all by itself.

'It's like that fairy tale. You know, *Beauty and the Beast*,' I said.

'You be Beauty. I'll be the Beast,' said Kendall, pulling what he hoped was a hideous face. He hobbled lopsidedly across the playground.

'Will you stop that, Kendall! They'll think you've got disabilities,' said Mum. 'Oh God, I'm dying for a fag. Do you think they'd mind?'

'You *can't*, Mum.'

But when we were shown in Ms Balsam's office we smelt a very familiar stale fug. I saw an overflowing ashtray on her desk. She saw me staring at it and emptied it quickly into her wastepaper basket.

'Sorry, sorry, sorry! *Horrible* habit,' she said. 'Never start smoking, Lola Rose. You'll end up looking like a smoked haddock, just like me.'

She did look a little fishy, her beady eyes magnified by the thick lenses of her glasses, and her long pale face was a bit yellowy. She wasn't a bit pretty but she didn't seem to care. She had a very posh voice but she didn't *act* posh and her clothes certainly weren't posh. She was wearing comfy old trousers and a creased jacket with bulging pockets.

She saw Mum looking longingly at the ashtray and patted her pocket. 'Shall we have a cigarette, Mrs Luck, and blow being a bad influence on the children?' She took out a packet of cigarettes and a novelty lighter in the shape of a fish. You flicked the head and the flame flared inside the jaws.

'Is that a shark?' Kendall asked.

'It doesn't look quite fierce enough for a shark,' said Ms Balsam.

'I love sharks. I don't care if they're fierce. I'm not a bit scared of sharks, am I, Mum?'

'Shh now, Kendall,' said Mum.

'No, it's OK, I want to have a chat with both the children.'

'I've seen *lots* of sharks. They're my friends. But silly old Jayni's scared of them!'

Mum and I froze. But Ms Balsam acted like she hadn't even noticed he'd called me by the wrong name. 'Could that *possibly* be a shark peeping out of your super-cool jacket, Kendall?' she asked.

'Yes! It's George the Second. I had another George but he ran away.'

'*Swam* away?' said Ms Balsam. She looked at me. 'I gather you don't care for sharks, Lola Rose?'

'I can't stick them,' I said.

'So what are you interested in?'

I shifted in my seat.

'What do you like doing best?'

'My scrapbook.'

Mum sighed. 'No, Lola Rose, she means hobbies. Well, you like crayoning and I've shown you how to do a little dance routine, haven't I?'

'What do you put in your scrapbook?' Ms Balsam persisted. 'Do you cut out pictures of your favourite band and football team?'

'I like cutting out all different bits and making it all look good on the page,' I said.

'Sometimes she goes a bit nuts and gives ladies animal heads and has a giant girl standing on the roof of a building,' says Mum, shaking her head.

'Collage!' says Ms Balsam. 'That's what it's called. Oh great, we'll do some collage work in art. I'll be taking you for art, Lola Rose. I'm helping out because we're a few teachers short. Right, I just need to take down a few details. Which was your last school?'

I swallowed. I tried to think of a name, *any* name. 'It was . . . London Primary,' I said stupidly.

'London *Park* Primary,' Mum said quickly.

Ms Balsam wrote it down, but she frowned a little. Maybe we weren't fooling her. I could just as easily have said Mickey Mouse Made-up School.

'And what about Kendall? Was he in the reception class at London Park?' she asked.

'Yes,' said Mum.

'No!' said Kendall, looking astonished. 'I'm at Molesfield Infants and I've got a blazer with a mole and a field on the badge.'

'Shut up, Kendall,' I said. I looked at Ms Balsam. 'He's making it up. He does it all the time. Doesn't he, Mum?'

'Yeah,' said Mum helplessly, drawing deeply on her cigarette.

Ms Balsam put down her pen and looked straight at me. 'We all make things up when it's necessary, Lola Rose. Or we simply keep quiet about things. *I* keep quiet about things. For instance, my lovely school might very well be closed down at the end of the school year because the silly inspectors feel we should be doing much better. We're on emergency measures at the moment.'

'Ah, I wondered how come you had spare places for the kids,' said Mum. 'So if the school's going to close there's not much point my two starting here, is there?'

'I'm determined we're *not* going to close,' said Ms Balsam. 'I'm very proud of my school and my staff and my wonderful pupils. They come from all different backgrounds and yet I like to feel we all fit together as a family. We're used to refugee children and others from troubled backgrounds, Mrs Luck. We don't always dot every 'i' and cross every 't' in our paperwork because we're too busy to pry into people's private affairs.' She picked up her form and tossed it in the wastepaper basket with the cigarette butts.

Mum smiled and raised her eyebrows at me. 'There now, isn't that lucky?' she said. 'That's very understanding of you, Ms Balsam. So, can I leave the kids with you today?'

'Certainly. I'll take them along to their classes – unless you'd like to come with Kendall to settle him in?'

'Lola Rose might be better. Our Kenny— Kendall tends to play up a bit with me.'

Mum gave us both a quick kiss and then dashed off with an airy wave before we could take in she was abandoning us. Kendall's mouth wobbled, the corners turning tight down. I had to fight not to cry myself. It was OK for Mum. She didn't have to stick it out at this scary new school with all these tough kids who would hate us because we were new and weird.

But it wasn't scary at all! Ms Balsam let me hold Kendall's hand tight while she took us into the reception class. There were loads of little kids messing around finger painting, bashing bricks, kneading red dough and trooping in and out of a little playhouse. A big girl with long fair hair in a ponytail and dungarees was having a funny paintbrush fight with a scabby little boy with a bristly head.

I thought she was an older sister like me but it turned out she was Ms Denby, the *teacher*. She gave Kendall a big smile as if she'd known him all her life. 'Hello, darling. What's your name, then?'

Kendall swallowed and looked at me, scared to speak in case he said something wrong again.

'His name's Kendall,' I announced.

The scabby boy sniggered. A plump little girl with a topknot stuck her chin out. '*I'm* Kendall,' she said.

'Kendall's a girl's name,' said Scabby. He laughed. The other boys did too.

'It's a girl's name *and* a boy's name. Didn't you know that?' said Ms Denby. 'Welcome to our class, Kendall. What would you like to do? How about finger painting?'

Kendall's hand screwed itself up inside mine. He hates getting his hands dirty.

'How about the dough?' said Ms Denby.

Kendall shuddered at the thought of getting it up his fingernails.

'He wants to build a big tower of bricks,' I suggested. I knew he should make a safe, boy's choice.

Kendall was staring at the playhouse. 'I don't want to do bricks,' he said. 'I want to go in that little house with George.'

I held my breath, waiting for the scabby kid to sneer. Surprisingly no one seemed to think it sissy to go and play house. When I led Kendall over I found two little boys and one little girl crouched inside, having a tea party.

'Do you want tea or coffee?' the little girl asked, laying a place for Kendall with her blue plastic tea set.

'Coffee. Black. And a ciggie too,' said Kendall.

'Coming right up,' she said, pouring imaginary coffee and lighting an invisible cigarette for him.

Kendall took it from her and inhaled thin air with appreciation. 'Thanks, babe,' he said.

Ms Denby and Ms Balsam and I were in silent stitches. Ms Denby gave me a thumbs-up sign. I nodded and went off with Ms Balsam. She patted my shoulder.

'There, he's settled in already,' she said.

We both knew it might not be so easy for me. I felt sick when we walked into the Year Six class-room. I thought I was quite tall but lots of the girls were much bigger than me, and so grown-up! They wore tight designer tops that showed their figures, and they had elaborate plaited hairstyles and nose rings and fantastic fingernails.

OK, not *all* the girls. There were a couple of little scruffy twitchy girls who looked sad. Then there were a clump of girls with big headscarves who all sat together. There was another Asian girl sitting by herself. She had her hair in a long glossy plait and when she grinned she had a gap in her front teeth. She was grinning at me.

She came up to me at play time. 'I love your jacket!' she said, stroking it admiringly. 'I'm Harpreet. What's your name again? Lola?'

'Lola Rose.'

'Cool name!'

I didn't need to worry. I wasn't sad old Jayni who got picked on.

I was cool Lola Rose in her fantastic furry jacket.

So now we were the Luck family – Victoria, Kendall and Lola Rose – and we had a whole new life going for us. It was strange how quickly it stopped feeling new. After a few weeks it was weird thinking back to the *old* life. I didn't feel fussed when someone asked me my name and wanted to know where I lived. I felt like I'd been Lola Rose for ever. I could have grown up in Flexley Park and been at Larkrise Primary all my school life.

Harpreet was the sort of best friend I'd always longed for. We sat next to each other in class and helped each other with all our work. She was brilliant at maths and IT and science. I'm OK at English and better at art so it worked a treat.

Ms Balsam *did* do a special collage lesson! She brought in a huge pile of old magazines for us to cut up. She suggested we do a picture with a family theme. Harpreet flipped through a big glossy magazine, trying to find photos of people who looked like *her* family. She had a huge family – her mum and dad, a little sister, a big sister, two big brothers, and hundreds of aunties and uncles and cousins and her grandma and grandpa out in India. She started moaning because all the people in the photos were too pink.

'You can colour them with brown felt pen if you like. Or maybe you can find stuff that kind of *represents* your family,' I said.

'Like what?' said Harpreet.

'Like … you could find someone with a big smiley mouth and cut it out and then find a white rabbit and a top hat and that could be your dad,' I said. I loved Harpreet's funny dad. He made a big fuss of me and did all these daft conjuring tricks, pretending to find eggs behind my ears and a string of coloured hankies from the sleeve of my new jacket.

'What about his body?' said Harpreet, who didn't quite get it.

'You don't need to show the actual people. Look, your mum could be represented by lots of gold jewellery and a television set because she can't miss any of her soaps. Your brother Amrit could be a state-of-the-art computer, right?'

'What shall I be?' said Harpreet.

'You can be sweets and a long plait and lots of little numbers because you're good at maths and you could find two linked hands and colour friendship bracelets round the wrists and they could be you and me.'

'You have such *good* ideas, Lola Rose,' said Harpreet. 'I'm so lucky having you as my friend.'

I helped Harpreet stick all her family on a bright pink background with a border of red hearts and yellow flowers. We outlined everything with a gold glitter pen. It looked lovely.

'I can't wait to show Dad,' said Harpreet. 'I bet he'll frame it and hang it in the lounge.' She paused. 'What about *your* dad, Lola Rose?'

'I haven't got one,' I said. I selected a large piece of turquoise paper for my own collage.

'You must have had a dad *once*,' said Harpreet. 'What's that blue for? Is that going to be sky?'

'It's going to be water,' I said.

I cut out a pink girl and added bright yellow hair way down past her waist. I fashioned a tail from a photo of green grass and made her into a mermaid. I cut little red roses for her hair and wound them round and round her long tail in a garland. I stuck her up at the top of the water, waving to a little green frog leaping up and down on a lily pad.

I searched for a woman pretty enough to be Mum but I couldn't find one, so I turned a beautiful white statue into a water nymph. I added lots more golden curls and inked tiny black musical notes coming out of her parted lips.

I cut out more red roses, a great fluttering drift of them, and stuck them in a big red heart round the mermaid and the frog and the statue. It looked like it was keeping them safe. The rest of the blue paper looked a bit bare so I stuck on some buried treasure and a little aeroplane sailing like a ship and ice lollies swimming along like a shoal of fish.

I wanted to stop there, but I couldn't. I cut out a shark from a nature magazine. I didn't like touching it with my fingers even though I knew it was only paper. I didn't want it in my picture. I wanted to rip it into little bits. But I stuck it down right at the very bottom of the page. It was looking up up up through the water at the three people caged in the heart.

'That looks scary,' said Harpreet.

It did look much too scary. I tried to ease the shark off the paper but the glue stuck fast. I tried pulling.

'Don't rip up your lovely picture!' said Harpreet. 'You'll spoil it.'

'I don't like the shark,' I said. 'I'm going to cover him up.'

I found a picture of some houses. I started cutting out a whole row of them, complete with little gardens. 'I'm going to have an underwater buried village,' I said.

I arranged it right along the bottom of the page, covering up every tooth and fin and scale. I put shells and seaweed hedges in the gardens and stuck anchors on the top of every roof as television aerials. I stuck and stuck until the bottom of my picture was twice as thick as the top, but it didn't stop me worrying about the shark swimming silently in and out the windows and doors, looking for his family.

I dreamt about the shark at night. I couldn't get back to sleep, even though I huddled close to Mum.

I hated her being out so much. I put Kendall to bed about eight but I stayed up until Mum came home, even though she sometimes didn't make it back till midnight.

'You should go to sleep, Lola Rose, you silly girl,' Mum said, rubbing her finger under my eyes. 'Look at these dark circles. You look like a little panda. You're a bad bad girl.'

But she didn't get cross with me. She was always in a good mood now when she came home from the pub. It wasn't just the drinks her customers bought her. I was scared she might have started a thing with the manager, Barry. She seemed to be very thick with him, especially since they had a karaoke night and Mum sang a special Kylie medley.

'He said I'm every bit as good as Kylie – and he said my bum's just as good as hers too,' Mum said, dancing round the bedroom in her underwear.

'Mum!'

'He says he might give me a regular singing spot. He's got this mad idea that I could stand on top of the bar counter and prance round a bit.' Mum waggled her bum and held her hairbrush like a mike, demonstrating.

'*Mum!*'

'Your face, Lola Rose!' said Mum. 'Look, darling, if I've got a nice voice there's no reason why I shouldn't show it off.'

'It sounds like this Barry guy is more interested in your nice bum,' I said sourly.

'Ooh, you cheeky girl,' said Mum, pretending she was going to smack *my* bum with the hairbrush. 'Nah, old Barry's a sweetheart but he's too much under his wife's thumb. She doesn't mind the singing idea if it brings in more customers but she'll make sure Barry behaves himself. Not that I'd let him get anywhere. He's way too old and dull for me. I've got other fish to fry.'

Mum grinned at herself in the dressing-table mirror we'd bought at the weekend at a hospice shop.

My stomach squeezed. 'What do you mean, other fish to fry?' I said.

'It's just a silly expression, sweetheart. Take no notice,' said Mum, brushing her hair.

'Have you got a new boyfriend?'

'No! Well, not exactly. You can't call him a boyfriend. We've not even been out together. But he's interested, put it that way. Well, a number of the guys down the pub have chatted me up, as a matter of fact – but Jake's different.'

'Jake?'

'He is *gorgeous*, Lola Rose. He's an artist. He says he wants to paint my portrait. Imagine, I might find myself hanging in an art gallery one day! It's Jake who's the oil painting though. He's got this thick dark-blonde hair, quite long, as lovely as a girl's, but there's nothing girly about Jake, *oh no!*'

My heart was beating so fast I felt dizzy. 'Mum, don't!' I was in such a panic I didn't think what I was saying. 'What if Dad finds out?'

Mum stared at me. 'Dad?' she said. She acted like she'd forgotten all about him. 'Your dad's got nothing to do with it, darling. He's in the past. Over and done with. We'll never see him again.'

'But . . .' I screwed up my face, struggling. I didn't know why I felt in such a panic. That's what I wanted to hear, wasn't it? *I* didn't want to see Dad. But it seemed so weird for Mum to talk about him as if he was an old film she could barely remember. Dad had always come first with her.

'Don't you love him any more?' I said, as Mum got into bed.

She wasn't listening properly, humming under her breath. 'You what? Do I love Jake? It's early days, darling, early days.'

'I said do you love *Dad*!'

'Shh! Don't shout, you'll wake Kendall. Why are you going on about your dad, for God's sake? Don't you remember what he was like? He's left me with lots of little mementoes – look.' Mum tapped the caps on her teeth.

'Yeah, I know, Mum. But that's just it. Why are you taking up with another guy when you've only just left Dad? Why can't you be happy with Kendall and me?'

'Oh grow up, Jayni – sorry, Lola Rose.'

'I *do* act grown up, you know I do,' I said, turning my back on her.

'Oooh, don't go in a huff, sweetheart.' Mum cuddled up to me.

I tried to pull away, stiff as a board. Mum tickled me until I squealed and doubled up.

'Shh, shh!' said Mum, though she was giggling too. She cuddled in quick and this time I didn't wriggle away. 'I just mean when you *are* grown up you'll understand. I love you and little Kenny with all my heart, darling – but I need a man too. Life isn't worth living if you don't have someone to make your heart flutter. You'll see when you're older.'

I was sure I wouldn't. My heart had done enough fluttering to last me a lifetime. I didn't think I'd ever want a man. Especially not the kind of guy my mum liked.

I hoped this Jake would fade out of sight as quickly as the footballer, but Mum started going out with him on her nights off. When she was working he stayed till closing time and then walked her home. He came into our flat sometimes. Whenever I heard two lots of footsteps I snapped the light off quick and pretended to be asleep.

I wasn't in any hurry to meet him. I was very glad we only had one bedroom, and Kendall and I were sprawled right across the only bed.

But then he came round on Sunday, Mum's day off. I should have suspected something. Mum got up early and showered and shampooed for ages. She got dressed in a new tiny turquoise top that showed off her navel diamond and put on her tight white jeans. Usually on Sundays we had a long lie-in until eleven or twelve and then Mum just muddled around the house barefoot, a big cardie over her nightie.

But that Sunday Mum nagged at Kendall and me to get up bright and early. Well, it *was* early but we weren't feeling bright. I didn't want to get dressed in *my* new jeans. They were already uncomfortably tight around my tummy. I always seemed hungry now, especially in the evenings when Mum was out. I'd eat three bars of chocolate on the trot, or go on buttering slice after slice of bread until I'd polished off the whole loaf.

I wanted to stay in my nightie and sit up in bed and stick stuff in my scrapbook. Ms Balsam had given me lots of her magazines. I was having fun snipping out heads and bodies and arms and legs and making new people on my page. Sometimes I invented strange new species with six arms or car wheels for feet. I'd cut the heads off the skinniest fashion models and stick them onto enormous elephants and whales.

'Come on, Lola Rose, stop that sticking and get *washed*,' said Mum, snatching my scrapbook. She pulled a face. 'You're definitely sick, you! One warped, weird little kid. What's with the whale lady? Tell you what, she's a dead spit of your Auntie Barbara.' Mum giggled and adjusted her jeans over her own tiny hips.

Kendall wanted to stay in bed too. He was involved in a complicated game with George under the covers, swimming in their own dark private ocean. Mum fished him out and carried him squealing to the bathroom.

'I want two clean, charming, well-dressed kids, *if* you don't mind,' she said.

'Why?' I whined. 'It's Sunday.'

'Exactly,' said Mum. 'It's Sunday. *Funday*. My Jake's coming round and we're all going out to have fun at Camden Lock market.'

Kendall and I were going to need some convincing. We got washed and dressed sullenly.

'For God's sake, smile!' said Mum, when Jake knocked on the door. She glanced at us anxiously. Especially me. It was as if she was suddenly noticing how big I was.

Jake came as a shock. He *was* good looking in a scruffy sort of way. His fair hair was longer than mine, tied back in a ponytail. But he was young. I'd imagined this big artist guy in his thirties. Jake was an art *student*.

'He's much younger than you, Mum,' I hissed in the ladies at Camden Lock.

'Not *that* much,' said Mum.

'How much?' I said. 'He's still at art college, isn't he?'

'Look, you're acting like he's still at school.'

'How old *is* he, Mum?'

'It doesn't *matter*. Now shut up and get a move on. I want to look round all the stalls. It's great here, isn't it? Jake told me all about it.'

When we came out of the ladies Jake and Kendall weren't there. We both stared at the wall where we'd left them as if expecting them to rematerialize. The spot stayed empty.

I clutched Mum's hand.

'They'll be in the gents,' she said.

'Kendall wouldn't let any stranger take him to the toilet,' I said.

Kendall was weirdly private. He hollered if Mum or I happened to burst in when he was on the loo. He'd often hang on grimly rather than use a public toilet. Sometimes he didn't make it in time.

'Jake isn't a stranger,' Mum said crossly.

She walked over to the gents. I followed her. We waited a minute. I started to feel sick. I must have gone white because Mum nudged me.

'It's OK, Lola Rose. For God's sake, they're just having a pee.' She shouted through the door. 'Oi, Jake, Kendall, get a move on in there! Lola Rose is getting worried.'

No one answered. Mum swallowed, pulling her white jacket higher round her neck.

'Jake? Kendall?' she shouted.

A strange man came out of the toilet, grinning stupidly. 'You lost someone, darling?'

'It's OK, it's just my boyfriend and my little boy. Maybe he's had a bit of an accident?'

'There's no one in there, pet.'

'What, not even in the cubicle?'

'There's only one and I've just come out of it.'

'Oh God,' said Mum. She looked at me. She chewed on her finger. 'Well, they've obviously gone for a little wander round. Boys!' she said, trying to sound jaunty. She gave me another nudge because I was crying. 'Stop it! Kendall will be fine. He's with Jake.'

'We don't *know* Jake, not properly. And what if Dad tracked us down and saw them together? Maybe *he's* got Kenny?'

'Oh my God, they've killed Kenny,' said the toilet guy, quoting *South Park*.

'Shut it, mate,' said Mum. She pulled me away.

'What are we going to do?' I looked at the heaving crowds in the market. 'How are we going to find them?'

'We *will*. Just shut up.'

'We shouldn't have left Kenny with Jake. Why did we have to go out with him anyway? He's not part of our family.'

'He could be one day,' said Mum. 'Don't look at me like that. And *you* were the one whining on about needing to go to the ladies.'

It was so awful thinking it was my fault. 'Kenny!' I yelled.

I rushed down the first little alleyway between the stalls. 'Kenny, where are you? *Kenny!*'

'I'm Kendall,' he said, bobbing up out of nowhere, laughing at me. 'Look what we've got, Lola Rose. Pancakes! Yummy yum.'

'Jammy crepes,' said Jake. 'Kendall chose the jams. He's got blackcurrant for you, Lola Rose, because he says you like purple.'

I love pancakes. I love blackcurrant jam. But my stomach was so stirred up, it was like swallowing an old sock. I only ate a mouthful and then threw it away.

Mum glared at me. 'You mean little cow,' she hissed. 'It was sweet of him to buy us pancakes. He hasn't got much money, Lola Rose, seeing he's a student. You could at least act like you're grateful. You're showing me up. At least *Kendall*'s behaving beautifully.'

That made me feel sicker than ever. Kendall was usually so shy and strange with anyone new. But now he was holding Jake's free hand, skipping along happily, George carefully tucked under his armpit. He was babbling non-stop, most of it non-sense, some me-and-George saga. Jake wasn't even *listening*, but every time he gave a little grunt Kendall's face lit up delightedly.

Jake's other hand was holding Mum's.

I wanted them to look ridiculous as a couple.

They looked great together. Mum seemed so different when she was around Jake. When she was near Dad Mum was always twitching, scared because the slightest thing could set him off. She was always glancing anxiously at him. She never dared look at anyone else. Dad went berserk if he thought she was eyeing up any other men.

But now Mum mucked about and giggled and sang little snatches of song. Heaps of men turned to look at her. Some of them said stuff. Mum waved and blew them kisses. Jake grinned and waved too. His new silver bangle slid up his slim arm when he waved.

It was a present. Mum bought it for him. She bought me some sparkly stud earrings that looked like real diamonds. She bought Kendall a real wristwatch even though he can't tell the time yet. She bought herself a moonstone pendant. She got Jake to fasten it round her neck as if *he'd* bought it for her.

'Aren't moonstones meant to be unlucky?' he said.

'Not on me. I'm Lady Luck,' said Mum. 'Don't you like it?'

'It's pretty, very pretty. *You're* pretty,' said Jake. He kissed her neck where he'd fastened the clasp.

'Um! Look at Mum and Jake, they're *kissing*,' said Kendall.

It was obvious what was going to happen next.

Ten

'Maybe it would be a good idea to rearrange the flat a bit,' said Mum. 'I've been thinking. You and Kendall might like your own den, more of a play space. So how about us turning the bedroom into *your* room. It's purple too, your favourite colour.'

'Lilac isn't purple.'

'It's *light* purple, Miss Picky. Anyway, I was thinking of getting a little portable telly for you two. You'd like that, wouldn't you? Then the living room could be more – well, my room.'

'And you want to put a socking great bed in it for you and Jake,' I said coldly.

'No I don't! Well. I was thinking about one of them sofa beds. Then if Jake should want to stay over . . .'

'Why can't he stay in his own place?'

'He hasn't exactly *got* his own place,' said Mum. 'He's staying with a friend at the moment.'

'Why can't he *get* his own place, then?' I said.

'Because he hasn't got any money. He's a student.'

'They give them rooms in the university, don't they?'

'Only the first year. For God's sake, Lola Rose, give it a rest. He's coming to live with us and that's that. I don't see why you've got such a problem with it. We're in love, can't you see?'

'He doesn't love you. He's just shacking up with us because he hasn't got anywhere else. And you spend a fortune on him. *Our* fortune.'

Mum slapped me straight across the face. Kendall was watching. He cried. I didn't cry. I stared Mum out.

'You only slapped me because you know it's true.'

'I slapped you because you're a spoilt little cow,' Mum snapped. 'What's the matter with you, Lola Rose? You can't be jealous, can you?'

'What, jealous of Jake?' I folded my arms. She was asking for it. 'Well, he is more my age than yours.'

I stepped back smartly in case she tried another slap.

She was meaner than that.

'Don't kid yourself *you'll* ever get a man like Jake,' she said, looking me up and down.

I didn't want her to see me cry. I slammed straight out of the house and down the path. I hoped she'd yell after me to come back but she didn't. So I went on walking, though I didn't really know where I was going.

I knew my way to school, I knew my way to the chippy and the Chinese, I knew my way to Mum's pub, I knew my way to the video shop. And I knew my way to Harpreet's house.

I could go and see Harpreet. She was my best friend now. We had our own special handshake and we each wore half of a Friends Forever locket. We told each other all sorts of secrets. We had very long whispered conversations about sex and often ended up giggling helplessly. But I didn't want to tell her about Mum and Jake. It was the one thing I couldn't talk about. My family.

Harpreet talked about her family all the time. She quarrelled with her brothers and sisters sometimes and she argued a little bit with her mum and dad, but they never had a proper *row*. They never ever hit each other.

I wished I'd been born part of Harpreet's family. I wished Harpreet's dad was *my* dad. I loved the way he put his arm round Harpreet and cuddled her close and called her his little girl. My dad had done all that with me. He called me all sorts of special things when he was in a good mood. I was his Princess Rosycheeks, his Fairy Doll, his Jay-Jay Jam Doughnut. But the good mood could change to bad, and then he'd call me other stuff, short, sharp, ugly words that stuck to me like slime.

I couldn't imagine Harpreet's dad turning like that. I asked her once to tell me the very worst thing he'd ever done to her. She thought and thought and then said he'd shouted at her when she was little because she'd run into the road. She'd cried and then *he* cried and gave her a great big hug.

Harpreet laughed and said he was a silly softie old dad, though he could be horribly strict about bedtimes and it didn't look like he was ever going to let her have a boyfriend. It seemed to me he was the best dad in the world.

I wasn't so sure about Harpreet's mum. She wasn't really pretty, though she had beautiful big eyes with long eyelashes. She had a way of rolling her eyes and sighing that made me nervous.

She seemed to be quite friendly with my mum, but she rolled her eyes expressively afterwards. I don't think she liked it that my mum got on very well with Harpreet's dad. She never *said* anything but she didn't need to. She just looked at my mum's hair or her tight top or her short skirt, she listened to my mum's giggle and her tales of what went on down the pub – and those eyes rolled like marbles.

I'd hoped I'd grow up little and pretty like Mum. I'd so hoped it might happen when I turned into Lola Rose. But now I wondered how I'd kidded myself. Mum had made it obvious. I wasn't ever going to look like her.

I'd end up like Auntie Barbara instead.

I walked straight past Harpreet's house. I walked faster and faster, as if I was trying to run away from myself. I wasn't even sure who I was any more. I couldn't believe how quickly Mum had settled into this new life. How could she fall in and out of love so easily? She acted like all those corny old love songs she sang, changing as quickly as a jukebox. She stood by her man but he was so cruel so it was all over and she did her crying in the rain and she would survive but then she met this stranger and then it was passionate kisses.

I thought of Mum and Jake kissing.

Then I heard kissing noises behind me. Loud, slurpy, silly lip-smacking.

It was a gang of boys hanging about outside the video shop. I knew one of them, a horrible boy called Peter who was in my class at school. He kept trying to pull all the girls' skirts up. He had a very pink face and big nostrils in a flat nose. Harpreet and I called him Peter Piglet.

'Give us a kiss then, Lola Rose,' he called.

I pulled a face at him. 'Get lost, Peter Piglet,' I said fiercely.

Peter went pinker than ever. The other boys laughed, and made more kissing noises. They were mostly older than Peter. That Ross was with them. He was famous in Flexley Park. All the girls fancied him. He was only thirteen but he got sixteen-year-old girls wanting to go out with him.

He was looking at me too. 'Yeah, fancy a snog, Lola Rose?' he said.

I didn't know if he was joking or not. The other boys were still making kissing noises.

I hurtled down the street away from them. I ran and ran away from their raucous laughter. I tripped and fell over and they laughed more. I tore the knees of my new jeans and got the sleeves of my beautiful furry jacket dirty.

I was sobbing by the time I got home. I wanted to make it up with Mum and have a cuddle with her – but Jake was there.

'Where've you *been*, Lola Rose? Don't you dare flounce off like that! I've been dead worried about you. Are you crying?'

'No!'

I tried to go into the bedroom but she caught hold of me.

'What's up with you? Look at the state of you! Your new jeans! And your jacket – look at the cuffs, they're filthy!'

I cried more then, but Mum rubbed at it with a damp tea cloth and cleaned up both cuffs. The jeans were so badly ripped at the knees she said she couldn't sew them.

'Maybe I can,' said Jake.

I thought he was joking, but he cut up an old flowery shirt he said he didn't want any more and made appliquéd flower patches on both knees.

'Wow,' said Mum, ruffling Jake's hair. 'You're a man of many talents.'

'Men don't sew,' said Kendall.

'He's a man, all right,' said Mum, kissing Jake. 'That's brilliant! Will you do mine too, darling? Lola Rose, don't you just love your new jeans! What do you say to Jake?'

'Thanks,' I said, as if he'd simply passed me the cornflakes. But I was secretly thrilled. I watched carefully to see how he did the appliqué stitch.

'I'll show you how to do it,' said Jake.

'It's OK,' I said, shrugging. I'd already worked it out.

I was determined not to be won over. I didn't see why Jake and I had to bond like Superglue just because Mum was nuts about him. She kept nagging at me to show him my scrapbook. I caught her lugging it out of the bedroom to show him herself. I flew at her and tugged it out of her arms.

'It's private!' I shouted.

'Ooh, what you got in there, then, Lola Rose? You been sticking in mucky pictures?'

The edge of my scrapbook had got bumped and the spine was torn a little in the struggle. I was furious.

'You're the only one who let guys take mucky pictures!' I said.

Mum went fiery red, even flushing down her neck. 'I never!' she shouted, like a little girl.

'Mucky pictures?' said Jake. 'Oh Victoria, you bad girl!'

'They weren't *mucky*,' Mum protested. She gave me a shove. 'I did some modelling once, that's all. Glamour pics.'

'Glamour!' said Jake, wiggling his eyebrows. 'Oh, show me, show me!'

'They were in these mags ages ago. I threw them all out,' Mum said quickly. She sighed, looking at Kendall and me. 'When I was young, before the kids ruined my figure.'

'I think it's gorgeous,' said Jake.

Mum beamed and nodded her head at me, as if to say, *So there!*

'Why can't you be happy for me?' she hissed in bed that night.

It looked like it was going to be the last night we were all tucked up together, Mum and Kendall and me. Jake had gone back to his mate's flat to gather his stuff together and have a few drinks. He was moving in with us tomorrow.

I didn't reply. I pretended to be asleep, but Mum pulled me over onto her lap.

'Do you really hate Jake?' she asked.

'He's OK.'

'Oh come on, he's flipping gorgeous! And he's so kind too. That's what I can't get over. Never loses his rag, never acts jealous. I thought you'd really landed me in it, going on about my glamour photos, but look how lovely he was. He's a man in a million, Lola Rose.'

'You've only known him five minutes, Mum.'

'I feel like I've known him all my life. The moment I set eyes on him I knew. We clicked, just like that.'

'You clicked with Dad. You clicked with the footballer. You click with any guy that's going,' I mumbled into the pillow.

Mum heard me. 'I'll click you right out of this bed if you don't shut up,' she said.

But she couldn't shut up herself.

'I couldn't wish for a sweeter guy. I never dreamt I could be so lucky. I'm getting on a bit now, I've got you two kids, my boobs are getting all saggy—'

'You're nuts,' I said.

'No, really.' She sat up in bed and stuck her chest out, feeling herself. 'Oh God, they *are*! I wonder how much a boob implant is. A thousand? More? I could afford it now!'

I snorted.

'What's your problem? It's *my* money and I've spent a fortune on you two.'

'And Jake,' I said. 'I bet he didn't buy his new cowboy boots himself. Or that new mobile. Or his new Walkman. Or that big set of oil paints.'

'He's an artist for God's sake.' Mum peered down at her breasts. 'Maybe I'd better have that implant if he's going to do a nude portrait of me. Do you think it hurts terribly? Would they have to cut you right open?'

'Oh no, of course not! They just unbutton your boobs, pop in the implant, and Bob's your uncle,' I said sarcastically. 'You're so stupid, Mum. Of course they cut you open. They cut right along underneath and then—'

'OK, don't go on about it,' said Mum. 'Maybe I'll put up with my boobs the way they are. Jake doesn't seem to have any complaints. That's what I mean, Lola Rose. He's so good to me. You don't think I was better off with your dad, do you?'

'I think you'd be better off without any bloke,' I said.

'You're starting to sound just like your Auntie Barbara,' said Mum. 'Watch out you don't start to look like her too!' She started poking my tummy. 'Ooh yes, podgy-wodgy!'

'Give over!' I said. 'You stop that, saggy-baggy!'

We tickled and poked, squealing with laughter. Kendall woke up and joined in. We had a wrestling match until Kendall fell right out of bed with a thump and the old lady downstairs started banging on her ceiling.

We hauled Kendall back into bed and then the three of us cuddled up close. We went to sleep just like that. I didn't even have the shark dream.

Eleven

Lipstick and High Heels

Jake moved in with us. Mum turned the living room into their room. She bought them a brand-new sofa bed. No community stores shabby old stuff this time. Mum bought a computer too. She pretended it was a present for Kendall and me. But it was Jake who sat at it all evening, playing games, while Mum was out working at the pub.

Kendall liked to loll against him. Sometimes Jake let him have a go.

'What about you, Lola Rose?'

'No thanks, it's boring,' I said.

I shut myself in my bedroom with my scrap

book. Mum had bought me a big pile of birthday cards, lovely flowers and seasides and sunsets and rainbows and fairy princess ladies with very long curly hair. They were brand-new birthday cards specially for me to cut up and stick in my scrapbook.

She bought them to stop me nagging her about the money. I'd found the envelope with the lottery winnings hidden under her tights. I'd peeped inside and panicked. There was hardly anything left. A fistful of five-pound notes. That was *all*.

I knelt there, Mum's tights squiggled all around me like black snakes. I felt so scared.

I stayed up and tackled Mum about it when she got back from the pub.

'Shut up, Lola Rose!' she said. She didn't want Jake to hear. 'How dare you nose round my things!' she hissed in my ear. 'It's *my* money anyway. It was my lottery ticket.'

'It's not anyone's money now. It's all gone.'

'Gone on lovely things for all of us,' said Mum. 'Now go to your bedroom this minute, you ungrateful little whatsit.'

I stormed off furiously. How could Mum be so stupid? What if she lost her job and couldn't get another? What if Jake started getting drunk and hitting her and we had to do another runner? The lottery money had made me feel so much safer.

I decided I wasn't speaking to Mum any more. But then she bought me the birthday cards and I couldn't stay cross. I spent hours cutting out and arranging and sticking. I wore a little groove at the side of my middle finger through gripping the scissors.

Kendall teased me because my mouth opened and shut as I snipped. 'Like a fish,' he said, and he made George attack me hungrily.

I was so startled I snipped straight through my favourite fairy princess. I made a great fuss and Kendall cried. I decided I didn't care. I found an African plains picture of giraffes and started creating a tribe of strange giraffe-girls, their abundant hair tumbling down their long spotted necks.

I called to Kendall, offering to tell him a giraffe-girl fairy story.

'I'm busy,' he shouted back triumphantly. 'I'm playing on the computer with Jake.'

I whispered bad swear words. Kendall liked being with Jake much more than being with me. So did Mum. They didn't seem to need me much any more.

I snipped snipped snipped at my magazine, playing guillotines. Heads tumbled into my lap. I crumpled them all together and threw them into the far corner of the room.

Well, *I* didn't need *them*.

I didn't need anyone. I was Lola Rose.

I just wished I *looked* more like my idea of Lola Rose.

I mooned in front of the mirror, experimenting with ways of doing my hair. I hunched my shoulders right up under my ears so that my hair seemed longer. I tugged at it, encouraging it to grow. Maybe next month, or the month after, or the one after *that*, it would have grown right down my back, fairy princess style.

I stole into the bathroom and squirted it with Mum's hairspray. Mum was so lucky having such thick hair. I could grow mine right down to the ground but it would always stay thin and wispy. It lay limp against my head now no matter how I tried to fluff it up.

I gave up on my hair and tried my face. I'd mucked about with make-up before, putting glitter on my eyelids and gloss on my lips, but I'd always wiped it off when Dad was due home. He said he didn't like to see his little girl all tarted up.

I could paint on make-up an inch thick now. I went crazy with Mum's make-up. I started properly with foundation and then pencilled in my eyebrows and smeared smoky grey on my eyelids. I outlined them with black pen, making it thicker whenever I wobbled. I put on two thick coats of mascara so I saw black fringe curtains every time I looked up.

Then I applied rouge on both cheeks. I knew you were supposed to follow the lines on your cheekbones, but my cheeks were so podgy I couldn't *find* my bones. At least I could see my lips. I attempted that special putting-on-lipstick smile but I got red all over my teeth, so I invented my own method, going slightly over the edge of my lips to make them look more voluptuous.

I hoped I looked much older. Twelve, fourteen, sixteen? I peeped in Mum's wardrobe and put on her high heels. We took nearly the same size now.

I stuffed the ends of the shoes with tissues. I stuck more tissues inside one of her bras so that I had an impressive bust when I pulled on my tightest T-shirt.

Jake and Kendall stared at me when I strutted into the living room.

'My goodness, Lola Rose,' said Jake.

'She looks silly,' said Kendall.

'You *are* silly,' I said. 'I'm going out.'

'Hang on,' said Jake. 'Are you allowed out by yourself?'

'I'm not going to *be* by myself. I'm meeting someone. Like a date.'

'Oh no you're not,' said Jake.

'Oh yes I am,' I said rushing to the front door.

Jake called to me to come back.

'You can't tell me what to do,' I shouted. 'You're not my dad.'

I met Steve and Andy down the road, coming back from a shopping trip, laden with Marks and Sparks carrier bags. Well, Andy was laden, two bags in either hand. Steve was swanning along carrying a plant pot. He raised his eyebrows at me and walked on, jasmine trailing decoratively down his arms. Andy stopped and balanced his shopping bags on the pavement. He mimed great delight to see me, clutching his heart.

'Why it's Lola Rose, looking *gorgeous*!'

'Hi, Andy,' I said. I tried to make my voice sound husky and provocative but it just sounded like I had a cold.

'Hi, Lola Rose,' he said, his own voice as gruff as

he could get. I laughed, even though he was taking the mickey.

I walked on down the road, though my ankles kept twisting in Mum's high heels. I decided to go round to Harpreet's house and show them off to her. I knocked at her door. I rang the bell too, in case they hadn't heard.

'Shh!' said Harpreet, opening the door. 'My dad's having a nap.' Then she looked at me properly. '*Lola Rose!*'

'Can I come and play?'

'Yeah. Well. For a bit. My mum's cooking our dinner.'

The wonderful hot savoury smell of it made my mouth water. I hoped I might get invited to share it. Harpreet took me into their front room. Her little sister Amandeep was sitting cross-legged in a corner, muttering to her Barbie dolls. Her big brother Amrit was hunched over the computer. He nodded in my direction without taking his eyes off the screen.

'Can I try your shoes on, Lola Rose?' Harpreet begged.

'Sure,' I said, slipping them off.

Harpreet wobbled around, roaring with laughter every step.

'Look, why don't you kids play shoe shops in another room?' said Amrit, sighing. Then he looked up and saw me. He stayed looking. He started telling me about the work he was doing on the computer. Then he went on about his football team at school. Then he started bragging about this band he and his mates had started up. He was the drummer. He didn't have his own drum kit but he started beating out the rhythm on the wall.

'Shut *up*, Amrit, you'll wake Dad,' said Harpreet.

'Dad's already awake,' said Mr Gabrie, coming into the room in his socks. He yawned. His mouth stayed open when he saw me.

'Good gracious, Lola Rose! No, it's not Lola Rose at all, silly me, she's just a little girl. You're her big sister. Good afternoon, Miss Luck, I'm delighted to meet you.'

I knew he was just kidding around, but it was fun, and Harpreet and Amandeep giggled. Amrit looked irritated.

'What's all this noise? Have you naughty children woken your poor father?' said Mrs Gabrie, putting her head round the door.

Her eyes rolled when she saw me. 'Does your mother know you're out like that, Lola Rose?' she said.

'This isn't Lola Rose, this is Lola Rose's beautiful big sister,' said Harpreet's dad. 'May I offer you a sherry, Miss Luck? Would you care for a cigarette?'

'Don't encourage her,' said Mrs Gabrie crossly. 'You'd better go home and wash your face, Lola Rose. Take those shoes off at once, Harpreet, and give them back to Lola Rose. Hurry up now, dinner's nearly ready.'

'Can Lola Rose stay for dinner?' Harpreet asked.

I looked at Mr Gabrie hopefully, but his eyes swivelled to his wife.

'I'm sorry, dear,' she said insincerely. 'There isn't enough for another person.'

'Lola Rose can eat mine. I'll be having a pizza with my mates later,' said Amrit.

I smiled at him with my shiny red lips, but Mrs Gabrie wouldn't relent.

'Nonsense,' she snapped. 'Lola Rose is going home for her own dinner now.' She looked at me beadily. 'You've got lipstick on your front teeth!'

I wanted to bite her with my stained teeth. I shrugged instead, pretending it was a totally cool new fashion to have bright red teeth. I stalked out of their house. I tripped going down their front path. I hoped they weren't watching.

My feet were hurting in Mum's shoes. It felt like I was getting a blister. Several. I knew I should go home but I'd only been gone half an hour. I'd never be able to convince Jake I'd had a real date.

I couldn't convince myself. I could call myself Lola Rose until the cows came home but I was still stuck being shy, soft old Jayni. I was never going to get pretty and sparky and sexy like Mum. I was going to get bigger and blobbier and end up like Auntie Barbara, just as Mum said. Poor elephantine Auntie Barbara who was so wibbly wobbly that no man would ever want her.

Maybe no man would ever want me. Amrit had acted like he was chatting me up, but maybe he was just having a laugh at me.

The gang of boys were hanging around outside the video shop again. Ross was there. Peter Piglet too. I knew I should run away quickly.

I didn't run. I walked towards them.

They started making the kissing noises again but I smiled this time. I walked right up to them, wobbling on Mum's high heels.

'You look daft in them shoes,' said Peter, his pink nostrils going in and out as he breathed heavily.

'You *are* daft, in shoes or out of them,' I said. I tried to sweep past him, but tripped.

'Whoopsie,' said Ross, and he clutched my arm to steady me.

He wasn't quite so good looking when you got close to him. His eyes were a little too close and his lips were too thin. I wasn't sure I wanted him hanging onto my arm. I tried to pull away.

'It's OK, I'm just helping you,' he said. 'It's Lola Rose, isn't it?

A tall boy in a torn T-shirt grinned. 'Lola Rose sat on a pin. Lola rose!'

It wasn't funny but they all fell about laughing. I knew they were laughing at me – but I grinned too.

'So you're in Pete's class?' said Ross. 'You look older than him.'

'I *act* older,' I said, tossing my hair.

He still had his hand on my arm. He wasn't gripping tight but his fingers felt weird on my skin. I wasn't sure if I liked it or not. He was obviously the boss guy of the gang. He was the best looking. He was the one all the girls fancied.

He was peering at me, head on one side. 'Where are you off to then, Lola Rose?' he asked.

I liked the way he kept saying my name. I loved

being reminded I was this new glamorous girl. She was so much more grown up than silly old Jayni.

I smiled back at Ross. 'Nowhere special,' I said casually.

'So hang out with us,' said Ross.

'OK,' I said, as if I couldn't really be bothered. I was fizzing inside. I wondered where we'd go. I hoped it might be McDonald's. I was starving hungry.

Ross didn't seem to be thinking about food. 'We'll go down the park,' he said, still smiling.

All the boys sniggered.

I took no notice. Ross was still smiling straight at me. His eyes were very blue with black lashes, and he had lovely smooth, rosy skin. He was big too, with muscles like he worked out. He could get any girl he wanted. He seemed to want *me*!

Ross and his mates strode off towards this park. I trotted along behind them, finding it hard to keep up in Mum's heels. Piglet Pete hung back, keeping pace with me.

I didn't want to be stuck with him. I wanted it to be a fairy tale. I looked almost pretty now I was Lola Rose. Maybe Ross wanted me to be his girl-friend. 'Push off, Pete,' I said.

'OK,' he said, shrugging. He ran ahead and joined the others.

'Hey, Lola Rose!' Ross called, peering back at me. 'Come on!' He beckoned with his finger, making little kissing encouraging noises.

The boys all laughed. I didn't like the way Ross was acting. He wasn't treating me like I was a girl. He was calling to me like I was his little dog.

I still followed him.

It wasn't a proper park, just a scrubby patch of grass and a tangle of bushes used as a rubbish dump. There was some woman walking her dogs way in the distance and an old man mumbling to himself, clutching a beer can. And all the boys, making stupid noises.

I wanted it to be just Ross and me in a beautiful big green park. We'd walk hand in hand and he'd be looking at me with those big blue eyes and whisper lovely things. But this was all so different. I was stuck by the bushes with all these boys and I didn't like it.

'It's getting late. I have to go home now,' I said.

'No you don't, Lola Rose. Come here!'

Ross bent his head and kissed me, right in front of the others. It wasn't gentle and loving, like he cared. He was just showing off. I struggled to get free but he held me tight. I twisted my head away and started yelling.

'Shut up, you idiot!' said Ross.

I wouldn't shut up. I shouted.

'Let that girl go!' someone called.

Ross hung onto me, but some of the others started running. A dog started barking furiously, getting nearer. Two dogs, leaping up at all of us, huge Alsatians.

Everyone was running now. I tried to run too, but I fell in my shoes. I huddled there on the grass, the dogs barking in my face, showing their sharp teeth. I started screaming.

'It's all right, Lola Rose! They won't hurt you. They just like to make a lot of noise – like me!'

I peered up past the two dogs. Ms Balsam was standing over me!

'Down, Bealey, down, Buss, down, girls! Stop barking, you're giving us both a headache. Give your paws to Lola Rose and show her you want to be friends!'

The two dogs quietened. They sat up on their back legs and politely offered me their paws. I took each one gingerly, giving it a tiny shake.

'There!' said Ms Balsam. 'See, I can control my dogs far better than I can control all you kids.'

'Hello . . . Bealey?' I said, patting the dog's head.

'This one's Miss Beale and this one's Miss Buss. They were amazing women who ran a school for girls in Victorian times. I called my dogs after them. I've had them since they were six weeks old. They're getting on a bit now but they can still make an impressive amount of noise. They scared off all the boys satisfactorily, didn't they? So what was going on, Lola Rose?'

'Oh, nothing,' I mumbled. I slipped Mum's shoes on and struggled to stand up.

Mrs Balsam put her hands under my elbows and hauled me upright. 'Are those your friends?'

'Sort of.'

'I know the big lad, Ross. I used to teach him. He was a real handful. Do you like him?'

'No,' I said, wiping my lips with the back of my hand.

'Here.' She fished in her pocket and found me a

tissue. 'You're all smudged. Have a good wipe.
Good god, you've got half of Boots' make-up
counter all over your face. Don't you dare turn up
at school like that. *Or* in those shoes. How do you
walk in them?'

'I can't, not properly. They're my mum's.'

'Doesn't she mind you borrowing her shoes?'

'Well, she doesn't exactly know.'

'Maybe you should scoot off home quick and put
them back in her wardrobe. So, Mum's out then?'

'Yeah, she works at the Coach and Horses.'

'So is there anyone at home to look after you and
Kendall?'

'Oh yes,' I said quickly. 'We've got Jake.'

'He's your babysitter?'

'Well, he's like Mum's boyfriend.'

'And you get on all right?' she asked, as we
walked towards the park gates, Miss Beale and
Miss Buss bounding after us.

I shrugged. 'He's OK, I suppose.'

'Did he say you could come out tonight?'

'I told him I had like a date.'

'With *Ross*?'

'No! I just met up with him and those others. And
he asked me to come down the park.'

'Did you think that was a good idea?' said Ms
Balsam.

'Yes. No. Well, I didn't know they'd start messing
about like that.'

'A smart girl like you?'

'Well, I suppose I went a little bit nuts because it
was Ross. I mean, he's so good looking and that. It

made me feel really special, like I was somebody.'

Ms Balsam stopped walking. She put her hands gently on my shoulders. She looked straight into my eyes. 'You *are* somebody, Lola Rose. You're a very special, clever, creative girl, and very mature for your age too. I'm very impressed with the way you look after Kendall. He's OK, is he?'

'Yes, he likes being with Jake. They play computer games all the time.'

'So do you feel a bit left out sometimes?'

'No. Well. Sometimes, yeah.'

'Lola Rose, I don't want to pry. I know there's probably a lot of stuff you don't want to talk about. But if ever you feel like a little chat you know you can always come and find me at school.'

'Yes, I know. Thank you, Ms Balsam.'

She gave me a lift home in her car, me in the front, Miss Beale and Miss Buss barking like mad in the back.

Ms Balsam nodded at me when I got out of the car. 'See you in school tomorrow. I saw Peter's in Ross's little gang. Do you want me to have a stern word with him?'

'Better not.'

'If you're really keen on getting a boyfriend wouldn't Peter be a better bet than Ross?'

'No fear!'

Ms Balsam chuckled. 'Oh dear. But I take your point. Bye for now then, Lola Rose. I hope you won't get into trouble for coming back late.'

'I'll be fine,' I said.

Kendall was still up when I got back even though it was way past his bedtime. It was way past mine too.

'Don't you *ever* go off like that again,' Jake said. 'Kendall's been crying for you.'

'No I haven't,' said Kendall, hitting him on the head with George. 'I don't want stupid old Lola Rose. I can't stick her.'

'Is that true?' I said. 'Can't we have a cuddle then?'

Kendall shook his head but I picked him up anyway. He feebly punched me to prove his point and then snuggled into me.

'Bedtime,' I said, nuzzling his soft, feathery hair.

'I'm not a bit tired,' Kendall said, yawning.

'I am,' said Jake. 'I reckon I've read *Thomas the Tank Engine* at least two hundred times.'

I got Kendall into bed. He went to sleep in seconds. Then I sidled back to Jake.

'Are you going to tell Mum I dressed up in her stuff and went out?'

'I should do. But I'm not going to.'

'Thanks!'

'I'm just saving my own skin. She'd be mad at me for letting you. Lola Rose, have you *really* got a boyfriend?'

'Well, I know these boys. But the one I liked didn't turn out very nice so I probably won't be seeing him again.'

'Maybe that's just as well.'

'Maybe it is.' I hesitated. 'Jake, you know you did the flowers on my jeans? Could you do flowers on my denim jacket too, on the pockets, like? Maybe pink, to match the furry bit?'

'Sure. If you're a good girl.'

'I will be now.' I didn't kiss him goodnight because I wasn't a little kid like Kendall, but I waved my fingers at him and he waved both hands back to me.

'Jake's OK really,' I whispered to Kendall when I cuddled up to him in bed.

'I know that,' Kendall mumbles. I thought he'd gone back to sleep but then he suddenly said, 'Is he better than Dad?'

'He's better for us,' I said.

Jake didn't tell tales to Mum but she found out anyway. I'd got her top a little bit dirty and torn one of the little rubber tips off her high heels.

'You've been wearing my clothes, you little whatsit!' she said the next morning, slapping at me with the crumpled top.

She was in a very bad mood. I'd heard her arguing with Jake in the middle of the night. I got scared though there wasn't a real fight.

'I just felt like playing at dressing up,' I said quickly.

'You went out all dressed up too, didn't you? Don't lie to me, Lola Rose. There's mud all over my best shoes, you stupid little cow. How dare you sneak off like that? What were you up to? You might be able to wind Jake round your little finger but it won't wash with me. I'm not having you going out by yourself like that. Or *were* you by yourself? You weren't going with boys, were you?'

'I went for a walk in the park with Ms Balsam,' I said.

Jake stared at me but didn't say a word. Mum said plenty.

'What was she asking you, eh? I bet she wondered what you were doing, out by yourself, teetering about like a little trollop in my high heels. Oh God, Lola Rose, you've dropped me in it now.'

'No I haven't, Mum. She's ever so nice. She says I'm special.'

'Special needs, more like, gabbing away to that nosy old bag.'

'She's not nosy. You've got her all wrong, Mum. She's just friendly.'

'Rubbish!' said Mum. 'Now listen here, Lola Rose. You keep right out of her way. Don't let her worm anything out of you, OK? Else you'll be put into care as quick as a wink – and Kendall too.'

'I don't want to be put into care,' Kendall wailed. He didn't know what 'care' was but he spilled cornflakes all down his T-shirt in his anguish.

'There. Now look what you've made him do!' said Mum. 'And we're late for school as it is. Come on, mucky pup, let's get you shifted.'

'Lola Rose can change him and take him to school,' said Jake. 'We're going to the doctor's, Vic.'

Mum went red in the face. '*You* might be going to the doctor's, matie. I'm certainly not going to waste my time sitting in some dismal surgery breathing in everyone's germs. Come here, Kendall.'

My heart was thudding. 'What's the matter, Mum? Are you ill?'

'Of course I'm not ill. There's absolutely nothing wrong with me,' she insisted.

'Victoria,' said Jake.

'Shut *up*, will you,' said Mum.

I kept on at her but she wouldn't tell me anything. I did as Jake said and took Kendall to school. I kept worrying about it all morning.

'What's up, Lola Rose?' said Harpreet at lunch

time. 'You're not in a huff with me, are you? Is it because my mum wouldn't let you stay for dinner? She's a bit funny like that. I'm ever so sorry.'

'It's not your mum I'm worrying about, Harpreet. It's mine,' I said. I stopped eating my half of Harpreet's banana. 'Jake was nagging at her to go to the doctor's this morning. They wouldn't tell me why. Mum kept saying she wasn't ill but why else would she need to go?'

'I know!' said Harpreet. 'She could be having a baby!'

I stared at her.

'Don't look so gobsmacked. Your mum could be having Jake's baby, right?'

'I–I suppose so,' I said. 'Though I don't think she wants any more children.'

'These things happen,' said Harpreet, in a very worldly-wise way.

I tried to get my head round the idea of a baby. I pictured this little squirmy pink creature with Jake's long hair falling right down to its toes. Maybe I could brush it and plait it and play hairdressers. Kendall wouldn't always let me pick him up and baby him nowadays. Maybe it would be fun to have a real baby to play with. Mum didn't have much patience with babies. I could look after it for her and pretend it was mine.

I gobbled up the rest of the banana and then got stuck into my six squares of Cadbury's chocolate. I stroked the wrapping paper. Maybe we could dress the baby in purple? I could get Jake to help me make little purple dungarees with red flowers on the pockets. The baby could have a tiny purple teddy to match . . .

I spent the afternoon designing baby outfits on the back of my school jotter. I went arm in arm with Harpreet to pick up Kendall and Amandeep from their after-school club. We talked babies all the way home.

'Who's going to have a baby?' Kendall asked.

'Mum. Well, maybe she is. Harpreet thinks so,' I said.

'Mum!' said Kendall, astounded. 'She's not! She hasn't got a big tummy.'

'Not yet. It'll grow.'

'Is *our* mum going to have a baby?' said Amandeep. '*She's* got a big tummy.'

'I know, but she's just fat. I hope *I* don't get fat like her when I'm grown up,' said Harpreet, rubbing her hands up and down her skinny hips. 'My sister's getting a bit fat around the tummy. If *she's* pregnant our whole family will go bananas.'

'I don't want Mum to have a baby,' said Kendall.

'Yes you do. You like playing babies in the play-house. I could show you how to bath the baby and feed it and change its nappy,' I offered.

'I don't want to change pooey nappies!' said Kendall.

'I changed heaps of *yours*!'

'Kendall wears a nappy!' Amandeep exclaimed.

'I don't!' Kendall shrieked. He punched me hard in the stomach. 'Tell her I don't.'

'Ouch,' I said, doubled up. 'Will you give over punching, it *hurts*. Listen, you must never ever hit

Mum in the tummy now. You could really hurt her – *and* the baby.'

'Kendall wears a nappy, a nappy, a nappy!' Amandeep chanted.

Kendall punched her too. She punched him straight back, her little fist as hard as a stone. Kendall howled. I ended up having to carry him half the way home.

'It's your own fault, stupid,' I said, after I'd said goodbye to Harpreet. 'You hit her in the first place. And she's much better at fighting than you are. You shouldn't take any notice when she teases you.'

'But I *don't* wear a nappy!'

'I know. And she knows. She was just being silly.'

'I don't like her any more. I want George!' Kendall butted my shoulder with his head, trying to turn me into turquoise plush.

George had been banished from school because he'd attacked too many children in the infants. He lurked behind Kendall and then bobbed out and gnawed their legs. Kendall's teacher kept telling him off. Kendall said it wasn't him, it was George, and sharks couldn't help biting legs, it was their nature.

Kendall's teacher had a word with me. I told Kendall to quit it. Kendall said he'd try, but he couldn't always stop George.

'Bitey bitey bitey,' Kendall shouted, while George attacked a big boy called Dean who said Kendall was a nutter. George couldn't *really* bite –

but Dean could. He bent down and sank his teeth straight into Kendall's skinny leg.

Mum was furious when she saw the bite marks on Kendall. She was all set to charge up to the school and have a punch-up with the teacher, big Dean and his even bigger mother. I told Mum the whole story and she backed down. She whacked Kendall over the head with George and said he had to stay shut up at home while Kendall went to school.

Kendall wept and wailed every morning when he had to say goodbye to George. Mum told him it was his own fault and wouldn't give in.

Jake bought Kendall special shark-shaped turquoise jelly sweets to cheer him up on the way to school. Kendall sucked the shark sweets but howled just as hard. Turquoise drool ran down his chin and dripped onto his T-shirt.

I tried to turn Kendall's bed into an aquarium for George, spreading Jake's blue denim jacket over the cover and draping my green socks here and there like seaweed. I said George could be a basking shark, so he'd love lolling around all day doing nothing.

'He'll miss me terribly,' Kendall wept.

'If he gets a little bit lonely he can always snuffle into your pillow and pretend it's you,' I said.

'What can *I* snuffle into at school?' Kendall asked.

I suggested snipping a tiny sliver off George's fin to go in Kendall's pocket to use like a very tiny cuddle blanket. Kendall didn't like the idea of a mini-amputation. He snuffled into me instead.

I sighed about it, but I quite liked being needed so much. I'd have to watch out for Kendall when the new baby came. I'd make a big fuss of *both* of them. I'd pick Kendall up from school and the baby from the nursery and take them for walks in the park. I'd find a *proper* park with swings and a duck pond and an ice cream van. I'd strap Kendall into one swing and then sit on another with the baby on my lap.

We'd feed the ducks. I'd hold the baby on one hip and hang onto Kendall's T-shirt tight while he chucked bread into the water. Then we'd feed ourselves, an ice cream for me, a red lolly for Kendall and a little lick of ice cream for the baby.

I'd be utterly Lola Rose, my hair down to my waist, and much much much thinner. Maybe people would think I was the baby's mother. Maybe I'd go ahead and have my own babies, seeing I was so good with little children. Or maybe I'd start my own nursery and we'd make collages out of sticky paper and macaroni and fruit gums . . .

I played this pretend game all the way home. My arms ached holding Kendall but I didn't care. I jiggled him up and down, singing the 'Lucky lucky lucky' song.

I'd stopped worrying.

I didn't know that the worst worry was just about to start.

The Lump

Mum and Jake were at home, sitting at either end of their new sofa bed. Mum's eyes were red and puffy. She pressed her lips together, like she was scared she was going to start crying again. Jake kept looking anxiously at her. His eyes were red too. *He* hadn't been crying, had he?

Mum looked at us. 'What are you staring at me like that for?' she said.

Jake reached out and tried to take her hand. 'Tell them!' he said.

Mum snatched her hand away. 'Shut up!' she said.

'Tell us what?' I said, getting really scared.

'We know anyway!' said Kendall.

'What do you know?' said Mum, looking startled.

'You're going to have a baby!' said Kendall.

Mum gave one high-pitched yelp of laughter. 'No I'm not.'

'Yes you are, Lola Rose said.'

'Well Lola Rose doesn't know what she's talking about,' said Mum, folding her arms and glaring at me.

My new baby withered away inside its flowery dungarees until it was just a little purple smear.

'So what is it then? Are you and Jake splitting up?'

'I wouldn't be surprised,' said Mum.

'No, we're not!' said Jake – but he didn't sound certain.

'Dad hasn't found us, has he?' I whispered. I looked wildly round the room, scared he was hiding, waiting to pounce.

'It's not your dad. It's not *anything*,' said Mum. She got up to fill the kettle, switching the tap on so fiercely she sprayed herself with water. 'Bum! I'm having a cup of tea. Who wants one?'

'Your mum's got a lump,' said Jake.

He mumbled it so I wasn't quite sure what he'd said. And then when the words echoed in my head they still didn't make any sense. A lump? I looked at Mum, trying to see this lump on her head, her arm, wherever.

'I told you to shut it, Jake,' Mum said furiously. 'The kids don't need to know.'

'They'll have to know if you're going into hospital.'

'I'm. Not. Going. Into. Hospital,' said Mum, dabbing her wet front violently with the tea towel.

'The doctor said—'

'Yeah, well, he was probably just talking rubbish to scare me. I'm *fine*, I keep telling you. Do I look ill? There's nothing wrong with me. And I'm not going into hospital so they can slice bits off me.' Mum stopped jabbing her chest and wrapped her arms round herself.

'Mum? What lump?' I went to her and tried to cuddle her but she pulled away from me.

'It's nothing nothing nothing,' she said fiercely.

It was something something something.

She'd had a lump in her breast for months and months. A lump that was getting bigger and bigger. She'd kept quiet about it, hoping it would clear up by itself. Then Jake felt it and said she should go to the doctor. We didn't *have* a doctor here so Jake dragged her to his.

'He says your mum needs to go to this clinic as soon as possible. He's getting her an emergency appointment.'

'Yeah, well, he can stick his emergency appointment because I'm not going. I'm not having some creep feeling me up and telling me I need my boob chopped off.'

I'd made the tea for Mum but she was shaking now. Her teeth clinked against the mug every time she tried to take a sip.

I started shaking too.

'He said it might not come to that. It could just be a cyst or something,' said Jake. 'And anyway, if it *is* bad news then it's just a little routine operation, that's what he said.'

'Little!' said Mum. 'I'm not having them cutting me, ruining my looks. Who'd want me then, for God's sake?'

She looked at Jake. I willed him to say the right thing but he couldn't come out with anything at all.

Kendall started to cry. I picked him up and hugged him tight.

'There, look, you're getting the kiddies all upset!' said Mum. 'Why can't you keep your big mouth shut, Jake?'

'I was only trying to help,' he said.

'Yeah, well, we don't need your help. We don't need *you*,' said Mum.

She put her hand over her mouth as if she couldn't believe she'd just said it. She looked at Jake, her eyes brimming with tears, just like Kendall. She didn't *mean* it – she was just saying stupid stuff because she was so scared. She needed Jake terribly.

He sat there like a dummy, fiddling with a strand of his long hair, winding it round and round his finger. Mum started crying. Jake didn't budge an inch so she had to crawl over to him. She leant on his chest and howled all over his shirt, making black smudges on the blue denim. Mum said she was sorry and Jake said it was OK and she was going to be fine. But he sounded like he was reading from the telephone directory and his eyes stared into the shadows in the corner of our living room.

I couldn't sleep that night. I ate my way furtively through a whole big packet of fruit gums in bed, even though I'd eaten an enormous cheese and pineapple pizza for tea. I lay this way and that, my mouth stoppered with sticky gums, my hands clutching my swollen tummy.

Kendal snuffled in his sleep beside me, George clasped to his chest. Mum and Jake were awake for ages. I heard them whispering, on and on. Mum started crying and I sat up in bed, wondering if I should run to her. But then I heard Jake saying stuff and lots of sighing and then the bed started creaking.

I put my head under the pillow, not wanting to hear any more. I wanted to burrow right through the pillow into some sugar-candy sleepland where nothing bad ever happened and everyone lolled on great soft sofas and sucked sweets. I started to dream it, lying on a sofa, but it started tipping crazily, making me feel sick. A stream of strawberry-orange-lemon gushed out of my mouth. I was whirled round in this lurid water, hurtled out to a vast ocean where huge dark shapes were swimming.

Mum tried to act as if nothing were wrong the next morning. She wouldn't talk about the lump. She kept it up for days, pretending she didn't have a worry in the world. She sang loudly all round the flat but she wasn't fooling anyone, not even Kendall.

One night I woke up in the middle of the night needing to pee. I walked into the bathroom. Mum was in there, nightie in her hand, staring at herself in the mirror. She had her head tilted, hands on her hips, breasts stuck right out as if she were posing for a glamour photo. She had a silly smile on her face but there were tears trickling down her cheeks.

She gasped when she saw me and covered her chest with her arms. I wondered if the lump stuck out and looked scary.

'Knock, can't you?' Mum said crossly, turning her back on me and tugging her nightie over her head.

'Mum, are you going to go to that clinic?'

'Nope.'

'But what if the lump gets bigger? What if—?'

'Just shut up about it, Jayni.'

'Lola Rose,' I whispered.

'Yeah, Lola Rose, whatever. Just go back to bed, *now*.'

So I went back to bed even though I badly needed to pee. I hunched up, holding myself, wishing I knew what to do.

I hadn't told Harpreet. I'd let her burble on about babies. I didn't want to tell her about the lump because it was so scary. I didn't want to make it seem real. But it was getting so I couldn't think of anything else. Harpreet caught me crying in the school toilets and kept on at me until I told her why.

'Will you swear not to tell anyone?'

Harpreet swore solemnly on her little sister's life. 'What is it, Lola Rose? Is it about the baby?'

'There isn't a baby,' I said.

Harpreet blinked at me with her beautiful eyes. 'Did she lose it?' she whispered.

'No, she was never having a baby. You got it all wrong. She's . . . she's got this lump. Here.' I gestured in the air above my own flat chest.

'Oh help,' said Harpreet. 'Is it *cancer*?'

I jumped as if she'd said a very bad swear word. No one had dared say it before.

'I don't know. She's supposed to go to this hospital clinic to find out. But she says she's not going.'

'She'll have to go! Is she nuts?'

'She's always been a little bit nuts about stuff like that.' I washed my hands in the basin very slowly, rubbing the soap until it made bubbles.

'My great-auntie had breast cancer,' said Harpreet.

'Did she get better?'

There was a horrible pause. I rubbed and rubbed my hands until they wore white lather gloves.

'Well, I don't want to say this, Lola Rose, but actually she died.'

I clasped my soapy hands.

'But she was much older than your mum.'

'Does that make a difference?'

'Well, it's bound to. My great-auntie was an old lady. And she had all these strokes too. That's how she got the cancer my mum said. She had a fall and hit her chest. She was bruised all over. And then she got the cancer.'

I stopped still, thinking about my mum's bruised breasts. 'Is that how you get breast cancer?' I whispered. 'Could you get it if someone hits you hard?'

'Well. Maybe. I don't know. It's just what my mum says and she's not always right. Oh Lola Rose, don't cry again.'

'I'm not,' I said. I knew Harpreet was totally wrong. But I still didn't like her saying it. I rubbed my eyes fiercely and then screamed as the soap stung them.

Harpreet had to slosh water in my face and rub the soap away with the hem of her school skirt. It hurt horribly but I didn't really care. Harpreet put her arms round me when she'd got the soap off.

'I bet your mum doesn't have cancer at all, Lola Rose. It'll just be some silly old lump that doesn't *mean* anything.'

'That's what Jake says. But he says Mum should still go and get the lump taken out.'

'Well, obviously.'

'What do you think will happen if she doesn't? Will the lump get bigger and bigger and bigger?' I saw an awful image of Mum with one breast blowing up like a balloon, all warty and revolting.

'Maybe,' said Harpreet. 'Don't look so scared though. Your mum will be all right, honest.'

'Do you promise?' I said foolishly, as if Harpreet was a medical expert *and* a fortune teller.

'I promise promise promise,' said Harpreet firmly.

                              *   *   *

Mum was out when Kendall and I got back from school.

'Has she gone to the hospital?' I asked Jake.

'You know she won't go near the place. She's mad if you ask me,' said Jake. He had Mum's make-up mirror propped up in front of him, so he could draw himself. He stopped, looked at the piece of paper, sighed and crumpled it up. He started on a fresh page, screwing up his eyes to look at himself.

'Let's play on the computer, Jake,' said Kendall, tugging at his arm.

'Leave off, mate. No, the computer's stuffed. You've been mucking about on it, haven't you?'

'No!' said Kendall. 'Well. Not much. You can fix it, Jake. You always fix it.'

'I can't fix it this time,' said Jake. 'Will you leave off, Kendall, you're jogging me.'

Kendall's face crumpled.

'Come on, Kendall, I'll see if I can get the computer working,' I said, switching it on, though I knew zilch about boring old computers.

'It's stuffed, I tell you,' said Jake, switching it off again.

'Well, couldn't you just play with Kendall for two minutes? Look, he's crying.'

'He's always bawling,' said Jake. 'I've never known such a crybaby. I've got this portrait assignment, OK? I'm late handing it in as it is. Very very late. You do realize I've hardly set foot in college since I met your mum?' He said it as if we'd sellotaped him to the chair.

'You could do Kendall's portrait, couldn't you? Or mine? Look!' I copied one of Mum's favourite poses, head tilted up, mouth slightly open, chest thrust forward, hand on hip, one knee slightly bent.

'For God's sake,' said Jake cruelly.

I rushed off to the bathroom, not wanting Jake to call me a crybaby too. 'I hate him,' I muttered, hugging myself.

I wanted my mum.

She didn't come back for tea. Jake didn't seem to care too much. They'd obviously had another row. He went on moodily sketching until way past tea time. I made baked beans on toast for Kendall and me. I didn't make Jake anything to show I was mad at him.

'Mum will be late for her evening shift down the pub,' I said.

'That's her look-out,' said Jake. 'As if I care.'

'Why are you being so *horrible*?'

'Look, it's not me. I'm not the one that's changed. This is all getting so heavy.'

'Mum can't help having this lump.'

'Yeah, but she won't deal with it like any normal woman. She has to make all this into such a drama. It's probably nothing. Women have lumps all the time, it doesn't mean it's – it's—'

'Cancer,' I said.

'What's cancer?' said Kendall.

'It's an illness,' said Jake.

Kendall paused, pushing baked beans from

one side of his plate to the other. 'Is Mum really sick?'

'Sick in the head, more like,' said Jake.

'She's sick in the head putting up with *you*,' I said. I golloped my baked beans and ate Kendall's leftovers too. I still felt empty so I ran my finger round the baked bean tin to lick up the juice.

'Don't do that, you'll cut yourself,' said Jake.

I took no notice – and then caught my finger on the jagged edge of the tin. 'Ouch!'

'You idiot,' said Jake. 'I *told* you.'

He held my throbbing finger under the cold tap and then wrapped it up in one of Mum's scarves because we didn't have a bandage or a hankie.

'Mum will create if I get blood on it,' I said.

'Tough,' said Jake. 'She should be here to look after you.'

'Don't you love her any more, Jake?'

He tied the scarf in a neat bow, frowning. 'Look, I never said I *loved* your mum. I mean, it's been great – she can be so cute and silly and funny when she's not in one of her moods. But this was never like a for ever thing.'

I pulled away from him so abruptly that the scarf unravelled. '*Mum* thinks it's for ever.'

'You could have fooled me. You should have heard the things she said to me this afternoon,' said Jake sulkily. 'Watch out, you'll make your finger bleed again. Give it here.'

'I'll do it,' I said, fiddling with the end of the scarf. 'I *knew* you two had had a row.'

'Your mum's certainly got a big mouth on her,' said Jake. 'Was she that lippy with your dad, eh?'

I stood still. I pressed my lips together.

'What is it with your dad?' said Jake. 'Your mum gets that exact expression if I ever mention him.'

'Yeah. Well. We don't talk about him.'

'You kids don't get to see him ever?' Jake looked over at Kendall, who was sitting in the corner, muttering to George. 'Kendall misses him a lot, you know. I guess that's why he's all over me.'

'He *likes* you. He thought you were for ever too. Like a new dad.'

'You must be joking! I'm not *old* enough to be a dad. I'm only twenty, for God's sake.'

'My mum had me when she was seventeen. Jake, where *is* she? Do you think she's gone straight to the pub to do her shift?'

'I tell you, I don't know. She just went storming out. She's lucky I didn't do the same. What would you kids have done then, eh?'

'We'd be fine. Mum knows I can look after Kendall.'

'I suppose you can. Better than your mum!'

I couldn't help being pleased he said that, even though it was mean to Mum. I didn't know what to do about her. I knew she'd *probably* be all right. She'd run off before, several times, sometimes when we were living back with Dad, sometimes since. She was often away for ages but she always came back.

I *knew* that. But I still worried. Maybe she'd gone storming off in such a rage she hadn't looked when she crossed the road. Maybe she'd seen a car coming and she was in such a state she'd darted across anyway. Maybe she was so scared about the lump and losing her looks she *wanted* to get knocked over . . .

I put on my denim jacket.

'What are you up to, Lola Rose?' said Jake, as I walked towards the door.

'I'm going out.'

'Oh no, you're not playing that trick on me again.'

'I'm going looking for *Mum*.'

'No you're not. You're staying right here. Don't even try arguing with me this time.'

'You can't stop me,' I said.

Maybe he could. He wasn't scary like my dad but he was quite strong. I'd seen him lift Mum up in his arms as easily as I lifted Kendall. I didn't feel like lucky Lola Rose who might sweet-talk her way round him. I felt like stupid, sad Jayni. So I took my denim jacket off again and played with Kendall for a bit and then put him to bed.

I cuddled up beside him. My hand was sore so I stuck it into my armpit. It was very painful just getting a tiny cut. I wondered what it would feel like to have a large lump of breast sliced off your body.

I hugged Kendall tight, his feathery hair tickling my chin. I breathed in his sweet, warm smell. He moaned in his sleep and fought himself free, stretching out in a windmill shape so I couldn't cuddle him. It felt as if he was abandoning me.

I must have gone to sleep at some time – and then woke with a start when the door banged. I heard voices, Mum laughing, sounding funny. Jake said something. Then someone else spoke. Another man.

Kendall sat bolt upright. 'Is it Dad?' he asked.

I crept to the door, Kendall following. I listened, the blood drumming in my head. The man spoke again. He sounded uneasy and embarrassed.

It wasn't Dad.

Mum laughed again but she sounded as if she might also be crying. I went rushing through to the living room. She was staggering in those high heels, her arm draped round the neck of a strange fat man, his shirt tight over his big belly. He had dark sweat circles under his arms. It was obviously a strain keeping Mum upright. Jake was staring at them, his eyes screwed up. He looked as if he was watching an awful television soap and couldn't wait to change channels.

'Mum?'

'Ah! My little L-L-Lola Rose!' Mum said. She spoke as if she had a mouthful of sweets. I knew that voice. She was very drunk.

'Go to bed, Kendall,' I said. 'I'll put you to bed too, Mum.'

I tried to unhook her from the fat man.

'I don't *want* to go to bed. I want to *party*,' said

Mum, clinging to the man. 'L-L-Lola whatwasit? – ah yes, Rose. My Rosy Posy. I want you to meet my boss Barry.'

Barry bobbed his head. 'I'm not actually. Not any more,' he said, reaching round to unwind Mum's arm himself.

'You're not *Barry*?' said Mum, trying to focus on him. 'Well, blow me, you *look* like Barry, and you sound like Barry too.'

'Yeah, I'm Barry all right, but I'm not your boss, not any more, Vic.'

'*Victoria!*'

'Whatever. I've given you fair warning, darling. No more drinking on the job.'

'But you and me are mates, Barry,' said Mum, pursing her lips and pecking her head forward, trying to kiss him. 'I'm your little lark, remember?'

Jake grunted in disgust and turned his back on them.

'You're my little liability,' said Barry.

He pulled himself free so violently that I wasn't ready and nearly dropped Mum.

'Whoops!' said Mum, staggering.

I staggered too, trying to support her.

'Shall we dance?' Mum said.

Kendall came rushing over in his T-shirt and pants. 'I'll dance, Mum,' he said, hanging onto her legs.

'Yes, let's all dance,' said Mum, patting him fondly on the head. 'My little boy, my big girl – my lovely lovely kids.' She stopped swaying and looked straight at Barry. Maybe she wasn't quite as drunk as she was pretending to be. 'I've got to work to feed my kids, Barry, you know that. So I'll be in to work tomorrow usual time, right? Stone cold sober, I promise.'

'You can be sober or you can be roaring drunk. It's all the same to me,' said Barry. 'You're not working for me any more. You're Trouble with a capital T.'

Mum came out with a mouthful of abuse. Kendall giggled nervously at the rude words.

'That's nice, isn't it?' said Barry. 'Swearing like that in front of your precious kids. And after I took the trouble – and the flak from my old lady – to drive you home. You make me sick, Victoria Luck.'

'You make *me* sick,' Mum shouted as he slammed the door. She kept yelling it, over and over.

It was the wrong thing to say in the circumstances. I got her to the bathroom in time and held her forehead. She knelt over the toilet and was sick again and again.

'It's OK, Mum,' I whispered as she moaned. 'It's OK, Mum, I'm here.'

But she kept looking round, tears dribbling down her cheeks, mouth puckered.

She was looking for Jake. But he wouldn't go near her, not even when she kept calling his name.

Fourteen

Us Three

Jake left the next morning. He could see it was a good time because Mum could barely move. She groaned when she sat up in bed and she still couldn't even drink a glass of water without being sick. She watched Jake packing up his paints and drawing pads and jeans and cassettes. He was wearing all the extra presents she'd bought him – hand-tooled cowboy boots, the thick silver bracelet, a denim jacket.

He glanced at the computer.

'Yeah, walk off with that too, why don't you,'

Mum whispered, watching him. Her eyes were sad slits.

'No, no, it's for the kids,' said Jake. Maybe he remembered it was broken.

'Mr Big Heart,' Mum murmured.

'Look, don't be like that, Vic—'

'Like what? My guy clears off because I've got cancer and I'm supposed to be what? Happy?'

'You don't know you've *got* cancer. I bet you anything you like you haven't. And I'm *not* clearing off because of that.'

'It's because the money's run out,' I said.

I got into bed beside Mum. She winced as I made the bed move. I edged further in very slowly and put my arm round her. She smelt bad but I knew she still needed holding.

'You've got it in one, Lola Rose,' she said.

'That's rubbish. I'm not like that. Look, this was never meant to be permanent. We just had fun together, that's all. I couldn't have stayed once term is over anyway – you know I'm going travelling.'

'Well, get on your travels now,' said Mum. 'Get lost.'

She wouldn't kiss him goodbye. Maybe it was because she hadn't had a chance to brush her teeth. I wouldn't kiss him either. I ducked my head when he tried. But Kendall came running. He threw himself at Jake and hugged him hard, clinging to him like a little monkey.

'Don't go, don't go, don't go,' he begged.

'I've got to go just now, Kendall. But I'll come back and see you, little mate, OK?'

I had to drag Kendall off him. I got kicked and punched for my pains. I had to fight back a bit because he was really hurting. Mum dragged herself out of bed to help. Then we heard the front door bang. We stopped and stood like statues, all hanging onto each other.

'He's gone,' said Mum. She ripped the moonstone necklace off and threw it on the floor.

'He's coming back, he said,' Kendall sobbed.

'No he's not,' I said. 'We don't want him back. Good riddance.'

'Then . . . will Dad come back?' said Kendall.

'No! We don't want *any* men – not Dad, not Jake, not that big fat Barry, *no one*.'

'That's right,' said Mum. 'To hell with the lot of them.' She leant against the wall, groaning.

'Mum? Are you all right? Is it the lump?' I asked, panicking.

'My head's hurting, that's all,' said Mum. 'Will you just *forget* my bloody lump.'

She went back to bed and pulled the covers right up over her head. I knew she was just wanting to hide but it looked awful, as if she were in a shroud. I screwed up my face and hit my forehead to stop myself thinking it.

'Lola Rose?' said Kendall.

'It's OK. I've got a headache too. No wonder – all that yelling, you little monster!'

Kendall pulled a goofy monster face, curling his fingers into claws. He didn't really *want* to play. I saw him glancing fearfully at Mum. But he roared and ran round the room while I played the monster catcher with my big net.

'For God's sake, clear off to school, you kids,' Mum moaned.

I didn't want to leave her on her own. 'I'll stay and look after you, Mum. I'll take Kendall to school but then I'll nip back. I can make you black coffee and fix you some soup for lunch.'

'I'm not ill, I've just got a hangover. All I want to do is sleep. You go to school, do you hear. I don't want old Bossy Boots Balsam ringing me up and giving me grief.'

So I went to school, though I couldn't get my head round any of the lessons. Kendall was in a state too. I shouldn't have started him off on the stupid little monster game. He wouldn't stop roaring in the classroom. They had to call for me to calm him down.

'Has anything happened to upset him at home?' Kendall's teacher asked.

'No, miss,' I said quickly.

'He was really starting to settle down, making a few friends – but now we seem back to square one. Maybe I should talk with your mum, Lola Rose.'

'Well . . .'

'Or Dad? Kendall seems so very fond of him.'

'He talks about our *dad*?'

'Well, your step-dad.'

'We haven't got a step-dad,' I said firmly.

When I got Kendall on his own I gave him a

good shake that set him off howling. 'It's your own fault! Just keep your mouth shut at school, right?'

Kendall whined all the way home. I wished I could run right away from him. And Harpreet. She was going on and on about her mum and how she'd thrown a fit because she'd caught her putting make-up on.

'Not even proper make-up, just that glitter stuff, you know. But my mum goes bananas, right, acts like I'm this total slag. She goes on about her daughters bringing disgrace on the family. You are just so *lucky*, Lola Rose. Your mum doesn't care.'

'My mum does care,' I said stiffly.

'Yeah, but she lets you do what you want. Don't go all snotty on me! What's the matter?' Harpreet nudged nearer, lowering her voice. 'Is she worse, your mum? Is she getting really sick?'

'No!'

'Yes,' said Kendall, snuffling. 'She was ever so sick, I saw.'

'That was because she was drunk, stupid.'

'Your mum was *drunk*?' said Harpreet, rolling her eyes like her mother.

'Not really *drunk* drunk,' I said quickly. 'She's had a hard time. You don't understand, Harpreet. And neither do you, Kendall, so you just shut up.' I gave him another shake. 'Telling people Jake's our step-dad!'

'He is! What is he, then?'

'He's nothing. He's gone now anyway.'

'He's gone! You mean he's left your mum?' said Harpreet.

Her eyes looked like they were going to pop right out of their sockets. I hated the way she was hanging on my every word. It was like she couldn't wait to hear more scandal. I wasn't sure I wanted her for my friend after all.

'My mum chucked him out. And good riddance,' I said, slapping my hands together.

'My mum said it could never last,' said Harpreet.

'I wish you and your mum would keep your noses *out* of our business,' I said.

I seized Kendall by the wrist and hauled him along, running away from Harpreet and Amandeep. Kendall yelled because I was pulling too hard but I didn't ease up. I ran faster and faster, my heart pounding. Every beat said Mum-Mum-Mum.

I thought she'd still be cowering under the covers – but her bed was empty. The whole flat seemed empty.

'Mum?' I called. '*Mum!*'

'Hiya,' said Mum, coming out of the bathroom. She was wearing her white jumper and leather skirt and high heels, looking a million dollars.

'Oh Mum!' I said, and burst into tears.

'Oh my Gawd, what's up with you?' said Mum, shaking her head. She'd just washed her hair and it bounced on her shoulders.

'Are you all right, Mum?'

'Of course I am, you silly sausage,' said Mum, putting her arms round me. Kendall scrabbled to get in on the cuddle too. Mum picked him up, laughing. 'What's up with you, babe?'

'Lola Rose … has … been … horrid!' he gasped, out of breath with running and crying.

'Rubbish,' said Mum, tickling him where his neck joined his shoulders.

Kendall hunched over, squealing with laughter though his eyelashes were still stuck together with tears. I looked at his damp little face and felt awful.

'*I'm* rubbish. I *have* been horrid. Kendall, I'm really really sorry.'

Kendall blinked up at me. 'I *might* forgive you,' he said, sounding so funny that we all laughed.

'Are you hungry, kids? Let's have tea, eh?' said Mum.

She fixed us this lovely treat meal just like a birthday party, with sausages on sticks and crisps and baby pizzas and ice cream in new glass bowls, purple for me, red for Kendall, with our new names written on our puddings in strawberry sauce.

'See this, Harpreet!' I said inside my head. 'My mum cares for us big time!'

'You're the best mum ever,' I said, tucking in.

'No, I'm not,' said Mum, nibbling crisps. 'I haven't been very mumsie at all recently. I've left you kids alone too much. I'm going to be here for you now. No more shifts down that stupid pub of an evening. I'm well shot of that. I'll get a day job. I was thinking, maybe I could work on a make-up counter, or be a hairdresser, say – I'm good at doing hair, aren't I, Lola Rose?'

'You're the best, Mum. You do your hair beautifully,' I said, patting her blonde curls. I thought you probably had to train for those jobs first but I didn't like to say anything to spoil Mum's mood.

'I'm well shot of J-A-K-E too,' Mum said, raising her eyebrows at me significantly.

Kendall hadn't caught on to spelling yet and carried on licking his sausage like a lolly.

'You bet, Mum,' I said.

Kendall experimented, dipping his sausage in his ice cream.

'Eat your sausage properly, Kendall!' I said. 'That looks totally disgusting.'

'It gets mixed up in my tummy,' Kendall said. 'So why can't I mix it up in my mouth too?'

'OK OK, but don't be surprised if no one ever wants to sit down and eat a meal with you.'

'I don't want anyone. Apart from George,' said Kendall, dipping George's furry jaws into the ice cream bowl too.

'You're getting him all *mucky*,' I nagged, but I was relieved he wasn't throwing a tantrum about Jake.

I couldn't get over how calm Mum was about him. We had a girly heart-to-heart after Kendall was in bed.

'I'm glad to be rid of him,' Mum said bravely.

I looked at her.

'OK, I was nuts about him at first. Well, he is

gorgeous. You must admit it, Lola Rose, he looks an absolute dreamboat – that hair, that flat stomach, that little bum—'

'*Mum!*'

'Well, you know what I mean. But I suppose I knew it wouldn't last, what with me being a little bit older and you kids and everything.' Mum sighed, smoothing the skin over her forehead. 'Am I getting all wrinkly, Lola Rose? I've got frown lines, haven't I? What do you reckon on that Botox treatment? Do you think it would work? Maybe I'll treat myself if I get lucky on the lottery cards again, eh?'

'You're bonkers, Mum. You haven't got any wrinkles!'

'I *have*. And I'm getting all saggy and baggy too,' said Mum, sticking her chest out and staring down at herself critically. She patted her breasts as if they were two puppies. 'Poor things. Still, I don't think this one's going to have to be sliced off.' She looked at me, her eyes very big and blue. 'I went to the hospital today and saw this consultant.'

'Mum! You didn't say!'

'Well, I wasn't going to keep the damn appointment. But then I thought maybe I ought to. I mean, if it's just us, Lola Rose, then I can't take chances, can I? And if I *have* got something serious then I need to get it treated, right?'

'I wish you'd told me you were going. I'd have gone with you. You hate hospitals,' I said, taking Mum's hand.

'It *was* a bit scary. But I kept thinking I had to show Jake I'm not gutless. I had to wait *ages* and I was still feeling a bit groggy with the drink so I very nearly walked out. But I got talking to these other women waiting with me and it made me feel a bit better, knowing we'd *all* got lumps. And then the consultant himself was *gorgeous* – quite old, of course, but so good looking, lovely suit and beautiful hands with very sensitive, long fingers. It felt very weird taking my top off for him. I went all giggly and blushed like a schoolgirl.'

'Mum! You're not meant to flirt with your doctor.'

'Oh, you know me, I'll flirt with a floormop if no one else is around. But Mr Key is the bee's knees, I swear. He says he's not going to cut my boob off even if it is . . . cancer.' She said it in a whisper. 'He's just taking the lump out, and some little thingies under my arm, in case they've got it too. So isn't that great? He swears he'll be able to cut kind of *under* my boob so it'll hardly show.'

'When's he doing it, Mum?'

'He said he'll put me at the top of his list.'

I thought about Mum in hospital. Then I thought about Kendall and me. My throat dried. I swallowed and waggled my tongue around to make a bit of spit.

'Don't pull those silly faces. You look like poor old Bubble,' said Mum.

'Mum, what about Kendall and me? When you're in hospital?'

'Don't you worry about it, sweetheart. I asked a nurse and she said people only stay in a day or so. Well, I reckon I can have the little op and then discharge myself. So you'll only be on your own one night. You can manage that, can't you darling?'

I wasn't sure. I knew I'd be scared. But I wasn't baby Jayni any more. I was supercool Lola Rose. 'Of course I'll manage, Mum, no bother,' I said.

'That's my girl,' said Mum. She put her arms round me. We hung onto each other and hugged until our arms ached.

Mum stayed lovely day after day. She didn't go for another job just yet. She said she'd wait until after her operation. We used up the last of the lottery money. Mum kept treating us. Kendall had red ice lollies cut up in his cornflakes for breakfast and red ice-lolly soup for his tea. She read him *Thomas the Tank Engine* until she was hoarse. She took him swimming and let George take a dip too, though he reeked of chlorine for ages afterwards.

Mum made me Cadbury's chocolate sandwiches for breakfast and Ribena cocktails for my tea. She did my hair in a different elaborate style every day and made me up properly so that I looked almost pretty.

She also bought me my very own pair of purple high heels! I still couldn't walk in them properly even though they fitted, but I didn't care. I staggered round and round the flat in them, my bum sticking out, my ankles wobbling. I kept sticking out a leg, admiring the tautness of my calves, the arch of my foot, the glossy sheen of the purple leather, the dizzying splendour of those soaring high heels.

'Walk naturally! You look as if you're on a tightrope,' Mum laughed.

Kendall kept begging to have a go in them. He looked a scream as he minced around like a miniature drag queen, his lips bright red from the lollies.

'What a weird pair of kids,' said Mum, lighting a cigarette and inhaling deeply. Her eyes suddenly welled up. She said it was the smoke from her ciggie but I think that was an excuse.

I kept crying at odd moments too, even when I wasn't thinking about Mum. I missed an easy catch playing rounders and my team moaned at me and I burst into baby tears. Some of the girls in my class said catty things about my new hairstyles and I rushed to the toilets to cry. I got stuck doing some new maths problems and slumped in my desk, snivelling.

I didn't really care about dropped balls and dopey girls and decimals.

'What's the matter, Lola Rose?' everyone kept asking.

I couldn't tell them I was scared my mum was going to die.

No, of course she wasn't going to die. She probably didn't even have cancer. She was just going to have a tiny lump taken out, then she'd be as right as rain. I imagined Mum in a rainstorm, hair plastered to her head, hunched in her white jacket. She was soaked to the skin but she was smiling and singing, tap-dancing through the puddles in her high heels.

Voice of Doom

The letter came from the hospital. It was the first letter we'd had at our new address.

Mum tore open the envelope, her hands shaking so badly she tore the letter too. She held a half in either hand helplessly.

'Oh God, this is it, kids,' she said. 'I'm going in on Thursday. *This* Thursday. They don't give you much notice. Still, my Mr Key said he'd slot me in as soon as possible.' Mum smiled as if Mr Key was keen to make a date with her.

'I don't want you to go into hospital, Mum,' said Kendall. 'Not Thursday. You take me swimming on Thursdays. You can't go.'

'I have to go, little mate,' said Mum.

But she didn't seem so sure on Wednesday night. She started drinking. I got scared she'd make herself sick again.

'You can't get drunk, Mum, not when you're going into hospital tomorrow,' I said, trying to sneak the bottle away.

'You put that right back, Lola Rose. In fact you can pour me another glass.'

'But Mum—' I poured her the tiniest measure. Then I deliberately dropped the bottle.

It made a horrible mess on the carpet. I cut my fingers trying to clear it up. Mum slapped me hard for being so clumsy. I cried. Then Mum cried too. We had a long, mournful cuddle. I carried Kendall into Mum's bed and we all huddled up together. I don't think Mum slept. She was wide awake whenever I woke up.

I kept having nightmares. George's chlorine smell made me dream we were all in the water, clinging to each other as we sank down and down where the sharks were waiting.

We got up very early. Mum had bought us croissants and Danish pastries as a treat for breakfast. She didn't eat a bite herself. Kendall picked out all the currants, licked the icing, but only ate a mouthful himself. I ate my way through three pastries, even though they'd gone a bit stale overnight. No matter how much I ate I couldn't stop the huge, empty feeling inside me.

Mum wouldn't let us say goodbye properly. 'We

won't make a thing of it or we'll all start howling. Go on, kids, off to school. I've got a treat in the fridge for you for tea. You be a good boy for Lola Rose, Kendall, and go to bed when she says. I'll be home as soon as I can make it. Don't come to the hospital just in case anyone asks why you're on your own. Go on then. Scram. Don't look so scared. I'll be fine. I promise you. I'm Lady Luck.'

I took Kendall to school – but then I came scurrying back home. Mum came rushing to the door at the sound of my key. Her face was pink with hope. I think she thought I was Jake.

'Lola Rose!'

'I'll help you pack your bag for the hospital and see you off properly.'

Mum sighed but she didn't have the energy to send me back to school. She got her case out. 'God, wasn't it weird, throwing all our things together that night your dad went for you,' she said. 'I wonder what he's doing now?'

'He'll be getting drunk. Singing. Chatting up girls. Fighting.' I opened Mum's chest of drawers, looking through her stuff.

'You don't think I should tell him, just in case . . .' Mum stopped.

I stopped too. 'No.'

'But he *is* your dad. He does love you, darling. And there's Kendall, he was always so gentle with him.'

'*No!*'

I held up her best black nightie. 'You can't wear this, Mum. It's see-through,' I said.

'No it isn't,' said Mum. 'Well.' She put her hand up inside the filmy nylon. 'I suppose it is a bit. Still, maybe I'll give Mr Key one last sneaky peep at a perfect pair of boobs before he goes digging for lumps.'

'Shut up, Mum,' I said.

'It might look weird with bandages underneath though,' said Mum mournfully. 'Oh Gawd, maybe I'd better buy a new nightie on the way.' She looked in her purse. 'Maybe not. I'm going to have to get my act together work-wise the minute I get out of hospital. I should have done something about it sooner, but I just wanted to be with you kids.'

'That's what we wanted too, Mum. Look, what about *my* nightie? It's clean – well, I've only worn it a couple of times. It would fit you easy-peasy.'

It was a white T-shirt with a teddy bear on the front. Mum looked at it and then folded it into her case. 'OK, I'll take it. I'll look a bit daft but I'll be decent. It'll be like I'm cuddled up with you, Lola Rose. I'll like that.' Mum looked at me. 'You will be all right, won't you, lovie? Look, I'll leave you my mobile just in case of emergencies. Don't you run up a big bill though, there's a good girl. You won't mind being by yourselves tonight, will you?'

'Of course not,' I said quickly.

'It's not as if you're really alone in the house,' Mum said. 'I mean, there's Miss Parker downstairs and the two boys up above.'

'Yes, Mum,' I said. We both knew poor smelly Miss Parker couldn't look after herself, let alone anyone else, and Mum and Steve and Andy weren't on speaking terms any more. (Mum thought Steve was being overly friendly to Jake and told him to stop making eyes at her boyfriend. She said some other stuff too. Steve and Andy were mortally offended.)

Mum started biting the skin round her thumb. I gently took it out of her mouth.

'Quit that, Mum. We'll be fine.'

'You could always try to get hold of Jake. Though his mobile's switched off at the moment, the little whatsit.'

'Don't try to phone him, Mum. We don't need him. We don't need anyone.'

'You're such a good, grown-up girl, Lola Rose,' said Mum.

I tried hard to feel grown up. I made Mum a cup of tea and sat her down with a stale croissant while I packed her washing things and her hairbrush and her make-up. I slipped in a card at the bottom of her case. I'd made it for her.

I'd cut out a sad-looking baby bunny and stuck it in the middle, with little bits of tissue stuck on its ears and paws to look like bandages. I'd wondered about a bandage across its chest but decided that would be too literal. I surrounded him with flowers and butterflies and birds and wrote 'Get Well Soon, Mum – With Lots of Love from Lola Rose and Kendall' in my best handwriting. Kendall had added lots of kisses. He didn't do them carefully enough. The kisses were all different sizes and spoilt the symmetry of the design but I hoped Mum wouldn't mind.

I gave her my own kisses at the bus stop. I got a bit carried away.

'That's enough! You'll wipe all my powder off,' said Mum. She looked at my watch. 'Oh to hell with this. I'll go up the high street and get a minicab.'

'But it's miles to the hospital, Mum.'

'Look, I'm an invalid! Why should I have to bum around on buses?' said Mum.

So I went with her to the minicab firm. I kissed her again and gave her one last hug – and another and another – and then she got in the car and they drove off. I waved long after the minicab had gone down the street and round the corner, out of sight.

Then I stood there.

I kept seeing Mum waving back from inside the car, sending herself up, doing one of those slow, spread-fingered, fancy waves like royalty as she mouthed goodbye.

The terrible Voice of Doom spoke inside my head. *What if this really is goodbye? What if this is the last time you ever see your mum?*

I ran like mad to get out of earshot. I went into the HMV shop in the arcade, ramming on the headphones, turning the volume right up. My head started throbbing. It was only eleven o'clock but I decided to go and get some lunch. Mum had given me ten pounds, which seemed heaps. I had a burger and French fries and a large Coke. I crammed it down quickly and felt just as empty when I'd finished. It seemed too mean to Kendall to spend much more on myself. So I sat where I was, watching a mum with two little kids across the way from me. The kids were just picking at their food. The moment they were wheeled off in their double buggy I whizzed over to their table. They'd left half a burger, heaps of French fries and most of a McFlurry ice cream. I stuffed them down so quickly I felt sick – even though I *still* felt empty.

I mooched round the shops for a while, nibbling at a bar of Cadbury's. I meant to save half of it for Kendall but I couldn't quite manage it. I didn't know what to do with myself. I didn't want to go back home in case it would feel too weird without Mum, even though I was used to her being out a lot. So like some sad little wimp I scuttled back to school. At least I got another lunch. I told the teacher I'd had a tummy upset but I was better now.

'Were you really sick?' Harpreet whispered.

She was trying to make friends with me again. I wanted to be her friend – but I was still mad at her.

'Yeah, I was sick because I was drunk like my mum,' I whispered back. 'We split a whole bottle of vodka.'

Harpreet's mouth opened in a big O. 'You never!'

'Of course I never,' I said. 'You're so thick some-times, Harpreet. You'll believe anything.' Then I relented. 'No, you're not thick. You're thin as a pin. I'm the one who's thick, look.' I punched my big tummy. 'Yuck, I'm getting so fat, look!'

Harpreet giggled. 'Maybe *you're* pregnant,' she said.

We both laughed. It was OK now. We were friends again.

I told her my mum had gone into hospital.

'You poor thing, you must be so worried.'

'Yeah. Well. Obviously.'

'She'll be all right,' said Harpreet, patting my hand. 'So who's looking after you and Kendall if Jake's done a runner?'

'He hasn't. My mum got rid of him, I *said*.'

'Well. Whatever,' Harpreet said. 'So, who's coming? A granny? An auntie?'

I knew I shouldn't say but I couldn't help wanting to show off. 'No one's looking after us,' I said airily.

Harpreet boggled at me in a satisfying manner. 'You can't manage by yourselves!'

'Sure we can. It's only overnight.'

'My mum would never let me stay by myself. She wouldn't even let my *sister* stay home by herself last holidays and she was eighteen.'

'Don't tell your mum,' I said hurriedly, scared there might be trouble.

'I won't.'

'Promise?'

'Yeah, I swear,' said Harpreet, gesturing sealing her lips and cutting her throat. Her forehead wrinkled as she thought it all out. 'Who will cook your tea?' she said.

'*I* will. I often cook.'

It all depends what you mean by 'cook'. I could open a tin and make toast. That was kind of cooking. I knew Harpreet was thinking of the complicated curries she had at home.

'You're so cool, Lola Rose,' she said. 'It's like you're an adult already.'

She made me *feel* cool.

But then I had to go home and face the empty empty empty flat.

'I want Mum,' said Kendall, sitting down in the middle of the floor, burying his nose in George's matted fur.

'Yes, but you know Mum's in hospital. It's OK, you've still got me.'

'I don't want you, I want *Mum*,' said Kendall, screwing up his face.

'Shut up. And don't you dare cry! I'm fed up with you being such a grizzleguts. Now listen, *if* you're good I'll make you some tea. But if you're going to blub I'll think you're just a little baby and put a nappy on you and put you to bed.'

Kendall scowled at me. 'I don't like you.'

'I don't like you either,' I said. 'I wish I had a different brother. *Harpreet's* brother, he'd be great. But I'm stuck with you, Kendal mint cake, so I'll just have to get on with it. OK, let's check out the fridge.'

There were two cardboard boxes. One was a big pizza with a smiley face squiggled on the top in tomato sauce. The other was a vast chocolate cake with two layers of butter cream. Mum had pressed pink and purple Smarties on the frosted chocolate icing, spelling out YUM YUM.

I looked at the pizza. I looked at the chocolate cake.

I was the one who burst into tears.

Kendall watched me warily. 'Don't you like pizza and chocolate cake?'

'I love them,' I said, blowing my nose on the kitchen towel.

'Why are you crying then?'

'Because Mum's tried so hard. And I want her too. So that makes *me* Mrs Grizzleguts, right? You can call me that as much as you like.'

'Grizzleguts!' said Kendall.

I let him go on saying it until he was sick of it. It seemed like hours. But then everything seemed to last hours.

I heated the pizza and we ate half of it, and a big slice of chocolate cake each. I read *Thomas the Tank Engine* and drew Kendall a train picture, rubbing out again and again until I got all the wheels in a straight line. Then he coloured it in (ruining it). We ate some cold pizza and had another slice of chocolate cake. And another. Well, I did. Kendall just ate the Smarties.

It seemed like a whole day had passed but it was less than an hour. I switched on the telly to check the time because I was sure our clock had stopped.

Kendall and I watched for a while but then there was a hospital programme and I changed channels. We watched some comedy but we didn't laugh. It was like we were tuned into our own hospital channel, watching our mum being wheeled off to an operating theatre where men in masks attacked her with sharp instruments.

Kendall nudged nearer until he was sitting on my lap. I rested my chin on his head. His crewcut was growing out. He looked like a little baby duckling.

'You hair's so cute now, Kendall.'

Kendall stiffened. 'I want it cut off!'

'No, it's much nicer now.'

'I don't want to look nice. I don't want to look cute. I want to look tough.'

Dad had always marched him to the barber's for a number one hair cut. He didn't look tough. He looked like a bald little baby but Dad went on about him being a real tough nut.

'We don't see Dad now,' Kendall whispered to George. He turned round to me. 'We will still see Mum, won't we?'

'Of course we will! Tomorrow, when she comes back from the hospital.'

'Promise?'

'I promise,' I said.

The Voice of Doom mocked me. *How can you promise that? Maybe she won't ever come back.*

The Voice talked to me half the night. I felt so lonely, even cuddled up to Kendall. I clutched my Pinkie teddy bear like a sad little toddler. I heard Miss Parker's radio rumbling away underneath me. Then I heard the creak of floorboards above my head and the gurgle of water pipes when Steve or Andy went to the loo. Cars went past. Cats yowled. Drunks shouted. Then there were footsteps outside.

Every time anyone walked along the pavement I tensed up.

The night went on and on for ever.

Sixteen

Home Alone

The mobile rang when Kendall and I were having breakfast.

'Mum! Oh Mum!' I said. 'Are you OK? Does it hurt? Are you coming home now?'

'I wish!' said Mum. 'I haven't had the blooming operation yet. They faffed around yesterday with blood tests and X-rays. They're doing the operation this morning. They're not letting me have any breakfast and I'm *starving*.'

'So – so when will you be back?' I said, all my relief draining away.

'Well, that's the problem, sweetheart. This nurse

says I won't come round from the anaesthetic for hours, and even then I'll be so groggy I won't be able to put one foot in front of the other. And they'll have to change the dressings and there might be a drain too—'

'What's a drain?'

'*I* don't know. Look, darling, I can't go into all the ins and outs of it. I've borrowed the mobile from the lady in the bed next to me seeing as you've got mine so I'll have to be quick. Let me say hello to Kendall.'

I handed the phone over to him. Mum was obviously asking him questions because he kept nodding.

'*Say* something, Kendall – Mum can't see you,' I said.

'Hello, Mum,' said Kendall. 'Mum, can I go and see the real George again? Will you take me? And can I have some more toy sharks and then if we got some glass I could have my own aquarium and – Ouch! Stop it, Lola Rose! Give me the phone back, it's *my* turn to talk to Mum.'

'She doesn't want to listen to you burbling on about your stupid sharks,' I said. 'Mum?'

'You kids,' said Mum. 'Look, Lola Rose, I'll try to give you a ring tomorrow morning some time. I'll have to go now. Bye, darling. Be a good girl, eh?'

The phone went dead.

'You hurt me when you pushed me!' Kendall said, rubbing his chest. 'I think you've given me cancer now.'

'Shut *up*, Kendall.'

'You're so mean to me. *Everyone's* mean to me,' Kendall whined. '*Mum's* mean. She said she'd be back today and I need her.'

'I need her too,' I said. 'Now stop complaining, finish your cornflakes and get ready for school.'

I was glad to get there. It made everything seem more normal. I didn't want to discuss Mum with Harpreet. Luckily we had a sex education lesson and we didn't discuss anything else all day. We watched a film where you actually saw this family undressed, totally naked. The whole class got the giggles, especially at the dad. The teacher got a bit narked and said she was disappointed in us for behaving so immaturely. She said there was nothing funny about human bodies.

'I think they're hilarious!' Harpreet whispered. 'That dad's willy! Yuck! Imagine him just walking around like that – it's disgusting. And the mum was just as bad showing off her boobies. I've never seen my mum and dad bare. I did walk in on my brother once in the bathroom and he got really really mad at me.'

'What's your brother look like then, Harpreet?'

Harpreet went into a peal of giggles – and when she found a banana in her lunch box at break we laughed so much we nearly wet ourselves.

I wanted to keep on and on laughing. I whispered to Harpreet all afternoon. I got told off twice and ended up being sent to Ms Balsam.

I thought I was going to get told off big time now. I didn't really care. I thought I might argue back, even throw a tantrum like Kendall.

But Ms Balsam simply sat me down and offered me a chocolate. I shook my head although they were posh chocolates in a big gift box.

'Go on, help me out. I'm supposed to be on a diet but they're so tempting. You eat a couple for me, there's a good girl.'

I helped myself to a milk chocolate truffle. 'Everyone keeps telling me to be a good girl,' I said, with my mouth full.

'I take it you've been behaving like a bad girl today?' said Ms Balsam. She picked out a dark chocolate cherry. 'Just to keep you company,' she said, popping it in her mouth.

She rattled the box at me and I chose a raspberry cream – white chocolate with a little raised tip of pink. It looked like a tiny doll's breast. I wondered what I was doing, stuffing my face with chocolate when my mum was in hospital. The sticky chocolate stuck to my teeth. My stomach lurched. I clapped my hand to my mouth.

'In here, quickly,' said Ms Balsam, leaping up. She steered me rapidly across the room. She opened a door and I was sick into her private toilet. Ms Balsam tucked my hair behind my ears and held my forehead. 'There, there,' she murmured.

When I was done she wiped my face with her own flannel and gave me a glass of water to sip. 'Bit of a waste of my chocolates!' she said. 'Still, you did it very neatly. Well done!'

I giggled weakly.

'So what's the problem, Lola Rose?' Ms Balsam sat on the edge of her desk, looking at me.

'I suppose I've got a tummy bug,' I said.

'Hmm,' said Ms Balsam. 'There's certainly something bugging *you*. You're not still hanging around with Ross and his little gang, are you?'

'No. I can't stick them now.'

'What about Peter? He's a good lad at heart. If you fancy a friend he'd maybe fit the bill.'

'I don't want a *boy*friend. I'm happy with Harpreet.'

'Yes, I like Harpreet too – lovely girl. You're both lovely girls – but I gather you've been very giggly girls today. Giggling about sex, is that right?'

'Sort of.'

'Well. It *can* seem a bit funny at times. But let's hope you're over the giggles now. I should pop back to your classroom and apologize nicely, unless you think you might be sick again. Maybe I should send you home to Mum.'

I bit my lip. 'No, I'm fine,' I said, getting up quickly.

Ms Balsam put her hand on my shoulder. 'Mum's OK, isn't she, Lola Rose?'

The walls closed in. The floor wavered. I wanted to clutch Ms Balsam and weep against her chest. But I remembered what Mum had said. *Don't let her worm anything out of you else you'll be put into care.*

'Mum's fine,' I said, shrugging my shoulder away.

I went back to class and said sorry and sat meekly for the rest of lessons, head down, keeping out of trouble. Harpreet and I had a giggle again on the way home. I kept whispering worse and worse things to set her off. I hated saying goodbye to her when we got to the Gabries' house.

Then it was just Kendall and me.

'Tell me something to make me laugh, Kendall,' I said. 'Go on, tell us a joke.'

'I know an elephant joke. Well, I think I do,' said Kendall.

He didn't. His joke went on for ages and then he forgot the punch line.

'OK, I'll tell you a joke,' I said.

'I don't think I like jokes,' said Kendall.

'Yes you do. I'll tell you one you'll like. What's yellow and dangerous?'

Kendall peered at me, his face screwed up anxiously.

'What's yellow and dangerous?' I repeated.

Kendall gave a high-pitched laugh.

'Why are you laughing?'

'Because it's a funny joke.'

'I haven't told it yet! Think, Kendall. What's yellow and dangerous?'

The Voice of Doom suddenly spoke, right behind my eyes, making them blink. *If he guesses the right answer your mother will be all right!*

I shook my head to try to shake myself free of it. Kendall shook his head too, copying me. His head looked as if it might snap straight off his little stalk neck.

'Don't, Kendall.' I grabbed his head and held it still. 'Now listen. This is such an easy-peasy joke. I'm sure you've heard it heaps of times

194

before. What's *yellow* and *dangerous*?'

I saw Kendall mouth *yellow* and *dangerous*. He was trying, I knew he was.

'I'll give you a clue, shall I? George would like this joke.'

'No he wouldn't. George doesn't like jokes either,' said Kendall.

'He'd like this one because it's about him. And you'll like it because it's about a yummy pudding. The old-fashioned sort that grans make.'

'I wish we had a gran,' said Kendall. 'Then she could look after us. Why haven't we got a gran?'

'She died.'

'Did she get run over?'

'No, she died of . . .' I couldn't say the word.

The Voice of Doom started up again.

'Think about the joke, Kendall!' I said, gripping him by the shoulders. I knew I was being ridiculous. It didn't make any difference whether Kendall knew the stupid joke or not. But I couldn't help myself. I went on saying it over and over again until Kendall cried.

'It's shark-infested custard!' I screamed at last.

I had a mad vision of Mum struggling in thick yellow custard, surrounded by sharks. I tried to argue with the Voice.

'Mum's going to be all right,' I said inside my head. 'She had the operation this morning and now she's right as rain and she'll come back home as soon as she can. She might even be home already, lying on her bed, waiting to give us a big surprise.'

I knew there wasn't much chance but I couldn't help hoping.

I ran down the road, Kendall trailing after me. The Voice of Doom changed tack, telling me if I could get indoors before it counted one hundred then Mum would really be there. I got in the front door just as it reached ninety.

Mum wasn't there. I ran into every room, calling.

Kendall stood just inside the front door, nibbling at his thumb. 'Mum isn't coming back, is she?' he said.

'Yes, she is! As soon as she can. She'll phone us any minute now, because she'll know we're home from school.'

I put the mobile on the table. We looked and looked and looked at it.

'I expect she's having her tea,' I said. 'We'll have *our* tea, shall we?'

I opened the last tin of baked beans and made some toast. The bread had gone a little mouldy but I picked off the blue bits. I needn't have bothered. Kendall just fiddled about with his beans, spearing them on his fork one at a time, licking them and then lining them up on his plate. He didn't even touch his toast.

For once in my life I didn't feel like eating either. I could barely swallow my cup of tea. I kept watching the mobile. The battery was getting low. I didn't know if you could still take calls while it was recharging.

I stared until my eyes watered. Why wasn't she

phoning? She knew we were waiting. She knew we were worried. Maybe the woman in the next bed wouldn't let her use her mobile.

Then I had a brilliant idea. I looked in the call register of the phone and found the number. Then I dialled it. I had to give it several goes because my hands were trembling.

'Hello?'

I took a deep breath. 'Hello. Look, you don't know me. I'm Lola Rose, the daughter of the lady in the bed next to you. Oh please, can I speak to her?'

'Sorry?'

I wondered if I'd got the wrong number. 'I'm Victoria Luck's daughter. She's in hospital with you.'

'Oh right! I'm sorry, dear, I didn't quite get you at first. What's the matter?'

'I want to speak to my mum!'

'Well, darling, I can't help you.'

'Oh *please*, just for a minute. Couldn't you pass the phone over?'

'But I'm not in the hospital. I came home this morning.'

'Oh! But – but my mum hasn't come home. What's happened to her?'

'She'll be fine, dear, I'm sure. She was only having her op this morning.'

'She said she'd come home.'

'No pet, not today. She won't be up to it.'

'But is she all right? The operation went OK? She is better now?'

'I don't know, dear. She hadn't even gone up to theatre when I left. Look, get your dad or grandma to ring the hospital, they'll know.'

'Right. Yes. Well, thank you,' I said, and I touched the END CALL button.

Kendall was looking at me, biting hard at his thumb.

'She's fine, I'm sure she is,' I said. I cleared my throat, sank my head down into my shoulders, and spoke from right inside my chest. 'Do I sound old, Kendall?' I growled.

'Are you being a monster?' Kendall asked anxiously.

'I'm trying to sound like a grown-up,' I said.

I practised my voice ringing Directory Enquiries. I wrote the hospital number on the back of my hand and then rang. A lady at the other end said the name of the hospital.

'Can I speak to Victoria Luck, please?' I said. I spoke so deep down in my chest that I had to repeat myself twice before she understood.

'Which ward is she on?'

'I – I don't know which ward.' I didn't want to say the word but I didn't have any choice. 'It's the cancer ward.'

'It'll probably be Florence. I'll put you through.'

I breathed out, my hand over my pounding heart. After a long time someone answered on Florence Ward.

'Can I speak to Victoria Luck?' I asked, my throat hurting.

'Who's speaking, please?'

I didn't know what to say. Her mother? Her sister? 'Her friend.'

It was the wrong decision.

'Well, I'm sorry, I'm afraid it's not possible.'

'But I'm grown up, honestly.'

'I'm afraid we don't use the ward phones for friends.'

'Can't you just tell me if she's all right? Please!'

'I suggest you contact Mrs Luck's husband and ask him,' she said.

'Well, you can suggest all you like, Miss Snotnose Meaniepants, but Dad doesn't know and I wouldn't ring him even if he did,' I shouted and then switched the mobile off.

Kendall blinked at me. I wondered if I could coach him till he sounded like Dad. I knew it was hopeless.

I tried to think of all the possibilities. I could go upstairs and ask Andy to ring for me. Though Andy and Steve weren't speaking to us. And if they knew Kendall and I were on our own they'd maybe tell someone.

I could try to find Jake. But I didn't know where he was living now.

I could go along the road and ask Harpreet's dad to ring for me. He'd help. But Harpreet's mum would *definitely* report us.

'I don't know what to *do*,' I wailed. I slumped on the floor, my head on my knees. I could feel my blood beating, even ticking in my eyelids, Mum-Mum-Mum-Mum-Mum.

'Are you crying?' Kendall whispered.

I didn't answer. I kept my face hidden. I could hear Kendall breathing noisily above me. He nudged me with his shoe.

'Lola Rose?'

I didn't feel like Lola Rose. I didn't even feel like Jayni. I was withering away into no one.

I wanted Mum so badly. I had to bite my lips to stop myself calling for her. What if she wasn't all right? What if the operation had gone wrong? What if she'd died?

'You *are* crying,' said Kendall.

'I'm not. I just need to know if Mum's all right.'

'Let's go and find her then,' said Kendall.

I thought about it. Mum had said we mustn't. But we had to know. We couldn't just wait day after day.

Seventeen

'OK. We'll go to the hospital,' I said. 'We'll find Mum and see how she is.'

I wiped my eyes, stuffed Kendall into his jacket, tucked George under his arm, and then we set off. I didn't have enough money for a minicab so we went to the bus stop.

I asked the driver how to get to the hospital. He said he didn't have a clue, it wasn't on his route. But an old woman witting at the front said she'd been sent to the eye clinic there, and we needed to get out at the flyover and change to a number 88. She made me sit down beside her and pulled

Kendall right onto her lap. He fidgeted tensely. She clasped him tightly round the tummy. He can't stand his tummy being touched. I hoped he wasn't going to make a fuss.

She was trying to be kind but she kept asking nosy questions. I made up this whole story about visiting our sick granny, our mum meeting us at the hospital. Kendall frowned.

'Keep still, Mr Fidget-bottom,' said the old lady. Kendall slumped sideways, whispering to George.

The bus ride lasted for ever but we got to the fly-over at last. The old lady waved to both of us. I waved back, trying to look grateful, but Kendall ducked his head.

'I didn't like her,' he said. 'I could feel her knicker elastic through her skirt. Yuck!' He shuddered. 'She's not our gran, is she?'

'Of course not. We haven't *got* a gran.'

'But you said we had.' Kendall sighed. 'You keep telling stories. I can't remember who we've got and who we haven't.'

'We haven't got anyone except you and me and Mum. And we're going to see Mum now. It will be a lovely surprise for her.'

'Is that true or is that another story?'

'It's true as true as true,' I said over and over.

I chanted it on the 88 bus all the way to the hospital. It was a huge place. It took us ages even to find our way across the car park. A man at the entrance told us we couldn't come in without an adult. I said quick as a wink we were with our dad but he was still trying to find somewhere to park. He'd sent us ahead to buy our mum some flowers from the gift shop. The man nodded and let us in, but he watched as we squeaked along the polished floor in our trainers.

'We'll really buy Mum some flowers,' I said.

'How did you know to come out with all that stuff?' Kendall hissed.

'I'm just inventive, I suppose.'

My inventions meant we spent nearly all our money on a bunch of flowers that already looked a bit droopy. I told Kendall it was the thought that counted.

We got in a lift, having to squash up against the wall because a lady in a bed on wheels was already inside. She looked very ill. Every time the lift jerked she groaned. Kendall slipped his hand into mine. The nurse pushing the bed gave us a smile.

'Where are you off to, kids?' she asked.

'We're going to see our mum.'

'Where's Dad?'

'He's up there already,' I said.

I seemed to be inventing multiple dads – in the car park, in the ward. I had it all worked out in my head that Dad could also be in the gents toilet or feeding our baby sister or held up talking to a neighbour on another ward.

I was all set to lie until my tongue turned black but I didn't have to say a thing when we got to Florence Ward. There were two nurses sharing a bunch of grapes in a little side room but they didn't spot us.

We hurried past bed after bed, looking for Mum. Some of the women were lying down looking grey like the lady in the lift. Some were sitting chatting to their visitors, eating chocolates and opening cards. Some were shuffling up and down the ward in their dressing gowns, attached to weird pull-along drips.

'What are those bag things for?' Kendall asked.

'It's to make them better.'

'Mum won't have one, will she?'

'I don't think so.'

'Where *is* Mum?'

'She'll be just up here,' I said hoarsely.

The Voice of Doom was shouting in my head. I saw an empty bed stripped of its covers. I stopped still, staring at it.

'Ouch, your nails are digging in,' Kendall said.

Then he pulled away from me. 'Mum!' He went charging down to the end of the ward.

I blundered after him, looking around wildly. Then I saw her too, her blonde hair fanned out on her pillow. She had her head turned to the wall so we couldn't see her face. The bedclothes were right up over her shoulders. She was lying very still.

'Mum?' said Kendall.

'She's asleep,' I said. I put my hand on Mum's shoulder and shook her gently. 'Mum?'

She mumbled something and tried to pull the covers up over her head.

'Mum! It's us, Lola Rose and Kendall.'

Mum opened her eyes. She looked at us blearily.

I wondered if she'd forgotten our new names. I bent right up close so that my lips were against her ear.

'It's Jayni and Kenny, Mum,' I whispered.

'Hello,' she said. She didn't sound particularly pleased to see us.

'How are you, Mum?' I asked.

'Bloody terrible,' she said.

She sounded as if she had the worst hangover in the world – but she still sounded like herself. She wasn't lying back, all grey and groaning. Though she did groan when Kendall nuzzled up to her for a cuddle.

'Mind out! It's *sore*!'

Kendall froze. 'Have they chopped your boobie right off, Mum?' he asked.

'Christ, I hope not,' said Mum, scrabbling under the covers. 'No, I'm all here under the bandages. They've hacked at it, they've hacked under my arm too. He's a bloody butcher, that Mr Key.'

'But it's to make you better, Mum. You are better now, aren't you?' I said.

'I don't know. I don't *care*. I just want to go to sleep.' She tried to burrow back down.

I tapped her shoulder. 'So will you come home tomorrow, Mum?'

'Look, I'll try – but at the moment I can't even get up to go to the loo, let alone get myself all the way home.'

'But – but what are we going to do, Mum? We haven't got any money left. We spent the last of it on your flowers.'

I laid them on the pillow beside her. Mum looked at them.

'That was a bit stupid then. Look, they're wilting already.'

I swallowed hard. 'I'm sorry, Mum. But what *are* we going to do?'

Mum's eyes were closing. 'Look, ask your dad,' she murmured.

'Dad? Mum, wake up! We don't live with Dad any more, remember?'

Mum moaned. 'Oh God,' she said.

She started crying. She didn't make any noise but tears leaked out of her closed eyelids. Kendall started crying too, his mouth puckered. I was scared someone might call a nurse.

'Don't cry, Mum,' I said. My throat was so tight it hurt to talk. 'It's OK.'

'It's not OK. Oh God, I'm so useless. Maybe you kids would be better off in care than stuck with me.'

'No, we wouldn't! You're a lovely mum. You can't help being sick. Don't you cry now. We'll manage. I'll think of something.'

Mum's face contorted.

'What is it, Mum? Is it the pain?'

'I can't stand it when you're so bloody *brave*,' Mum sobbed. 'I'm sorry, kids. I've screwed everything up.'

'No you haven't. You're the best mum in the whole world and you're going to get better ever so quick and we'll stay lucky lucky lucky.'

I went on talking to her like she was my little

girl, stroking her soft hair. She sighed, snuggled down and went to sleep. I stood still, feeling her shoulders rise at each breath. I told myself that I didn't care about anything else, just so long as she was alive.

Kendall snuffled behind me. He had one hand between his legs and a desperate expression. I didn't get him to the loo in time.

'My trousers are all wet,' Kendall wailed.

'Never mind. It's getting dark outside. No one will notice.'

'Are we going home now?'

'That's right.' I gave him a big smile. I was Lola Rose. I'd get us home somehow, even though we didn't have any money.

We waited for the first bus and got on. I opened my purse and then looked astonished to find it empty. I gave a little gasp and told the bus driver that my mum had given me two pounds for the bus journey and now they weren't there.

'Spent it on sweets, have you?' he said, but then he grinned. 'Go on, kids, hop on.'

The second bus driver wasn't anywhere near as kind. He said we'd have to fill out a special form with our name and address. I got very worried but a lady with a lot of shopping standing behind us said, 'Oh for God's sake, *I'll* pay for them' – and she did.

We both said thank you very much. She gave us a little lecture about being out late by ourselves and didn't our mother know?

'Our mum's in hospital,' said Kendall.

She looked at his tear-stained face. 'Oh dear, I'm so sorry,' she said.

So we got all the way home for nothing. It was very late when we got back. Kendall was starving hungry. So was I. I looked at the last few slices of bread in the packet but they were bluer than ever and smelt funny. Kendall opened his mouth hopefully, like a little bird.

'No, it's gone bad. You'll get a tummy ache if you eat it.'

'I want to eat *something*,' said Kendall.

I thought hard. 'Wait here.'

I went downstairs and knocked on Miss Parker's door. Her television was blaring but she didn't answer. I tried calling through her letter box.

'There's nobody in,' she called, which was a pretty daft thing to do. Still, she *was* daft, so what did I expect? She wouldn't come to her door. I gave up on her and went upstairs to Steve and Andy's.

I felt sick with nerves. Mum had called Steve and Andy a lot of bad names. Maybe they'd yell rude things at me when they saw who was knocking. I prayed it would be Andy who came to the door. He was so much nicer than Steve.

It was Steve. He raised his eyebrows when he saw me. He didn't say anything at all, just folded his arms.

'I'm sorry to bother you, Steve,' I said.

'You don't bother me, though I seem to bother you, judging by all the names I get called.'

'I didn't ever call you names.'

'No, but your mum certainly came out with a mouthful.'

'I know. I'm sorry. She's sorry too. She was just upset because of that Jake.'

'I haven't seen him around recently.'

'He's gone.'

'Oh dear.' He didn't sound very sympathetic. 'I bet your mum's in a bit of a state.'

'Yes. She is. So she didn't get to the shops today and I wonder – I know it's a bit of a cheek, but could we borrow a carton of milk?'

Steve's eyebrows shot up further. 'So she's sent you on this little begging mission?'

'She's not feeling very well.'

'Mm,' said Steve.

'Who is it, Steve?' Andy called from inside their flat.

'It's little Lola Lollipop from downstairs,' said Steve. 'Come to beg a pint of milk off us.'

'Borrow,' I said. 'We'll pay you back when . . . whenever.'

'Hi, Lola Rose,' said Andy, gently pushing Steve to one side. 'You OK, sweetheart?'

'Yes, I'm fine.'

Andy still looked concerned. 'Come in for a minute,' he said. 'Would you like a cup of tea? A Coke and crisps?'

My mouth watered at the thought. 'I can't really leave Kendall,' I said.

'Isn't your mum home?' said Steve, narrowing his eyes.

'Yes! Yes, but she's in bed, not very well. I want to make *her* a cup of tea, see, so if I could just borrow that milk?'

'Sure,' said Andy. He brought me a big two-pint carton, plus a couple of cans of Coke and a big bag of Kettle crisps. 'Take these back for you and Kendall.'

'Oh thank you, Andy, thank you!'

'What about breakfast? Has Mum got something in?'

'Well, the bread's gone a bit stale . . .'

He gave me half their loaf *and* a big packet of muesli.

'You're so kind.'

'Yeah, he's Mr Soft Touch,' said Steve, but he didn't sound too cross about it.

Kendall and I devoured the Coke and crisps. I felt we should save half as it was such a big bag but we were so hungry we ended up munching every scrap and licking out the bag. Kendall drank his Coke too quickly and got the hiccups. He found this uproariously funny at first. Then he got tired and tetchy.

'Stop me!' he begged.

I tried making him sip water but he hiccuped in mid swallow and choked. Even that didn't stop him. I knew you were supposed to be able to frighten someone out of hiccups so I tried creeping up on him and going boo. This didn't work either.

It seemed so stupid trying to frighten him when we were in such a scary situation already. The Voice of Doom was laughing its head off.

Eighteen

Auntie Barbara

Kendall was still hiccuping when I put him to bed. I made him lie on his tummy and then I patted his back.

'I used to do this when you were a little baby,' I said. 'It always made you burp.'

'Me a lickle baby now,' Kendall lisped. 'Burpy burpy burp.' He made George jump up and down. 'Poor George. He's got the burpy hiccups too.'

'I'm not surprised he's got hiccups. Tell him to stop snacking on poor little Bobby Blue Bear.'

'He gets hungry,' said Kendall. 'And Bobby *likes* being eaten.'

'Well, tell George he'd better not start on Pinkie. I don't want shark slobber all over *my* bear.'

Kendall giggled, hiccuped one last time, and fell fast asleep. I took my clothes off and lay down beside him. I'd put Kendall to sleep. I'd put Mum to sleep. I wanted someone to come along and put *me* to sleep.

There were too many worries circling round and round my head. I knew Mum couldn't come home tomorrow. Maybe not even the day after. And when she did come home she'd probably still feel poorly. She wouldn't be able to work for a while. So what were we going to do for money?

I couldn't keep begging food from Steve and Andy. I couldn't think of any way I could earn money myself. You had to be thirteen before you could do a newspaper round. I'd seen a few kids helping out in the market, but they were all boys. I could filch a few bruised bananas and rotten apples as the market closed up each day but that wouldn't be enough to feed the three of us. I could hang about outside McDonald's and grab left-over French fries and half-eaten burgers. I could sidle round Sainsbury's and pinch a packet here, a tin there . . . ?

No, I couldn't. I didn't have the bottle. What if I got caught? It was wrong to steal. But Mum needed good food to build her strength up. She'd looked so *little* lying there in hospital. What if I had to watch her losing weight day after day? What if she died?

What would Kendall and I do then? Would they make us go back to Dad? He'd be kind to Kendall but I wasn't his little Jayni any more. I was big enough for him to batter.

I moved my jaw gingerly. It still sometimes ached from that one punch. I couldn't take it like Mum. I was a terrible baby. I'd cry, and that always made Dad madder.

I curled up small and felt for Pinkie bear. I hugged her hard against my chest. I thought of Dad's fists. Tears trickled onto Pinkie's fur. I wished she could grow bigger, big as my pillow, big as the bed. I wanted her to lift me up and cradle me against her pink fur.

Auntie Barbara had given her to me when I was born. Maybe Auntie Barbara looked like a giant Pinkie without her clothes.

I clutched Pinkie tight.

Auntie Barbara!

I couldn't remember her properly. I last saw her at Grandma's funeral when I was younger than Kendall. Mum talked about her size so much she seemed like a character in a cartoon. It was weird remembering she was real.

Would she help us? I knew Grandad would have nothing to do with us. But maybe Auntie Barbara was softer? She must like us a little bit if she sent us special teddies. She used to send books too, before we moved to the flats. I remembered a big book about an elephant and one about a little bear and a funny one about jelly with a hole in the pages. I'd loved those picture books but

Kendall tore them all when he was a toddler. Auntie Barbara hadn't sent us any presents for years. But maybe she simply didn't have our address.

I didn't have *her* address. I couldn't ask Mum. She'd go mad if she thought I was going begging to the sister she couldn't stand. I wondered why Mum didn't like her. Maybe Auntie Barbara had been really mean to her. But she wasn't just Mum's sister, she was my auntie. Aunties were meant to help you, weren't they?

Harpreet had heaps of aunties. They made a big fuss of her and invited her to tea and bought her special sweets and hair slides and bangles. Maybe my Auntie Barbara wouldn't mind if I asked her to send a few fivers to tide us over until Mum could work. She must have quite a lot of money if she lived in Grandad's pub.

I couldn't remember the name. It was some sort of fish. The Cod? No, that sounded stupid. The Salmon? That wasn't right either. The *Trout*, that was it! And I knew the town, even if I didn't know the street.

I sat up in bed and rang Directory Enquiries on Mum's mobile. I wrote the number down and then dialled it quickly before I could change my mind. The phone rang and rang. I hoped Grandad wouldn't come to the phone. I was about to give up – but then someone answered. A woman.

'The Trout. Can I help you? Though it's after closing time—'

'I'm sorry. I forgot it was so late. Can I speak to
– to Barbara, please?'

'Speaking.'

'Oh! Well, you don't really know me but – but I
think you're my auntie.'

'Oh, good lord! Is that Jayni?'

'Yes.'

'Oh Jayni, how lovely that you phoned!'

'You don't mind?'

'Of course not! I've been hoping and hoping
you would all get in touch. What's happened,
Jayni? Are you all right?'

'Well. Sort of. It's just . . .' I didn't know where
to start.

'Let me have a word with your mum,' said
Auntie Barbara.

'Well, that's just it. She's not here.'

'Where is she?'

'In hospital.'

'Oh God. Did your dad catch her then?'

I sat up in bed, startled. How did Auntie
Barbara know we'd run away?

'No, she's had to go to hospital to have a lump
taken out. She said she'd come straight back but
she didn't. So we went to see her and she's all
sleepy but I *think* she's all right. We're back home
now, Kenny and me, but we haven't got any
money left. I don't know what we're going to do
for food. We've got some muesli but I don't think
Kenny will eat it. The bread's gone mouldy so I
was wondering if you could send us some money,
Auntie Barbara, just for a few days. We'll pay you

back the minute Mum gets work. She doesn't know I'm phoning and I'd be ever so grateful if you don't tell Grandad because I know he doesn't like us but I thought you might just be kind enough to—'

'Jayni! Let me get a word in edgeways, sweetheart! Now calm down. I'm going to help, don't worry. Hang on while I get a pen and paper. Then you can give me your address.'

'Oh Auntie Barbara!' I said, and I burst into tears. She sounded so *nice*.

I cried so hard I could barely stammer out the address. Auntie Barbara repeated it back to me to make sure she'd got it right.

'There now, Jayni, don't cry, pet. It's going to be all right. You can count on me. Now, have you got the door locked, you and Kenny? Then I should try to go to sleep now. Don't worry any more. I'll get everything sorted out, you'll see.'

So I went to sleep, clutching Pinkie to my chest, Kendall breathing softly by my side.

Then Kendall woke me up, shaking my shoulder and tugging my hair.

'Leave off, Kendall.'

'There's someone knocking at the door, Lola Rose! It's the middle of the night!'

'What? It'll be someone for Steve and Andy. One of their mates will have been at a party.

'They're calling out for Jayni and Kenny.' Kendall paused. 'Is that still us?'

'Oh help!'

I flew to the window, thinking it was Dad. I saw

a very large woman peering up at me in the moonlight, clutching great carrier bags. 'Auntie Barbara!'

I ran down the stairs, tripping and nearly falling in my eagerness. Miss Parker poked her head round her door. She had a hairnet pulled right down to her eyebrows.

'I'm telling the housing people on you,' she said. 'Waking a body at all hours! It's disgraceful.'

'I'm sorry, really sorry, but it's my *auntie*,' I said, hurrying towards the front door.

'I don't care if it's little green men from Mars, they shouldn't come knocking in the middle of the night!' said Miss Parker.

I took no notice, fiddling with the bolts on the door. 'Don't go, Auntie Barbara, I'm coming!' I called.

I got the door open at last. Auntie Barbara dropped the bags and held out her arms to me. I fell against her.

Whenever I hugged Mum hard she always teetered on her heels and said, 'Careful, you'll knock me over.'

No one could knock Auntie Barbara over. She didn't budge an inch. She stayed still, like a well-upholstered sofa, while I leant against her and cried on the big soft cushion of her chest.

A small fist pummelled at my bottom.

'Do we know her?' Kendall asked.

I stopped snivelling and stepped back, reaching for Kendall. 'Of course we do! This is our auntie. Auntie Barbara, this is Kenny.'

'I'm Kendall,' he said.

Auntie Barbara stooped, arms open. Kendall backed rapidly.

'I don't hug strange ladies,' he said.

'Kendall!' I hissed.

Auntie Barbara laughed. 'Quite right, Kendall. And they don't come any stranger than me.'

She *did* look strange. She had long blonde hair, thick and soft, like Mum's, but Auntie Barbara's was really long. She wore it caught up and coiled and twisted into a bun at the top of her head, though little tendrils escaped and hung down like earrings. She had a very pretty face with Mum's big blue eyes. She didn't wear any make-up. Her skin was very pink as if she spent a lot of time scrubbing it. If you chopped Auntie Barbara off at the neck like one of those old hairstyling doll heads she'd win any beauty contest. But things started to go weird past her shoulders. There was just so much of her. She was the BIGGEST LADY I'd ever seen. She wasn't just fat, she was vast, so massive she seemed a different species altogether.

She wasn't wibbly-wobbly like the lovely maid at the hotel. She looked like she was made of pink marble, a great monument. She was wearing a vast silk top in a wonderful deep purple, with a matching wrap-around skirt. It could have wrapped round Kendall and me a dozen times. Her toenails were painted purple too, shining in her silver sandals. I wondered at first how she could stretch down over her huge stomach to

reach her toes, but she proved amazingly agile
for such a large lady. She bounded up the stairs to
our flat, swinging the great bags.

Miss Parker watched, open-mouthed. 'Who's
she when she's at home – the Queen of Sheba?'

Auntie Barbara laughed and gave her a regal
wave. She had a great silver ring on either hand
and a huge chunk of amber hung on a thick silver
chain. It was easy enough to imagine an amber
crown on top of her coiled hair.

Kendall and I followed in her wake. Her bottom
was enormous above us. Kendall's eyes met
mine. We struggled not to giggle.

Steve and Andy peered down from their land-
ing above, in little shortie Japanese dressing
gowns. Auntie Barbara waved to them too. When
we got inside our front door, Auntie Barbara said,
'I wonder if they realized we could see right up
their dressing gowns!'

We could all giggle together.

'Right, Jayni, where's the kettle? I'm dying for a
cup of tea. And biscuits.'

'I'm afraid we haven't got any.'

'*I* have,' said Auntie Barbara. She opened one of
the carriers and brought out tea bags, chocolate
Hobnobs, a walnut cake, fairy cakes, doughnuts,
a multipack of sandwiches, bananas, apples and *a
giant bar of Cadbury's chocolate*. 'I think we could
all do with a bit of sustenance,' she said, smiling.
'I went to the all-night supermarket on the way.'

'How did you know I like that chocolate, Auntie
Barbara?' I asked her, awed.

'*I* like it,' said Auntie Barbara. 'I've been known to eat a whole bar by myself.'

'Not a *giant* bar?'

'You bet a giant bar,' said Auntie Barbara, bustling around making tea as if she'd lived in our flat all her life.

'But aren't you worried that—?'

'That it'll make me fat?' said Auntie Barbara, she hooted with laughter. 'Bit late in the day to start worrying!'

She sat herself down on Mum's sofa bed, filling it as if it was her own armchair. Kendall and I sat cross-legged in front of her. We had cups of tea too, and started on Auntie Barbara's picnic. It tasted wonderful. Even Kendall ate heaps, properly too, swallowing the crusts on his sandwiches and eating the sponge as well as the icing on his fairy cake.

Auntie Barbara ate the most though. It was plain she could out-eat anyone. She saw me watching every mouthful she took. 'I'm a very bad example, Jayni,' she said. 'It's very unhealthy to eat as much as me and get so terribly fat.'

'Then why do you do it?' Kendall asked.

'Don't be so rude, Kendall!' I said, nudging him.

'No, it's a perfectly sensible question. Shame is, I haven't got any answers. I eat because I'm greedy. I like food.'

'I like food too,' I said, biting my lip.

'Don't look so worried. I'm sure you won't take after me,' said Auntie Barbara, happily biting into a big éclair, cream oozing everywhere.

'I don't take after Mum,' I said, reaching for an éclair too.

'I don't think you need take after anyone. You're yourself. Unique. The one and only Jayni.'

'She's not Jayni,' said Kendall.

Auntie Barbara wiped the cream from her mouth. 'Who is she then, Kenny? Whoops, sorry, Kendall.'

'I call myself Lola Rose now,' I said shyly. 'And Kenny's Kendall, like he said, and Mum's Victoria Luck.'

Auntie Barbara nodded. 'Are these new names to stop your dad tracking you down?'

'How do you *know*?'

'Because he came barging into my pub weeks ago, effing and blinding and generally doing his nut. He said your mum's gone off with a footballer. *Has* she?'

'No! She stopped seeing him ages and ages ago. No, we had to do a runner because my dad hit my mum, and then he went for me.'

'My dad didn't hit *me*. My dad said I'm his little champ,' Kendall said, sticking his chin up. 'He's the big champ and I'm the little champ.'

'Little chump, more like,' I said.

'You shut up, Lola Rose,' said Kendall, clenching his fist.

'I think Lola Rose is an absolutely lovely name,' said Auntie Barbara. 'Did your mum think that up?'

'I chose it myself,' I said proudly. 'You won't tell Dad, will you, Auntie Barbara?'

'What do you think I am, daft?' said Auntie Barbara. 'I had a few sharp words with him.'

'He didn't hit *you*, did he?'

'I'd like to see him try,' said Auntie Barbara, flexing her big arms. 'I don't think any man would dare take me on. Even your grandad thought better of it once I'd got to a certain age. He had a really nasty temper too, just like your dad. He didn't mellow in old age either. He was a crabby old beggar up until the day he died. In fact he died in mid rant, yelling at me because I was changing the beer barrels—'

'So he's dead, our grandad.'

'A couple of years ago. I tried to let your mum know but she'd moved. She isn't a girl for keeping in touch. We didn't really get on when we were kids, your mum and me. We were so different, chalk and cheese. We had this awful row over something – and I got really mad at your mum. But that was long ago. I'm not mad at her now – and I've *never* been mad at you two. I'm so happy you phoned me, Jayni. Sorry, Lola Rose.'

'How did you get here so quick? There aren't any buses this early, are there?'

'I drove, sweetheart. I'll pop back down to the car in a minute and get my case.'

'Your case?'

'I'm staying to look after you, darling. Until your mum gets better. I've got it all organized at the pub. I've got this lovely Australian couple working as bar staff, and they're going to manage things for me till I get back. You didn't think I'd just lob a few pounds and a packet of biscuits at you and then disappear? I'm your auntie. You're *family*.

Nineteen

Treats

'I'll go and see your mum this morning,' said Auntie Barbara.

'I'm coming too,' I said.

'And me,' said Kendall.

'Will it upset him?' Auntie Barbara mouthed.

'Probably,' I mouthed back.

I was worried *Mum* might be upset. Upset with me for calling Auntie Barbara.

We went to the hospital together, Auntie Barbara striding confidently down the ward, Kendall and I scuttling along behind her.

Mum was lying on her back, looking towards

us. Her face screwed up. 'Oh Gawd, what are *you* doing here?' she said rudely.

Auntie Barbara blinked – but then she laughed cheerfully. 'Good to see you too, Nikki,' she said, and bent down to give her a kiss.

I was sure Mum would wriggle away. She didn't. Her good arm hooked round Auntie Barbara's neck and she hugged her hard.

'So how are you?' said Auntie Barbara.

'Fine!' said Mum. She still had great wads of bandage on her breast and under her arm. Her face was ghostly pale without her make-up and her hair hung in limp strings.

She pulled me close for a hug too, whispering in my ear. 'Has Jake been in touch?'

'No,' I said wretchedly.

Mum sighed as if it was somehow my fault.

'Lola Rose has been a little star, Nik. She's been so responsible and grown up.'

'Yeah yeah yeah. Takes after you then, doesn't she?' said Mum.

'Kendall's been brilliant too,' said Auntie Barbara. She was laying it on a bit thick now. Kendall had been a right pain.

Mum just gave a little snort.

'Mum?' said Kendall. He climbed up onto the bed, wanting to see her face. He frowned at her. 'You look horrid, Mum.'

'Thanks a bunch,' Mum muttered, pushing him away. 'Get off the bed, Kendall, I don't want you breathing all over me.'

Kendall slid off the bed, tears in his eyes. He

looked at me to make it better. I knew he hadn't meant to be unkind. He was worried that Mum still looked so ill.

'I don't like you,' he said, his lip trembling.

'I don't like you either,' Mum said, shutting her eyes.

'I don't want you for my mum any more,' Kendall said, tears spilling. 'I want Auntie Barbara.'

I covered his mouth up quick. 'He doesn't mean it, Mum,' I said hurriedly.

Maybe he did. He thought Auntie Barbara was wonderful. She knew all about sharks for a start. She'd been on holiday to America and seen the island where they made that old movie *Jaws*, the one where the shark chews people's legs off when they're swimming in the shallows.

Auntie Barbara got it out the video shop for Kendall that evening. He watched it sitting on her vast lap, George clutched to his chest. Auntie Barbara was worried that he might be frightened but he didn't seem to mind a bit. He only got upset at the end, when the shark died.

I couldn't watch any of it. I sat cross-legged with my back to the telly, working on my scrapbook, a pile of magazines by my side. I was doing a 'Favourite Food' page for our family – Mum, Auntie Barbara, Kendall and me. It was difficult to balance the page. Auntie Barbara had heaps and heaps and heaps, I had lots, Mum had hardly anything if you didn't count wine and ciggies, and Kendall just had a red ice lolly.

'Did you see sharks when you were on holiday, Auntie Barbara?' Kendall asked.

'Not swimming in the sea. I saw whales though, lots of humpback whales. I've got photos at home, I'll show you sometime. I went out in this special whale-watching boat. The whales like to eat plankton so they blow out this sticky stuff and all the little fishy things get stuck and then the whales come along and go chomp chomp chomp.'

Auntie Barbara mimed it for us. Kendall did his best to imitate her and blew sticky stuff out of *his* nose by mistake.

'Have you ever been to Disneyland, Auntie Barbara?' I asked. 'My friend Harpreet has and she says it's the best place in the whole world.'

'I haven't ever been there. Still, maybe we could go some day?'

'You mean, you and Kendall and me? And Mum? But how could we afford it? The lottery money's all gone.'

'I could treat us,' said Auntie Barbara.

'Are you rich?' Kendall asked excitedly.

'Not *rich*. But I'm reasonably well off, I suppose, now your grandad's passed the pub on to me. I don't spend much on clothes and posh cars and stuff, but I do like to go on good holidays. I went to Thailand last year. It's a fantastic country and lovely lovely people. I've got this smashing Thai family who do the meals in my pub now. Have you kids ever had Thai food?'

'We have Chinese takeaway. I like chicken chow mein,' I said.

'You wait till you try Thai. It's truly scrumptious.'

'Truly's in *Chitty Chitty Bang Bang*,' said Kendall, proud because he'd remembered.

'We had the video at our old home,' I said.

'It's a play now too, with a real car that flies right up in the air. We could go sometime if you like,' said Auntie Barbara.

We stared at her. It was as if she was taking *us* in a magic car, flying us out of our own dull life to a dazzling magic land where everything seemed possible.

She took us up to town on Sunday morning and said we could go anywhere we wanted. Kendall chose the aquarium, surprise, surprise. Auntie Barbara was very understanding when I explained I couldn't go in. She sat me on a bench overlooking the river.

'You sure you'll be OK?'

'Yeah, of course,' I said.

I wasn't. The sharks were shut up in the aquarium but I couldn't shut all my other worries up. They swam round and round my head. I felt really guilty that Kendall and I were having a good time with Auntie Barbara while Mum was stuck in hospital, still not better. She'd looked so small when we'd said goodbye. I was scared she'd shrink every time we went to see her, until one day she'd just be a hank of hair, a few bones and a bandage.

I was scared I might start crying so I tried to distract myself. I gathered up some sweet wrappers and started tearing them up and sticking them with spit onto my arm like tattoos. I'd seen a picture of a snail made out of coloured paper at school so I copied that. Then I did a butterfly and a ladybird and a rose.

Auntie Barbara sucked in her breath when she saw. I thought she'd make me pick all the papers off and give me a lecture about licking dirty bits of paper. Mum would have. But Auntie Barbara held my arm up and inspected it closely, smiling.

'Do you like Matisse?' she said.

I'd never even heard of Matisse so she took us to the Tate Modern. Kendall moaned and said it was going to be boring-boring-boring, but when we'd walked all along the river bank to this huge gallery he ran around all over the place and no one seemed to mind.

There was a special Matisse exhibition. I wasn't sure I liked his work at first. All the paintings were a bit squiggly and didn't look real though I liked the bright colours. Auntie Barbara liked a picture of a big lady lying back on a sofa in funny floppy trousers. She said she'd have a go at making some similar trousers for herself. She makes most of her clothes because she's so huge she can't find anything in the shops.

'I'll make you a pair of stripy trousers too, Lola Rose,' said Auntie Barbara. She saw the look of horror on my face. 'Joke!' she said, laughing.

We turned a corner – and there was the school snail picture, absolutely huge, bigger than Auntie Barbara.

'It's a collage!' I said.

'Do you know something? I think *your* collage work knocks spots off old Matisse. I love that food picture you did last night. Hey, talking of food, I'm starving! Let's go and find the café.'

We all had sausages and mash. Kendall turned his sausages into sharks and made them swim in the mashy sea but then he ate them all up. I ate mine too, and then a big strawberry cheesecake, but on the bus to the hospital I started to feel sick. Kendall went quiet too. Auntie Barbara put her arms round us.

'Will Mum be better now?' Kendall asked.

'Let's hope so,' said Auntie Barbara – which wasn't quite the same as a straight yes.

When we got to the ward Mum was propped up on her pillows, her hair carefully brushed, her make-up pink and pretty, almost her old self.

'You *are* better, Mum!' said Kendall.

'Yeah, I'm going home tomorrow, they've promised,' said Mum.

'That's great news, Nik,' said Auntie Barbara.

'*Victoria*,' said Mum.

'Victoria Luck. Lady Luck,' I said.

'That's right, that's me,' said Mum, but she wasn't looking at me. Her eyes kept swivelling past all of us.

We stayed for a while, Auntie Barbara and me trying to chat to Mum, Kendall sitting on the floor muttering to George. Mum slid further and further down the bed, barely replying.

Then she suddenly sat up straight. She licked

her lips and then bared her teeth in a big smile.

I looked round. Jake was shuffling up the ward, clutching a small bunch of carnations, the sort you buy outside a garage for £2.99. Mum behaved as if he'd given her an armful of hot-house lilies. She gave him a really smoochie movie-star kiss right in front of us. Jake's mouth was all wet when he pulled away. He lifted his arm as if he wanted to wipe it. Mum was gazing up at him. His arm froze. He looked like a statue saying hello. Then he waved it awkwardly at Kendall and me.

'Hi, kids,' he said. He nodded nervously at Auntie Barbara too.

'Hi, I'm Victoria's sister,' she said.

Jake looked astonished. Auntie Barbara watched him, waiting for some crass comment. She seemed utterly composed but I saw her fingers fidgeting behind her back, digging hard at a hangnail. It must be awful – everyone always amazed that two sisters could look so different.

Jake managed to hold his tongue. Mum patted the bed, making him sit beside her. I saw her wince slightly when he sat down heavily but she didn't say a word. He could have used the bed as a trampoline and she wouldn't have complained.

'How lovely of you to come and see me, Jake,' she said, like it was a huge surprise – though I found out later she'd begged a loan of a mobile from another patient and left urgent messages at his art college.

I suppose it was good he came. Maybe he

loved Mum a little bit. Maybe he thought she was about to die and might leave him something. Not that she *had* anything. Just a suitcase of clothes, a few bits of furniture – and two kids.

Mum seemed to have forgotten all about us. She chatted non-stop to Jake, two pink smudges of rouge standing out on her pale cheeks. Jake hardly said a word. He looked relieved when Kendall edged towards him.

'How's my little pal, eh?' said Jake. He picked Kendall up and plonked him on his lap. Kendall kicked his legs happily.

'Careful!' said Mum, frowning at Kendall.

'Does it hurt a lot?' Jake asked, looking stricken.

'No, no, hardly at all. And don't worry, I'm still all in one piece,' said Mum, patting her bandages gingerly. 'It's all thanks to you, Jake darling. If you hadn't found the little lump and made me go to the doc then I'd have been up the creek without a paddle.'

'I want to paddle,' said Kendall, not understanding. 'Mum, Auntie Barbara's taking us to the seaside to see sharks and whales and then we're going to Disneyland.'

'Oh yeah? What's that whizzing past? Whoops! It's a flying pig,' said Mum.

Kendall lost track altogether but didn't seem to mind. 'Paddle paddle paddle, George and me are going to paddle,' he sang. He kicked his legs again, pretending to paddle. He caught Mum on her side. It wasn't her sore chest or arm but it must have hurt. Her eyes blinked but she stayed smiling bravely.

Jake eased Kendall off his lap and stood up.

'Where are you off to?' said Mum.

'I'm sorry, Vic, I've got to go.'

'But you've only just got here!'

'Yeah, well, I've things to do. You know how it is.'

Mum knew. She couldn't bear it. She waited until he was out of sight and then started sobbing. Auntie Barbara reached out to hold her hand but she snatched it away.

'Don't, Nik, he's not worth it,' Auntie Barbara said softly.

'How would *you* know?' Mum sobbed.

'Yeah. How would I?' said Auntie Barbara. She put her arm round Kendall and me. 'Come on, kids.'

'Stop making such a fuss of those kids, they're *mine*,' Mum cried.

'Mum's tired,' said Auntie Barbara. 'We'll go now. What time do you think they'll let you out tomorrow? I'll come and collect you in the car.'

'It won't be till lunch time – and I'll get myself home, thanks very much,' Mum sniffed.

'Sure, sure,' said Auntie Barbara. 'But I'll come at lunch time even so.'

Auntie Barbara made us both go to school on Monday, even though we argued.

'No, I'll need to concentrate on your mum. We've got some stuff to sort out. And I don't want you to miss any more school.'

'It'll be a waste of time sitting in lessons. I won't be able to take anything in,' I said.

I was right. I kept thinking about Mum. I told Harpreet Mum was getting out of hospital. She gave me a big hug and said she was very happy for me.

'So she's better now?'

'Yes, of course she is. Or they wouldn't let her out of hospital, would they?' I said.

'That's right,' said Harpreet, patting my shoulder. 'Here, Lola Rose, Mum's put an extra bar of chocolate in my lunch box. You can have it if you like.'

I had extra everything in *my* lunch box because Auntie Barbara had packed it for me. Harpreet and I shared a wonderful feast of cream cheese and date and banana rolls, chicken salad sandwiches, vegetable chunks with their own special dip, salt and vinegar crisps, blueberry muffins, buttered fruit bread, rosy apples, cranberry juice – and a giant bar of Cadbury's chocolate.

'I'm going to get so *fat*,' Harpreet said, rubbing her flat tummy.

'I *am* fat,' I said.

'No you're not. Well, not really,' said Harpreet. 'You're bound to slim down a bit in your teens. You'll take after your mum.'

'I hope so,' I said. 'But if I don't, it's not *so* bad being fat, is it?'

'No, of course it's not bad at all,' said Harpreet comfortingly.

But when we came out of school at the end of the afternoon Harpreet stopped dead in the playground. 'Oh my goodness, look at that fat woman!' she gasped.

She put her hand over her mouth and giggled. She wasn't the only one. Half the kids were gawping and nudging each other.

'Is she someone's *mum*?' Harpreet spluttered. 'She's like an elephant! Whoever is she?'

'She's my Auntie Barbara. And you can just shut up,' I said.

I ran across the playground to the school gate where Auntie Barbara was waiting. She was wearing a blue denim shirt that could have sailed a ship. She held out her big blue arms and I rushed up and hugged her in front of everyone.

'You look lovely, Auntie Barbara. I like that shirt. It matches your eyes,' I said.

Auntie Barbara hugged me harder.

'So where's Mum? Did you go and fetch her? Why isn't she here?' I said, my heart starting to pound.

'It's OK. She's at home, resting.'

'And she's all right, really?'

'Well,' said Auntie Barbara. 'She's OK. For the moment.'

Her words clanged in my head. The Voice of Doom repeated them. *For the moment*. I needed it to be *for ever*.

Harpreet was hovering, looking at me beseechingly with her beautiful big eyes. 'I'm so sorry,' she mouthed at me.

'Auntie Barbara, this is my friend Harpreet,' I said.

Harpreet looked very relieved. She held out her hand politely. 'Pleased to meet you, Auntie Barbara,' she said. She looked at me. 'You never said you had an auntie! Is she a real blood auntie or just a friend?'

'I'm a real auntie *and* a friend,' said Auntie Barbara.

We went to collect Kendall and Amandeep from their after-school club. Amandeep hung back and acted shy, sucking her thumb.

'She can't help being a bit babyish,' said Kendall, taking hold of Auntie Barbara's hand. 'Auntie Barbara, I love you.'

'I love you too, Kendall,' said Auntie Barbara.

'Will you take us to the aquarium?'

Auntie Barbara laughed but I was shocked.

'Kendall! We're going straight home. Mum's back!'

'Well, she can come too,' said Kendall.

'Don't be silly, she's not well enough yet.'

'She's always ill now,' said Kendall, as if it was Mum's fault. 'Can't we go to the aquarium now and see Mum after?'

'No, it's straight home, sweetheart, but we'll get you a red ice lolly on the way, how about that? What about you, girls? What's your favourite ice cream?'

I had a white Magnum and Harpreet and Amandeep both had soft Cornettos. Auntie Barbara had a double-choc Magnum. She nibbled the chocolate off bit by bit just the way I do. She made little *Mmm* noises. I do that too.

'We should have bought an ice cream for your mum,' she said. 'What does she like?'

'She doesn't often eat ice cream – she watches her figure,' I said without thinking. Then I felt terrible.

'I watch my figure too,' said Auntie Barbara. 'I watch my figure getting bigger!' She said it like it was a poem. Then she pointed to places on herself and said, 'Cornetto, Cornetto, and Magnum Magnum Magnum!'

When we got to Harpreet's house she whispered in my ear, 'I love your Auntie Barbara, Lola Rose.'

'I love her too,' I whispered back.

I wished I was young enough to swing on Auntie Barbara's hand like Kendall. He started whimpering to go to the aquarium the minute he'd finished his ice lolly.

'Now who's acting like a baby?' I said crossly.

I knew why he was. I almost wished we *could* go to the wretched aquarium. I was sort of scared of seeing Mum even though I'd missed her so much.

I was scared that she'd still look really ill.

But when we let ourselves in the front door we heard Mum talking. Someone was with her. I thought it must be Jake.

It wasn't Jake.

It was Dad.

Twenty

The Fight

The flat started spinning. I nearly fell over.

I heard a harsh laugh.

It *was* Dad.

No, it couldn't be Dad. He didn't know where we were. He couldn't possibly find us. He couldn't be real. This couldn't be happening. I had to be dreaming. If I closed my eyes tight and then opened them really really wide I'd wake myself up.

I closed my eyes. The flat stopped whirling. Dad's voice stopped too. It *was* a dream.

I opened my eyes wide. And there was Dad,

right in front of me, his mouth a great grin, showing all his teeth.

I gasped. Kendall cried out too. 'Dad! Dad! It's my *dad*!' he whooped.

He hurtled forwards, skinny arms elbowing me out of the way. Dad caught him and whirled him round and round. Kendall's shoes hit me hard on the head, making me reel again.

I felt hands gripping my shoulders, holding me up. Auntie Barbara.

'Did *you* call Dad?' I whispered.

She shook her head. She looked over at Mum, lying on the sofa, white jacket over her black nightie, her face a mask of make-up.

Mum?

I dodged past Dad and Kendall and ran to her. She put her hands up quickly to stop me.

'Careful, careful! I'm still blooming sore, like I've done ten rounds with Lennox Lewis. Hello, darling. Glad to see your mum safely home? And Dad too? Isn't it a lovely surprise, eh?'

I stared at Mum. She stared back at me, her chin up, but she couldn't quite meet my eyes.

'It's time we got together again, Jayni,' she said. 'We've all missed Dad terribly, haven't we, Kenny?'

'Yeah! Yeah! Oh, Dad, you're the greatest! Wheee!' Kendall yelled, as Dad stuck him on his shoulders. 'I'm the king of the whole world! Look, I can touch the ceiling.'

'Watch that light fitting, Kenny, you'll electrocute yourself,' said Mum.

I felt as if Mum had stuck us all into an electric socket. Fear sizzled through me, making my hair stand on end.

Why had she done it? We'd spent all these weeks hiding from him, taking such care to start a new life so he couldn't trace us.

I knew why. She'd been so scared in the hospital. She needed someone to make her feel good. To make her feel she still *looked* good. Jake had been useless. So she started thinking about the one man in the world who was crazy about her.

She started spinning a little fairy tale, the way she always did. She'd kid herself it would all be so different now. Dad would be shocked she'd been so ill. He'd feel really bad and want to make it up to her. He'd have missed us so much. He'd realize just how much we meant to him. So he'd come back and he'd treat Mum like a queen. He'd never ever raise his hand to her again. He'd love her and cherish her and make her feel his special babe. We'd all play Happy Families and live Happily Ever After.

Mum had done her best to turn herself into a fairy princess. She couldn't raise her bad arm but somehow she'd bent over the basin and washed her hair one-handed. She'd painted her face with elaborate care. Her eyeliner was smooth, her lips outlined without a single smudge, though her hands were shaking now. She'd shaved her legs and painted her toenails pink.

She lay back in her careful pose, her jacket hiding the bulky bandage over her breast. She wanted the fairy tale to be real. Her eyes were going blink blink blink. She was wishing it inside her head.

I wished it for her too.

Maybe it really would come true. Dad wasn't laying into us, he was all lovey-dovey.

'I've been doing my nut without you, babe,' he said, sitting down beside Mum. Kenny stayed squealing on his shoulder. 'I couldn't credit it when you played that vanishing trick on me. I thought OK, you were teaching me a lesson, you'd stay away a couple of days, but you really meant it, didn't you, darling?' His voice thickened.

Mum snuggled up to him, touching his face with her carefully painted fingers. 'Not really, Jay, sweetheart. I don't know what I was think-ing. I was scared, you know? I suppose I just flipped. I needed to protect the kids.'

'But you know I'd never lay a finger on my kids,' said Dad. He yanked Kendall onto his lap and tickled him. 'I love this kid of mine to pieces, can't you see that?'

I felt as if I was falling down a tunnel. Dad was acting like he only had one kid. What about *me*? And what about the last time we'd been together? He didn't just lay a finger on me. He clenched his fist and punched me on the jaw, nearly knocking me out.

I stared at Dad, shouting inside my head. He

looked over at me as if he could hear. He smiled. It was a shark smile.

'Ah, Jayni,' he said, as if he'd just clapped eyes on me. 'Aren't you going to give your old dad a kiss and tell him you're pleased to see him?'

Mum held her breath, staring at me pleadingly.

I pretended for her sake.

I pretended for my sake too, because I was scared out of my wits. I wanted to run right out the room, down the stairs, down the road, run away for ever. But I walked up to my dad. He put his arm round me. His lips nuzzled my ear, my neck.

'That's my good little girl,' he whispered. 'Was it you who put your mum up to all this, eh?'

I didn't know what to say. I started shaking.

'Hey, are you shivering? You shouldn't be cold in that natty furry jacket. Nice little bit of clobber, that. So where's my fancy jacket, eh?'

'We'll buy you one, darling,' said Mum.

So she hadn't let on that the money was all gone.

'That's my babe. And my boy and my girl. My family, safely come back to me,' said Dad, arms round us all. Imprisoning us.

Auntie Barbara was standing free, watching us. She had her arms folded across her chest, hands gripping her elbows as if she was trying to hold herself in. She was looking at Mum like she couldn't quite believe it. Mum wouldn't look back at her.

But Dad did.

'So, Barbara,' he said. 'You were telling me porky pies when I came round to your pub.' He put his head on one side, puffing out his cheeks, his voice a silly high-pitched imitation. '*Oh no, believe me, Jay, I haven't got a clue where Nikki is. I haven't seen her for years. The last time I saw the kids Kenny was a baby.*'

'That was true, Jay,' Auntie Barbara said steadily. 'I didn't even have *your* address.'

'Liar!'

'You can call me all the names you like. I'm used to it.'

'Ooh, what sort of names do you get called, little Barbie?'

'I'm sure you're familiar with most of them,' said Auntie Barbara. 'I'll go and make us all a cup of tea, eh, Nikki? How are you feeling?'

'Fine,' said Mum. She looked grey underneath her make-up. 'Barbara just came to look after the kids when I had to go into hospital for the op.'

'So who called her then?' said Dad.

I stayed very still.

'I did,' said Mum.

'Why didn't you call *me*? They're my kids, for God's sake.'

'I know, darling, but I thought you might be freaked out by the whole hospital bit. Barbara, I'd love that cup of tea—'

'Yeah, OK, Barbie, you pop the kettle on like Polly, and then you can pop off back to your pub,' said Dad. 'We don't need you now. We're going home too.' He peered round the room, sniffing. 'Whatever made you pick this dump, Nik? Are you sure this tumour isn't in your head?'

'There's no tumour anywhere, darling. They've dug it all out of me. I'm as good as new,' said Mum.

'I hope so, babe. I couldn't bear it if you had to have one of your lovely boobies chopped off.'

'That's a really helpful attitude,' said Auntie Barbara.

We all tensed. Dad pushed Kendall so he slid off his lap.

'She didn't mean it to sound like that, Jay,' said Mum.

'What do you think I am, thick? Don't look so worried, babe. Jayni, stop that silly shivering. It's OK. I'm not going to blow my top. Even with your fat freak of a sister. Hear that, Barbie? You trot off back to Big Daddy.'

'He's dead and gone,' said Auntie Barbara, 'and I don't think any of us should trot off tonight. Nikki's exhausted. She needs to rest. And she has to go back to the hospital next week for the results of her tests.'

'What tests?' said Dad. 'I thought you said the tumour had gone, Nik?'

'It has, it has,' said Mum. 'They cut it all out. I'm fine now. Just a bit tired.' Her voice cracked and tears started dribbling down her cheeks.

'Don't cry, sweetheart, you know I can't bear

it,' said Dad. He pulled her close so her head was against his chest. 'There there, my little babe. It's OK, your Jay's here now. He'll take care of you.'

He stroked her hair and kissed the tip of her nose as if she was a little girl. Mum hung onto him.

'Oh Jay, you promise? You really will take care of me?'

'I swear I will, darling. You can count on me. You're my little babe and I'm going to keep you safe. Now you lie back. No wonder you're tired. I'll tuck you up, eh? You could do with a little nap. We'll stay here for the night if that's what you want. We'll get you back home tomorrow. I'll carry you in my arms if necessary. I'd carry you clear across the world, babe. You mean all the world to me. I was ready to top myself when you left. But I don't blame you, sweetheart. I'm not angry any more. You were obviously getting sick already, not thinking straight. You panicked, I know. I understand. But now you can relax. We're going to start all over again, you and me and our little lad.'

'And Jayni,' Mum said.

'And Jayni,' Dad said.

I hated the way Dad was looking at me. I couldn't be his little girl any more. He thought it was all my fault.

Maybe it *was* my fault.

My head felt as if it was being crushed. I couldn't hear, I couldn't see, I couldn't think.

Then I felt those two steady hands on my shoulders.

'Come and help me make the tea, Jayni,' said Auntie Barbara.

She steered me out into the kitchen. I leant against her. She wrapped her arms round me, bending over.

'You can come and live with me if you like,' she whispered.

'He wouldn't let me.'

'We'll work it out somehow. I'm not going to let him hurt you, I promise.'

'But he'll hurt *Mum*.'

'Maybe they'll work something out,' said Auntie Barbara. 'Maybe he really will take care of her. Maybe this is his last chance and he's taking it.'

When we went back into the living room Dad was trying hard, plumping up the pillows behind Mum and straightening the covers on the sofa bed.

'That's my girl,' he said. 'There! Is that comfier?'

'Yes, Jay, much.'

'We'll tuck you right up, eh?' Dad said tenderly. 'Let me take your jacket off. There now, don't worry, I won't hurt your poor chest. My brave little babe, you never make a fuss, do you? Well, you're not ever going to get hurt again, I promise. We'll tuck you up tight and you can have a lovely long snooze.'

'You're so good to me, Jay,' Mum said.

'That's right, babe. No one's ever looked after you the way I do,' said Dad, tucking the cover in firmly.

He felt something stuck under the mattress. He pulled it out. He held something crumpled and blue. He looked at it incredulously. 'What the bloody hell are these?' he said.

Dad held the blue boxer shorts out and waved them in the air, so that the legs flapped. It looked comical but no one laughed. Even Kendall ducked his head, elbows pressed against his sides.

Mum stared at the shorts helplessly.

'What are they?' Dad asked.

'They're underpants,' Mum whispered.

'Yeah. Right. I can see they are,' said Dad, holding them out, practically thrusting them in Mum's face. 'That's not really the issue, is it, Nikki?'

Mum swallowed.

'*Is it?*' Dad yelled.

'Don't shout, darling, please,' Mum begged.

'I'll shout my head off until you tell me whose pants these are,' said Dad.

They were obviously Jake's. I hated him for being so careless, so forgetful.

'They're Kendall's,' I blurted out.

'Oooh. *Kendall's*, are they?' said Dad. 'Why the fancy name, Kenny?'

Kenny tried to shrug, his shoulders wiggling.

'Are they your pants, *Kendall*?' said Dad. 'Bit big for you, aren't they?' He held up the boxer shorts. They'd have reached right down to Kendall's ankles.

'I think you're telling me porky pies, Jayni,' said Dad.

'Leave the kids out of it,' said Auntie Barbara. 'For God's sake, what does it matter whose stupid pants they are? Forget it, let's have our tea.'

She passed Dad a mug but he batted it away, so that hot tea sprayed everywhere, spattering Auntie Barbara's Thai silk two-piece.

'Whoops!' said Dad. 'Aha! Are they *your* pants, Barbie? No, I don't think so. A little on the small side this time.'

'You're labouring the point, Jay,' said Auntie Barbara, dabbing at her wet wrap-around.

'Too right I am. I want an answer.' Dad scrunched the pants up and wiped them round Mum's face like a flannel. 'Whose are they, Nikki?'

'I don't know,' Mum whispered.

'You don't *know*? So you've had so many men taking their clothes off since you've been here you've lost track, have you?'

Mum shook her head, clutching her sore chest. 'Jay, I'm sorry. Please don't be angry. There was just the one guy,' she wept.

'You slag,' Dad yelled. He raised his hand, his fist clenching.

I ran towards Mum.

Auntie Barbara was quicker. Her own fists were clenched. She didn't hit Dad. She *kicked* him. Her foot shot up in its big purple suede sandal. She kicked him hard, right in the crotch. Dad gasped and doubled up. Auntie Barbara balanced herself on the balls of her feet, ready for when he got up.

Dad got to his knees, clutching himself.

'You raise your hand one more time to Nik or the kids and I'll kill you,' said Auntie Barbara.

Dad staggered to his feet, his face contorted. He grabbed the tea mug and smashed it against the wall. Then he turned and came at Auntie Barbara again, the broken shards clutched in his hand. He went for her face – but she whirled her arm and chopped him hard on the shoulder with the side of her hand. He swayed, dropping the broken mug, his mouth open.

'I mean it, Jay,' said Auntie Barbara. 'Now get out. Get out of this flat. Get out of their lives.'

Dad looked at Mum.

'I'm sorry, Jay,' she sobbed. 'Just go now. Please.'

Dad stood there, sobbing with rage. He looked round at all of us – and then he ran out, slamming the door behind him. We heard Miss Parker downstairs calling out, complaining at the noise. The front door slammed harder.

Then there were footsteps and a banging on our door. We all thought Dad was back but it was Andy and Steve from upstairs.

'You OK, Victoria? We heard the ruckus.'

Steve had grabbed an umbrella, Andy a saucepan. They weren't great weapons, especially not for a fight with my dad. But Auntie Barbara had beaten him! She stood in the middle of the room, breathing hard, tidying her purple top.

'We're fine now, but thanks so much for coming to protect us.'

Steve and Andy were obviously dying to stay and find out what had been going on, but Auntie Barbara gently but firmly told them Mum needed to rest now. They shuffled back upstairs obediently.

'I think we need a fresh pot of tea,' said Auntie Barbara. She looked at Kendall. He'd wet himself he'd been so scared. 'And you need a change of trousers, Kendall. OK, Lola Rose. I'll do the tea, you do the trousers.'

I looked over at Mum. She had her head buried in her hands. I hesitated.

'Let Mum have a little cry,' said Auntie Barbara.

I took Kendall into the bathroom. He started crying too.

'I'm a baby. I wet myself!'

'No, it's OK, Kendall. *I* nearly wet myself. It was so scary.'

'That man *was* Dad, wasn't he?'

'Of course he was.'

'I remembered him different,' said Kendall.

'Yes.'

'He shouted at me.'

'He shouted at everyone.'

'I thought he was going to hurt us. But then

Auntie Barbara hurt him!' Kendall wriggled out of his wet trousers and kicked his leg in imitation. He waved his arm, nearly whacking me on the head as I washed him.

'Watch out, Kendall!'

'*You* watch out, Lola Rose, or I'll go kick-chop-thump like Auntie Barbara.'

'How did she *do* that?'

I was glad Kendall had seen it too, otherwise I'd have wondered if I'd imagined it. Already Auntie Barbara seemed to fly through the air in my memory, arms and legs whirling, like a martial arts movie.

'*Thai* martial arts,' said Auntie Barbara, when we asked her. 'I went to see Thai boxing when I was in Thailand. It's amazing. They do it to music and they use so many parts of their bodies as weapons – their fists, elbows, knees, shins and feet. When I came back I saw there were some Thai boxing evening classes. I went along just to watch, but I ended up joining in. I'd done some judo before so it wasn't like I was starting completely from scratch.'

'You joined in just like that? You are brave, Auntie Barbara.'

'No I'm not. I used to be scared to say boo to a goose when I was your age.'

Mum sniffled. 'You were Daddy's little darling.'

'*Big* darling.'

'You're so big you can even beat my dad,' said Kendall.

'Will you really kill him if he comes back?' I asked.

'No! Look, I'm thinking of becoming a Buddhist. They don't believe in killing anything, not even little creepie-crawlies.'

'But you *could* kill him if you wanted? If he was really really hurting us?'

'I don't know. Maybe.'

'Auntie Barbara, can you stay with us for a bit, *please*? Just in case Dad comes back?'

Auntie Barbara looked at Mum. 'I don't think your mum wants me to stay,' she said. 'But she hasn't got much choice. It looks like you're stuck with me.'

Twenty One

Treatment

Mum cried and cried. I couldn't work out why. Auntie Barbara had rescued us! Mum didn't *still* want Dad back, did she? She'd been just as scared as we were.

I asked Auntie Barbara.

'I expect she's just worn out with everything, pet,' she said.

'She *is* better, isn't she? They *did* get all the tumour out?'

'Yes, I think so. But she might have to have some treatment.'

'What treatment?'

'Let's just wait and see, shall we?' said Auntie Barbara.

'But she is going to be all right, isn't she?'

'I hope so, darling.'

'You promise?'

Auntie Barbara wavered. 'I wish I could promise you that, Lola Rose,' she said.

Mum seemed fine the next day. When Kendall and I came home from school she was looking lovely, her hair newly coloured and styled. She was wearing her white jeans, but now they had embroidered pink roses up and down the seams.

'Has Jake been here?' I asked.

'Has he heck,' said Mum. '*I* did them. You're not the only one who can be creative, Lola Rose.'

'They look lovely, Mum. *You* look lovely.'

'Do I?' said Mum, preening. 'Well, I've got to tart myself up. I'm going job-hunting tomorrow.'

'Why don't you wait a bit, Nikki?' said Auntie Barbara. 'Give yourself time to get better.'

'I *am* better,' said Mum. 'And I need a job as soon as possible. I've got to feed these kids.'

'I can take care of the bills for a bit,' said Auntie Barbara.

'I don't want you to,' said Mum. 'Haven't you been lecturing me all day about standing on my own two feet and not depending on anyone?'

'I don't *lecture*,' said Auntie Barbara, giving Mum a tiny push. 'And you'll never be able to stand on your two feet, not wearing those ridiculous high heels.'

Mum blew a raspberry at Auntie Barbara. 'Nag nag nag.'

'Whinge whinge whinge,' said Auntie Barbara.

Mum pulled a hideous face.

Auntie Barbara pulled a worse one.

They were like two silly kids.

'Aren't they childish, Kendall,' I said, winking.

I started singing Mum's 'Lucky' song as I helped get tea ready – steak and chips and a watercress salad to build Mum up, and then strawberries and cream. I washed the watercress and took the stalks off the strawberries and whipped the cream. Kendall licked the bowl, singing the 'Lucky' song too. Mum joined in *and* Auntie Barbara.

I thought she'd have a great big powerful singing voice, but she sounded sweet and girly, just like Mum. They started singing all these daft duets together. Mum didn't have the energy to dance but she took off her high heels and kicked them up and down in the air.

Auntie Barbara *did* dance, larking about, light on her toes in spite of her bulk. She picked Kendall up and danced with him. Then it was my turn. She whirled me round and round the room until Mum and Kendall blurred, and the room whirled with me.

I felt so happy then, eating my treat tea, sure we really were lucky lucky lucky.

Mum still had to go back to hospital to get the results of her tests. Auntie Barbara went with her. I hoped they might come to meet us from school. I wanted them to be waiting by the gate with big smiles on their faces. But they weren't there.

Kendall and I walked home with Harpreet and Amandeep. I nattered to Harpreet – all sorts of stupid stuff about boys and football and rock stars – but all the time I was chanting inside my head. *Let her be all right, please please please.*

I tried not to walk on any cracks in the pavement in case it was bad luck.

'Are your shoes hurting you?' Harpreet asked.

'No.'

'So why are you walking funny, picking your feet up like a pony?' said Harpreet.

'Am I?' I threw back my head and neighed. 'Give me a carrot. And a sugar lump.'

'You're nuts,' said Harpreet, giggling.

'I'm a shark, not a pony,' said Kendall. 'Watch me, Amandeep.'

He held his arm out like it was part of his head, opened his mouth as wide as it would go, and circled round us.

'Shut your mouth, Kendall, we can see your tonsils,' I said. 'Hey, Harpreet, you should see my Auntie Barbara do her whale imitation.'

'I like your auntie. So where is she today?'

'She's with my mum,' I said. My voice went wobbly.

Kendall looked at me. He stopped being a shark. He put his hand in mine and hung on tightly all the way home.

I knew it was bad news the moment we got in the door. Mum was hunched up on the sofa, chin on her knees, all her make-up cried away. Auntie Barbara tried to smile at us but her eyes were red too.

'Oh Mum!' I cried.

She held out her arms and we went rushing to her. She cuddled us close, while Auntie Barbara hovered.

'It's awful news,' said Mum. 'The lump *was* cancer, and now it's advanced. And it was in all the lymph nodes under my arm too. So I've got to have chemotherapy so I shall puke all the time and I'll probably lose all my *hair*.' She started weeping again.

'You'll look funny without hair,' said Kendall.

'Shut *up*. Mum will still look pretty no matter what,' I said fiercely. 'Just so long as she gets better.'

'But will I get better?' said Mum.

'Of course you will,' said Auntie Barbara.

'And I could just as easily say of course I *won't*,' said Mum. 'Do you know what the odds are, Lola Rose?'

'Nikki, stop it. You shouldn't tell her all this.'

'Look, she's my daughter. I'll tell her what I want. I don't have secrets from my kids. I've got a fifty-fifty chance, Lola Rose, even if I let them do all this chemo and radiation treatment. Fine sort of Lady Luck I am.'

I felt as if the Voice of Doom had burst out of my head and was booming the bad news from a loud-speaker. It was so loud I couldn't think of anything else.

Kendall didn't seem to understand properly and whined to watch television. He wouldn't eat his tea and got very boisterous at bedtime, leaping about all over the place, refusing to put his pyjamas on. Mum yelled at him. Kendall burst into tears and wouldn't stop. He screamed for hours until we were exhausted.

When he finally settled, still snuffling in his sleep, Mum got Auntie Barbara to go down to the off licence for a couple of bottles of wine. She drank steadily, swallowing the wine as if it was medicine, until her head lolled and her eyes closed.

'Time you were asleep too, Lola Rose,' said Auntie Barbara.

'I don't think I can,' I said.

'Come here.' Auntie Barbara held me tight. I couldn't feel safe even with her arms round me.

'It's so *unfair*,' I mumbled into her shoulder.

'I know, I know.'

'I hate feeling scared all the time.'

'It's awful, isn't it.'

'I just want Mum to be better and Dad to stay away and for us to be happy, just like anyone else. And – and it's so bad of me, but I feel so cross with *Mum*.' I burst out crying. 'I know it's not her fault, she can't help having cancer, but it's like she's spoiling everything. Oh God, I'm sorry, I shouldn't say that. It's wicked. *I'm* wicked.'

'No, you're just worn out with worrying, darling. You're not wicked at all, you're the best girl ever. I'm so proud of my special niece. This is the one great thing for me, you know. I've met up with you and Kendall again.'

'Will you really stay with us?'

'I'll have to nip back home soon to sort out the running of the pub and get some more clothes and go to my bank but I'll come straight back, I promise. I'll be here for you, Lola Rose, no matter what.'

I put my hands either side of her big, sweet face. Her blue eyes stared straight back at me. I knew she really meant it. I leant against her and knew I loved her.

Mum's treatment frightened me. She had to go to the hospital to have the chemicals dripped into her. Auntie Barbara stayed with her and drove her home. Then the sickness started. She had to have a bucket in bed because she couldn't always get to the toilet in time. They gave her more drugs to stop the sickness but she still *felt* sick, yawning all the time, all white and sweaty and sad.

'I'm being bloody poisoned,' she groaned. 'I'm sick of puking all over the place. I'm not going back to that hospital. I'm not going through with all this.'

'Yes, you are,' said Auntie Barbara. 'You're going to have all the treatment and get better, do you hear me?'

'I'd sooner take my chances,' said Mum. 'Poor as they are.'

'Yes, but you can't just think of yourself. There's the kids.'

'They'll be better off without me,' said Mum.

'No we wouldn't!' I cried. 'We need you, Mum.'

'And I need you, darling,' said Mum. 'I love you,

sweetheart, and little Kendall. I haven't always been a good mum to you. Do you think getting ill like this is a punishment?'

'No! You've been the best mum *ever*,' I said.

'I haven't always been the best sister,' said Mum, as Auntie Barbara held a cold flannel to her head.

'True,' said Auntie Barbara briskly. 'But cancer cells don't start multiplying just because you've been a bad girl in the past. Now stop whining and cuddle down and try and get some sleep.'

'Bossyboots,' said Mum. Then she reached out and grabbed Auntie Barbara's hand. 'I'm sorry, Barbs. For everything.'

'I know. It's OK. It was all over ages ago. You actually did me a favour.'

'What favour? What did you do, Mum?' I asked.

'Never mind. Forget it,' said Auntie Barbara.

'I can't forget it. What if I'm going to die? I don't want to go to hell!' Mum wept.

'You're not going to die. Not yet. Not for years and years and years,' said Auntie Barbara firmly. 'And what's all this hell nonsense?'

'Dad said I'd go to hell.'

'Oh well, Dad was a warped old beggar.'

'I thought you and Dad were always so thick. You were always the favourite,' said Mum.

'*Why* did Grandad say you'd go to hell, Mum?' I persisted. 'Because you ran off with Dad?'

'I ran off with Barb's boyfriend first,' said Mum.

I stared at Auntie Barbara.

'He was her fiancé. Michael. They had the wedding all planned, honeymoon booked, everything finalized. And I was going to be the bridesmaid,' Mum howled.

'In a lilac dress with freesias in your hair,' said Auntie Barbara. 'And I was going the whole hog, marrying in ivory lace, with a bouquet of purple freesias and white roses. I was much too big for white lace even in those days but I was on a strict diet, scheduled to lose three stone in three months. Yep, it was all planned, every detail.'

'You didn't plan for me to ruin it all,' said Mum. 'I didn't even *like* him much. I thought he was a bit boring really.'

'He *was* boring,' said Auntie Barbara. 'I always knew exactly what he was going to say.'

'But you didn't know what he was going to *do*.'

'Well, certainly, he didn't seem the type to go after my little sister.'

'Did you love him, Auntie Barbara?' I asked.

'Maybe I thought I did. At the time,' she said, sighing.

'I didn't mean things to get out of hand,' said Mum. 'I was just having a little flirt with him. Only things kind of escalated.'

'You were only sixteen. You were just messing about. I blamed Michael more than you.'

'Why wouldn't you take him back? He begged you. He never really stopped loving you, couldn't you see that?'

'I'm not so sure. Anyway, it was beside the point. *I* stopped loving *him*. I didn't want him any more.'

'Maybe you'll meet someone else, Auntie Barbara,' I said.

'I don't think I want anyone now,' said Auntie Barbara. 'I like being on my own, totally independent. I *would* have loved children though.'

'Well, you can share mine,' said Mum. 'And if I don't make it—'

'Stop it.'

'You *will* make it, Mum.'

'*If.* You'll look after the kids, Barbs?'

'You know I will.'

'Jay might make more trouble.'

'I'll sort him out,' said Auntie Barbara. 'And I'll sort you out too if you don't stop rabbiting. You need some sleep.'

Mum kept to her bed for a few days. We tiptoed round the flat. Kendall had to keep the television turned right down. We couldn't always turn *him* right down too. He kept crying over the slightest thing.

'Couldn't you try to be a good boy, Kendall?' I begged him.

'No, I want to be bad,' said Kendall.

He kept pestering me while I was working on a very special get well card for Mum. I'd designed a beautiful country landscape with bluebirds and apple blossom and newborn lambs and a stream with white swans. I'd cut out four figures walking into the sunset hand in hand – Mum, Kendall, Auntie Barbara and me. I used up the whole of a Cadbury's chocolate wrapper for Auntie Barbara's purple party frock. I stuck little pink feathers round Mum's shoulders to make a furry jacket and sequins on her feet for sparkly shoes.

I stuck her a bit too high up, so that she floated a few inches above the ground even after I turned her shoes into very high stilettos. The feathers looked a bit odd too. They looked too much like angel's wings.

'Let me see,' said Kendall. 'Let George see too, Lola Rose.'

'Look, get that filthy toy out of my face,' I said irritably. George was covered in jam and glue and general grime. 'He needs a wash.'

'He doesn't like washes. He wouldn't mind a proper swim though. Can we go and see the real George soon, Lola Rose?'

'No, of course we can't. Not with Mum so ill.'

'Auntie Barbara could take us.'

'She's looking after Mum, you know she is.'

'*You* could take us.'

'Oh yeah, sure.'

'Why won't you? Is it because you're scared?'

'Shut *up*, Kendall. Quit bugging me. Go and see if Mum's awake and wants a drink.'

Auntie Barbara was taking a nap too because she'd been up with Mum half the night.

'I don't want to see Mum. She's scary now.'

'Don't be silly.'

'She could be sick on me.'

'No, she won't. I think she's stopped being sick now.' She'd eaten boiled eggs and toast and then soup for lunch and kept them all down.

I warned Kendall I'd throw George in the rubbish if he dared touch my get well card and went to check on Mum myself. She was propped up on her pillows, having a cigarette.

'You shouldn't be smoking, Mum!'

'Why? Will it give me cancer?' she said, laughing at me.

Auntie Barbara stirred. She was wedged tightly into the armchair, her head resting on her arms.

'I think she's stuck there for ever!' Mum whispered. 'She'll have to walk round with a great big chair stuck on her bum.'

'Mum! You are dreadful!'

'Yeah, yeah. Hey, Lola Rose, I'm starving. What can I have to eat?'

'I could make you boiled egg and soldiers.'

'I'm sick of all that kiddie muck. How about running down the chippy, eh?'

We still didn't have any money of our own so I had to take Auntie Barbara's purse out of her bag. I knew she wouldn't mind.

I skipped like a little kid down the road to the chip shop. I came charging out holding a big, warm, greasy bag of chips – and barged straight into Ross.

'Hey, it's little Lola Rosy Posy. Coming for a snog, then?'

'No thanks,' I said dodging past.

I ran up the road, my feet barely touching the pavement, like Mum's stilettos in my picture. Mum seemed so much better. She was over the worst now. Wasn't she?'

Twenty Two

Terror!

I woke in the middle of the night. I could hear footsteps, whispering, groaning. I slid out of bed and ran into the living room.

'Is Mum sick again?'

Auntie Barbara was bending over Mum. 'She's very hot,' she said. 'Put the light on, Lola Rose, so I can have a look at her.'

I put the light on. Mum seemed OK at first glance, pink cheeks, bright eyes. Too pink, too bright.

'She's got a fever. I think we'd better get her to the hospital,' said Auntie Barbara.

'No, no, I hate that hospital,' Mum mumbled.

'You're ill, lovey. You need to get that fever down,' said Auntie Barbara. 'Help me bundle her up, Lola Rose. I'm going to drive her to the hospital.'

I wrapped the duvet round Mum. She was burning hot but shivering.

'What the bloody hell is wrong with me now?' she wailed.

'It'll be your white blood cells. I've been reading up about cancer treatment,' said Auntie Barbara, wringing out a cold flannel and putting it on Mum's forehead. 'The chemo's knocked them for six so you haven't got any resistance to infection.'

'You're such an old brainbox,' said Mum. 'So what happens next, Dr Barbs? Is it curtains?'

'Of course not! You're such a drama queen. You'll be better in no time,' said Auntie Barbara, though she didn't sound too sure.

'Kiss Mum goodbye, Lola Rose.'

I kissed both her hot pink cheeks. 'You *are* going to get better, Mum. You have to.'

'Yeah. We wish,' said Mum.

Auntie Barbara lifted her up in her arms as if she were a baby. She carried her out the front door and down the stairs to the car. I watched from the window as Auntie Barbara got her car door open and stowed Mum carefully in the back seat. They drove off. I watched the red back lights. Then I watched the darkness where they'd been. The Voice of Doom started up.

That's the last time you'll see your mum.

'Shut up. That's rubbish. *You're* rubbish. Auntie Barbara said she's going to get better.'

She would do, wouldn't she? But you know she's wrong. Your mum's going to die.

'She's not, she's not, she's not,' I said. I put my hands over my ears but it was inside my head.

She's going to die and there's nothing you can do about it.

'I'll wish, I'll pray, I'll promise anything.' I thought of all the fairy tales I'd read at school, the dangerous quests, the impossible tasks. 'I'll do anything.'

Anything at all?

'Yes, anything!'

Right. What are you most afraid of?

'My dad?'

He doesn't scare you so much now.

'Then . . . what?'

What gives you nightmares?

'Sharks.'

You got it. So go back to the aquarium. Stand at the shark tank. Lean against the glass so they swim right up close.

'I can't!'

Stay there and count sixty seconds. And again and again, sixty times, till you've stayed a full hour.

'But I'll scream. I'll be sick. I can't!'

Not even to save your mother?

I knew the Voice wasn't real. I knew it was me, making it all up. But I couldn't control what it was saying.

I thought of those great fishy heads gliding past,

those awful staring eyes, the rows of jagged teeth. I started shaking as if they were swimming just the other side of the window. I couldn't do it.

Yes I could. It wasn't much to ask. Any other child could do it, easy-peasy. I had to try for Mum.

I went to the sofa bed and buried my face in Mum's pillow, breathing in her sweet, musky scent. Auntie Barbara came back as dawn was breaking. Her face was screwed up. When she saw me she tried to smooth it out into a smile.

'It's OK, Lola Rose. Mum's being looked after in hospital. They're pumping antibiotics into her.'

'I'm not going to school today. We'll come to the hospital, Kendall and me.'

'You can't, my love.'

'Yes we can!'

'No, Mum's being nursed in a side room. You can't see her in case you pass on another infection to her.'

'Did I give it to her then?' I asked, appalled.

'No! Well, it could have been any of us. Your mum's just so vulnerable at the moment.' Auntie Barbara struggled, shutting her eyes. 'I'd give anything to make her better, Lola Rose.'

'Do you love her, Auntie Barbara?'

'Of course I do!' said Auntie Barbara, wiping her eyes.

'But she was awful to you. She stole your boyfriend.'

'Yes she did. She was very naughty even as a little girl. I had a special china doll with a long silky crinoline and a parasol—'

'I've got a picture of one. I love those dolls!'

'Well, your mum cut off all her golden ringlets and scribbled blue biro tattoos all over her arms. She said she'd turned her into a punk. I made a fuss, even though I was a bit old for dolls by that age. Dad heard me and saw the doll and then he laid into your mum. He was so hard on her. I cried buckets because it was my fault your mum had red slap marks all over her legs. Yes, I've always loved her. Like you love Kendall.'

'I don't think I'd love him if he mucked up *my* doll.'

'Yes, you would. You'd *hate* him but you'd love him too. It was awful when I lost touch with your mum. And now that I've found her . . .' Auntie Barbara let her voice tail away. She took a deep breath. 'I'm so glad I found her. And you and Kendall. Now, darling, we'd better go to bed for an hour or two before we have to get up again for school.'

Auntie Barbara set her alarm clock but didn't stir when it started ringing. I switched it off quickly. I got Kendall washed and dressed and then organized myself.

'Where's Mum?' he asked. 'She hasn't died already, has she?'

'Kendall! Shh! No, she's had to go back to hospital because she's got a fever.'

'Is she going to die there then?'

'No! She's not going to die – how many more times? Now, we're going to have breakfast *quietly*, OK? We don't want to wake Auntie Barbara.'

'But she'll be late taking us to school.'

'I'll take us, like I used to. Auntie Barbara needs to sleep, she's been up all night.'

Kendall nodded and started eating his breakfast, George on his lap. George got smeared with butter and sprinkled with crumbs. Kendall had dreadful table manners, especially this morning.

'Don't suck your toast. It's not an ice lolly.'

'You said I had to eat quietly. Toast goes crunch crunch crunch if you bite it,' said Kendall.

I had to smile at him. At least I was going to be doing him a favour this morning.

I wrote a note to Auntie Barbara telling her we'd gone to school. I sent our love to Mum. Then I let us out of the flat, shutting the door behind us very gradually so it didn't bang.

Kendall ran down the garden path and turned right.

'No, this way,' I said, grabbing his hand.

'But school's *that* way.'

'I know. But we're not going to school.'

'Where are we going then? To the hospital to see Mum?'

'No, we're not allowed to now. Not till the fever's gone.'

'So where *are* we going?'

'You wait and see.'

I bought two children's travel cards at the tube station. I was using Auntie Barbara's money again but there was nothing else I could do.

'We're going up to town?' said Kendall. 'All on our own!'

'Yes. It's an adventure, OK?'

'It won't get scary, will it?'

'Not for you.'

He didn't know what I was getting at. He didn't twig until we were walking along the embankment.

'This is the way to the aquarium!'

'Yep.'

'Oh, Lola Rose, are you taking me to see George?'

'That's right.'

'But you hate sharks.'

'Yes.'

'You won't go in.'

'I will this time.' Though I wasn't so sure now. I stood still for a moment.

'What's the matter?'

'I feel a bit funny.'

Kendall peered up at me. 'You *look* funny. All whitey-green. Like you're going to be sick.'

'I do feel a bit sick.'

'You'd better wait outside. I'll go in all by myself. *I'm* not scared,' Kendall bragged.

I knew you wouldn't dare!

'I'm coming in too.'

I stumbled into the reception area and paid, pretending we were with another family up ahead of us. It was very dark. There were watery sounds all around us, as if we'd dived straight into an ocean. There suddenly seemed no way out. I saw a door but it said STAFF ONLY, NO ENTRY — TRESPASSERS WILL BE FED TO THE SHARKS.

'Come on, it's downstairs,' said Kendall, rushing ahead.

'Wait for me!' I cried, grabbing his hand.

'Your hand's all wet, Lola Rose. Let go.'

'No. Please. Wait, Kendall!'

'I want to see George!'

He jerked his hand free and hurtled down the stairs to the next level. I ran after him, fish wriggling and squirming in tanks on either side of me. Then I saw the great tank looming, crowds gathered round.

'George!' Kendall cried, rushing to the glass.

I cowered at the other side of the walkway, narrowing my eyes until I couldn't see the dark shapes gliding through the water. I couldn't breathe. It was as if I were in the water too, drowning.

I wanted to walk up to the shark tank and spread myself fearlessly against the glass window, but I couldn't, I couldn't.

I heard Kendall calling, 'George! Here, George! Here, boy!' as if he were calling his pet dog. Then I blinked and saw George swimming towards him, his mouth opening wide.

'Kenny!' I screamed.

It looked like he was about to be swallowed whole. I ran towards him, trying to snatch him from those terrible jaws.

'Stop it! Stop grabbing at me! I'm fine. I'm not a bit scared,' Kendall said furiously, pushing me away.

I was scared. There I was, against the glass,

George darting past, his cold, alien eyes acknowledging me.

'It's me. I'm here. Lola Rose,' I whispered. 'I can do it. I can outstare you. You can swim past again and again. You can open your awful mouth and bare all those teeth at me, but I'm not going to move. I'm going to stay here nose to nose with all of you for an entire hour. I'm going to make my mum better, you'll see.'

I counted the seconds, over and over and over. Kendall watched with me for a while but then he hunched up in a corner, chin in his knees, just waving languidly every time George came into view. He was sometimes stepped on. The shark tank was the major attraction of the aquarium. People kept trying to elbow me out of the way but I stood fast. I wouldn't even let little toddlers in front of me.

I couldn't understand why they weren't all terrified. Some of them grinned at the sharks as if they were goldfish. A few of the adults were scared though, squealing and running away.

I stuck it out as the fish swam round and round and round, never once colliding. The ghost-like stingrays followed each other as if they were doing a slow dance routine. The golden trevallies swam in shoals. The sharks swam independently, as if they were each all alone in the tank, the nurse shark, the zebra shark, the sand tiger shark and the brown sharks.

I watched them, and every single time they swam past my heart thumped and sweat sprang out on my forehead. I felt sick, I needed the toilet, I couldn't stop shaking – but I stayed there.

I counted each second until I got to three thousand six hundred. Then I moved. I'd made a misty impression against the glass. It looked like a ghost Lola Rose had pushed her way right through the glass and was in the tank swimming with the sharks.

'You're obviously a real shark enthusiast,' said an attendant in a bright yellow T-shirt.

I smiled at him weakly, rubbing my forehead.

'You should come one time when they're being fed.'

I imagined those jaws ripping, chewing, swallowing. I shuddered. 'How do you feed them? You don't get in the tank with them, do you?'

'No. We feed the conger eels in the tank, but not the sharks.'

'You'd end up as food yourself,' I said.

'No, not these babies. We do swim among them sometimes but not when the public's around.'

'You don't!' I didn't know if he was kidding me or not.

'Yes we do,' he said. He reached into his pocket and pulled out something white and pointed. 'Shark's tooth!' he said. Then he held out his hand. 'Go on, you can have it, seeing as you're so interested.'

'Really?' My hand closed round the tooth before he could change his mind.

'They're meant to bring you luck.'

'Thank you so much,' I whispered, clenching

the tooth tightly in the palm of my hand.

The attendant walked off with a nod and a wink.

'What did that man give you?' Kendall asked.

'Oh, just a peppermint,' I said quickly. I put my hand up and pretended to eat it. 'You don't like peppermint, do you?'

'I like Kendal mint cake,' said Kendall.

'I do too,' I said. 'Come on, we'll buy you an ice cream because you've been so good.'

I kept the shark's tooth hidden in my hand all the way home. I felt mean because I knew Kendall would be thrilled if he knew about it, but he'd want it for himself. I had to keep it safe until I could give it to Mum.

I was sure it was a lucky talisman, able to work magic and make Mum better. I'd endured the hour-long torture of the shark tank. This was a sign that I had completed my task. I had shown the Voice of Doom.

Mum was going to get better.

Twenty Three

Lady Luck

Auntie Barbara was out when we got back, obviously at the hospital. I wished we'd stayed up in London. It was a long, long afternoon. Then Auntie Barbara came back at last. I heard her hurrying up the stairs. When she burst through the front door she could barely speak she was so out of breath. Her hair was tumbling out of her ponytail and there were damp patches on her blue shirt.

'Where have you *been*?' she gasped. 'I went to the school to pick you up and you weren't there. Ms Balsam said you hadn't been at school at all today. How could you do this to me, Lola Rose – at a time like this?'

'I'm sorry. I – I had to go to the aquarium. I didn't want to worry you. I left a note.

'Don't you dare do that ever again!' said Auntie Barbara. 'You went to the *aquarium*? For goodness' sake, hasn't Kendall been there enough times already?'

'It wasn't for Kendall. It was for me. To make Mum better,' I said. 'She *is* better, isn't she, Auntie Barbara?'

I held the shark tooth so that it dug into my palm. Auntie Barbara looked at me. She was struggling. Then tears started splashing down her flushed face.

'No, she's worse,' she said, starting to sob. 'They can't get her temperature down. The antibiotics don't seem to be working. That's why I came to collect you. You're not allowed to see Mum but I thought you could call to her from the corridor.'

'She's dying, isn't she?' said Kendall.

'No!' I said.

'Maybe she might be dying, Lola Rose,' said Auntie Barbara. She put her arm round my shoulder.

'She can't be! I made her better! I stood right next to the sharks. They swam right up close, but I didn't run away. I've got the magic tooth. She *can't* be dying!' I sobbed. 'What did I do wrong? Should I have stayed longer? *What?*'

'Stop it, Lola Rose. You haven't done anything

wrong. You haven't made Mum ill – and you can't make her better, no matter what you do.'

'I *can*. I've tried so hard. I've got the lucky shark's tooth, look!'

'Let me see! Where did you get it? *I* want it,' Kendall cried, trying to snatch it.

'It's *Mum's*,' I said, holding it high above his head.

'Then we'll go and give it to her,' said Auntie Barbara. 'But it's a present, Lola Rose. It's not magic. It can't make her better.'

'It can!'

'Well . . . we can give it a go,' said Auntie Barbara. 'I'm going to have the quickest wash and change ever, kids, OK? Ready in five minutes.'

I decided to change too. I put on my best black top and purple velvet skirt. It was too hot for a furry jacket but I wore it anyway. I dressed Kendall in his black leather jacket although he complained. And he went on and on about the shark's tooth.

'I keep telling you, Kendall, it's for Mum. But when we go back to the aquarium I'll ask for one for you.'

'*Not* when you're meant to be at school,' said Auntie Barbara, bright pink from her quick bath. She wore her purple Thai silk two-piece edged with silver braid and her silver flip-flop sandals.

'You look lovely, Auntie Barbara.'

'Thank you, Lola Rose. So do you. And you too, Kendall. OK, have you got your shark's tooth? Right then, darlings. Off we go.'

We met Andy and Steve coming up the stairs.

'You look like you're going to a party,' said Steve.

The Voice of Doom bellowed through the banisters. *A farewell party*. I clutched my shark's tooth so hard all the way to the hospital that it scored a deep red scratch on my palm.

'It's bitten you,' said Kendall.

We trailed along endless polished corridors. Kendall's sandals squeaked, my heels tapped and Auntie Barbara's flip-flops slapped at every step. When we got to Mum's ward Auntie Barbara made us wait while she went into the side room where they were now nursing her.

We waited a long time. I took Kendall's hand.

'That's not the shark's-tooth hand, is it? I don't want it to bite me too.'

'It's in my other hand. It's OK.'

'It isn't OK, is it, Lola Rose?' Kendall said, weaving his fingers into mine. 'What have they done with our mum? Why won't they let us go and see her?'

'We might be too germy. But Auntie Barbara says we can call to her. Shall we try calling now?'

'What will we say?'

'Anything. Stuff like "We love you, Mum. Get better soon."'

'I shall feel silly, calling out,' said Kendall. 'All these ill people will stare at us.'

'We'll go right up close, by the door. Come on.'

We walked to the door of Mum's side room. It was half open. I peeped round fearfully. Mum was there in the bed, but she had a mask over her face and tubes running in and out of her. I could only be sure she was Mum because of the blonde hair tumbled on her pillow. A nurse was taking her temperature and arguing with Auntie Barbara.

'It's more than my life's worth to let the kids in, you know that,' she said.

'What does it matter now?' said Auntie Barbara. 'Think of the children. They need to see their mum. And it could just help her. She loves those kids so.'

'I think she's out of it already,' said the nurse.

I started crying and the nurse looked up. She saw me – and then nodded.

'OK. Quick. Come and see your mum for two minutes. But I'm scooting out of here, right?'

Kendall and I tiptoed towards the bed. Auntie Barbara carefully threaded her arm through all Mum's tubes and stroked her clenched fist.

'Nikki, sweetheart, the kids are here. Jayni and Kenny. Lola Rose and Kendall. They've come to say hello.'

Mum's eyes stayed shut. Her hand didn't unclench.

'Mum?' I said. 'Can you hear me, Mum? Listen, I want you to have this.' I reached for her clenched hand and gently prised her fingers open. I squeezed the shark's tooth inside. 'There! You'll never guess what it is, Mum. It's a shark's tooth, a real one. It's really really lucky. I did this hour-long ordeal and it was my reward. It's going to make you better.'

Mum didn't stir.

'I haven't got a shark's tooth to give you but you can have a whole shark if you want,' said Kendall. He thrust grubby George under Mum's arm.

'Did you hear that, Mum? Kendall's given you George,' I said.

'Not for ever and ever,' Kendall said. 'It's just a borrow.'

'But you can keep the shark's tooth. When you're better we could bore a hole in it and hang it on a piece of string round your neck.'

'I'm not wearing a tacky bit of *string*,' Mum mumbled, making us all jump. She opened her eyes.

'You're still alive, Mum!' I sobbed.

'Of course I am. And I'm going to get better. I've got to look after you two, haven't I? Now clear off, kids. I've got a lousy headache and you're doing my head in.'

We kissed her burning forehead, Auntie Barbara, then Kendall, then me. I took George back because I knew Kendall wouldn't be able to sleep without him – and George was a total germtrap too.

'I've made you better, haven't I, Mum?' I whispered.

'*I've* made me better,' said Mum. 'I can do anything. I'm Lady Luck, aren't I?'

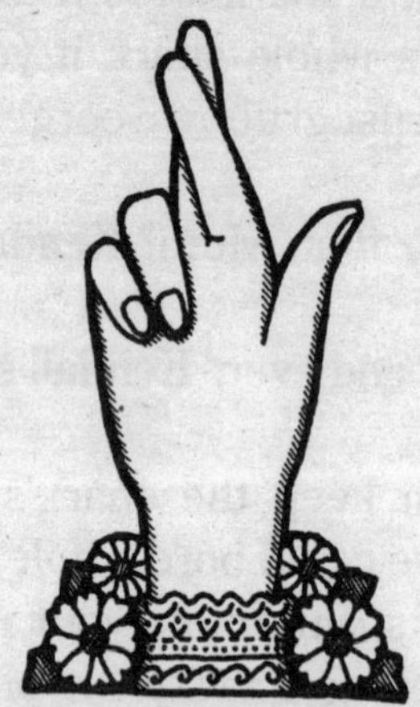

Twenty Four

Fingers Crossed

Mum's fever went down, but she had to stay in hospital a while. Then she was well enough to come home, though she still had to go for her treatment. First the chemotherapy, weeks of it.

All Mum's beautiful long blonde hair started falling out after the second treatment. It was so scary at first. Kendall and I were cuddled up with her in bed in the morning and when she sat up great long locks of her hair stayed on her pillow.

'Oh my God,' Mum gasped. She put her hands to her head, feeling the bald patches. 'This is just like being in a bloody horror movie!'

'Never mind, Mum. It's only a few curls,' I lied.

Mum's fingers ran along her scalp, feeling. More hair fell out there and then, fluttering down over her nightie in long pale strands. Mum started whimpering, hanging onto her head with both hands as if she were trying to keep the rest of her hair in place.

Kendall started crying too, his eyes screwed up so he couldn't see Mum properly.

'What's up now?' said Auntie Barbara, sailing into the room in the great black silky caftan she wore as a nightie.

'Look!' Mum wailed.

'Oh God, your hair, you poor love,' said Auntie Barbara. 'Right. I know what we can do. Lola Rose, you've got a pair of sharp scissors, haven't you?'

'It's cut-my-throat time, right?' Mum sniffed.

'I'm going to cut your hair, Nik.'

'No! I've always had long hair. It's part of me.'

'Not any more, darling,' said Auntie Barbara sadly. 'Come on, sit on the chair, and we'll get snipping. It'll be less strain on the roots if it's very short. Maybe we'll be able to keep some of it that way.'

Auntie Barbara cut Mum's hair really short. I gathered up all the locks and twisted them into a big soft plait and tied it up with purple ribbon.

'You can pin it back on, Mum,' I said.

'It's not going to work. I look awful. Like a skinhead,' said Mum, crying.

'No, you know who you *do* look like, Mum?' I

said, staring at her ruffled short hair and pale face on her little stalk neck. 'Kendall!'

'Great!' said Mum. But then she wiped her eyes and stuck out her bottom lip and lisped, 'I want George!' Her Kendall imitation was spot on and we all laughed.

Cutting her hair so short didn't really work. It all fell out anyway until poor Mum was completely bald. Her head looked horribly naked. The hospital gave her a wig but it didn't look right and Mum said it itched like crazy. She cut up some of Auntie Barbara's Thai silk into scarves and wound them round and round her head, and then she pinned the plait I'd made her at the back.

'That looks ever so pretty, Mum!' I said.

'Pretty frightful,' said Mum, peering into the mirror and sighing. She puffed out her cheeks. 'And I'm not just an old baldy-bonce. I'm getting *fat*.'

I always thought you got thin when you got cancer. Mum really *was* getting fatter. The chemotherapy drugs gave her a big round face and a big round body too.

"Yuck! Look at me,' she said, struggling to pull her zip up over her stomach. 'I'm going to have to buy some new jeans. New everything.' Even her lovely white jacket was too tight for her. 'You'd better have it, Lola Rose,' she said.

'It's yours, Mum. You'll get thin again when you're better.'

'I don't think I'm ever going to get better. And

what's the bloody point if I end up looking like a freak? I can't *stick* being so fat!'

Auntie Barbara sniffed. 'Shut up, skinny. Try being me!'

But Auntie Barbara wasn't quite as fat as she had been. She wasn't on a diet, but she didn't have time to eat so much while she was running around looking after us and rushing back to see to the pub at weekends.

'Maybe I'll fit into real clothes soon,' said Auntie Barbara. 'If so I'll turn my purple silk wrap-around into a bedspread for you, Lola Rose.'

'No, I'll need it. I'm blowing up like a bouncy castle,' said Mum.

'You're not. You're still weeny compared to me,' said Auntie Barbara.

'Well, that's not hard,' said Mum.

'Mum! Don't be mean!' I said.

Mum pulled a face. 'I'm allowed to be mean. I'm the one that's ill. And at least Barb's still got a full head of hair.'

'Yours will grow back, I promise. It'll be as blonde and curly as ever,' said Auntie Barbara, giving Mum a hug. 'Just wait till you've finished your chemotherapy.'

'Then it'll be radiotherapy. Therapy! Is that a fancy word for torture? First they poison you and then they burn you.'

'But they make you better,' said Auntie Barbara. 'Now quit your moaning!'

'You quit your nagging!'

They weren't really arguing. It was just their little game with each other. They started singing their 'Sisters' song, harmonizing beautifully.

'We'll have to do a star turn down The Trout,' said Auntie Barbara.

'Oh yeah, and do a spot of lap-dancing too?'

'I'm serious.' Auntie Barbara looked at Mum, her eyes very blue. 'Why don't you and the kids come and move in with me? You'd go down really great with all my regulars. I'll give you a half share in the pub. You should have had it in the first place. You can help me to modernize it. What do you think?'

I held my breath. Mum's face screwed up. She blinked and tears spilled down her cheeks.

'Yeah, all right,' she said, like she'd just been offered a cup of tea – but she reached out and clasped Auntie Barbara's hands tight.

'What do you think, Lola Rose and Kendall?' asked Auntie Barbara. 'How do you both fancy living in the pub with me?'

'Can I drink beer?' Kendall asked.

'No, but you can drink Coke and have lots of packets of crisps,' said Auntie Barbara. 'And I've got a lovely big pub garden. Tell you what! We could have a little pond with goldfish. I don't think we could have real trout, even though it would be appropriate. And no sharks!'

'Except for my George! Could he swim in it?'

'If he really wants to,' said Auntie Barbara. 'Lola Rose? Would you like to live at The Trout? There's lots of little attic rooms. You could have your own bedroom. Purple, of course. And there's a big old screen somewhere – maybe you'd like to decorate it with scraps?'

I took a deep breath. She didn't need to try to persuade me. It sounded like a fairy tale. 'It would be wonderful,' I said.

I'm going to miss my friend Harpreet, of course. I've never had a best friend before so it will be horrible saying goodbye. Still, maybe her mum will let her come and stay in the holidays. Mrs Gabrie still doesn't think much of my mum but she approves of Auntie Barbara. She actually invited her in for a cup of tea the other day!

I'll miss Ms Balsam too. I like it at Larkrise, especially the art lessons. Still, I'll have a new school to go to now. I'm going to stay Lola Rose and then maybe I'll make lots of new friends.

I won't miss this house much, though I *will* miss Andy upstairs. He and Steve are getting this new place soon. And Miss Parker might be going into a home. We're all moving on. It's definite now. Mum and Kendall and me are going to live at The Trout. Though it's not going to be called that for much longer.

'I could never stick the name,' said Mum. 'And if we're going to run it together, Barb, we don't want all the guys to call us the two old trouts.'

'So we'll change the name, no problem,' said Auntie Barbara. 'What shall we call it, eh? What about the Singing Sisters?'

'Big Sister and Little Sister,' said Mum. 'Only I'm the blooming Big Sister now.'

'Stop it!' said Auntie Barbara. 'You'll get your figure back soon enough, you'll see. Though it'll be hard for you to go on a diet living at the pub. Wait till you try our Thai green chicken curry!'

We all knew Mum could still pull any bloke she fancied, fat or thin. She'd like it at the pub because she'd meet lots and lots of men. I wish she didn't need them so much, but she can't seem to help it. Still, I don't think she'll ever want Dad back again.

I don't really worry about Dad now. Auntie Barbara will protect us if he ever comes back.

I worry about Mum. Even though she's getting better. She really is. The hospital is very pleased with her progress. Mr Key says her chances are very good now.

I don't know why. It was probably the treatment. Even though she nearly died after that first week.

She was lucky.

You can't *make* lucky things happen. You can't win the lottery every day.

I know it was just chance that Mum got better after I'd endured the shark ordeal. A lucky co-incidence. But I still feel good every time I look at the shark's tooth hanging on the fine silver chain around her neck.

We're going to live happily ever after, Mum and Auntie Barbara and Kendall and me. Fingers crossed.

The Diamond Girls

Jacqueline Wilson

For Nick and Jon

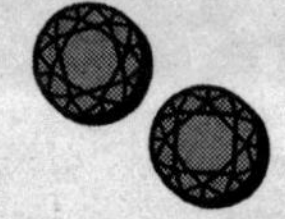

1

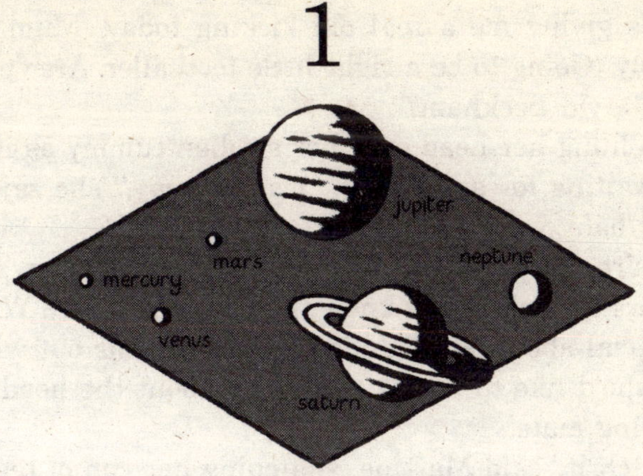

'I've got a surprise for you girls,' said Mum. 'We're moving.'

We all stared at her. She was flopping back in her chair, slippered feet propped right up on the kitchen table amongst the cornflake bowls, tummy jutting over her skirt like a giant balloon. She didn't look capable of moving herself as far as the front door. Her scuffed fluffy mules could barely support her weight. Maybe she needed hot air underneath her and then she'd rise gently upwards and float out of the open window.

'Quit staring at my stomach, Dixie,' Mum snapped.

'How can she *help* staring?' said Jude. 'It's so gross.'

'Oh yuck, it's *moving*!' Rochelle squealed.

Mum cradled her tummy, patting the little bulgy bit wiggling about beneath her navel. I hoped it wouldn't wiggle too much. Mum's navel looked ready to pop out like a cork.

I used to think that's how babies were born. That was weird enough. The real explanation seems worse. I'm sure I don't want any babies myself, ever.

'He's giving me a real old kicking today,' Mum said proudly. 'Going to be a right little footballer. Aren't you, baby David Beckham?'

She hung her head over her swollen tummy as if she was waiting for an answer. '*Yes, Mummy!*' she said, in a tiny baby voice.

'You're nuts, Mum,' said Jude. 'You've been a bit bonkers ever since you knew the baby was a boy. What's so special about *boys*?' Jude threw her arms out wildly, as if she'd like to whack every boy about the head just for being male.

'Watch it,' said Martine, snatching her cup of tea out of Jude's way. 'What are you on about anyway, Mum? We don't want to move again. We've played musical chairs all round the blooming Bletchworth Estate.'

We started off in South Block. We moved there when a three-bedroom flat became vacant, but then Mum had a row with the people on our landing. We swapped to the ground floor of North Block, but it was so damp we had rotten colds and coughs all winter, so then we moved up to the top floor. It wasn't a good idea to be right under the roof. Whenever it rained Jude and I had to squeeze into Mum's room because we had too many leaks coming through our ceiling. The council never came to get it fixed no matter how many times we phoned.

We liked living there even so.

Martine liked living on the top floor because her boyfriend Tony lived right next door in number 113. Martine's the oldest of us Diamond girls. She's just sixteen. She says that makes her an adult and she can do whatever she likes. She looks exactly like Mum but she tries very hard not to. She's got Mum's lovely thick black hair but Martine dyes hers blonde. Mum likes to wear short skirts so Martine wears jeans, low slung so you can see the top of her thong when she bends forwards.

Jude liked living on the top floor because she knew how to get through a secret trapdoor onto the roof. She claimed it as her own private territory. Lots of the boys in our block wanted to climb up there too but Jude wouldn't let them. She can get the better of all the boys, even though she's smallish and only fourteen. She might be small but she's squat and very very tough. Jude looks out for me and squashes people flat if they start teasing me. We're not supposed to have favourites in our family but if I did have a favourite sister then it's definitely Jude.

Rochelle liked living on the top floor because Martine was round at Tony's so often she generally had the bedroom to herself. She could prance around pretending to be a pop singer, hairbrush for a mike, watching herself in the wardrobe mirror. She's always watching herself. I suppose I'd want to watch myself if I looked like Rochelle. She's only twelve but she tries to look much older. She's very pretty with long curly blonde hair and a heart-shaped face and pink pouty lips like one of those loveheart sweets. There is absolutely nothing else sweet about her. A lot of the time I simply can't stick my sister Rochelle.

I liked living on the top floor because I could stare out the window and pretend Bluebell and I were flying over the rooftops, high above the tower blocks, over the ocean, all the way across the world to Bluebell's birthplace in Australia. I knew that was where real budgerigars came from. When I made Bluebell talk she always started off saying, 'G'day, Dixie.' However, if you were rude enough to look up Bluebell's bottom she had this little white label saying 'MADE IN CHINA'. She didn't talk Chinese but I sometimes fished out left-over cartons of chow mein and chop suey from the dustbins and Bluebell dug her beak in very happily.

I felt for Bluebell up my cardie sleeve. I didn't often walk round with her perched on my finger now, even at home, because everyone acted as if I was a total nutcase. I stuffed her up my sleeve instead like a little paper hankie. I gave her feathers a secret stroke every now and then. I needed to stroke her now because Martine and Jude and Rochelle were all shouting and I knew it bothered her.

'We want to stay here, Mum, OK?' said Jude, sticking out her chin. 'North Block's much the best. South Block sucks. *And* Middle Block. North Block's my *territory*.'

'I've got my bedroom just the way I like it,' said Rochelle. 'It's not fair, Mum – you never think about us.'

'We can't leave this flat, not now Tony helped do it up so swish,' said Martine. He just helped her paint her and Rochelle's bedroom but she acted like he did a complete *Changing Rooms*. 'We'll never get as good a flat, not on this estate.'

'You're right,' said Mum. She eased her legs down onto the floor, rubbing at her big blue veins. Then she sat up as straight as she could and folded her arms across her big bosom. She gave us such a look that we all shut up, even Jude.

'We're not getting a better flat on this estate, OK? We're moving, like I said. It's all planned, in all my star charts. Every time I read the tarot cards the wheel of fortune comes up, symbolizing a new beginning. We have to act on it. It's like our destiny.'

'You and your stupid fortune-telling, Mum. You're like a blooming gypsy. *My* fortune's right here,' said Martine.

'There are too many bad vibes here,' said Mum, shifting on her chair and patting her tummy protectively.

'Yeah, and whose fault is that?' said Jude. 'Why did you ever have to get pregnant again?'

'I can't help fate, darling. It's all in the stars.' Mum looked up, as if the Milky Way was shining across our kitchen ceiling.

'We did a project on the stars at school. And the planets and all their little moons. We had to draw them but my compass didn't work so mine went all wobbly,' I said.

'I did that project when I was back in primary school. I got an A,' said Rochelle.

'Why do you always have to show off, Rochelle?' I said. 'Who cares about your stupid A grades?'

I cared. It was horribly unfair that Rochelle got to be very pretty *and* very clever. Jude wasn't pretty but she was very clever, even though she didn't try much at school. Martine was pretty but she wasn't any good at lessons and couldn't wait to leave.

I was plain and most people thought I was stupid.

'Pipe down, girls. Now listen. We're going to have a fresh start. We're leaving this old dump altogether.'

'No we're not,' said Jude, folding her arms too. 'You can't make us.'

'Oh yes, we are moving,' said Mum, and she nodded at the letter in front of her.

We'd all thought it was just another bill or some silly

letter from the social. We hadn't taken any notice when Mum was reading it, though I had wondered why she hadn't scrumpled it up and thrown it in the rubbish bin.

Martine snatched the letter. 'The Planet Estate?' she read.

'Isn't it just perfect?' said Mum. 'See, Jude, it's fate.'

'Oh my God, it's not even in London! We can't go there. How can I see Tony?'

'I think you've been seeing way too much of that Tony, if you must know,' said Mum. 'You're too young to get serious.'

'Oh, that's great, coming from you! You had me when you were – what, sixteen?'

'That's my point, I know what I'm talking about.'

'You're moving us all to some weird estate in the middle of nowhere just to split Tony and me up?' Martine wailed, starting to cry.

'Oh for God's sake, stop being such a drama queen! The whole world doesn't revolve around you and your boyfriend. I'm doing this for all of us. We need a bigger place, now you're all having a little brother.' Mum patted her stomach.

She said it as if we'd all begged for a brother. We'd all been appalled and embarrassed when she told us she was going to have another baby.

'You can't *get* bigger than three-bedroom flats, not council,' said Jude.

'I've got my whole bedroom wall like this big pop collage. It'll ruin it if I have to tear it all down,' said Rochelle.

'You can make another one. You'll have more space. We're moving to a *house*,' said Mum. 'A proper family house with our own garden.'

We all missed a beat, taking it in. I clutched Bluebell. 'Will we be allowed pets?' I asked.

'Yes, Dixie.'

'Real ones? Birds?' I saw a green garden of trees with red and purple parrots and yellow canaries and blue budgerigars flying freely, cheeping and calling. Bluebell quivered, trying to stretch her faded feathers.

'OK, if you're having a bird I'll have a big fluffy cat,' said Rochelle. 'I'll have *lots* of those Persian cats with white fur. I'll call them Snowy and Sugar Lump and Ice Cream and Ivory.'

Phantom cats, as big and white as polar bears, were stalking through my garden, climbing the trees, pouncing on all my helpless rainbow birds.

Jude saw me clutching my sleeve. 'And *I'll* get a big Rottweiler and he'll swat those pesky cats with one blow of his big paws. Then I'll put him on a lead and he'll be our guard dog and he'll always look out for you, Dixie,' said Jude.

'What are you on about?' said Martine, still crying. 'This is just crazy talk – dogs and cats and bogging budgies. It isn't a *game*. We can't move. I *won't!*'

'Yes you will,' said Mum. 'Stop shouting at me! I don't want my blood pressure going up, it's bad for the baby.'

'That *badword* baby,' said Martine. She said so many badwords we all blinked.

'Stop that!' said Mum. 'I won't have it, do you hear? I know you're just upset because of Tony. You can't really think that about your poor little baby brother.'

'Yes I do!' Martine shrieked. 'You're so selfish, Mum. You act like none of us girls matter. You're just so obsessed with wanting a stupid boy you're mucking up all our lives. You should hear what they say about us on the estate – what they say about *you*.'

'Well, I won't have to hear, because we're moving. You can swear at me all you like but it's settled and signed for, totally official,' said Mum, rolling up the letter and smacking it on the table. She hit her wrist by mistake and rubbed it furiously. 'Ouch! Now look what you made me do.'

'Good!' Martine shouted and she marched out, slamming the front door.

'As if I care what those boring old bags have been saying about me,' said Mum, having a sip of her tea. 'Anyway, what *have* they been saying?'

I looked at Jude and Rochelle. Rochelle opened her big mouth but Jude gave her a quick nudge.

'So, this Planet Estate . . .' Jude said to distract Mum. 'How did you hear about it?'

People are always saying things about her, but we don't tell Mum, even when we're mad at her.

'I went down the council telling them all about the baby, wanting a swap, and this girl diddled away at her computer and the moment she mentioned the Planet Estate I had this weird tight feeling in my chest—'

'Indigestion,' said Jude.

'*Intuition!* I just knew it was the place for us, especially when she said that all six blocks also had streets of houses with gardens, for big families.'

Rochelle was counting on her fingers. 'Six blocks? There are *nine* planets – I remember from when we did them at school.'

'Yeah, you'd better get off to school, you're all late,' said Mum.

'No point going though, is there? Not if we're moving,' said Jude.

'You bunk off half the time anyway, you bad girl,' said Mum. 'Well, you can make yourself useful going down to Tesco and bringing back as many cardboard boxes as you can manage. We'll need them for packing.'

'*I'm* going to school,' said Rochelle. 'I'm telling all my friends we're moving. We're really going to be living in a proper house with a garden, Mum? Can I have my very own bedroom? It's not fair I always have to share.'

We *all* share. We started off Martine and Jude, and Rochelle and me, but it didn't work. It's better with Martine and Rochelle, and Jude and me. But it would be best if we all had our own bedrooms.

'Can I have my own bedroom too, Mum? Can all of us?' I asked.

'We'll have to see, darling. Maybe. I don't know exactly how many rooms there are, or how big they are.'

'I bags the biggest bedroom,' said Rochelle.

'No, no, I've got to have that for me and the baby. I've been thinking about taking out another loan. I hate all that cheap second-hand crap. Who wants gungy old stuff for their little baby son, eh? I saw this cot with a cute little blue bear motif—'

Mum was off on one of her baby-boy rants. She'd be talking Mothercare catalogue for the next ten minutes. Jude yawned, poured herself another bowl of cornflakes and went to watch one of her *Buffy* videos on the telly. She pulled her school tie off, rolled up her shirt sleeves and kicked off her shoes.

Rochelle packed her school bag ostentatiously, playing at being the good little girl.

I was still trying to think of nine planets. I hadn't really been concentrating when we'd studied them at school. I'd been too busy dreaming up my own planet. Bluebell and I lived there all alone in perfect peace. There'd be hardly any gravity on Planet Dixie so I could fly just like Bluebell. We shared a special mossy nest at the top of the tallest tree. It bore multi-fruit all the year round, apples on one branch, pears on another. Raspberries and blackberries and strawberries grew in leafy clumps around the trunk and grape vines dangled downwards, so that we didn't have to leave our nest to peck at breakfast.

'Dixie! Close your mouth! Stop that daydreaming, you look gormless,' Mum snapped.

'I was just trying to think of all the planets, Mum.'

'We're going to live in Mercury. Then there's Venus, Mars, Jupiter, Neptune and Saturn.'

'They've left out Pluto and Uranus,' said Rochelle.

'Yeah, well, who'd want to live in Mickey Mouse's dog or something that sounds very rude,' I said. I was still counting. 'So what's the last planet?'

'Earth, stupid. Where we live. Though you're generally on a different planet altogether, Dixie. Planet Loony.' Rochelle stuck out her tongue and made for the door.

'Hang on, Rochelle, take Dixie with you.'

'Oh *Mum*. I haven't got time to do a blooming school run. I'm *late*,' Rochelle said, on her way to the bathroom.

'I don't want to go to school today, Mum. Like Jude said, there's no point, not if we really *are* moving to this Planet place.'

'You'll get me into trouble,' said Mum, but she reached out for me and cuddled me into her. I leaned against her, though I was careful not to touch her tummy.

'OK, OK, little Dix, you can stay off school today.'

'Hurray!'

'Why don't you like school, eh?'

I shrugged. There was no point getting started.

'Who's your teacher? Is she giving you a hard time? You tell her it's not *your* fault you're a bit of a dilly-dream, it's just the way you were born.'

'Mmm,' I said, playing with Mum's hair.

It wasn't the teacher, it was the other kids. This girl had spotted me whispering into my cardie cuff and she'd pounced on Bluebell. She told all the others and they all did budgie squawks and screwed their fingers into their foreheads and called me Birdbrain.

'Well, you'll be at a new school soon when we're living in Mercury. It's the smallest planet, always associated with children – and here I'll be, having my baby boy in Mercury. Come to that, I've always liked Freddie Mercury too,' said Mum, chuckling. She sighed when I looked blank. 'You know, the singer with all the teeth in Queen. Freddie . . . How about that for the baby's name? Or what about Mercury?'

'If you call the poor kid Mercury he'll be teased rotten,' Jude called.

'Call him Justin,' said Rochelle, coming out the bathroom. 'Or Craig. Or Robbie.'

'I want something really special. Unusual,' said Mum.

'What other singers do I like?' said Rochelle. 'I know, Baby Busted!' She cackled with laughter and rushed off to school.

I relaxed and started plaiting Mum's long black hair.

'Help me think up a good name, Dixie. I tried hard with you girls. You're all so lucky – dead individual.

There aren't any other Martines or Judes or Rochelles or Dixies round here. I'm stuck with stupid old Sue. There are *heaps* of Sues.'

'There's only one of you, though, Mum,' I said. I finished one plait and tied it with a piece of string from the kitchen drawer, adding a few paperclips too as silver decoration.

'What are you doing? Turning me into whatshername – Pocahontas?' Mum said.

'Hey, you could spell your name differently. S-i-o-u-x, like the native American tribe. *That's* individual,' I said.

'Oh well, I'll give it a thought. Hey, leave off now, it's making me go all itchy. What about cowboy names for the baby?' Mum thought. 'Butch Cassidy?'

'Yeah, but what if he's a bit little and wimpy, Mum? You can't call him Butch.'

'The Sundance Kid? Hey, Sundance, that's a glorious name! And the sun is a perfect symbol of male energy, right? Little baby, are you Sundance?'

Mum put her hands on her tummy, peering at it intently, as if she could see the baby inside dancing in the sun.

2

I got packed in a jiffy. I crammed my clothes into one
big carrier bag. They got a bit squashed but I didn't care.
I don't like my clothes much. They've mostly been
Rochelle's before me and she likes pink and glitter, tight
skimpy stuff that shows off her figure. I haven't *got* a
figure. I'm so small that even miniskirts come way past
my knees, I'm so skinny that everything looks baggy on
me, and I'm so pale that pink makes me look sickly
white. I got born too early. I was smaller than a bag of
sugar and I had to stay in hospital for weeks and weeks.
I never really caught up with everyone else my age.
Rochelle says I'm the runt of the litter.

The only garment I really like is my blue cardigan.
It's magic because it stretches every time it's washed so
it's grown with me the last two years.

My dad bought it for me. He took me out for the day,
just him and me, and he saw I had goose pimples up
and down my arms so he bought me my big blue cardie.
I've worn it every day ever since. I've even worn it to

school, though we're supposed to wear navy sweatshirts
or jumpers. I got told off, but I insisted that blue's just
like pale navy, so what was the problem? The teachers
didn't bother to send a note home. They'd had enough
arguments with my mum in the past when Martine and
Jude and Rochelle were at our school.

I packed all my possessions into one of the cardboard
boxes Jude had brought home from Tesco. There was
my big book of fairy tales at the bottom. I didn't bother
with the words, I just looked at lovely pictures of
princesses with hair waving down to their knees, and
made up my own stories. Then there were my notepads
and fibre-tip colouring pens and my red gel pen that
smelled of strawberries and my yellow gel pen
that smelled of bananas. I had a Miss Kitty writing
set too but I didn't really have anyone to write to. I
had Martine's old one-eyed panda and Jude's monkey
with the missing paw and Rochelle's old Barbies. I
didn't play with them any more but I'd have felt mean
if I'd chucked them out.

Rochelle had done *heaps* of chucking, but she still had
two suitcases and three cardboard boxes brimming over
with her bits.

Jude had even less clothes than me, and just one box
containing her baseball bat and her biker boots and her
videos and all her fantasy novels.

Martine was still refusing to pack. She wasn't speaking
to Mum. She wasn't speaking to any of us, because we
were all getting excited at the idea of a house with a
garden now. Martine spent almost every second next
door with Tony and his family. Mum got so mad at her
she went and banged on Tony's mum's front door and

they had an argy-bargy right on the landing, Martine joining in too.

'Slagging off her own mother in front of everyone!' Mum wept afterwards. 'And me in my condition too.'

Jude and Rochelle and I had to do most of Mum's packing but we divided it up easily enough. Jude got all the heavy house stuff organized, Rochelle did Mum's clothes and make-up, and I did Mum's mystic paintings and her crystal ball and her tarot cards and astrology charts and *Every Woman's Easy Guide to Fortune Telling*.

I had to pack for little Sundance too. Mum had started buying enough little blue dungarees and sleeping suits and weeny fleeces for an entire nursery of baby boys. All brand new. Someone from the social had given her a black plastic rubbish bag full of old baby clothes but Mum wasn't grateful.

'It's a blooming insult, giving me this washed-out rubbish,' she said, tipping them out all over the carpet and stirring them disdainfully with her long pointed fingernails. 'For God's sake, look – sick stains!' she declared, stabbing at a faint white shadow on a little jacket. 'Right, this is all going in the bin where it belongs.'

She still hadn't decided on Sundance's nursery furniture. She'd gone off the Mothercare selection, and now wanted something more special.

'What, like Harrods?' said Jude.

She was being sarcastic but Mum took her seriously. 'I could check out their nursery stuff, certainly, but I think it might be a bit too traditional, you know? It would be great to get something specially designed, but that might be a bit too pricey.'

'Just a bit,' said Jude. She paused. 'Don't forget you've got to pay for the removal van.'

'Well, I was thinking of asking one of your dads for a bit of help.'

I sat up proudly. The only one of our dads Mum was still in touch with was *my* dad.

'I'll see if he can help us hire a van,' said Mum.

'Or loan us his hearse,' said Rochelle, cracking up laughing. Jude joined in. I stared at them, stony-faced.

'You shut up!' I said, so fiercely that they all took a step backwards, even Jude. 'Don't you dare laugh at my dad! I don't know why everyone thinks his job's so funny.'

'It's not funny, it's downright creepy,' said Rochelle, shuddering. 'It's a good thing you're not a little kid any more. Imagine holding his hand after he's been doing his day's embalming!'

'Yeah, actually, I had a bit of trouble with that aspect myself,' said Mum. 'I made him have a very long bath every time he came near me, but I still seemed to smell something weird on him.'

'He doesn't smell a bit!' I shouted, nearly crying.

'Of course he doesn't smell. *Mum's* the one that smells,' said Jude.

'Oi, you! I don't blooming well smell.'

'Yes, you do, of all those weird little oils,' said Jude.

'They're lovely, and they're doing me good too. I need neroli and lavender to calm me. No blooming wonder when I have to deal with you lot! Here, Dixie, take that scowl off your face. I didn't really mean it about your dad, darling, you know that. Come here.' Mum held her arms out and pulled me to sit on her lap, though her huge tummy meant I had to perch right at the end of her knees.

'Your dad's a very sweet guy,' Mum said softly. She divided my long hair until she found my ear. 'I think he's the best out of all my special guys,' she whispered.

Rochelle's got sharp ears. 'You always said *my* dad was your all-time favourite, Mum,' she said.

'All your dads were lovely guys,' Mum said. She sighed and settled back in her seat, patting her bump. She started chanting the dad story.

We all knew it backwards. She had soothed us to sleep telling us the tale when we were little. It was like our special bedtime story.

'First there was my lovely Dave, Martine's dad. We were childhood sweethearts. We first went out in Year Ten – imagine! We were so in love. Thought we knew it all too, as you do. I couldn't help being thrilled when I knew Martine was on the way, though I knew *my* mum would create. She always had a down on me, my mum, said I'd go to the bad. Dave did his best to stand by me, bless him. But how could he cope with a baby when he was still a kid himself?

'Then Jude's dad came along,' said Mum.

Jude blew a raspberry, but she listened all the same.

'Dean knew where he was going all right, and for a while he took care of me. He did his best to be a dad to Martine too. He could be so sweet and tender with us, he made my heart melt. But he could be a tricky guy too, especially if he was crossed. I loved him with all my heart but I knew I had to leave him when he started slapping me around.'

'Good riddance to him,' said Jude.

'Then there was *my* dad, Jordan,' said Rochelle. 'He was the best looking, wasn't he, Mum? I bet you'd have stayed with him for ever if he hadn't died.' She looked at me. 'Then *you* wouldn't be here today, Dixie. You wouldn't even exist.'

I knew she was just trying to wind me up, but I suddenly felt panicky. I looked down at myself, scared my arms and legs would start fading away as I turned into a ghost girl.

'Of course there was always going to be a Dixie,' said Mum. She waved her fingers in the air, squinting at five little lines on her palm. 'Read my hand! Four gorgeous girls – and one beautiful bouncing boy! It was always my destiny, darling. Maybe it's just as well I didn't sort out how it was all going to happen. It was so sad, losing my Jordan. You're right, Rochelle, he was so handsome my heart started hammering just at the sight of him. He was so talented too. He'd have been a real star in the music world if he'd only had the right breaks. It wasn't really his fault he got into the drug scene. It goes with the territory, right? Oh God, it was so awful awful awful when the police called me.' A tear slid down Mum's cheek. She always cried when she talked about Jordan.

Rochelle snuffled and puckered up like she was crying too. She always acts like losing her dad was the big tragedy of her life, but as he took his overdose when she was two years old I don't think she can even remember him.

Mum ran her hands through Rochelle's lovely long blonde hair and gave her a kiss on the cheek as if they were both still grieving.

I perched Bluebell on my finger and started grooming her feathers. Mum turned to me. I elbowed Rochelle out the way. She pouted and pinged her fingers at Bluebell, making her fall off and land on her head.

'You pig,' I said, hitting out at her.

Rochelle dodged, laughing.

I cradled Bluebell, stroking her poor beak. 'You've bent it, Rochelle, look!'

'Oh dear, how will the poor little soul pick up all her birdseed now?' said Rochelle. 'Though I forgot, she doesn't *actually* eat, does she? And she clearly can't fly to save her life. Pretty duff sort of budgie, if you ask me.'

'And you're a pretty duff sort of girl to tease your poor sister so,' said Mum. 'Don't let her get to you, Dixie darling.'

'Tell me about *my* dad, Mum,' I said.

'That's just what I'm going to do, sweetheart. Dear Terry. I was so out of it, crying over Jordan, and Terry was so kind and talked to me for hours and hours, helping me sort everything out—'

'The oak coffin or the ash coffin or the deluxe mahogany lined with purple satin,' said Rochelle.

'Bog off, bad girlie,' said Mum. 'You can mock, but if it wasn't for Terry's sweetness I think I'd have gone right out of my mind. I was heading that way anyway, going a little bit bonkers every lonely evening—'

'And so you had a little bitty bonk with creepy old Terry,' said Rochelle.

'You're getting *way* too lippy, madam. Just you watch it. I might be eight months pregnant and the size of a flipping elephant but I can still sort you out, *no* problem,' said Mum. 'Terry is a lovely lovely guy and if only he didn't already have a family I'm sure we'd be together now. Though maybe I'm not destined to shack up with any of my guys for long. I figure it's us Diamond girls together – and we'll have to look to Junior here to look after us when we're all old ladies.'

'What about Junior's dad?' Jude said.

Mum sighed. 'I knew it was just going to be a brief encounter. He was so lovely and so artistic. Imagine, a painter! I wish he'd got to know you girls. I'd have loved him to do a portrait of all us Diamonds.'

'Why won't you tell us his name, Mum?' I said.

'Maybe she doesn't even know it,' Rochelle muttered.

'Honestly, Mum, why do you always have to get involved with all these guys?' said Jude.

'I'm not involved with anyone right now, Miss Priss. I must admit, I haven't been very lucky with my guys.'

'That's putting it mildly,' said Jude.

Mum pulled a face but refused to react. She rang my dad at his work to see if he could help us. It didn't sound as if he was pleased to hear from her. Mum kept sighing and pulling faces and going 'Yeah, yeah,' and 'Look, I don't ever bother you at home, darling, so quit nagging me. We do share a daughter. Do you want to have a little word with our Dixie?'

My throat went tight. I kept swallowing, trying to get enough spit into my mouth so I could speak. But I didn't have to. Mum nodded more.

'Sorry, Dixie, Dad sends his love and he'll be in touch very soon but he's up to his eyes in work right now,' said Mum.

'Up to his eyes in *corpses*?' said Rochelle.

Jude shoved her. Rochelle shoved back, squealing.

'Shut up, girls!' said Mum. 'No, no, listen, Terry, it'll

just take half a second – we're moving, we need a van. *Please*, darling, be a mate and help us.'

I waited, clutching Bluebell, just in case he changed his mind about having time to talk to me.

Mum put the phone down. She smiled reassuringly. 'There! All fixed!'

'Is Dad coming with a van?' I asked.

'No, he can't make it at the weekend, sweetie. It's difficult for him. I can understand. But he's got this mate, he'll get him to come. He might charge a bit, but it should just be peanuts. Dixie? Dad says he misses you a lot, sweetheart, and he told me to give you a big hug from him.'

I sloped off to my bedroom after Mum gave me the hug. My bed had all my stuff stacked on it so I curled up under Jude's duvet. She came in a few minutes after me.

'What are you doing in my bed? Hey, I sound like the three blooming bears!'

I kept my head in her pillow.

'Are you crying, Goldilocks?'

'No.'

'Fibber! Don't get my pillow all wet and snotty.'

'I've stopped now,' I said, sitting up and wiping my eyes on my cardigan sleeve.

'Were you crying just because you wanted to see your dad?' said Jude. 'You're daft, you. I don't *ever* see my dad and do I care?'

'Yeah, but your dad was nasty and hit Mum. And Martine. I expect he hit you too, even though you were just a baby.'

'I'd like to see him try now,' said Jude, punching the

air violently and making the bed bounce. 'I'd soon sort him out. Mum's much better off without him. She's much better off without *any* of them.'

'How come Mum can't see they're going to let her down when she looks into her crystal ball and reads the tarot and works out all her star charts?'

'Mum and her stupid crazes! Don't take it so seriously, Dixie. It's just a bit of glass and some old cards and some silly figures about stars. How can Mum possibly tell the future with that silly old rubbish?'

'Because she's psychic?'

'She's no more psychic than I am,' said Jude. She grabbed my hand. It was the one clutching Bluebell. She gave him a little stroke and then acted like he'd pecked her finger.

'Ouch! Keep your stunted little eagle under control, our Dixie! OK, let's see if I can read your palm. Ah! I see change on the horizon. Change of scenery – it says so in the stars. Or is it the planets? Here's your Mount of Mercury' – she tickled my palm – 'look how pronounced it is. It definitely features in the future. Ooh, what's this I see? Look at this wiggly line here. How significant is that!'

'What? What does it mean?' I knew Jude was only fooling around but she said it all in exactly Mum's tone of voice, making it sound so special, as if she really could read my palm.

'It means you're going to have fun on your new planet. See, the line squiggles around, just like a smile.' She traced the line for me.

I twisted my hand. 'But if you look *this* way it's a frown,' I said anxiously.

'Well, you'll have to keep your hand the right way up,' said Jude, tickling me. 'Now, what about this young budgie here? Hold out your wing, if you please.' Jude pretended to examine Bluebell's feather tips. 'Aha! Someone will be spreading their wings and flying off into the great blue yonder.'

'But then flying back to me?' I said.

'God, you're such a worryguts,' said Jude.

We heard Martine coming in. Mum said something, then Martine.

'I'm not bogging well going and that's that!' she yelled.

'Hm,' said Jude. 'It's easy predicting there's trouble ahead for *someone*!'

3

Martine still wasn't packed on Saturday, when we were moving. She stayed out all Friday night with Tony.

'She's simply making her point,' said Mum, wearily making us all tea and toast. She was still in her black silky nightie. It used to look slinky but now it was strained to the utmost, one of the seams starting to split.

'How come you're so cool about Martine staying out when you went absolutely bonkers when I came in at midnight that time?' said Jude, chewing toast.

'I knew Martine was safe next door, silly. You were skyrocketing around fighting with a lot of wild boys,' said Mum.

'What if Martine doesn't come back?' said Rochelle, licking honey off her toast with her pink pointy tongue.

'Quit messing around with your food like a toddler,' said Mum irritably. '*Eat* that toast. It's going to be a long day and we've got a hell of a lot to do.'

'If Martine stays with Tony's folks then I'll have our bedroom all to myself,' said Rochelle. She sounded hopeful.

Mum glared at her. 'Quit talking rubbish. Of course Martine's not staying at Tony's. Now come on, eat up, all of you. We've got to be all set and this tip cleared up by ten o'clock when the guy with the van comes for us.'

'My dad's pal,' I said proudly.

'I hope he's not another undertaker,' said Rochelle. 'He'll turn up wearing black and he'll carry our table on his shoulders very slowly, like it's a coffin.'

'My dad's not an undertaker, he's an embalmer,' I said.

'And he's not going to do all the humping around, apparently. He's got a bad back. It's our job to get the van loaded,' said Mum.

We stared at Mum in her tight black nightie. She looked like she'd explode if she lifted so much as a tray of teacups. Mum rubbed her stomach anxiously, pressing her lips together.

'Don't worry, Mum, we'll get it sorted,' said Jude.

'Yeah, Jude and I will carry all the furniture,' I said.

'You, pet!' said Mum, grabbing hold of me by the wrist.

I'm horribly small and scrawny for my age and I've got particularly stupid matchstick arms and legs. Jude's tried to teach me how to fight but I'm rubbish at it. I just duck if anyone attacks me. I've done a lot of ducking in the playground, especially after Jude went to secondary school. It didn't seem to make much difference when Rochelle left. She was sometimes the one doing the attacking.

'I'm not loading any stupid van. I'll break my nails and I've just got them perfect,' said Rochelle, waving her beautiful long pink nails, the thumbs decorated with little glass hearts.

'You're not loading the van, you're going to be doing

the scrubbing. Wear my Marigold gloves if you're fussed about your nails,' said Mum. 'No arguing, now! Let's all get cracking.'

Jude went out and rounded up some of her gang. She didn't like any of the boys but they all looked up to her. She soon had half the lads from North Block getting our furniture along the balcony, into the lift and out onto the courtyard.

I tucked Bluebell down the neck of my T-shirt, rolled up my cardie sleeves, and started heaving and shoving the cardboard boxes out the door. I tried lifting a couple, gasping and panting, but Mum made me stop.

'You're too little, Dixie. You'll do yourself an injury. Your womb will drop and you won't be able to have any babies.'

'Good!' I said. 'Look, I'll *shove* the boxes along the balcony, OK, Mum?'

'OK, pet, have a go. We're a bit strapped for time. I'll pack up all our Martine's gear seeing as her ladyship has failed to do it herself.'

'Shall we knock at Tony's door, Mum? Maybe she's overslept?'

'I'm not talking to his rubbish mother, not after the mouthful she gave me. I wouldn't graze my knuckles on her front door. No, Martine will just have to put in her appearance when she's good and ready.'

'But what if she doesn't?'

'I don't think she will,' Rochelle said, still hoping. 'Oh bum, I've got my jeans all gungy kneeling on the kitchen floor. My *best* jeans!'

'Why wear your best jeans when we're moving? What are you *like*, Rochelle?' Mum fussed, spilling Martine's clothes on her bed and then rolling them up in her duvet.

'I didn't know I was going to be doing the bogging scrubbing. It's not fair, you always give me the worst jobs, Mum. How come Martine gets out of doing her fair share? She made just as much a mess so she should be scrubbing too, even though she's maybe not coming with us.'

'There's no blooming maybe, I keep telling you!' Mum said fiercely, emptying Martine's drawers into a big laundry bag. She shook the drawer vigorously, so that little rolled-up socks and wispy thongs and snaky tights bounced all over the carpet. 'Of course she's coming. She lives with us. She's family.'

We heard footsteps along the balcony and then a tap at the front door.

'There she is!' said Mum triumphantly.

It wasn't Martine. It was a small skinny guy with a bad haircut and round glasses. They didn't sit comfortably so he had to wrinkle his nose and hitch them up every few seconds.

'Hi,' he said, glancing at Mum's stomach anxiously. 'I'm Terry's matc.'

'Oh yeah, great. You're the guy with the van,' said Mum.

'I'm Dixie,' I said, pushing past her. 'You're my dad's best pal, aren't you?'

'Well, I know Terry, yes, through work.'

'I *said* he'd be an undertaker,' Rochelle whispered, giggling behind me.

'No, no, I've got this florist's business. Hence the van.' He pointed over the balcony way down to a white van with FREDA'S FLOWERS in fancy gold lettering.

'Oh, I see. You're Freda, are you?' said Mum.

We all sniggered. He sighed. It was obviously a joke he'd got sick and tired of long ago.

'Freda was my mum. It was her business. Now she's gone, I run it. I'm . . .' He hesitated for a second. 'I'm Bruce.'

'Hello, Bruce. I'm Sue Diamond and these are all my girls. Well, shall we get cracking?'

Bruce looked anxious. 'Terry did tell you I can't lift anything, didn't he? I mean, I'd like to help, seeing as you're . . .' He gestured tactfully.

'Yeah, no worries, mate, we've got everything under control,' said Mum. She tucked her hand through his arm like they were great pals already. 'You're a sweetheart to help us out.'

'Well, it's just a business deal,' Bruce said nervously. 'I drive you there with all your stuff for fifty quid, right? I need to be back at the shop this afternoon though. I'm short-staffed, and there might be deliveries – bouquets and that.'

'Sure, sure, we'll be all moved into our dream house by then,' said Mum. 'So let's get cracking, girls, and get the last of the stuff downstairs.' She gave Bruce's arm a squeeze. 'How about you carrying these clothes, darling?'

'But I've done my back in, Mrs Diamond, like I said.'

'Call me Sue, silly. I've never been a Mrs in my life, I'm my own woman. I know you've got a bad back, mate. So have I, as a matter of fact. You try having a big bruiser of a baby boy leaning up close and personal against your spine! I'm not asking you to shift a blooming wardrobe, just a few little flimsy clothes that hang inside it. You can do that, can't you, Bruce?'

Bruce saw he didn't have any choice. He let Mum thrust the duvet containing all Martine's clothes into his arms.

'I'll help you carry some,' I said, seeing as he was still sort of my dad's friend.

'No, Dixie, you start rolling up the rugs. Look at that fluff! Rochelle, you were meant to sweep under them, you dodo. Jude, you get all your boy pals loading our stuff into the van, OK?' Mum said, giving us all little pokes as she organized us.

She prodded Bruce too and so he started plodding along the balcony, Martine's clothes flapping over his arms.

Then there was a bang of a door, and a lot of shouting. Bruce shuffled back again, looking bewildered. Martine was yelling at him.

'Mum? What's going on? What's this creep doing with all my clothes?' she shouted.

'He's not a creep, he's my dad's friend!' I said indignantly.

'Yes, don't you dare come marching in here, yelling and screaming and showing us all up, madam,' said Mum, folding her arms above her stomach.

'I'm yelling because you're getting rid of all my clothes!' said Martine. She had dark circles under her eyes and her hair was sticking up all over the place, like she'd tossed and turned all night. 'I know you're mad at me, Mum, but I never thought you'd throw all my clothes out!' She was breathing heavily as if she might start crying any minute.

Mum was working herself up too, her face blotchy with rage. 'What do you think I'm doing, sending them all off to Oxfam?' she shouted.

'Well, that's what it looks like, doesn't it?' said Martine. 'Look, even my leather jacket!' She plucked it from Bruce's arms, starting an avalanche of clothes all over the hall. Bruce shrank back against the wall, bracing himself for another onslaught.

'What do you want me to do?' he asked helplessly.

'You pick up all those clothes and take them down to the van,' Mum snapped, as if he'd dropped them deliberately.

Bruce gathered up the clothes and sloped off, side-stepping Martine as she made a half-hearted grab at them.

'Stop it, Martine!' said Mum.

'You stop it, Mum. There's no point putting all my stuff in the van. I'm not coming. Can't you get that into your head? I'm staying with Tony, no matter what. I love him.'

Mum raised her hand. I was sure she was going to slap her. Martine thought so too and tried to dodge. But Mum's hand curved gently round Martine's flushed cheek, cupping her chin.

'Martine, pet, can't you learn by my mistakes? I know you love Tony — but it won't last.'

'It will, it will! We're going to love each other for ever.' Martine brushed Mum's hand away. Mum's arm swung sadly, her fingers still outstretched. She took a deep breath.

'If you're going to love each other for ever then can't you give me a month or two? I need you to help settle us into the new place. I can't manage just now, not with the baby making me so bulky. I can't lift or carry or stretch. See what I'm like,' said Mum, acting it out.

'We'll help you, Mum,' I said.

'Oh, Dixie! You're too little, like I said.' Mum lowered her voice. 'And Jude's not girly enough and Rochelle's too scatty.' She looked deep into Martine's eyes. 'I need you, darling. You're my girl, my eldest. You and me together, Martine, making it work. You don't have to stay once your baby brother's born and I can run around all over the shop. Help me. Please. I can't make it work, not without you.' Tears started dripping down Mum's cheeks. She didn't blink or try to wipe them away. She stared steadily at Martine.

Martine suddenly started crying too. 'Oh Mum,' she said. She threw her arms round Mum's neck. 'All right, I'll come.'

'I knew you would,' said Mum, hugging her tight.

'Just till the baby's born.'

'Well, give me a week or two after to recover. I'm not getting any younger, you know. I can't snap straight back into action the way I did when I had you, darling. Still, they say boys are easier. I hope the little whatsit sleeps soundly. I don't fancy all that two-o'clock-in-the-morning feeding caper.'

'Well *I'm* not doing it!' said Martine, but she clung onto Mum, nuzzling her head against her neck as if she was still a baby herself.

'My big girlie,' Mum said softly, running her fingers through Martine's tufty hair.

'Typical!' said Rochelle, pushing past to wave her grubby mop over the balcony. 'I do all the hard work, scrubbing away like stupid Cinderella, ruining my only decent jeans in the process, and *she* gets all this fussing. How come manky old Martine's your favourite, Mum?'

'You're *all* my favourite Diamond girls,' said Mum.

'Little sparkling gems, the lot of you – especially the pretty one with the Marigold gloves.'

Rochelle peeled off her pink rubber gloves and flapped their flabby fingers at Mum. Mum grabbed one for herself and they had a silly Marigold glove slap-and-flap fight.

Bruce came back empty-armed and stepped warily round them, shaking his head. 'I'm not sure I like all those young lads getting in and out my van,' he said. 'I know some are helping load your stuff but there's others just generally mucking about. One of them was fiddling with the steering wheel and when I ticked him off he gave me a mouthful you'd never believe.'

'Oh, I'd believe it all right,' said Mum. 'Don't you worry, Bruce, mate, just tell our Jude and she'll soon sort them out for you. We're nearly done anyway. I can't wait to get out of this dump and start out in our lovely new house, eh, girls?'

Martine didn't look like she agreed one little bit. She went to tell Tony she was coming with us after all. He came down to see us off when the van was fully packed. He didn't say a word to any of us, but he took Martine in his arms and gave her a really passionate twirly-tongue kiss.

Mum tutted but didn't try to stop them. All Jude's gang hooted and catcalled, while Jude herself mimed being sick. Rochelle looked envious. I wasn't sure what I felt. I rather wanted someone to love me lots, but I thought it would feel very wet and squirmy kissing like that. I decided I preferred budgies to boyfriends as they just gave you neat dry pecks of affection.

The biggest boy in Jude's gang suddenly caught hold of her by the wrist and started kissing *her*. Jude wasn't having any of it. She gave him such a shove he staggered backwards onto his bottom. Jude rubbed her lips with the back of her hand, shuddering, like she was removing slug-slime. All the other boys howled.

Rochelle sidled up to them, tossing her fair curls over her shoulder. She sucked her mouth into a little pink pout to show that *she* wouldn't mind a kiss. The boys jostled around her, some of them making kissy-kissy noises, but they were just teasing her. Rochelle flounced into the van.

'Honestly, what creeps,' she said. 'I don't know why you hang round with that crowd, Jude.'

'I don't hang round them. They hang round me,' said Jude.

'Yeah, well, say goodbye to your little gang,' said Mum. 'We're off now. Put Tony down, Martine, and get in the van. Let's get going.'

Bruce steered the van very slowly round all the blocks while we did our best to steady all the stuff in the back. Mum wound down a window.

'Bye, boring old Bletchworth!' she shouted at the top of her voice.

People turned and stared. Some of the women shook their heads and tutted. Mum blew raspberries at them all. Lots of the men wolf-whistled. Even the decorator guys painting the windowsills on South Block bent down from their cradles and waved. Their little gang had been painting the whole Bletchworth Estate for months. All the girls were crazy about the youngest guy, who was dark with a cheeky grin. He went out with a different girl every night and he was already a dad, even though he was only seventeen.

He seemed to have taken a shine to our Martine because he called out, 'Bye, gorgeous, nice knowing you!' He waved so wildly he dropped his paintbrush and it landed with a thump on the top of Bruce's van.

'Blooming heck! What an idiot! I hope he hasn't made a dent in my van,' said Bruce. 'Let's get out of here before he starts hurling his paint pots too.'

Mum was laughing but she was crying too.

'Are you sad, Mum? Don't you want to go now?'

'I'm fine, Dixie. Of course I want to go. This is the start of our brand-new life. Let's get that wheel of fortune whirling!'

4

'Are we nearly there yet?' I said.

'For God's sake, Dixie, we've only been driving ten minutes!' said Mum.

'I think I'm starting to feel sick,' I said.

'Breathe deeply and look straight ahead,' said Bruce. 'I'll buy you some barley sugar at the next service station.'

'Thank you, Uncle Bruce.'

'I'm not your uncle, dear.'

Still, he acted like an uncle, buying us all sweets when he stopped for petrol. I still felt sick. It didn't help that I was squashed up the wrong way, but I was so wedged in with boxes I couldn't turn round. Martine was practically sitting on top of me, texting Tony non-stop on her mobile. Jude and Rochelle were fighting over who had more room, fiercely shoving each other. I sometimes got in the way of their shoves. I clutched Bluebell and pretended we were flying right out of the window, soaring straight into the sky, up to our own silent, sisterless planet.

It seemed a very long way to the Planet Estate. Mum started to get as bored as us girls.

'I'm starving,' she said.

'Have a barley sugar,' said Bruce, offering her the packet.

'I'm eating for two, mate. I need more than a blooming barley sugar. Come on, let's stop for a snack. We could have an early lunch, give us a bit of energy for all the unpacking.'

She made Bruce stop at the next service station. We wandered round and round the food court in a daze. There was so much to choose from, not just the same old stuff you get down the chippy or the Chinese.

Martine said first of all that she was too miserable to eat. Then she said she'd just have a salad. And maybe a piece of cold chicken. And a packet of crisps. And some fruit. And maybe a KitKat and a coffee.

Jude had a large plateful of spaghetti bolognese.

Rochelle had a Cornetto and a cream doughnut and a Mars bar.

I had prawn sandwiches. I didn't like the sandwich part but I enjoyed picking out the little pink prawns and making them swim across my plate. Then I had a bowl of strawberries and whipped cream. I spent ages spooning on the cream so that each red strawberry mountain had its own cap of creamy snow.

Mum had macaroni cheese for the baby's benefit and a big bowl of chips for herself. She tried to get Bruce to have chips too and a big mixed grill. 'I like to see a man eat a proper plateful,' she said. Bruce said he could only stomach tea and toast mid morning. He paid for it hurriedly, counting it out in coins.

Mum nudged up close with her tray, calling for us all to come over quick. It looked like she was hoping Bruce might pay for our lunch too. Bruce looked terrified and made for a table so quickly he bumped his tray and spilled half his tea over his buttered toast. Mum had to pay. The bill came to £36.99.

'Rubbish!' said Mum. She said a worse word, actually.

The lady at the till blinked at her. 'Language!' she said.

'Yeah, well, the Queen herself would start effing and blinding at this sort of rip-off,' said Mum. 'You add that up again. You must have added at least a tenner.'

'Mum!' Martine hissed. 'You're showing us up!'

'We could put some stuff back,' I suggested, though I'd already winkled a couple of prawns out of my sandwich and eaten the biggest strawberry.

'I've only got a snack – unlike *some* people,' said Rochelle, nudging Jude.

'I bet my spag bol cost less than all your rubbish,' said Jude, nudging her back.

'Shut up, girls. No, you're not putting anything back. OK OK, we'll pay for our food, but let's hope you've got gold knives and forks to eat it with,' said Mum, fishing two twenties out of her purse.

She didn't have much money left, yet she still had to pay Bruce for driving us. I hoped the Planet Estate would have a good chippy because that's what we'd be eating all week.

Bruce hunched up small when we all sat down with him, holding his plate of soggy toast as if we were about to snatch it away from him. Mum tried to chat to him to show she had no hard feelings over him not forking out for our meal, but he kept shrugging and shaking his head. He kept peering round to see if people were looking at us. Maybe he was embarrassed to be seen out with us in case people thought he was our dad.

'How's your toast, Uncle Bruce?' I asked, squeezing up beside him.

'It's OK. It's just toast. I'm not your uncle, I said.'

'Do you know any of my real uncles? Or aunties? Or maybe my gran and grandad?' I asked, leaning up so close I could whisper in his ear. I didn't want Mum to hear me. She always said we didn't need any other family. She said we were a fine family all by ourselves, the Diamond girls.

So how come she was so desperate for this baby *boy*?

'I don't know your dad's folks, Trixie. I don't even know your dad that well. We're just work mates, really. I deliver the wreaths.'

'So you've never been to his house?'

'Well, a couple of times. Socializing. He's always having people round, your dad.'

'He's never had *me* round,' I said. 'Tell me what his place is like, Uncle Bruce, please!'

'Well, it's just . . . just a house. It's modern, quite comfy. Maybe a bit too full of satin cushions and ruffled curtains, but then I'm a bloke, so I wouldn't really go for anything too frilly and feminine.'

'Why does my dad want frilly stuff then?'

'It's Stella's taste, dear.'

'Who?'

'You know. His wife,' said Bruce, buttering his second slice of toast. 'She's very girly, like. And his girls are all fluffy curls and lipstick too. Even the baby's a curlyknob, all dainty and dimples.'

I felt as if he'd stabbed me straight in the ribs with his knife. I put my prawn sandwich down. I tore at the crusts, turning them into breadcrumbs. I remembered the fairy story of Hansel and Gretel and how they were abandoned in a forest because their mum and dad didn't want them. They left a trail of breadcrumbs so they could find their way back. I didn't get that. Why would they want to go back to such horrible parents? I decided I'd stay in the forest. I wouldn't go near that gingerbread cottage and get caught by the wicked witch. I wouldn't even have a lick of her candy-cane door knocker. I'd clear off and make my own cottage. Bluebell would live with me. I'd have a trapeze in my garden and she'd have her perch and we'd swing in unison and turn somersaults just like a circus act.

'Dixie! Stop daydreaming. You look so gormless with your mouth hanging open. Do you have to mangle your food like that? Especially when that sandwich cost me a fortune! Pull yourself together! Bruce is talking to you.'

I knew Bruce was talking. I'd been trying to get him to tell me stuff about my dad all morning but now he'd started I didn't want to hear. I knew my dad had a wife and two other daughters but I didn't want to think about them. I hadn't known he had a new baby. I didn't want to think about her. It was the one thing I'd always counted on. *I* was his baby.

I'd been a dreadful baby. Mum and Martine and Jude and Rochelle had told me often enough. I'd been premature, like a little skinned rabbit, all purple and shrieking my head off. I went on shrieking for months and months, wanting to be fed every three hours, night and day.

'Tiny little thing, but you had the lungs of a bull-moose,' said Mum. 'God, you didn't half bellow! And then you were forever *ill* – jaundice and eczema and croup. I'd walk you up and down, up and down, and you'd yell and wheeze and scratch and scream until I very nearly chucked you out the window.'

It was no wonder my dad never wanted to see much of me.

I muttered something about going to the toilet and mooched off while Bruce was in mid-sentence. I was sick of hearing about babies.

I sat in the toilets a long time, reading all the rude rhymes on the door. I stroked Bluebell on my lap and pretended she was flying up above every cubicle, peeking at everyone peeing. I heard Mum and the girls come in, calling for me. I kept quiet and clutched Bluebell by the beak.

I waited until Mum's voice got high and panicky and then I pulled the chain and sauntered out. I tried to look surprised when Mum rushed at me.

'There you are! Oh dear lord, we've been calling till we're hoarse. I was about to phone the police. I thought someone must have whipped you away with them.' Mum hugged me hard. 'Didn't you hear me calling, Dixie?'

'Course she heard. She was just winding us all up,' said Rochelle, tossing her hair.

'I *didn't* hear,' I said. Well, I'd tried hard not to.

'So what were you doing all this time?'

'I had a funny tummy,' I said. This wasn't exactly a lie. My tummy had screwed itself up into a knot the moment Bruce mentioned my dad's baby.

'There! I bet it was that prawn sandwich,' said Mum.

'It wouldn't affect her immediately,' said Martine, putting blusher on her pale cheeks. 'God, I look such a sight. I'm scared Tony's going to go off me. What if he clicks with some other girl while I'm away?'

'Oh shut it, Martine,' said Jude. 'What if *you* click with some other guy?'

'Tony's my one and only,' said Martine. She said it seriously but it sounded so silly we all laughed, and even Martine sniggered a little.

'*Ton-eee's my one and oh-oh-onleee,*' Rochelle sang, camping it up.

'You are so *wet*, Martine,' said Jude.

'So are you – now!' said Martine. She flipped her hand under the running tap and squirted Jude in the face.

They started having a grand water fight until Mum bashed them with her handbag.

'For God's sake, girls, stop acting like little kids. Look at you, you're soaked! Come on, let's get going. Bruce will be wondering what the hell has happened to us.'

He was prowling nervously up and down outside the Ladies. He looked astonished to see Martine and Jude dripping wet but didn't bother to pass comment. He did edge up to me, though.

'You all right, Trix— Dixie?' He fidgeted. 'Your mum pointed out I wasn't being tactful, going on about your dad's family. I didn't mean any harm. I thought you *wanted* me to tell you stuff about him. I didn't mean for you to get upset.'

'I'm fine, I'm fine,' I said. I fiddled around up my cardigan sleeve, feeling for Bluebell.

'You looking for a hankie?' asked Bruce.

I shook my head. I remembered I'd stuffed Bluebell

down my T-shirt. I felt for her, pretending I had an itch. She slipped through my fingers and swallow-dived to the floor. I picked her up quickly, blushing.

'Is that a budgie?' said Bruce. 'I had a budgie when I was a little boy.'

'A real one?'

'Yes, our Sammy. We used to let him out of his cage and he'd perch right on the top of my head, singing away. He could do all sorts of tricks.'

'I'm going to have a real budgie but I won't keep it in a cage because I think that's cruel. I'm going to train it like a hawk so it flies around wherever it wants but comes when I whistle to it.'

'Oh yes? I think you might have to do quite a lot of whistling,' said Bruce. He ruffled my hair. 'I'll tell your dad you're a really cute kid when I see him.'

'Did he ask how I was then?'

I saw his eyes flickering behind his glasses.

'Yes, he did. That's right, and he also asked me to tell him exactly what you look like now.'

'Oh!' I fiddled with my hair, and turned over the grubby cuffs of my cardigan. 'I look a mess.'

'No you don't. I'll tell him you look little, but very pretty.'

I stared up at Bruce. 'I think maybe you need new glasses!' I said.

Bruce smiled at me. He had rather goofy teeth and they showed a lot when he smiled. He remembered and put his hand over his mouth to hide them.

'I'm glad you and my dad are mates,' I said.

He didn't point out they weren't mates this time. He nodded at me and gave me a little pat on the shoulder.

Mum was busy rounding up the girls. Martine was on the phone again, Jude was looking at action videos in the shop and Rochelle was flicking through magazines.

'Put that back, Rochelle, I'm not buying it. I don't care whose pin-up they've got inside. I've just spent a small fortune on a meal. We've got a whole house to fix up now.'

'How do you mean, fix up?' said Jude.

'Well, they said it might need a coat of paint, a little bit of work here and there. Nothing major. We could give a painting party, all hands on deck, eh?'

Mum was looking at Bruce's hands in particular. His fingers became fists.

'It's council, isn't it? They'll get it painted for you,' he said.

'Oh bless! Yeah, if you're prepared to wait ten years. I'm having a baby, sweetheart, and my little boy needs a nice new blue nursery. And all my girls want lovely bright bedrooms too, don't you, darlings?'

'Count me out, Mum. You know I'm just here till the baby's born,' Martine said.

'You sound like a stuck CD. I've got the message,' said Mum. 'But wait till you see the house, Martine, you might just be tempted to stay. It's going to be lovely, you'll see. I can just picture it. The Planet Estate's practically out in the country. We can get a buggy with really big bouncy wheels and take the baby for long country walks, get some roses in his little cheeks—'

'And there's a garden, isn't there, Mum?' I said.

'We'll make it a lovely garden. Maybe grow roses. And what's that creeper stuff that smells good? Honeysuckle! We'll drape it all round the front door.

Maybe we could have a water feature like Charlie with the chest, though that might be a bit dodgy when the baby starts to walk.'

We talked houses and gardens for ages in the van. We didn't seem to be getting near any countryside. We stayed stuck on grim motorways for a long time and then we branched off into a bleak grey town of ugly square buildings and torn-down posters and scribbled-over walls. There were six enormous concrete tower blocks on the horizon.

'God, what a dump!' Mum muttered.

Bruce glanced at her. I didn't like his expression.

We drove on down smaller streets of terraced houses and corner shops with iron shutters. Black plastic rubbish bags were strewn all over the pavements, many of them leaking.

I hunched down to see the six tower blocks. They were getting nearer. I knew what their names were: Mercury, Mars, Venus, Neptune, Jupiter and Saturn.

Jude was sitting very still too, craning her neck, a look of horror on her face. Martine stopped texting Tony and stared too, her finger blindly stabbing the air. Rochelle stopped singing, though her mouth stayed open. We didn't say a word, hoping we were wrong.

Mum prattled on, chatting to us, chatting to Bruce, even chatting to the baby. 'Who's my gorgeous boy, then? Stop that kicking now and listen to Mummy. Who's going to be brought up in a lovely new house then, with his own blue bedroom and his own beautiful big garden? You can run about all you please, my little darling, play footie to your heart's content. You're going to live happily ever after, my little Diamond boy.'

Bruce turned down a street of sad falling-down houses, half of them boarded up. Brambles rioted in the gardens. We all saw the street sign. Mercury Street.

5

Thirty Mercury Street had rude words spray-painted all over the front door and the brickwork. Two of the upstairs windows were broken and boarded up with cardboard. Water dripped forlornly from the toilet overflow, staining the grey-pebbledash underneath. The front garden was a rubbish tip of McDonald's boxes, Kentucky Fried Chicken cartons and empty beercans. There were no flowers, no grass, just knee-high dandelions.

Bruce switched off the ignition. We sat motionless inside the van. No one said a word. Then Mum shook her head.

'This *can't* be it,' she said. She opened the van door and heaved herself out. She blinked at the house, shaking her head. 'It isn't our house,' she said, her hands clasped protectively round the baby.

'Yes it is, Mum. Number thirty. And this is Mercury — it said so back there,' said Jude, jumping out and standing beside Mum. She looked round warily. There didn't seem to be anyone about but it wasn't the sort of place where you left things to chance.

I wriggled out beside them and held onto Jude's hand. She didn't try to swat me away.

'I'm not getting out. It's way too scary,' said Rochelle.

'I can't believe it, Mum,' said Martine. 'You've messed up my entire life and got rid of our lovely flat for *this* dump?'

'It's *not* our house! I saw it. The girl down the council showed me photos on her computer, I swear she did. It was lovely, all prettily painted with flowers in the garden. The houses weren't wrecks, they all looked brand new,' Mum said wildly, whirling round and round as if she might suddenly spot the real Mercury houses on the horizon.

'It *was* brand new – once,' Martine said. 'She obviously showed you photos from years and years ago, when the estate was newly built. Why didn't you *realize* that? If the houses were really that special there'd be a waiting list, wouldn't there? But no one else would ever be mad enough in a million years to put their names down for this dump.'

'Let's all get back in the van and go *home*,' said Rochelle.

'We can't,' said Mum. 'It's allocated already. *This* is our home.' She stared at it and started crying. 'Oh my God, what have I done?'

'You're so stupid, Mum. You don't ever think,' said Martine.

'Shut up,' said Jude. She put her arm round Mum. 'Don't cry. It's not good for the baby. It's OK. It's maybe not so bad inside. Let's go and look.'

Mum had the keys in an envelope, but you didn't really need them. It wasn't worth locking 30 Mercury Street.

All self-respecting thieves would give it a wide berth. It smelled damp and stale and musty. I nuzzled my nose into my cardigan sleeve.

The stained carpet had been half ripped up and lay curled over on itself in the middle of the living room. Someone had used it as a picnic bench. There were screwed-up fish and chip papers and empty lager cans littered all round it. The walls were all scribbled over. Some giant graffiti artists had even left their tag marks right across the ceiling.

We went into the kitchen. Someone had been sick in the sink.

'Yuck!' Rochelle squealed. 'Quick, let's get *out* of here. We can't stay here, we simply *can't.*'

'Let's see the bedrooms,' Martine said grimly.

We trooped up the stairs, Jude taking Mum by the arm and leading her, like she'd suddenly become an old lady. There was one big bedroom, two smaller rooms and a tiny cupboard room.

'Which do you want, Rochelle?' Jude asked.

'I don't care,' said Rochelle tearfully. 'They're all rubbish. I'm not stopping here.'

'Well, *I'm* only here till the baby comes. I did say so, all along,' said Martine.

Mum looked dazed. 'How can I have a baby here?' she said. 'How can I look after you girls in a place like this? How can I? How?'

No one knew how to answer her. We trailed downstairs again, where Bruce was waiting in the living room, glancing anxiously out of the window at his van.

'I'd better keep an eye on it,' he said. 'Shall we start unloading now?'

'I can't put our stuff in this house. It's filthy!' said Mum.

'Well, I can't keep it in the van, Sue,' said Bruce. 'I'm sorry, but I've got to get back sharpish. I thought this was going to be a simple moving job, cash in hand, not all day with lots of humping furniture around.'

He was hinting to Mum he wanted his money now, plus a tip for his trouble, but she wasn't connecting with him. She was looking at the letter in the key envelope and then trying to make a call on her mobile.

'Oh Gawd, I haven't topped it up. Martine, here, lend us yours.'

'But I want to phone Tony.'

'Just hand me the blessed phone for two minutes, will you? I'm sick of you moaning on that mobile, telling tales on me to your wretched Tony. You're acting like I've done this on *purpose*. I wasn't to know.'

'You should have found out first. You're the mother. Though a fat lot of use you are as a mother,' said Martine, shoving her mobile in Mum's hand.

'Shut it, Martine, I'm telling you,' said Jude.

'I'm trying my best,' said Mum, sniffing. She dialled the number and then breathed out in an angry hiss. 'Typical! They've put me on hold and they're playing "We All Live in a Yellow Submarine". It has to be some sick joke, right? We want to know where *we're* going to live. Because it ain't *here*. Don't worry, kids. We'll get this sorted soon.'

Mum had her head up, her chin jutting, her chest thrust out, her huge belly heaving. For a moment she looked like a comic book super-hero, able to snap her fingers and make our beautiful house appear as if by magic. But then I blinked and she was just my mum again, starting to bite her nails, her face screwed up with worry. It wasn't going to happen.

Mum did her best. When she finally got through to the Housing Department she ranted, she raved, she wept, she pleaded. She said she had four children and was about to give birth to her fifth any minute. It didn't make any difference.

Mum stabbed the off button on Martine's mobile so hard she hurt her finger and had to nurse it in her armpit. 'Pigs! Rotten useless unfeeling pigs!' she said, rocking with the pain. 'They say they sent a team to clear up the house once I'd signed for it and they can't help it if someone's broken in and mucked it up meanwhile.'

'Can't they give us another house, Mum?' said Rochelle.

'They say they've hardly got any now, they've all been sold off. It's this stinking dump or one of them huge hostels full of refugees,' said Mum. 'They won't offer me anything decent because I signed for this tenancy.'

'Yes, well, you were mad to sign, weren't you?' said Martine relentlessly.

'I know. OK? You're right. Do you think I feel good about it?' said Mum. 'I feel bloody terrible.' She collapsed onto the rolled-up carpet and started crying, her head in her hands. We stood round her in a ring, watching helplessly. Bruce stood in the doorway, holding his van keys.

'Don't upset yourself,' he mumbled.

Mum cried harder.

'You'll make yourself ill,' Bruce said, trying to sound firmer. 'And you've got to get organized.'

It was clear Mum was past organization now.

'Well, *someone*'s got to sort things out,' said Bruce. He looked at Martine, because she's the eldest.

'Don't look at me,' she said furiously.

Bruce's eyes swivelled to Jude. She glared at him and went to sit beside Mum on the carpet. She put her arm round her.

Bruce looked at Rochelle. She was in tears too.

'This is a horrible horrible horrible house and I hate it. I want to go *home*,' she wept.

I was the only one left. Bruce looked at me. He shook his head and sighed. He took a deep breath. 'OK. Here's what we'll do,' he said. 'You two little girls, Rosanne and Dixie, try to get the house cleared up a bit. You two big girls help me unload the van. I can't do too much. If I do my back in again there'll be hell to pay.'

'I'm not a little girl! I'm *Rochelle*, not Rosanne! I'm not cleaning! I did all the rotten cleaning back home. And this is disgusting. I'm not touching *sick*!'

'OK, OK, I'll do the sick in the sink,' said Bruce, starting to roll his sleeves up. 'Then we'll *have* to get the van unloaded. I've got to get back. I'm very very late as it is. If you lot don't co-operate I'll just have to drive off with all your stuff still on board. I don't want to, but you're leaving me no option. You're not being *fair*.'

'No, we're not,' I said. 'I'll help, Uncle Bruce.'

'I don't think a little titch like you can hump furniture, sweetheart,' said Bruce, but he nodded at me gratefully.

'Little *squirt*,' said Rochelle rudely. She felt in her shoulder bag, found her pink Marigolds and threw them at me. 'Here you are then if you're so eager to get cleaning. *I'm* not having some weirdo guy telling *me* what to do.'

Her aim wasn't good. One of the gloves landed on Mum's head, sticking to her long black hair like a giant water lily. Mum swatted it away wearily. She wiped her eyes with the back of her hand and smeared mascara across her cheeks.

'Oh bum. I must look a right sight. Quit showing off, Rochelle. Take no notice, Bruce, she's always been a stroppy little cow. Now come on, girls, chop-chop, do like Bruce says.' She smiled up at him, all tears and smudges. 'Thank you, sweetheart, you're a star. I *knew* you'd help us.'

Bruce sighed. He threw his van keys to Jude. 'You make a start with the furniture then. You look like you're the strong girl of the family.'

It was exactly the right thing to say to Jude. She jumped to it. Bruce thrust his fingers into the rubber gloves and strode resolutely to the kitchen.

We watched Jude opening the van doors and reaching in for the first of the boxes. She staggered a little as she hauled it to the pavement.

'She'll hurt herself. I'll help her,' said Mum, trying to get up.

'Oh for God's sake, you can't shift huge boxes in your condition. I'll have to do it,' Martine said, and she stomped out to help Jude.

'Well, I'm not doing *anything*,' said Rochelle.

'Yes, you are, darling. You're going to ferret in the van for the carrier with the cleaning stuff because all them sinks and toilets are going to need a lot of bleach. *I'm* going to do that. *You're* going to be chief clothes girl, getting all our gear unpacked out of all the boxes and bags.'

Rochelle huffed and puffed but did as she was told.

'What can *I* do, Mum?' I asked.

'You can help me up for a start, Dixie. I'm stuck here like Little Miss Muffet on her blooming tuffet,' said Mum.

I held her hands and pulled hard. Mum staggered to her feet. She straightened up slowly, rubbing her tummy.

'Phew! I'll be glad when he's born. Three weeks to go! Still, I'm glad it's all plain sailing this time. Not like when I had you, little darling. You came two months early and scared me silly.'

'Does it hurt horribly when you have a baby?'

'Well, it's no picnic,' said Mum.

'Worse than being punched?'

'It's different.' Mum reached out with her fingers and gently poked the corners of my mouth. 'Hey! Where's my smiley babe? Don't worry so, I'll be fine. Your little brother will pop out no problem. Boys are meant to be much easier than girls.' Mum rubbed her face. 'Am I still all mascara smudges?'

'A bit. Here.' I licked my finger and rubbed hard. 'It was scary when you cried like that, Mum.'

'Oh tosh. I wasn't *really* crying. I was just putting it on so old Bruce would stop fussing and fretting and make himself useful,' said Mum, giving me a hug.

'Oh yeah. I knew that really,' I fibbed.

'No, you didn't! You'll believe anything, my baby girl.' Mum held onto me, rocking me. 'I know I'm having my baby boy but you're still my baby girl, Dixie.'

'Come off it, Mum. I'm not a baby any more.'

'Yes you are! You'll be my baby when you're a little old lady of eighty and I'm an ancient old bag of a hundred and goodness knows what. OK! Let's get cracking. Maybe I can't hump furniture but I can clean.'

'I'll clean too, Mum. Not the sick though.'

'Well, old Bruce seems to be tackling that,' said Mum, cocking her head and listening to running water in the kitchen. 'I knew he'd turn up trumps.'

'He's got to get back though. Urgent.'

'I bet I can twist him round my little finger. You wait and see, little Dix.' Mum rubbed her tummy as if she was Aladdin and it was her magic lamp. 'He's a gentleman, our Bruce. He's not going to abandon a pregnant lady.'

She suddenly doubled up, her face contorted.

'Mum?' I said. '*Mum!*'

Mum looked up and burst out laughing. 'Fooled you! And I'll fool Bruce too.'

'Oh Mum, you are *bad*!' I pretended to smack her.

Mum caught hold of me and gave me a big hug. 'Bless your dad for finding him. He never lets me down.'

I gave Mum a big hug back.

'You're always there for me too, babe. You and all my girls. Diamond girls stick together through thick and thin. Even Martine!' Mum got closer, so she was whispering in my ear. 'She won't go back, you'll see. She'll go off that dull boy Tony soon enough. She'll meet some nice new boy. It's plain as day in her charts.' Mum glanced out of the window uncertainly. 'Maybe not from round here. At her new school! She'll settle down and sit her exams and surprise herself by doing really well. I'm sure she's bright enough to go to college and make something of herself. I want all you girls to have proper careers. I don't want you just being a mum like me and doing rubbish jobs like cleaning and bar work. I reckon Martine could get a job in the City – one of these business women in Armani suits earning pots of money.'

'And Jude?'

We both had a giggle at the idea of Jude in a designer suit.

'Something outdoorsy and adventurous for our Jude. She could maybe be a skiing instructress or run her own stables.'

Jude had never strapped on skis or sat on a horse in her life, but we could both see her doing just that.

'And it's obvious Rochelle has to be an actress. She's got the looks and she's certainly enough of a drama queen,' said Mum.

'What about me, Mum? What am I going to do?'

'You're my little dreamer. Maybe you'll make up stories. Yeah, write books like those *Harry Potter*s. You can keep us all in the lap of luxury, eh?' Mum looked all the way round the room, and then shook her head. 'We'll get this place fixed up, Dixie. I know it's a dump but we've always got our home sorted and looking lovely, and we'll do it here too. It *could* be a lovely house, once it's all clean and painted. It's got nice big rooms so we'll have more space. And we've got the garden! You wanted a garden, didn't you, Dixie? Run out into the back garden, see what it's like. Quick, before Rochelle sees you.'

I ran through to the kitchen. Bruce was labouring at the sink, his face screwed up.

'Poor Uncle Bruce,' I said.

'Yeah, poor silly old fool Bruce,' he said, but he didn't stop scrubbing.

'Mum says I'm to check out the back garden,' I said. I scrabbled with the key in the back door.

'Hang on, I'll do it,' said Bruce.

'No, *I* can do it,' I said, wrenching the key and scraping

the skin off my fingers. I still couldn't get the door open though I pulled and pulled.

'There's a bolt at the top, little 'un,' said Bruce, peeling off one of his rubber gloves. He reached over me and tried to budge it. It was a struggle even for him.

'Doesn't look like the garden's used much,' he said, shoving the door hard. It opened. We saw outside. Bruce whistled. 'Understatement of the century,' he said.

It wasn't a garden at all. It was a jungle. The grass came right up to my waist. Brambles grew everywhere like crazy hedges, turning the whole garden into a maze. I gazed at purple and blue and yellow plants.

'Flowers!' I said.

'Weeds, darling,' said Bruce.

'*I* think they're flowers,' I said, wading through them.

'Careful! Steer clear of them nettles. You'll be in over your head if you don't watch out. Come back indoors, Dixie,' Bruce called.

'Not yet! It's lovely here,' I said, thrusting my way through shrubs and ferns. There were great white flowers that really were way above my head, shading me like umbrellas.

'You watch where you're stepping,' Bruce muttered, but he went back indoors.

I fumbled for Bluebell and helped her soar up into the air, flying round the umbrella flowers, sweeping round the brambles, skimming the long tangled grasses. I imagined a flock of parrots to keep her company. Monkeys climbed the trees, swinging from branch to branch. Lions stalked through the undergrowth but I snapped my fingers at them carelessly. They bowed their great heads and let me stroke their beautiful golden backs. The largest lion raised his nose, opened his mouth and roared right in my face, his hot breath scorching me. I didn't flinch, though Bluebell fluttered away as fast as she could.

I trekked on fearlessly through entire continents until I came up against the Great Wall of China. It was a real brick wall, marking the end of our garden. I tried several running leaps at it to hitch myself up on top. I scraped all up and down my arms and dropped Bluebell in the grass. I tucked her down my T-shirt, and leaped at the wall again, getting the knack of it now. I hung on tight, heaving one leg up, then the other.

I was up there, sitting on the Great Wall of China itself. I peered up and down the gravelled alleyway, looking for Chinese people and rickshaws and chop suey restaurants.

'This is your birthplace, Bluebell,' I whispered down my neck.

The alleyway looked disappointingly ordinary and English. There was black creosote fencing the other side, and if I craned my neck like a meerkat I could see over a big gate into another back garden. It was very very different from my jungle garden. The grass was bright green and mowed into stripes. They looked as if they'd been drawn with a ruler. The beds of flowers were impossibly neat too, planted in a pattern, each plant so perfect I wondered if they might be plastic.

Down at the end of the garden there was a swing. It looked very fancy, with a white canopy and a padded seat. I wondered how high you could swing on it. I *loved* swinging. Jude used to take me to the rec back at Bletchworth, but then all the junkies started hanging out there and so we had to stop going.

I looked longingly at the swing. I could jump down off the wall, run across the alley, nip through the gate and jump on the swing. I pretended I was perched on that padded seat, rocking backwards and forwards.

Then a little girl walked down the garden, straight to the swing. I blinked, wondering if I was making her up. No, she was real, a very clean, tidy little girl of about six. She had the neatest plaits tied with pink polka-dot hair ribbons, and a pink dress to match. I saw her knickers when she climbed on the swing. They were snowy white with pink lace round the legs. She had white socks too and white sandals. I saw the rubber soles as she started swinging. Even they were spotless. It was like she lived on another planet altogether where dirt had been banished.

I jumped down off my wall and ran across the alley. I went to the gate and stuck my chin over the top.

'Hiya!' I said.

She was so startled she nearly fell straight off the swing. She looked back towards her house anxiously. It didn't look real either. It was a big black and white house with a red pointy roof and flowers growing up a trellis in a regular pattern, like wallpaper.

'It's all right! I'm not going to hurt you. What's your name?'

She stopped swinging, her chin on her chest. 'Mary,' she said, in this tiny little voice.

'I'm Dixie,' I said. 'And this is Bluebell.'

She raised her head a little.

'Here she is,' I said, holding Bluebell out on one finger over the gate.

She sucked in her breath. 'A little bird!' she whispered.

'Yes, she's my budgie. Want to stroke her?'

Mary nodded. She slid off the swing and came over to the gate. I could see she'd been crying. Her blue eyes were very watery and her little lashes were spiky with tears. She sniffed, wiped her eyes carefully and then held up her hand. She had remarkably clean hands with pearly fingernails, as if she was fresh out of the bath. I wished my own fingernails weren't so grimy. I noticed my cardie cuffs were grey too. I turned them over to hide the worst of the dirt.

I dangled Bluebell over the fence. Mary could just about reach. She tickled the back of Bluebell's head with one delicate little finger. Then she stopped, looking worried.

'Is it . . . dead?'

'What? No!'

'It's cold like it's dead. My kitten's dead now.'

'Oh, how sad. Is that why you're crying?'

'No, it died weeks ago. It got run over. It was my fault. I was very bad.'

'Why was it your fault?'

'Mummy said I left the front door open.'

'But you didn't *mean* to.'

'No, I loved my kitten.'

'Did you have a funeral? I love funerals. I had this mouse once. It wasn't really a pet mouse, but I caught it and kept it in a box. I tried to make it a special little mouse house and I fed it lots of cheese but it kept trying to eat the cardboard box instead. I should have let it go free but I really wanted a pet and so I kept it and then it died. I turned the house into a coffin and painted it black with a tiny portrait of the mouse on the top in a little oval with REST IN PEACE underneath. I put the mouse in one of my socks and then lined the coffin with Mum's old silky petticoat and I had a proper funeral. My sister Jude came to it, though she said I was weird. She helped me dig a hole down the rec and we buried the mouse. I made a little cross out of lolly sticks. My other sisters teased me and said I was taking after my dad. He's an embalmer, you see. They always tease me. You know what sisters are like.'

She was staring at me as if I was talking a foreign language.

'Do you have a sister?'

She shook her head.

'I'll lend you one of mine if you like! I've got three.'

She took me seriously and shook her head, her little plaits bobbing on her shoulders. They were pulled so tight they looked like they might give her a headache. I could see a little blue vein throbbing on her forehead.

'Here,' I said, reaching right over the gate to untie a plait for her.

She stepped backwards, fending me off. 'No! Don't! You mustn't!'

'I'm only going to loosen your plaits and make them comfier for you.'

'No! Please don't. I'm not allowed to untie them,' she said.

'OK. Sorry. You've got very pretty hair. I wish mine was really blonde, not mouse. Rochelle's got blonde hair too. She's the sister next to me. I'm the youngest so far. Until my brother gets born. Have you got any brothers?'

'There's only me.'

'That must be so peaceful! And you get brand-new toys

and clothes and never have to take turns. You can have a go on your swing whenever you want.'

I waited hopefully, wishing she'd invite *me* to have a swing. She didn't take the hint.

I sighed, leaning further over the gate, though it was starting to cut into my chest. 'We're always arguing, us four. Soon we'll be five. Like I said, my mum's having a baby. She says he's going to be called Sundance but maybe she'll change her mind.'

'Is Sundance a real name?'

'Well, it's weird, isn't it? We've all got funny names. Not like Mary. That's a nice sensible name.'

'It's a holy name. Jesus' mother was called Mary. She was very very holy and good. But I'm not.' Mary hugged her chest. There were goose pimples on her little white stick arms.

'You're cold. Here, put my cardie on.'

I fiddled with the latch on the gate, and suddenly it swung open. 'There!' I said, marching in.

Mary looked very worried.

'It's OK. I'm not going to do anything. I won't even have a swing, not if you don't want me to. I just want to warm you up with my cardie.'

Mary hunched her elbows against her sides so I couldn't get her arms in the sleeves.

'Go on, I'm ever so warm.'

'I'm not allowed,' said Mary.

'Yes you are. I'm not *giving* you my cardie, it's just to warm you up a bit.'

Mary let her arms grow limp. I draped the cardigan round her.

'There! It's a lovely blue, isn't it? It's gone a bit bobbly now but it's still beautiful. My dad bought it for me. Do you have a dad, Mary?'

'Yes, but he drives a coach so he's not home much,' said Mary. 'I wish he was home all the time.'

'Never mind. I don't get to see my dad much at all. He doesn't live with us, see. But it's OK, not having a dad around, just so long as you've got your mum.'

Mary stayed very still. She shivered, even though she was smothered in my cardigan.

I looked over at the swing. I took a step towards it. Mary looked more and more worried.

'It's OK, Mary. I just want to play.'

'I'm not really allowed to have someone in to play,' she said. 'Mummy might be cross.'

'Ah. Is she in a bit of a mood, then?'

Mary nodded.

'Well, look, can I just have one teeny swing? Is that all right? You don't mind?'

Mary looked as if she minded very much but she didn't try to stop me. I sat on the white padded seat and kicked my legs. I soared upwards. It was just as good as I'd imagined.

'Wheeee!' I sang.

'Shh! She'll hear,' said Mary.

'OK, OK. Just one little swing more, then I'll go, I promise,' I whispered.

I held the ropes and thrust my feet forwards, flinging back my head until I felt wonderfully dizzy. I felt as if I was flying right over the garden and the red pointy roof. Bluebell flew with me, high into the sky.

Then I saw Mary hunched under my blue cardie. 'OK, it's all right, you can have a go now,' I said, jumping off.

I staggered. 'Hey, look at me, I'm drunk!' I reeled around, putting it on now.

Mary stared but then started giggling.

'You play at being drunk too, Mary. Pretend to fall over!'

She squatted down obediently but was careful not to crumple her clothes. 'Daddy got drunk once,' she said.

'My mum sometimes gets drunk. She gets ever so funny and giggly. But she doesn't drink now, because of the baby. I suppose I'd better go now. I'm helping her get the house sorted. She can't do much because she's so big. Thank you for letting me have a swing.'

'That's OK.'

'I'll have to take my cardie back now. Did it warm you up?'

'Yes.'

'There, I knew it would! Can I can come and play again?'

'Well. I suppose. If Mummy doesn't find out.'

'What's up with your mum then? Is she often in a bad mood?'

Mary blinked. Then she took a deep breath. 'No, she's a lovely mummy. She's the loveliest kindest nicest mummy in the whole world.'

'That's good,' I said. 'Well, bye, Mary.' I made Bluebell give Mary's nose a very gentle peck. 'That's the way budgies say goodbye,' I said.

Mary giggled. 'You are funny, Dixie.'

I pulled a silly face at her and staggered out of her garden, pretending to be drunk again. Then I dashed back across the alleyway, leaped up and over the wall at the very first go, and went back through the jungle.

'*My* mum's the loveliest, kindest and nicest,' I said to Bluebell. '*And* my dad.'

I pretended that Martine and Rochelle and even Jude didn't exist. I lived in a beautiful black and white house with a garden and a swing with my mum and my dad and my real budgie Bluebell. I had my very own bedroom with a sky-blue ceiling and a rainbow round each wall. The carpet was green as grass with an indoor swing so I could soar backwards and forwards across my room.

Mum and Dad loved each other for ever and they loved me too. They said they didn't want to risk having any more children, girls or boys, because they could never never never love them as much as me. Dad still worked in a funeral home, and maybe Mum worked there too, carefully dressing all the dead people and powdering their faces and combing their hair. Each night, if there were any lilies left over from Uncle Bruce's wreaths Mum would plait them into her long black hair and look like a flowery princess.

6

Mum didn't look like a princess when I went back indoors. She was scrubbing away at the toilet upstairs, sitting on the floor with her legs stuck out comically either side of the loo.

'Hey, babe,' she said. 'What have you been up to, eh?'

'I've been in the garden. And I've made friends with a little girl over the way.'

'That's nice, darling. OK, are you going to help your old mum?'

'Yep.' I rolled up my cardie sleeves and started trying to clean the basin. The taps were stiff with black grime that wouldn't come off.

'Try using an old toothbrush,' said Mum. 'There's some bathroom stuff in that cardboard box.'

I couldn't find any really old toothbrushes. Rochelle's pink toothbrush was a *bit* bristly.

'Rochelle will kill you,' said Mum, when I started scrubbing. 'So what's your new friend called?'

'Mary. She's very shy. But we played a bit. I think she likes me.'

'Is she about your age? You could go to school with her.'

'I don't want to go to school, Mum. I want to stay home and help you. I could look after the baby when he comes.'

'You need your education, pet.'

We heard Jude shouting outside. Boys were shouting too. There was a lot of swearing, mostly from Jude.

Mum sighed. 'It looks like living here is going to be an education in itself. Help me up, Dixie. I don't know what's up with Jude but she's effing and blinding fit to show us all up.'

I ran down the stairs in front of Mum. Martine had to catch hold of me as I ran for the door.

'Hang on, Dixie, there's a whole gang out there. It's not *safe.*'

'Jude's there,' I said, dodging past Martine.

There were six boys out in the street by the van. Four had hoodie jackets, the hoods pulled over their baseball caps so they looked like fierce birds with beaks. There was one big fat guy with a very rude phrase scribbled across his enormous sweatshirt. The last boy had dark curly hair and a black scarf and an earring, a bit like a pirate. He was standing with his hands on his hips, shaking his head at Jude, looking pitying. Jude was swearing away at him, not seeming to notice she was outnumbered. These weren't boys like the kids at Bletchworth. They were older, and much scarier.

Rochelle was standing beside Jude. She looked angry too, her cheeks bright pink, her eyes glittering. 'Will you just bog off!' she yelled. She wasn't yelling at the boys. She was yelling at Jude.

'Yeah, push off, big sister,' said Pirate Boy.

'OK, when you've stopped hitting on my little sister. Do you know how old she is? *Twelve!*'

'Shut up, Jude! I'm very nearly thirteen.'

'And very well developed too, darling,' said Big Fat Guy.

'You talk to her like that and I'll punch you straight in your fat chops,' said Jude.

He said worse. Some very rude things about Rochelle *and* Jude. Her fist clenched and she punched him right on the chin. He shook his head, looking dazed.

'Right, she's asked for it,' said one of the Hoodies. 'Let's teach the stroppy little cow a lesson.'

Two of his mates seized Jude by the shoulders and slammed her up against Bruce's van. Jude lifted her leg and tried to kick them, but the others caught her. The first Hoodie stepped forward, grinning.

'Leave her be, she's only a silly little kid,' said Pirate Boy.

Jude unwisely said something very rude and insulting back. Then she spat in the Hoodie's face. He clenched his fists. I screamed and started running, but someone pushed me out the way. This person elbowed his way through the boys. The biggest Hoodie lunged at him but he blocked the punch with an arm that seemed made of wood. Then he used this bionic arm to strike sideways at his ribs. The Hoodie fell to his knees, gasping.

'Now clear off!' he shouted. 'Leave these girls alone!' They went running for it.

I stared at this amazing Superman. It was *Bruce*!

'Wow, Uncle Bruce, you were simply *brilliant*! That was just like a cartoon fight, *wham-bam-bash*! And it was you doing all the bashing! You saved Jude from getting beaten up.'

'I didn't need saving,' said Jude sourly, sucking her fist. Her knuckles were bright red from punching the Big Fat Guy.

'Let's see that hand,' said Bruce.

'It's fine,' said Jude. 'Just keep your nose out of things, right?'

'*You* keep your bogging nose out of things, you stupid interfering pig!' Rochelle yelled. 'How *dare* you come charging up acting like a total idiot! You can't tell me who I can talk to!'

'He obviously wants to do a lot more than talk, idiot. He's way too old for you. And he looks a complete plonker too. What does he think he is, an extra in *Pirates of the Caribbean?*'

'I think he's really cool,' said Rochelle. 'And I think he liked me, until *you* mucked it up telling him how old I am.'

'Yeah, *twelve* – but you've got the brains of a six-year-old,' said Jude, poking Rochelle.

'Don't you dare start hitting me!' said Rochelle, pushing Jude.

'Someone needs to slap some sense into you! Can't you see what those boys are *like?*'

'You're just jealous because they were chatting to me, not you,' said Rochelle. 'You can't stick it if someone fancies me, Jude Diamond.'

'Oh for God's sake, stop being so *idiotic!*' said Jude, shoving her in exasperation.

Rochelle was wearing her best red suede high heels. She found it hard to balance on them at the best of times.

She tottered backwards and ended up on her bottom with her legs in the air.

Pirate Boy was still lurking at the end of Mercury Street. He was looking back over his shoulder. Rochelle went as red as her shoes. She swore furiously, staggered upright and flew at Jude, trying to scratch her face with her long fingernails.

'Hey, hey, cut it out, girls!' Bruce cried.

They both told him to mind his own bogging business and carried on fighting. Jude could normally floor Rochelle in seconds but now Rochelle was so angry she was almost a match for her. I screamed, begging them to stop. Martine pocketed her phone and tried to wade between them. Jude accidentally punched her on the shoulder. Martine whipped off her shoe and started trying to whack them both about the head.

'Stop it! Please stop it, you crazy girls!' Bruce shouted hoarsely.

'This will put a stop to it,' Mum gasped, waddling up to us with a brimming bucket.

Suddenly we were all drenched in soapy water, screaming, sobbing, soaking wet.

'My cardie's all wet! And Bluebell!' I wailed.

'How *dare* you, Mum!' Martine said furiously.

'If you're all going to act like little wildcats you'll get treated like them,' Mum retorted.

'*I* wasn't fighting, I was trying to stop them. Look, my mobile's soaked! I'll kill you if you've ruined it!'

'My best suede shoes! They're sodden! You've spoiled them. You've all utterly humiliated me. I hate you all!' Rochelle screamed.

'Shut up, you stupid little show-off, you're the one that

started all this,' said Jude. Her wet hair stuck flat to her head so she looked like a seal. She felt her face and looked at the smear of blood on her fingers. 'You've clawed me, you little cat!'

She gave Rochelle another push. Rochelle retaliated by trying to scratch her again.

'Mum, Mum, stop them!' I shrieked, shaking my wet hair out of my eyes.

Mum didn't seem to be listening to any of us. She let the empty bucket fall to the ground with a clank. She put her hands on her stomach. Her face screwed up.

'Oh no!' said Bruce. 'Are you all right?'

'No I'm not bloody all right,' Mum muttered. She made little whimpering noises, her eyes screwed up.

'Oh Gawd, it's not the baby, is it?' Bruce asked.

Mum nodded, bending right over. Water trickled down her legs, as if she'd wet herself.

Bruce took two steps backwards, greasy-white with shock. Martine stopped wiping her mobile and stared at Mum. Jude started biting her thumb, one cheek still bleeding. Rochelle stopped shrieking and stood still, patting her damp hair into place.

'It's not due yet, Mum,' said Martine.

'Can't help that,' Mum said, breathing out weirdly, blowing *whoo-whoo-whoo*.

'Stop it, Mum, you can't be actually having it!' said Rochelle. 'It must be indigestion or something.'

'Indigestion, my bottom,' Mum gasped, though she used another ruder word. 'My waters have broken. I'm having the baby now!'

'Oh God, oh God, what are we going to do?' Rochelle

said, staggering around on her silly suede heels. 'How can you have a baby *here*?'

'We'll need the bedding out of the van. And we've got the kettle. We need lots of hot water,' said Bruce.

'What for?' said Jude.

'I don't know. That's what they always do in movies – get clean linen and hot water,' said Bruce.

'I'm not in some stupid old cowboy film, you berk. I'm having my son in hospital. I'm not booked in anywhere yet but they can hardly turn me away when I'm about to give birth any minute,' said Mum. She straightened up, breathing more slowly. 'God! I'd forgotten what it's like. Right, I'd better dig out a nightie and my washing stuff. And make-up. And the little blue sleeping suit, the one with the tiny teddies, for his little lordship. And the big blue shawl. Go on, jump to it, girls, I haven't got much time, judging by the strength of these contractions.'

Bruce was shifting from one leg to the other, still horrified. 'You're going to hospital, you said?'

'Yes, of course I am. You'll drive me there, won't you? Because I'm not up to tottering off down the bus stop, matey.'

'Yes, of course I'll take you. But then I'll *have* to get cracking. You'll have to find someone else to look after the girls. I'm no use. They don't do a thing I say.'

'*I* do what you say, Uncle Bruce,' I said.

'One out of four isn't that promising, Dixie,' said Bruce, but he smiled at me. 'Anyway, let's get the rest of the furniture out the back of the van, girls, so your mum can stretch out properly. Or should we leave one of the beds so she can lie on that?'

'Not *my* bed! I don't want it getting all icky with blood and baby stuff,' said Rochelle.

My three sisters went to sort out the back of the van with Bruce. I let out my own breath like I was having a baby myself.

'It's OK, Mum,' I whispered. 'I think he might be staying. You can stop pretending now.'

'Mm?' said Mum, clutching her stomach again. 'Oh Gawd, here it comes already. Tell them to get a move on, Dixie. My boy's going to pop out here on the pavement at this rate.'

'You mean you're really having the baby now?' I said, my heart starting to thump.

'Oh lord, Dixie, don't be so daft. I'm not that great an actress,' said Mum, running her hands through her hair. I saw the beads of sweat on her forehead. She screwed up her eyes against the pain and started *whoo-whoo-whoo*ing again.

'Mum?' I said, getting really scared.

She clutched me tight, struggling to keep upright. 'Oh, Dixie. It hurts so. It's too quick. Everything's going wrong. It is going to be all right, isn't it? My boy's going to be all right?' She sounded just as scared as me.

I took a deep breath and put my arm round her. 'Don't you worry, Mum, everything's going to be fine,' I said. 'You know it is. It says so in the stars.'

7

'All right, all right, the van's ready,' said Bruce, wiping his forehead and looking at Mum anxiously.

'Any minute now!' said Mum.

Bruce gave a little moan.

'Don't worry, I'll keep my legs crossed,' said Mum.

'You'll have to have one of the girls with you just in case the baby starts coming when I'm driving,' said Bruce.

'I was *joking*,' said Mum.

'I'm not,' said Bruce.

'I'll come, Mum,' I said, holding her hand.

'Don't be so silly, sweetheart. They wouldn't let you in,' said Mum.

'I'll come,' said Jude, but she looked a bit queasy.

'You wouldn't even know which end it came out of,' said Mum, laughing, even though she was doubled up in pain. 'I know babies aren't your thing, Jude, don't worry.'

'They're not my thing either!' Rochelle said hastily.

'No, no, you three must stay at home.' Mum looked at Martine, pleadingly.

'*OK*,' said Martine, sighing. She took Mum's arm and helped her into the van.

'Now, darlings, you behave yourselves, right? You'll be OK, won't you? Jude, here's two tenners, you nip out to the nearest chippy for your tea. Then I want you to lock yourselves in until Martine gets back. No more chatting up the local lads, Rochelle. No fighting, Jude. No treks over the garden wall, Dixie chick. And no more quarrelling, do you hear me? Rochelle, I'm talking to you!'

'She hit me. Mum!'

'Yeah, and who did this? said Jude, tapping her cheek. But then she nodded. 'I promise we won't fight, Mum.'

Rochelle pulled a face, but muttered 'Promise' too.

'You promise you'll be all right, Mum?' I said, trying not to cry.

I couldn't stand seeing her with her face all crumpled up with pain. I'd never been in a hospital but I'd seen *Casualty* and *ER*. I imagined Mum on a trolley, her vast belly under one of those flimsy white gowns like a giant bib, while scary masked people cut her open.

'Will they cut you, Mum?' I asked.

'No, no, not if I can help it! I still want to wear a bikini when I get my figure back. Don't look so worried, Dixie, I'll be fine. I promise. I'll probably be back here this time tomorrow with your little brother all tucked up in my arms, OK?'

'So who's going to look after the girls while you're in hospital?' said Bruce.

Mum looked at him as if he was simple. 'You are, Bruce, babe.'

'Oh no. No, look, I made it clear right from the start. I've got to get back. I should have been back at the shop hours and hours ago. I can't hang around babysitting your girls.'

'We're not babies,' said Jude. 'You push off. We don't need you.'

'Yes, they do need you,' said Mum. She doubled up again. 'I haven't got time to argue. You take me to the hospital, Bruce. I haven't got a clue where it *is* but you'll have to get me there sharpish, mate.'

She started her *whoo-whoo-whoo*ing, so loudly she sounded like a steam train. Rochelle sniggered. I dug my elbow in her and she punched me hard.

'Cut it *out*,' Mum gasped, and then she lay back in the van. 'Oh God, I think it's coming.'

'Hang on,' Bruce said grimly, slamming the van door shut behind Martine and starting up the engine.

We could hear Mum moaning inside as the van hurtled away. Jude and Rochelle and I stood on the pavement, staring after her. An old lady in a headscarf and matted fleece and bedroom slippers came out of a house three doors away. She looked us up and down like we were monkeys at the zoo.

'Did they kick you out your old place then?' she said.

'No they didn't!' said Rochelle, flouncing.

'Don't kid me. I've never seen the like. Fighting and brawling in the street the minute you get here! You girls acting like alley cats and your mum practically giving birth in the gutter!'

'You mind your own business, you old bag,' said Jude.

'I'm complaining about you to the council. This used to be a decent estate. When me and my late husband moved in we were proud to live here. Now look at this dump. And it's used as a dumping bin too, for all you problem families.'

'We're not a problem family!' I said.

'Come indoors, Dixie, Rochelle,' said Jude, grabbing us and pulling.

When we'd shut the front door I looked at Jude. 'We're *not* a problem family, are we?' I said.

'Of course not.'

'That's what they called us at school,' I said.

'It was a crap school.'

'I liked it,' said Rochelle. 'I liked Bletchworth High too. It's not fair. I really liked it. Mr Mitchell was my best ever teacher and he said if I really put my mind to it I could pass all my exams and go to university, but with my looks maybe modelling school could be an option.'

'Yeah, yeah, Mr Mitchell was just a pervy old creep,' said Jude. 'You are so *thick*, Rochelle. You act like you know it all and yet you haven't a clue. Why do you think those boys were chatting you up, eh?'

'They *liked* me. And if you hadn't poked your nose in I'd have copped off with that dark guy with the earring,' said Rochelle, poking Jude.

'Don't you poke me with those poxy pointy nails! Look at my face! That old bag was right, you're just like an alley cat.'

'Don't you call me a cat, you cow!'

'Stop it!' I shouted. 'Please please please don't start fighting again.'

Jude and Rochelle stared at me. I don't usually go in for shouting.

'Who pulled your chain?' Rochelle said rudely, but she stopped poking Jude and let her arms dangle limply.

'Are you feeling left out, Dixie?' said Jude. 'You can join in the fight too.' She punched me very lightly in the chest.

I knew she was joking. I acted out staggering and sank down onto the dirty carpet, pretending she'd floored me. Jude waved her fists in the air in mock victory. Rochelle sniffed at us. Then I stood up and we all stood staring at each other, wondering what to do next.

'Mum'll be all right, won't she?' I said.

'Of course she will. She's used to having babies. She's had enough practice, after all,' said Jude.

'But she said it was coming too quickly.'

'That's good, isn't it?' said Rochelle. She started sniggering again. 'Imagine if it comes before she gets to hospital! How will old Bruce cope?'

'I hope she doesn't hook up with him, he's such a creep,' said Jude.

'I *like* him,' I said.

'He looks like a frog,' said Rochelle. She pulled a stupid froggy face that was *nothing* like my Uncle Bruce. 'He talks like a frog too, all croaky.'

'And he puffs up like a toad when he's trying to boss us about,' said Jude.

'No he *doesn't*! Look, he *protected* you from those horrible boys.'

'They *weren't* horrible,' Rochelle huffed.

'Don't start again,' I begged her. I looked up and down the dark hall. I tried the light switch. I clicked it up and I clicked it down. It didn't work.

'Oh no,' I said. 'The light bulb isn't working.'

Jude edged her way into the living room, where most of our furniture had been dumped in everyone's haste to empty the van. She switched on the living-room light switch. It wasn't working either.

'Uh-oh,' she said.

'There's no *light*,' said Rochelle. 'What are we going to do? We can't stay in the dark. Jude?'

'What do you expect me to do? Turn into a torch?' said Jude, biting the skin of her thumb.

'Maybe the light works upstairs?' I suggested.

'It's not working anywhere, stupid,' said Rochelle, but she still went clattering upstairs to check.

'We can't go to bed in the *dark*,' she said, running back downstairs.

'We haven't got the beds up there yet,' said Jude. 'Maybe we'd better all stay downstairs tonight. She put her arm round me, seeing I was shivering. 'It's OK, Dixie, it'll be like camping. Look, you two start hunting around for all the duvets and start sorting them out and I'll go out for some fish and chips. Put the kettle on, Rochelle.' She paused. She bit her thumb again.

Rochelle was having the same thought. She ran into the kitchen and tried fiddling with the switches on the filthy cooker. 'Oh God, nothing electric will work! We can't even have a cup of tea. Or a hot bath. Or watch the telly.'

'Maybe Uncle Bruce will fix the electrics when he comes back?' I said.

'Not if it's all switched off. Anyway, I don't think he's going to *come* back. I bet you he'll just dump Mum and Martine at the hospital and then do a runner,' said Rochelle.

'Well, good riddance. We'll find someone else to fix it. The council,' said Jude. 'If only Martine had left us her mobile I could ring them now. Tell you what, I'll find a phone box and give them a bell while I'm out for the fish and chips.'

'You don't know the number,' said Rochelle. 'Oh God, what are we going to *do*?'

'Stop panicking, Rochelle, you're frightening Dixie,' said Jude.

'Oh, poor little poppet,' Rochelle mocked. 'Why do we all treat her like a blooming baby? She's nearly as old as me. She just looks so stupidly immature.'

'And you *act* so stupidly immature,' I said.

'That's great, coming from a girl with a stuffed toy birdy friend perched on her finger,' said Rochelle, flicking at Bluebell.

'Cut it out,' said Jude. 'Now get cracking with the bed stuff, both of you.'

'I want to come with you, Jude,' I said.

'No, you're better off here. Especially if those lads Rochelle's so crazy on are lurking close by.'

'Yes, that's *why* I want to come too,' I said.

'Oh bless! You're going to protect me, Dixie?' said Jude. 'I'll be back soon. Don't look so worried.'

She waved at us jauntily, but her face was pinched and she took a very deep breath as she went out the door, like she was about to dive off a cliff.

Rochelle and I looked at each other when she'd gone.

'So now there are just the two of us,' I said. 'It's like one of those creepy detective stories where people keep disappearing.'

'Horror story, more like. How could Mum dump us

here? She's so *stupid*,' said Rochelle. She squeezed in and out the furniture, kicking it with her spoiled suede shoes. 'I can't stand her sometimes.'

'Shut up, Rochelle. She's in the middle of having a baby and it looks like it's going all *wrong*.'

'What is she doing having another baby when she's got all of us? Serves her right if she has a bad time. It might make her more careful,' said Rochelle, fumbling her way through cardboard boxes.

'*Don't!* Look, all sorts of stuff could be happening to her,' I said. I remembered all the childbirth scenes I'd seen on the television. I saw Mum panting, purple in the face, screaming out. I saw a hospital bed and blankets spattered with bright-red blood. I saw Mum lying very white and still, and then the sheets being pulled over her head.

'Don't *cry*,' said Rochelle. 'Look, help me, birdbrain! Shove that silly budgie up your jumper and get searching for the duvets. They must have got jumbled up with the clothes.'

'What if she dies?' I sniffed, mopping my eyes on someone's T-shirt.

'Stop it, that's *my* T-shirt. Don't wipe your snotty face with it. And stop that silly boohooing, she's not going to *die*. She's not ill, she's just having a baby.'

'Some women do die having babies.'

'Trust you to be so morbid. You obviously take after your stupid dad. Aha!' Rochelle found one of the duvets at the bottom of a box, under Mum's clothes. She pulled it out, but got distracted by Mum's silky black kimono. 'She went without her night things,' said Rochelle, stroking the soft black material. She bent her head and sniffed Mum's scent. 'I didn't mean that about hoping Mum has a bad time,' She whispered. 'I was just saying that because I was mad at her.'

'I know,' I said.

I wiped my eyes with my own cardie sleeve. Bluebell gave me a little nudge with her beak as I did so. I clambered over the beds. They were mostly in bits so they could fit easily in the van. 'Shall we just fix Mum's bed and then we could share it tonight, you, me and Jude?' I said.

'Yuck, I don't want to sleep with you two,' said Rochelle, but she helped me fiddle with Mum's bed all the same. We couldn't get the headboard to stay slotted in properly and the mattress was too heavy for us to lift onto the base without Jude.

'We could just use the mattress tonight,' I said.

'I don't want to be down on the floor. Something might crawl over me. This place is so filthy. There could be cockroaches. Or rats.'

I wished Rochelle hadn't said that. She seemed to be regretting it too.

'What will we do if there *are* rats?' she said, standing up on Mum's armchair.

'We could . . . hit them with your high heels?' I suggested.

'I'm not having my best shoes made all manky with bits of dead rat!' said Rochelle, stepping down again gingerly.

'OK, OK. Well. We'll have to get all your cats – you know, the white ones: Snowdrop and Sugar Lump and Ice Cream, and they'll see the rats and they'll go, "Ooh, yum yum, tasty rat nuggets for our tea," and gobble them all up.'

Rochelle giggled. 'You're so weird, Dixie. I never know if you're funny or just plain bonkers.'

'Definitely bonkers,' I said, and pulled mad faces, miming being a crazy person as we wrapped a sheet round Mum's mattress and smoothed out the duvet and puffed up all the pillows.

Rochelle needed to go to the loo and made me come up the stairs with her and wait outside the door. We'd been running all over the house earlier on but now it was much more scary by ourselves.

I used the loo myself. While I was sitting on it there was a sudden thump at the door.

'Dixie! Quick, come to the door with me,' Rochelle hissed.

'I can't, I'm still going! You answer it. It'll just be Jude, with our chips.'

'What if it isn't? What if it's those boys? Dixie, do you *really* think they'd hurt me? The really good-looking guy with the earring? Don't you think Jude was just jealous?'

'Jude isn't the least bit jealous of you, you know that,' I said, bouncing up off the loo.

There was another thump at the door.

'Dixie, *please*, come with me.'

'OK, OK.' I rushed out of the loo, pulling my knickers up. 'Listen, we won't *open* the door, we'll shout first to see who it is. Only don't get too near the letter box or they could reach through and grab you.'

'Oh help help help, I *hate* this. Why can't we have an ordinary mum who looks after us and a proper dad and a *nice* house?' said Rochelle.

'I'd sooner be us Diamonds,' I said.

Rochelle and I edged towards the front door. We found we were holding hands.

There was another *thump-thump-thump*, loud and angry.

'Oh God,' said Rochelle. 'It *is* those boys. They've come to get me.'

'You boys can just bog off or my Uncle Bruce is going to get you,' I yelled.

The letter box opened. 'It's me, Jude! Why won't you open the door?'

We struggled to open it, our hands slippery with sweat.

'You two bananas,' said Jude, scoffing at us.

'It's not *our* fault. Why did you knock like that? Why couldn't you just let yourself in like a normal person? You just wanted to frighten us,' Rochelle sniffed.

'I couldn't let myself in, idiot, I don't have a key. Mum's got them all,' said Jude.

We stood still, thinking. We didn't even know where she *was*. Perhaps this town didn't even have a hospital. Maybe Bruce was driving round and round with Mum screaming in the back of his van . . .

'What if she doesn't come back tomorrow?' I said.

'Shut up, both of you,' said Jude. 'Let's eat. I got Coke too. And look, matches!' She held them up proudly.

'Have you got cigarettes then?' said Rochelle.

'No, you dumbo, it's so we can see when it gets dark.'

'Quit calling me names. You're the dumbo, you'll set the whole house on fire if you start playing around with matches. Why didn't you get a torch?'

'They don't sell bogging torches down the chip shop or the off-licence. I'm sure we've got candles somewhere in the kitchen box.'

We looked for them, without any luck.

'Maybe we can go and ask a neighbour for some?' Jude suggested.

'Oh yeah, like that old lady,' said Rochelle.

'Anyway, let's eat, for God's sake. The fish and chips are getting stone cold,' said Jude.

We ate them straight out of the paper because we didn't know where the plates were. We took turns swigging Coke out of the bottle. We used the rolled-up carpet as a table and chair.

'These chips aren't anywhere near as nice as the ones from our chippy at home,' Rochelle complained.

'Well, I'm sorry, Lady Muck. I should have trudged sixty miles all the way home to get chips more to your taste,' said Jude. 'Give us yours, then, I'm still starving.'

Jude finished up eating most of mine too. 'Doesn't Bluebell want any chips?' she asked.

'Oh, don't start her off. She doesn't half get on my nerves with that stupid toy bird,' said Rochelle.

'You get on *my* nerves,' I said. 'You just whinge and whine and moan moan moan but you don't help get things organized.'

'Oh yeah? So what's *your* major contribution, Ms Brain-dead Queen?' said Rochelle.

'I know a neighbour we can ask for candles,' I said proudly.

Jude and Rochelle stared at me.

'No you don't, stupid,' said Rochelle.

'I *do*. My friend Mary lives at the back of our garden. We can ask her mum. She says she's ever so kind,' I said.

Rochelle snorted. 'Oh God, she's really gone crackers

now. There are little friendies at the bottom of our garden! You'll end up in a loony bin if you don't watch out, Dixie.'

'She's real. I played with her in the garden. *I did!*'

Rochelle raised her eyebrows and sighed. 'My sister, the nutcase,' she said.

'You come and see,' I said, crumpling up my chip paper and throwing it at her.

'Yuck! Stop it, you'll get my top all greasy,' said Rochelle. 'I'm not going out into that jungle out the back. There'll be all sorts hiding in the grass – mice, toads, snakes.'

'I'll come with you, Dixie,' said Jude.

'No, don't! Don't leave me by myself!' said Rochelle.

'*Now* who's the baby?' said Jude. 'You'll have to stay, Rochelle, as we haven't got a door key. Besides, Martine will be coming back sometime.'

'I bet she doesn't. I bet she hitches a lift back to Bletchworth. She's not daft. I wish I could go with her.'

I wished she would too. I thought how peaceful it would be, just Jude and me. And Mum, of course. Though now there would be the baby too.

'It's all the baby's fault,' I said, as Jude and I went out the front door. 'If Mum hadn't got pregnant she wouldn't have wanted the extra room and we wouldn't have moved. I hope little Sundance is extra sweet or I shall seriously dislike him.'

'Sundance! I hope Mum's joking,' said Jude. 'No, it's not *his* fault. He didn't ask to be born, did he? I don't know why Mum wants to keep on having all these boyfriends and babies. I just don't get her.'

'Yeah, I know. But Mum says she's finished with

blokes now,' I said, skipping along beside Jude.

'As if!' said Jude.

'Well, if you get your Rottweiler – you know, to chase away Rochelle's white cats – then he'll maybe chase all the boyfriends away too.'

'That was just a game, Dix.' Jude turned round and looked at me. 'So this Mary, is she a game too?'

'No, she's real, I *said*. Look, see over the wall? That's her house. Doesn't it look clean and tidy? Mary's so clean and tidy too.'

I checked the grey cuffs on my cardie, the stain on my T-shirt, the hems of my jeans, black and fraying where they trailed on the ground. 'Jude, are we dirty?'

'What? Well, you're a bit grubby, certainly. *I'm* clean. Cleanish. And Rochelle's never out the blooming bathroom. Ditto Martine.' Jude climbed onto the wall. She stood right up on it, legs braced. 'So that's your Mary's house then? Wow!'

'The one opposite, with the black wooden fence. Jude, be *careful*.'

She'd started to tightrope-walk along the top of the wall, showing off.

'Whoops, whoops, I'm falling to my death,' Jude said, waving her arms around, winding me up.

'Stop it!'

What if something really happened to Jude? I imagined her pitching off the wall and breaking her neck. All my family was disappearing. I only had Rochelle left, and I didn't even like her . . .

'Dixie?' Jude held out her hand. 'Come on, don't look so worried. I'm only messing about, you know I am.'

'What about Mum?' I said.

'Mum will be *fine*,' said Jude, though she didn't sound sure. 'Come on, don't let's think about Mum just now. She'll be back safe and sound with the baby soon, you wait and see. Tomorrow. So let's get ourselves sorted out now, right? We'll go and see if your pal Mary's mum will give us some candles.'

Jude helped me over the wall into the alleyway. I stopped her as we got to Mary's back gate.

'Maybe we ought to go to the front?' I said. 'We can't just barge right into their back garden, can we?'

'Why not?' said Jude. She stood at the gate, looking across the neat green lawn. There were no toys scattered, no balls or bikes, no one sitting on the beautiful canopied garden swing.

'If we just wander in then Mary's mum might think we're burglars,' I said.

'OK, OK, we'll go round to the front and knock, if it makes you happy,' said Jude.

I don't think she was too keen on marching over that weirdly perfect lawn either.

We went down the alleyway to the end, turned left, and then went back down Mary's street. It was as if we'd walked into a different world altogether. The houses were *all* tidy and clean and freshly painted, with shiny door knockers and little porches and ruffled curtains at the spotless windows.

'I wish *our* house looked like these,' I said. 'Do you think they're one of the other planets?'

'No, silly, these aren't council houses, these are private. They're posh, can't you tell? Is Mary posh?'

I considered. I started to worry. 'She's not *snooty* posh,' I said.

'Which is her house, then?' Jude asked.

I couldn't work it out. I peered at the rows of identical black and white houses. I didn't know how to match up the fronts with the backs.

'It's this one,' I said, pointing at the nearest.

Jude clicked open the metal gate. I tugged at her sweatshirt.

'No! Next door. Or the one after. I don't *know*,' I said.

Jude sighed. 'What are you like, Dixie?' she said. 'Come on, which is it?'

I dithered. 'Maybe we should go back and try the back way after all?'

'Maybe we'll just knock on any old front door and *ask*,' said Jude.

She went in the next gate along. The hedge was growing out across the pavement and the car on the front drive was red and sporty.

'Not that one, Jude. This might be it,' I said, nodding at the next house with the metal gates. The hedge was clipped into a green wall, not a leaf out of place. It reminded me of Mary's plaits.

Jude swung the gate open and started walking up the crazy paving path. I hung back.

'What are you waiting for? She's *your* friend,' said Jude.

I trailed after her, wishing I'd held my tongue about Mary.

'Come *on*,' said Jude irritably.

She rapped loudly with the lion door knocker. We waited. My heart was beating as if I had a little knocker right inside my chest. Then the door opened, although the lady looking at us kept one hand on the latch so that she could slam it shut in a second.

She was very pretty, with lovely golden hair curling almost to her shoulders and very blue eyes. They were outlined with grey pencil, very carefully, without a single smudge. Her skin was peachy with powder, her lips pearly pink. Mum didn't often bother to do her face if she was staying in during the day, but she wore lots of black eye make-up and deep red lipstick when she went out on the razzle.

Mary's mum didn't look as if she'd do any razzling down the pub or the club. She was wearing a pink fluffy sweater and a white pleated skirt. She looked like a mum in a telly advert, the sort who'd make a meal on her cooker and then serve it up on a tablecloth.

She looked at Jude, she looked at me. 'Yes?' she said.

I swallowed hard. I tried to say something but only a mouse squeak came out.

'My sister's friends with your daughter,' said Jude.

'I don't think so,' she said.

'I'm her new friend,' I whispered.

She was shaking her head. Jude glared at me, thinking I'd made it all up after all.

'You're Mary's friend?' she said.

I took a deep breath, nodding.

'Where did you meet her? At school?'

I hesitated.

'They were playing together in your garden,' said Jude, not realizing she might be getting Mary into trouble. 'We've just moved in. We're on the Planet Estate.'

Mary's mother nodded, watching me with her corn-flower-blue eyes. She looked like a princess in my fairy story book.

'So Mary invited you into our garden?' said her mum.

I knew I had to be very careful. 'Well, no, I was in that lane at the back of our house and your house. Mary was in *your* garden. I talked to her.'

'Ah,' said Mary's mum. 'Well. That's very nice. I'm glad you've made friends. But I'm afraid she can't come out to play just now, dear. She's not very well so I've sent her to bed early.'

'Well, we really came round to ask you a favour,' said Jude.

'Oh?' said Mary's mother warily.

'I – I wonder if you could loan us—' Jude started.

'No, I'm sorry, dear,' she interrupted. 'I'm afraid I never give to anyone at the door.'

'We're not *begging*,' said Jude, fiery red. 'We don't ever beg. We were just wondering if you'd loan us a candle because the lights aren't working in our house.'

'A candle?' said Mary's mum. She looked surprised. Then she smiled. 'Yes, of course. Wait here a minute.' She shut the door on us.

'Why won't she let us in after her? Does she think we're going to nick her ornaments? Blow this. Blow *her*. Come on, Dixie, let's go back,' said Jude.

We started down the pathway again.

The door opened. 'Hey, girls! I thought you wanted a candle,' said Mary's mum. She was holding a whole packet of them, with some matches too.

'Thank you very much,' I said, bobbing back. 'We've already got matches, but thank you for the thought.'

She smiled as I took the candles, looking prettier than ever.

'Maybe Mary can come and play tomorrow?' I said.

'Maybe,' she said, still smiling.

She closed the door again. I waited, counting the candles.

I heard her in the hall, calling for Mary. Then I heard a sharp slap and someone crying.

8

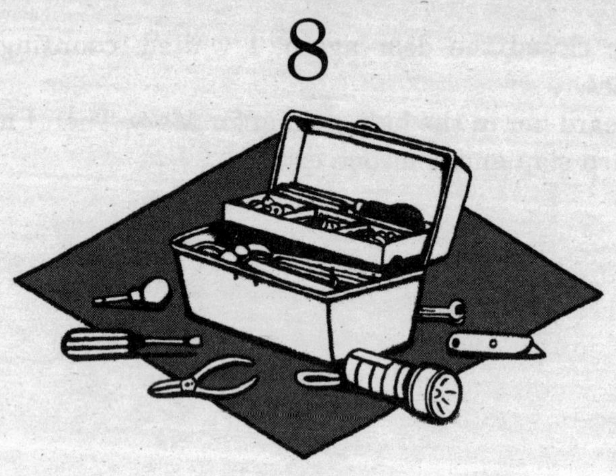

'You mean pigs! You've been gone such ages!' said Rochelle. 'I thought you weren't ever coming back. And it's getting dark and what are we going to *do*?'

'Candles!' I said, jiggling them at her. 'From my friend Mary's mum.'

I shivered. I hadn't told Jude about the slap or the crying. It seemed too private and shameful. I didn't see how anyone could hit a little girl like Mary. Maybe I'd made a mistake. I didn't *see* the slap, I only thought I heard it. Perhaps Mary tripped over, bumped herself and started crying. Her mum couldn't have hit her. She was the kindest sweetest mother in all the world.

I wondered about my own mum. 'Do you think Mum's had the baby yet?' I asked. 'How long does it take?'

'Don't ask me,' said Jude, with a shudder.

'It can take ages. Days, sometimes,' said Rochelle. 'It's the worst pain you can ever imagine. Far far far worse than the worst period pain ever, though of course *you* wouldn't know about that, Dixie.'

I thought about my worst pain ever, when some girls at my old school had punched me in the stomach until I was sick. I wondered what it would feel like to be punched in the stomach for days on end.

I cuddled in to Jude.

'*Baby*,' said Rochelle, but when we all flopped down on Mum's bed she wanted to cuddle up too. 'It's *Pop Idol* tonight,' she whined.

'Go on, we'll pretend like it's on the telly,' I said.

'You and your pretending, Dixie,' said Rochelle, raising her eyes to the dingy ceiling. 'Yuck! Look, it's filthy! We're all going to go down with some terrible disease like rabies.'

'You get rabies from mad dogs, you nutter,' said Jude. She bared her teeth and started growling and slavering at her.

'It's *scabies*. A boy in my class back at Bletchworth had them. Then I fell over and hit my head and had scabs and the teacher thought *I'd* got them,' I said.

I wondered what the school would be like here. Probably the kids would be even nastier, the teachers even meaner.

'*Sing*, Rochelle,' I said.

She started working her way through old Britney and Beyonce numbers, standing on the bed and wiggling her bottom. Jude and I cheered her at the end of each song and gave her glowing reviews. Jude's were way over the top, saying stuff like Rochelle had the voice of an angel and the figure of a she-devil, sending her up. Rochelle took her ultra-seriously and started preening, prancing all round the room.

Then she started singing one of Mum's old favourites, that weird Queen song like an opera with lots of strange words like Beelzebub and Galileo. We tensed up when she got to the 'Mama Mia' part. Rochelle stopped at the second Mama and rubbed her lips, as if she could wipe the sound away.

'This is stupid,' she said, flopping down on the bed.

It suddenly seemed very very quiet in the house. It was starting to get dark. I thought of all the tough boys on the estate, out on the prowl. I thought of the men who'd broken into this house and drunk themselves crazy and puked in the sink.

'Shall we push the cupboard against the door so no one can get in?' I whispered.

'What about the window?' said Rochelle. 'They could simply smash it and climb in.'

'No one's going to break in – but if they do I'll fight them off,' said Jude. 'Let's play the television game again. I know, I'll be *Match of the Day*.'

She jumped up and started dodging in and out of the crowded furniture, kicking a rolled-up sweater and yelling, '*Here's Jude Diamond with the ball, running with it – look at the girl go . . . talent on wheels, dodging, feinting . . . Come on, Diamond – yes, you can do it! She's diving at the net – yes, smack in the middle! What a goal – the girl done good, the Diamond sparkles!*' Jude jumped up and down between the boxes, waving her hands in the air.

'Right, Dixie, your turn,' she said.

'Don't do something wet wet wet on little kids' telly,' said Rochelle.

'I'm going to do a nature programme. And it *is* wet wet wet because it's a tropical jungle,' I said, getting off the bed and crouching low.

I clutched a hairbrush like a mike and started whispering into it, like that old man David Attenborough.

'*So here we are, in this hot steaming jungle, on the track of the lost tribe of giant gorillas,*' I whispered. I took Bluebell out of my sleeve and made her flutter past my face. '*Birds of Paradise flash their rainbow wings,*' I said. I took Jude's sweater-football and perched it on my shoulder, one sleeve swinging. '*Mischievous monkeys leap all around me, wanting to make friends.*' I made the sweater chatter and scratch. '*But remember, we are on a quest for the lost tribe of giant gorillas – and* hist! *I hear growling!*'

'Gorillas don't growl,' Rochelle muttered. 'They're shy and gentle.'

'Pipe down, we're watching Dixie,' said Jude.

I carried on winding my way in and out the furniture, my hand cupped behind my ear. 'Definite *growling,*' I whispered. '*Which is distinctly odd, because world gorilla expert Rochelle Diamond has led us to believe that gorillas do* not *growl. She has appeared on my programme, giving us the benefit of her knowledge, informing us all again and again and again that gorillas are sweet, shy creatures that wouldn't say boo to a goose – but I* think *the growling sounds very aggressive. It's coming from over here. Could this be a giant gorilla lair?*'

'They don't live in *lairs,* idiot. They build nests in trees,' said Rochelle.

'In *trees?*' said Jude. 'Jeez, I wouldn't want to be walking underneath in case they turned over too quickly and fell out of their nests. Imagine being squashed to death by a furry gorilla.'

I was scrabbling in Mum's clothes bag for her fun-fur

winter coat. I shoved it over my head, then jumped up on top of two boxes and thumped my chest. 'Grr! Grr! I am the leader of the lost tribe of giant gorillas! I don't give a toss what Rochelle says about *other* gorillas. I am very very very aggressive and I hate know-all girls who think they're clever and I'm going to *get* her!' I leaped right on top of Rochelle on Mum's mattress, growling fit to bust.

Rochelle squealed and tried to fight me off, the fur coat slipping so that neither of us could see. There was a loud banging somewhere. We both struggled up out of the coat depths, wondering what Jude was up to. But Jude was sitting up too, listening.

'Jude?'

'Someone's knocking at the door,' she said.

They banged again, fiercely, insistently. Two people knocking, one using their fists. Then someone opened the letter box and shouted through it.

'Open the door, you dozy lot!'

Martine! We ran to the door, Rochelle and I stumbling over Mum's fur coat. Jude got there first and slung the door open. Martine and Bruce stood there.

'At last!' said Martine.

'You've come back, Uncle Bruce! I knew you would. But where's Mum?'

'She hasn't had the baby yet,' said Martine wearily. She'd smudged her eye make-up so that she had great panda eyes, and her hair was sticking up in clumps.

'But it was practically popping out in the van!' said Jude.

'Apparently it slowed down once she was in the hospital. The nurse I spoke to said she wasn't in strong labour yet so we might as well go home,' said Bruce, rubbing his eyes and yawning. 'Look, I've *got* to get to *my* home now, girls.'

'Not strong labour!' said Martine, her fists clenched. 'It was so strong she was screaming. She was in agony!'

'Now, now, no need to go upsetting your sisters,' said Bruce. 'I'm sure she'll be fine. She had all of you OK, didn't she?'

'No she didn't. She nearly died having Dixie,' said Martine, glaring at me like it was my fault.

'Well, the nurse said she was doing fine – everything under control and proceeding normally. She wouldn't have fibbed to me, especially as she thought I was the father.' Bruce shook his head, sighing.

'I don't know why she even spoke to you. You're nothing to do with our family,' Martine said furiously.

'Yeah, well, I'm starting to go down on my knees and count my blessings on that one,' said Bruce. 'I don't know why you're all turning on me. I've gone out of my way to be helpful, and given up a whole day's work for you – for no financial recompense whatsoever, it seems. I've acted like a blooming saint, and yet you've all taken advantage of me.'

'I haven't, Uncle Bruce,' I said, taking his hand. 'Do you want some of my chips? I couldn't eat them all. They're a bit cold now but maybe you don't mind?'

'Thank you, sweetheart. No, I think I'll give your chips a miss. One of you big girls could go and make me a nice cup of tea though. I think we could all do with a cuppa while we try and sort out who's going to look after you.'

'*I'll* look after us. And you can't have a cup of tea, so there,' said Jude.

'She's not being rude,' I said quickly (though she was). 'It's just the electrics don't work in the house and so we can't plug the kettle in. We've got candles though. I got them, from my friend's house. Maybe if we lit them all and held them under the kettle it would start boiling.'

'It's your head that needs boiling, Dixie, you're so stupid,' said Rochelle.

'The electrics?' said Bruce, sighing. 'Let's see. Where's the fuse box?'

'Don't look at me. It's not *my* house,' said Martine. 'As soon as Mum's back and better, I'm off. This is a total *dump*. We got a bit lost and couldn't find Mercury at first, so we've been all over the bogging Planets, and they're all awful. There were some little boys peeing in the street, and some big lads – real thug types – whizzing all over on skateboards.'

'One damn near went smack into my van. Could have killed himself, but he just laughed!' said Bruce.

'*Some* parts are lovely,' I told him. 'Right at the back of our house there's this lane and some *beautiful* houses. What sort of house do you live in, Uncle Bruce?'

He wasn't listening. He was opening up a little cupboard in the hallway and peering into it. He sucked his teeth and then walked down the hall and opened the front door.

'Don't go yet!' I called.

'I'm just getting my tool box from the van, Dixie,' he said. 'But then I'll *have* to go, sweetheart. You'd better all be thinking who you're going to call. Have you got a nan?'

'She died. She didn't like us much anyway,' said Jude. 'She never even sent us birthday or Christmas presents

– imagine!' said Rochelle, tossing her hair and striking a tragic attitude.

'My heart bleeds for you,' said Bruce.

I *loved* the way he didn't seem to think much of Rochelle. I followed him out to his van. He found his tool box and lugged it out of the van.

'Do you think you can fix the electrics, Uncle Bruce?'

'I'll have a go,' he said. He took his big glasses off and gave the lenses a wipe on the bottom of his T-shirt. His face looked younger without them, though they left pink pinch marks on his nose.

'I used to wear glasses,' I said. 'Mum thought I couldn't see the board properly at school.'

'So did your eyesight get better?'

'No, some kid tripped me in the playground and my glasses broke and we didn't ever get them mended,' I said.

Bruce was frowning. 'Does your dad pay maintenance for you, Dixie?'

I shrugged. 'I don't know.'

'Maybe your mum could get the social services to pay for new glasses for you?'

'Oh no, I don't want them. They called me Goggle-Eyes at school.'

He put his own glasses back on, wincing. 'Snap! That's what they called me when *I* was at school,' he said.

'I hate school,' I said.

'Maybe this new school will be better?' he said, going back into the house.

'Maybe,' I echoed, though it didn't seem likely.

I *could* look out for my new friend Mary in the playground though.

I thought about that slap behind the closed door. I felt sad and wanted Mum.

Then I thought *properly* about Mum.

What was happening to her now?

'Don't look so sad, sweetheart,' said Bruce. He chucked me awkwardly under the chin. 'I bet school will be a doddle.'

'I'm not thinking about school now,' I said. 'I'm thinking about Mum.'

'Well, tell you what,' said Bruce, as I trotted after him. 'How about if I phone your dad? Maybe he could come and look after you for a few days?'

I so wanted to believe this could be true. 'I don't think so,' I said mournfully. 'He's got his other family.'

'Yes, well, you're family too.'

'But they don't know about Mum or me, see,' I mumbled.

'Ah. Well. Yes, I suppose that does make a difference,' said Bruce. 'It doesn't really let him off the hook though. He's still responsible. But under the circumstances we'd better not pester him. So, what about the other girls' dads?'

He started peering at the fuse box, taking stuff out and getting things out of his tool box. Jude came to watch, irritated that he seemed to know what to do.

'You'd be mental if you got in touch with *my* dad,' said Jude, peering. 'If you even knew where to track him down. Where do they put violent nutters? Broadmoor, maybe?'

'Oh well, it's good you don't take after him,' said Bruce. 'Pass us that screwdriver, Judy.'

'*Jude*!' said Jude crossly, but she did as he asked. She

held his torch for him so he could see into the gloomy box. He told her what he was doing and why. It was all gobbledegook to me, but Jude nodded, taking it in. Then Bruce flicked a switch inside the box, told me to try the hall light – and it worked!

'Well done, Uncle Bruce! You're brilliant!' I yelled.

'No, I'm not. Any fool could fix it,' said Bruce. 'You can do it if it ever happens again, Jude.'

'You calling me a fool?' she said, but she was only joking.

Martine came running from the bathroom, where she'd been washing her face. 'You've really fixed it!' she said. 'Does that mean the water will be hot now?'

'Well, we'll give it a go. Let's hope the boiler isn't bust. I doubt if I can fix that,' said Bruce. He stepped nearer Martine. 'Jude here says it's no use contacting your dad because he's a bit violent?'

'*My* dad isn't a bit violent – but the last we heard he's in Australia,' said Martine.

'We've all got different dads,' I said.

'Oh Gawd, your family isn't half complicated,' said Bruce, shutting up the fuse box. He nodded at Rochelle, who was rushing round the house switching on every single light.

'Don't go too mad, you'll overload the system again,' he called. 'So, Dixie, what about Princess All-too-pleased-with-herself? What's *her* dad like?'

'Dead,' I said. I paused. 'That's how my mum met my dad.'

Bruce raised his eyebrows. 'She's a one, your mum!'

I looked at him sideways. Rochelle switched the light on and off, on and off. Jude stood up straight, her chin in the air. Martine ran her fingers through her wild hair, glaring at him.

'Are you having a go at our mum?' she said, speaking for all of us.

'No! No, I was – admiring her, like. For – for getting on with life. I wish I could say the same.' Bruce blinked anxiously behind his big glasses.

I nodded at him. 'Tell us about your life, Uncle Bruce.'

'Nothing much to tell,' he said.

'Have you got children?'

'No, no.'

'Have you got a partner?'

'Not at the moment, no. No family to speak of.'

I gave him a great big smile. 'You could be part of *our* family, Uncle Bruce,' I said very quickly, before the others could stop me.

'Well, that's very very sweet of you, Dixie. I'm touched. But no – I mean, you've got your lives to lead, I've got mine. Such as it is. Anyway, I *must* get back. I'll just check the immersion. Gawd, they don't half install some rubbish in these council gaffs.'

'I suppose you live in a bogging palace,' said Martine.

'Well, it's hardly that, but it's a good solid semi – Victorian. It was my mum and dad's house, see. I grew up there. I've tried to keep everything in good nick. It's got a fair-sized garden, little rockery, vegetable patch at the end—'

'Yeah, yeah,' Martine interrupted.

'He sounds like an estate agent,' Jude whispered, too loudly.

Rochelle sniggered and tapped the immersion. 'Have you got it working? Because I want a bath,' she said.

'I'm not the general servant, you know,' said Bruce, running the kitchen tap. 'You girls should keep civil tongues in your heads if you want folk to help you. There!' He put his hand under the tap and lightly sprayed Rochelle. 'Warm enough for you?'

Bruce straightened up, unrolling the cuffs of his check workshirt. He let the sleeves hang down over his pink hands. 'Well, I'm off, girls. I reckon you'll have to cope by yourselves until your mum comes back from the hospital.'

'We can't cope, Uncle Bruce. Don't go!' I said, rushing to him.

I jumped up and put my arms round his neck. He took one little step backwards, looking startled, but then his arms came round me and he gave me a little hug. He smelled of sandlewood talcum powder and toffees, such a gentle, reassuring smell that I couldn't help clinging when he tried to unhook my hands.

'God, stop acting like a *baby*,' said Rochelle.

'Why are you making such a fuss? You hardly know him,' said Martine.

'Cut it out, Dixie!' Even Jude was irritated with me.

I couldn't help it. I felt like a baby. I couldn't stop fussing. I couldn't cut it out.

'You'll be OK, little 'un. Oh, there now, don't cry!' Bruce reached in his trouser pocket and brought out a very old-fashioned clean white handkerchief, carefully ironed into a square. 'Here, dear, blow on this.' He tried to blow my nose for me, without much success.

'I'll make it all mucky,' I said.

'Never mind, that's what it's for. You keep it,' he said. He looked at Martine. 'Look, I really *have* to go.'

'I know. Go on, then,' she said.

'I didn't mean to get into all this. I was just doing a favour for a pal.'

'My dad,' I sniffled.

'He's a lucky guy having a lovely little kid like you for his daughter,' said Bruce. He bit his lip, struggling with something. 'Tell you what. I'll go home now. I've got to see about the shop and do stuff, but I'll come back tomorrow. I could come back to your place late morning, say. Then I'll take you all over to the hospital and your mum will have had the baby by then and you can all meet your little brother. OK?'

'You bet it's OK, Uncle Bruce!' I said.

The other three nodded too. Jude even muttered 'Thank you.' Bruce nodded back, waved his hand awkwardly in the air, and then practically ran out of the house.

'Isn't he lovely?' I said.

'No!' said Martine.

'He's OK, I suppose,' said Jude.

'He's OK if you don't mind him looking and acting like a total geek,' said Rochelle. She twitched her nose and stuck her front teeth over her bottom lip, doing a cruel Bruce imitation. Martine and Jude giggled.

'Well, *I* think he's lovely,' I said. 'He's my third favourite grown-up, after Mum and my dad.'

Martine found the kitchen cardboard box and made a pot of tea. We ate a packet of biscuits between us. I felt sad we hadn't got around to making Bruce anything, especially as he had that long drive back. I decided I'd keep the kettle boiling all Sunday morning so that he could have a cup of tea the moment he got here.

Martine tried phoning the hospital on her mobile but

it took ages for her to be put through to the right ward
and then they said they could only give information to
Mr Diamond.

'Well, there isn't one,' said Martine furiously, and
zapped the phone off.

'Mum is all right though, isn't she?' I said. 'I mean,
they'd have said if – if—'

'Of *course* Mum's all right,' said Martine. 'Stop being
such a worryguts. Everything's fine.'

She was scared too though. I heard her get up very
early in the morning and rush to the toilet. She shut
the door, but I heard her being sick. She was shivering
when she got back into bed.

'Are you all right, Martine?' I whispered.

'Ssh! You'll wake the others,' Martine hissed.

I couldn't get back to sleep. I don't think Martine did
either. She tried to cuddle Rochelle to get warm, but
Rochelle kept tossing and turning, digging into me with
her bony elbows, suffocating me with her long curly hair.
I cuddled up as close as I could to Jude, Bluebell clutched
tight against my chest.

I don't think I've ever wanted Mum so much in all my
life.

9

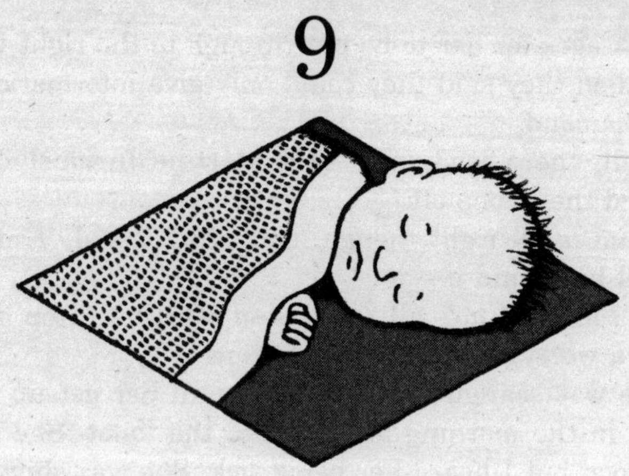

I heard a car draw up outside at ten o'clock the next morning.

'It's Uncle Bruce! He's here already!' I cried joyfully, running to the door. I opened it and stared.

It wasn't Bruce at all.

It was Mum getting out of a taxi. Our mum, back already, holding a blue blanket bundle in her arms.

I went flying out to her. 'Mum! Mum! Oh, Mum, you're all right!'

'Hey! Careful, Dixie! Watch out, you'll have me over. Mind the baby!'

Mum was holding the blanket close to her chest. I could just see a little tuft of black hair.

'Let's see him, Mum!'

Mum's face tightened, as if she was still in pain.

'Mum? What is it?'

'I'm sore, sweetheart, seeing as I've just had a baby,' she said.

'That'll be nine pounds eighty pence please,' said the cab driver.

'Gawd, for that piddly drive? I'd have been better off waiting for an ambulance,' said Mum. 'Here, Dixie, fish in my bag for my purse and give the guy a tenner. You can keep the change.'

'Oh, very generous, I'm sure,' said the cabbie.

I found the money and gave it to him.

'Thanks, darling,' said Mum, still hugging the baby close.

I was starting to worry terribly because she wouldn't show me his face. 'Is he OK, Mum?' I whispered, very gently touching the tuft of hair. It felt so soft. I could feel the baby's warm pink scalp, so small, so delicate.

'Dixie,' said Mum, like she was about to say something serious.

I looked up at her, my heart pounding. I decided I was going to love my new little brother no matter what.

'Did he get born too soon, Mum?' I asked, patting the blue bundle.

'Well, maybe I got my calculations wrong, darling. I got a lot of things wrong.'

'Mum!' Rochelle came hurtling down the path, screeching her head off.

'Ssh, Rochelle. He's asleep. Don't wake little Sundance. Is that his name still, Mum?'

Mum swallowed. Clutching the baby with one hand, she ran her fingers through her hair, tugging at it. It was as if she was tugging her face too, lighting up her eyes, making her mouth curl up into a big smile.

'Of course he's Sundance, darling,' said Mum. She

peeled back a corner of the blanket, showing us our little brother's face.

'Oh Mum!' I said, nearly in tears. 'Oh Mum, he's lovely!'

'He's so *sweet*!' said Rochelle. 'Look at his little nose and his tiny mouth! Oh, bless him.'

Mum still looked worried, but she rocked baby Sundance proudly. 'Yeah, bless him,' she said softly, and she bent and kissed his little tufty head.

Then Jude and Martine came running out the house too, and everyone circled Mum and kissed little Sundance. We went indoors and Mum sighed at all the furniture still crammed willy nilly in the living room. She collapsed on her mattress, the baby still swaddled in the blanket, clutched tightly in her arms.

'Was it really awful having him, Mum?' Martine asked.

'Well, it was no picnic, darling, put it that way,' said Mum.

'What time was he born?'

'One o'clock this morning.'

'Are you going to do his star chart, Mum?' I asked.

Mum had done all of ours, writing our fortunes in fancy italic writing and putting moons and stars all round the borders, and a clock at the top with the exact time of our birth and little pink baby-girl cherubs on either side.

'His star chart?' said Mum, looking dazed.

'Mum, are you all right?' said Jude, sitting down beside her. 'How come they let you out of hospital already? I thought you were meant to stay in for twenty-four hours?'

'Well, I discharged myself. I didn't fancy staying in there any longer than necessary, not when I needed to get back to you girls. And where's whatshisface? Did he clear off and leave you all by yourselves?'

'He's coming back this morning, Mum, he promised,'
I said.

'Yeah, to take us to the hospital, but obviously we don't
need him to do that now. Have you got his number, Mum?
We'll put him off,' said Martine.

'No! I want to see him!' I said.

'Oh God, Dixie, you're so *sad*. Imagine getting fond of
a geeky old twit like that,' said Rochelle, sitting the other
side of Mum. 'Can I give him a cuddle, Mum?'

'No, no, leave him be, lovie. I'm hoping he'll nod off to
sleep,' said Mum. 'We need to sweet-talk old Bruce back
again, Martine. We've got all sorts of baby stuff to get,
and I'm not up to running around much at the moment.
Plus we've got to get all the furniture shifted.'

'He's got a bad back, Mum,' I said.

'Yeah, so's every fellow I've ever met, when they want
to get out of a bit of hard work,' said Mum. 'Pathetic,
the lot of them. They should try having the babies, that'd
teach them. OK, who's going to make me a nice cup of
tea? That hospital cuppa was stewed to death. I need to
keep up my liquids if I'm feeding little Sundance.'

'Oh yuck, Mum! Are you really going to feed him
yourself? That's so, like, *animal*,' said Rochelle. 'Aren't
you scared it'll spoil your figure?'

'Well, I've done it four times over and everything's
bobbed back into place – or thereabouts,' said Mum,
patting herself.

Her chest was impressively big now but her tummy
was much flatter, nearly back to normal. She looked really
really tired, though. Her face was so pale, and she had
great dark smudges under her eyes. Her hair was all
tangled and greasy, hanging lankly about her shoulders.

'Shall I wash your hair for you, Mum?' I said.

'I could run you a bath. We've got lots of hot water. We got the electrics working. If there's any trouble I know how to fix it,' said Jude.

'Can I bath the baby, Mum? Oh please, let me,' said Rochelle. 'Give him here!'

'No, no, no!' said Mum. She said it so fiercely we all jumped and baby Sundance got startled, his little fists flying in the air. He wailed, and Mum rocked him in her arms.

'Ssh, ssh! There now, baby,' she murmured into his tiny red ear.

'Mum?' said Rochelle. 'Mum, I promise I'll be ever so careful with him.'

'I know, I know, but he's not a toy, sweetheart.'

'You let me bath Dixie when she was tiny.'

'I bet you banged my head on the bath!'

'I've bathed all of you,' said Martine on her way out to make the tea. 'Don't worry, Mum, I'll see to him. While I'm still here.'

'No, not just yet, Martine,' said Mum. She took a deep breath. 'Listen, girls, it's hard to explain, like, but we're still bonding, Sundance and me. *I* want to take care of him for the next few days, all right? I don't want any of you bathing him, dressing him up, changing his nappies—'

'Like we'd *want* to change his nappies?' said Jude, pulling a face. 'Mum, you look done in.' She put her hand on Mum's forehead. 'You're burning up. I don't think you should have come out of hospital so soon. When Bruce comes how's about we get him to run you back to the maternity ward, just so they can check you out?'

'No way,' Mum snapped. 'Will you girls quit fussing! All I want is my cup of tea.'

'Here you are, Mum,' said Martine, bringing it in from the kitchen.

Mum drank it down in three gulps and then lay back on her pillow, clutching Sundance. He was nodding off to sleep, his delicate eyelids drooping. Mum nuzzled him close, and in a minute she was asleep too.

The four of us stood watching, still a little awed, like shepherds in a Nativity painting. It seemed so weird that yesterday we'd just been Mum and us four girls. Now this new baby brother had changed everything.

'That's my little brother Sundance,' I whispered to Bluebell.

'And that's my brain-dead sister Dixie who still plays with cuddly toys,' Rochelle said, sighing.

'Ssh! Let's go in the kitchen. We don't want to wake them,' said Martine. 'Come on, we'll all have some tea.'

'Is she *really* going to call him Sundance?' Jude whispered. 'She's so hot, I'm sure she's got a fever. What's childbed fever? Do you think she's got it?'

'Of course not. Shut up, Jude. Come *on*,' said Martine.

We went and huddled in the kitchen. We'd got our own table and chairs in there but it didn't feel like our kitchen at all. The sink was clean now but none of us wanted to go near it. The floor was all stained and dirty, with half of the floor tiles cracked or missing.

I curled my legs up so my bare feet wouldn't touch it. I'd lost one of yesterday's socks in the messy sitting room and I didn't know where my clean ones were. I decided to go without. My trainers rubbed my feet so I left them off too.

401

I flew Bluebell round and round. She ended up perching on my big toe, gripping it with her wiry little claws.

'Do you *have* to sit like that, Dixie?' said Rochelle. 'Your feet are filthy. This whole house is a tip. Mum's mad bringing us here.'

'I'll say,' said Martine.

'Don't you *ever* stop moaning?' said Jude. 'We'll just have to get this house sorted, that's all.'

'Well don't look at me,' said Rochelle. 'I'm the one that did all the bogging scrubbing. I'm sick of it. I'm next to the youngest, so it's not fair I have to do all the hard work.'

'Not any more,' I said. 'You're in the middle now. Martine and Jude, then you – piggy in the middle! – then me, then Sundance. I'm not the baby any more. He is.'

'Yeah, and I bet he's a lot more clued up than you are already, Dixie. He's sweet, isn't he? So little.'

'I think he looks *big*,' said Martine, sipping at her tea. She pulled a face. 'Think of the size of his head and how it must hurt coming *out*.'

'Don't! Still, Mum's all right now,' said Rochelle.

'No she's not,' said Jude.

'Yeah, well, she's tired, obviously, but she'll be OK when she's had a good sleep,' said Rochelle.

'She looks awful. And she's acting weird,' said Martine. 'All that fuss about us not touching the baby, like we're going to hurt him. What's she on about, all this bonding lark?'

'She did go a bit funny when Dixie was born, remember?' said Jude. 'But then Dixie was in hospital for ages and Mum had to keep trailing backwards and forwards to visit her.'

'And she was still grieving for my dad. She got dead

depressed, she told me,' said Rochelle, nodding importantly.

'I hope she's not getting depressed now,' said Jude.

'*I'm* depressed, stuck here when I want to be back home with Tony,' said Martine.

Jude looked at her. 'Are you really going to walk out on Mum and all of us?' she said.

'I'm not going right this minute. But soon. I've got my own life to lead, Jude. I want to be with Tony.'

'How come he comes before us?'

'Because I love him,' said Martine.

'More than you love Mum and us?'

'Yeah, well, it's different. Look, one day you'll understand,' said Martine.

'*I* understand,' said Rochelle. 'I can't wait – though I wouldn't ever fancy a boy-next-door type like Tony. There's no need to shove me, Martine, he literally *is* the boy next door. No, I want some guy who's really good looking and dynamic and dead sexy.'

'Like that guy with the earring!' said Jude in disgust.

'Well, why not?' said Rochelle. 'I think he was pretty fit.'

'Yeah, fit to take you round the back of the house and mess around with you to show off to all his mates,' said Jude.

'Look, who are you to judge? You don't like boys. I do.'

'He's not a boy, he's a big lout – and you're just a silly little girl,' said Jude.

Rochelle shook her head pityingly, looking at Martine. 'She doesn't have a clue, does she?'

'I don't know,' said Martine, shifting uneasily. 'Maybe you should be careful, Rochelle. Jude's right, you're only a kid. You don't know what you're doing.'

Rochelle flushed. 'Don't you start ganging up on me

too, it's not fair.' She scrabbled in the empty biscuit packet, licking her fingers to get the last of the crumbs. 'I'm still starving. Why can't we have some proper breakfast? And what are we going to have for lunch?'

'Oh dear me, let's all go and ask cook what she's conjured up,' said Jude sarcastically.

I pretended in my head that we really did have a cook – a lovely cheery lady with a red beaming face. She let me lick her cake bowl and called me fond foodie nicknames like Pancake and Cherry Bun. I daydreamed we had lots of servants, a kind chauffeur who whizzed us to the shops and the seaside and all the amusement parks in a big white limo long enough for all us Diamond girls to fit inside.

We were very very rich and we lived in a huge black and white house and we all had our own bedrooms and Bluebell had her own aviary with lots of other budgies, but she always stayed my absolute favourite. I wondered about Bruce and whether he could come and live with us too. Maybe he'd just come and visit, seeing he was my uncle . . .

Then I heard a car door slam outside. It was the real Bruce come visiting! I rushed to the door, worried that the others might get there first and tell him to go away. He was looking anxious, hitching his glasses up and down, with a bulging carrier bag in one hand and a big bouquet of roses and lilies and freesias in the other.

He smiled when he saw me and handed me the bouquet with a flourish. 'Flowers for you, madam,' he said. 'Well, they're actually for you to take to your mum. But you can have a freesia just for you. Here, don't they smell pretty?' He pulled out a little lilac freesia and tucked it in my hair, behind my ear.

'You're all right then, you and your sisters? I was so worried about you stuck here all by yourselves. Martina did stay, didn't she?'

'Yes, we were fine,' I said, patting my flowery hair and then peering in his carrier bag. 'Wow, you've got those flaky roll thingies. And orange juice! Is this all *your* breakfast, Uncle Bruce?'

'Ha ha, as if I'm going to eat a dozen croissants all by myself! No, they're for you and your sisters. Then when you've had your fill we'll see about getting you all to the hospital to see how your mum's getting on.'

'We don't have to go to the hospital, Uncle Bruce. Mum's back already! Come and see.'

I tugged his arm and pulled him indoors. He dumped his bag and the bouquet in the hall and let me pull him towards the crammed living room.

'She's still asleep, don't go in!' Jude hissed.

'Just let him peep at the baby,' I said.

'The baby's nothing to do with him,' said Martine.

'Too right,' said Bruce.

I went on pulling, wanting to show off to him. I crept round the door. I expected Mum to be lying back on the pillow, the duvet up under her chin, but she was sitting up, cradling the baby in her arms. She was crying.

'Mum! Oh Mum, are you in pain?'

'Ssh! No, no, I'm fine, I'm just – over-emotional,' Mum sniffed, wiping her eyes with the silky corner of the baby's blanket.

'You should still be in hospital,' said Bruce.

'Who asked your opinion?' Mum said rudely. 'I had

to get back to my girls, didn't I, seeing as you scarpered?'

'Look, they're not *my* responsibility – even though I've come all the way back today and I've got breakfast *and* lunch and tea stuff, and even disposable nappies for the baby. I didn't know what kind to get. Did you have your little boy?'

Mum clutched Sundance tightly. 'Of course.'

'You look a bit rough, if you don't mind my saying so,' said Bruce.

'I do mind! Look, you be Mr Good-Guy and fix the kids something to eat and drink. I want a bit of peace to feed the baby and get him changed. Dixie, where's the box with all the baby things?'

I scrabbled at the hundred and one cardboard boxes all round the living room until I found the right one, crammed with little blue outfits. I fingered the little sleeping suits, making them kick their legs up and down as if they had tiny dancing babies inside them.

'They're all so sweet, Mum. Can Sundance wear these weeny stretchy dungarees? Look, there's a sun embroidered on the front – they're perfect.'

'OK, OK – and find me the little yellow and blue stripy top that goes with it.'

'Let me dress him, Mum, please!'

'No! I told you, *I'm* doing it. I'm doing everything for him. Off you go now.'

'Can't I even watch?'

'No you can't. You go and make yourself useful in the kitchen. He's *my* little boy.'

'He's *my* little baby brother,' I said, edging up to the bed. 'Can I just give him a kiss, Mum?'

'Go on then,' said Mum, sighing. 'But don't go poking at him with that damn budgie, OK?'

I gave Sundance a kiss on his little wrinkled forehead. He was very pink in the face.

'He's hot in that blanket. It can't be much fun for him, all bundled up. Can't he have a little kick without it?'

'You leave him be. I'm the one who knows all about babies,' said Mum, but she suddenly started crying again. 'I'm the one who knows beggar all about anything,' she wailed.

'Don't cry, Mum! Shall I get Jude or Martine?'

'No, just leave me be. Take no notice. You always get weepy just after having a baby. Nothing to worry about,' said Mum.

I couldn't help worrying.

I went into the kitchen and ate part of a croissant, sucking at the end, pretending it was a cigar. Then I stuck it under my nose like a moustache.

'You're a caution, Dixie,' said Bruce.

'Stop encouraging her. Don't play with your food, Dixie,' said Martine.

'Yuck, imagine eating that croissant with Dixie's snot dribbled all over it,' said Rochelle.

'I'm not the slightest bit snotty,' I said, but I went off the idea of eating it all the same.

Jude wanted to take Mum a croissant but Mum yelled at her to go away.

'She's got a mouth on her, your mum,' said Bruce.

'Well, she's not feeling too great, is she?' said Martine. '*You* try having a baby.'

'I'm never ever having babies,' I said.

'Me neither,' said Jude, eating Mum's croissant herself.

'Nor me. It mucks up your figure, makes you go all saggy,' said Rochelle, posing to show off her own perfect figure. 'What about you, Martine? You're Mum's last hope of being a granny.'

'Don't look at me!' Martine said fiercely.

'Don't you and Tony want to have little Martys and Tones?' said Jude.

'I wish you'd just shut *up* about it,' said Martine.

'I'm sick of people telling me to shut up and clear off,' said Jude. 'OK, I will. I'm going for a mooch around.'

'No, you can't! You've got to help get this dump organized,' said Martine.

'Watch me,' said Jude. She walked out of the kitchen, down the hall and out the front door.

'That's just typical of her,' said Martine. 'She's the strongest. How are we going to get all that furniture shifted without her?' She was looking at Bruce.

'I can't, Martina,' said Bruce. 'My back's really twingeing from yesterday. If I put it out I'll be flat on my back for a week, when I've got to drive up town for my flowers, keep the shop open, manage the deliveries. I can't risk it.'

'Well, we'll just manage ourselves, you and me, Rochelle,' said Martine.

'No way! If Jude can skive off, so can I,' said Rochelle, reaching for her denim jacket. 'I'm going out too.'

'No you're not.'

'If Jude can, I can.'

'Jude's older. She can look after herself. You're staying here. Rochelle.'

'You can't boss me about. You're not my mother,' Rochelle said. 'I'm just going down the road, that's all. OK?'

'No, it's not OK.'

'Well, tough,' said Rochelle, and she ran for it.

Martine ran after her, but gave up when Rochelle was out the door. 'It's not *fair*,' she said, nearly in tears. 'I get my whole life messed up and come here to help out and find I get left doing everything, just because I'm the eldest.'

'I hope you're not going to clear off too,' said Bruce. 'I can't stay too long, you know. You can't leave little Dixie in charge.'

'I'm *not* little!' I said.

'Oh yes, look at you growing, practically towering above me,' said Bruce, peering at an imaginary giraffe-necked Dixie.

'I know I'm small, but I'm not a baby,' I said firmly.

Maybe this wasn't a wise thing to say.

'OK, you can make yourself useful,' said Martine. She braved Mum in the living room and humped several boxes of pots and packets and china into the kitchen. 'You can scrub out all the cupboards and put our stuff in them. I'll make a start cleaning upstairs.'

Martine swished off with a broom and scrubbing brush, looking martyred. We heard her phoning Tony as she went upstairs: 'Yes, Mum's had the baby . . . Sure, they're both fine . . . Well, Mum's a bit whacked, obviously, so I'm having to do *everything* at the moment. The girls are no help whatsoever.'

'Cheek!' I said.

'Yes, double cheek! She didn't even mention me,' said Bruce.

'Exactly. We wouldn't have any light or hot water or breakfast without you, Uncle Bruce. We wouldn't even *be* here.'

'Ah. Maybe that's why she's so cross with me. Anyway,

I didn't come back here for her. Or your sisters. Or your mum.' He smiled at me, forgetting to hide his funny teeth. I smiled back.

'It's because you're my dad's mate, isn't it, Uncle Bruce?'

'I don't know about that. It's more this uncle lark. I'm getting to like the idea of you as my token niece, little Dixie.' Bruce sighed and stretched. 'But I'm also here to help out, so I'd better get on.'

'You mustn't muck up your back, Uncle Bruce.'

'No, I can't do any lifting, darling. I thought I'd busy myself checking out the whole house, making sure your washing machine's plumbed in properly, testing the cooker – boring stuff like that.'

'You are a total star, Uncle Bruce,' I said.

'Twinkle, twinkle,' he said, waggling his eyebrows at me, his glasses sliding down his nose.

I giggled and then sat down beside the boxes, poking about amongst the china and cutlery. I didn't know where to start. I got out all our different cups and lined them up on the floor, as if they were standing in a queue. Then I found the teapot and turned it into an elephant. The cup children took turns riding on its back, rewarding it with a sugar lump down its spouty trunk.

Bruce decided he needed his tool box and stepped backwards. He crushed a child and very nearly killed the elephant too. We picked up the pieces together.

'Maybe you'd better get the cupboards cleaned up, like your sister said. Then you can put all this china safely away,' Bruce said.

He stood me on a chair with a wet J-cloth and a tin of Vim. I scattered the white powder over the black grime and mouldy crumbs. I gave the shelf a little rub. Nothing much happened. It was like powdering a very dirty face.

'You need to give it a bit of elbow grease,' said Bruce, showing me how to scrub vigorously.

I tried to copy him but I couldn't reach comfortably. It made my arm ache and I rattled around on the chair so much I nearly skidded right off.

'Careful, Dixie! I don't think you're very safe wobbling about on that chair. Maybe you've done enough work now. I should go and have a little play in the garden.'

'But what about the cupboard?'

'I'll give it a going over for you when I'm done here,' said Bruce. 'Don't worry, we'll get this house shipshape in no time.'

'Shipshape?'

'Everything running smoothly.'

I thought about it. Things had never run smoothly, not even in any of our old flats. If we were in a ship it was always an old leaky one, and we were tossing up and down in a storm. Still, as long as we were all clinging together, safe inside the ship, that was all that mattered.

10

I skipped off out of the door and into the jungle. Bluebell came fluttering out of my Vim-crusted cuff and swooped up and down in delight. She sang a wild Australian song (I cheeped 'Waltzing Matilda') her wings spread wide.

'Don't fly too far, Bluebell. We're going to go and see Mary.'

We trekked through the jungle together and then I hauled myself up onto the Great Wall of China. There was Mary on the swing, in a blue-check dress, white ribbons fluttering on her plaits, lacy white socks and navy patent button shoes. She was peering round. When she saw my head above the wall she smiled and jumped off the swing, running towards the gate.

I clambered over the wall and ran across the alley.

'Hi, Mary!' I said.

'Hello, Dixie. I've been looking and looking for you! Do you want to come in and have a swing?'

'Yes please! But I don't want to get you into trouble.

You said your mum won't let you have friends round to play.'

'Mummy's out at church. Daddy's here, but he's still in bed. So you can come for a bit, but we have to be quiet.'

'As a mouse!' I said. I twitched my nose and went *'Squeak-squeak.'*

Mary giggled. She seemed happy to see me, but her eyes were red and sore, and her voice was husky, as if she'd been crying again.

'Are you all right, Mary?' I asked, wriggling onto the swing.

'I'm fine,' she said, though she didn't look fine at all.

She was as pin-neat as ever, her plaits pulled so tightly back behind her ears she could barely blink. There was something the matter with her hands. She had them curled into tight fists.

'Have you been crying?'

'No,' said Mary nervously.

'It's OK. I cry lots. We *all* cry in our family. My mum says it's a wonder we're not sloshing about ankle-deep in tears. Hey, Mary, guess what! Mum's had her baby. I've got my baby brother. He's so sweet. Maybe I can bring him round to see you soon. Do you like babies?'

Mary didn't look sure.

'I've got a baby boy,' she said surprisingly.

'No you haven't!'

'I'll show you.'

She ran off, her feet stiff in her patent shoes. She went in her back door and came out a minute later pushing a baby buggy almost as big as a real one. There was a peachy-skinned plastic baby doll sitting up in it, a fixed grin on his face.

'Oh wow! He's beautiful,' I said, though that grin looked a bit scary, and I didn't like the way his rigid pink fingers were reaching out, ready to grab at me.

Mary didn't seem too relaxed with him either. She pushed the buggy half-heartedly, and didn't touch the baby, even when he tipped over to one side.

'What's his name?' I said.

'Baby,' said Mary.

'Baby what?'

'Shall I call him Sundance too?'

'You could call him Butch, then they could maybe be friends. Do you take Baby Butch to bed with you?'

'Oh no. I'm not allowed. I might mess him up. I take my teddy to bed with me. I like my teddy best, even though he's old.'

'Old toys are much nicer.'

'Like Bluebell?'

'*I'm not a toy, I'm a* bird,' Bluebell chirruped. '*I like your garden, Mary. I think I might make a little holiday nest here.*'

I flew Bluebell round and round, looking for twigs. There were none on the velvet-green grass, so I had to snap some off the hedge. Mary looked tense. She didn't help me. Her fingers were still curled inside her palms.

I tried to bundle my little twigs together but they kept collapsing. 'I think birds must have secret gluepots,' I said. 'Oh, blow this for a game of soldiers. Hey, look, we could turn all the twigs into little soldiers and play armies.'

'I don't know how to play armies.'

'We'll just make it up.'

'I don't know *how*,' said Mary, sounding upset.

'OK, OK. Let's play families. Mother twig, father twig, lots of little kiddie twigs, yeah?'

'Yeah,' said Mary, but she kept her hands in little clenched fists, not taking hold of any of the twigs.

'Just watch me then,' I said. I took hold of a twig. 'Hello, hello, hello, I'm little Tilly Twig and I'm going to dance a jig,' I said, making her dance in front of Mary's face.

Mary smiled.

'You make little Tommy Twig dance with her,' I said.

'No, you do him too,' said Mary.

So I made Tilly and Tommy twirl for a minute.

'Find new little baby Titchy Twiglet and make him dance.'

'Babies can't dance,' said Mary.

'OK, he wants to crawl. Yeah, he can be crawling around and Tilly and Tommy keep falling over him.'

'You make him crawl, Dixie,' said Mary.

'You'll have to help. I haven't got three hands. There!' I snapped a tiny piece off a twig. 'Look, here he is, tiny Titchy. Isn't he sweet? Oh, he's crawling away from me. Catch him, Mary!'

I threw the little piece of twig. Mary obediently cupped her hands to catch him. The tips of her fingers were bright pink and sore, each small nail cut right back to the quick.

'Mary! Your nails!'

She dropped the little twig and curved her hands into fists again.

'Whatever did you *do* to them? Did you try and cut them yourself?'

'Yes,' Mary whispered, head bent.

'But it must have hurt awfully. Why did you *do* it? Why didn't you get your mum to cut your nails?'

Mary said nothing.

'Mary? Did your mum cut your nails?'

Mary said nothing. Her chin was on her chest, her white parting painfully obvious, raked into her head. I put my arms round her.

'She did, didn't she?' I said.

Mary started crying. 'They were dirty nails and Mummy said I'm a bad, dirty girl and I can't have nails like a little animal even though I act like one. So she cut them off,' Mary sobbed in a rush.

'Why didn't you run away?'

'She had me tight between her legs so I couldn't.'

'But it must be so so so sore.'

'I couldn't stop crying and that made Mummy cross.'

'Did she smack you?'

'You always get a hard smack if you cry.'

'My mum doesn't ever smack me.'

'My mummy smacks me lots. I deserve it because I'm bad,' said Mary.

'That's rubbish. You're not a *bit* bad. I don't know how your mum would cope with Rochelle. Or Jude. Or Martine. What about your dad – does he smack you too?'

'No, he gives me cuddles. But he says I've got to try not to be so naughty because it upsets Mummy.'

'But you're *not* naughty.'

'I am. I do really dirty things,' Mary said hoarsely.

'Like what?'

'I pick my nose. I scratch myself. And sometimes I don't get to the toilet in time.'

'You and everyone else in the entire world!'

'I get my clothes dirty.'

'You're the cleanest little girl I've ever seen. You always look like you've just jumped out of your bath. Heaps and heaps and heaps cleaner than me.'

'Mummy says I'm still dirty. Sometimes the dirt doesn't show but she can see it. Or the dirt's inside me and I have to take medicine to get it out.'

I stared at her. 'Your mum's nuts,' I said.

Mary looked startled. 'No she's not!'

'She's worse than nuts. She's cruel,' I said, gently picking up one of Mary's tiny hands. I blew softly on her poor pink fingers. 'I'm blowing fairy dust on them. That'll make them get better quickly.'

'They're better already,' Mary fibbed politely.

'I'm going to tell my mum what your mum did,' I said.

'No! No, you mustn't! Please please please don't tell, Dixie,' Mary begged. She seized hold of me, even though it must have really hurt her fingers. 'Promise you won't tell. I told a girl in my class at school and her mum said something to my mummy. She said it was all a mistake and I was just telling stories. But then when I got home she got the scissors out of her sewing basket and said she'd cut off my tongue if I ever told tales again.'

'She wouldn't *really* cut off your tongue, Mary,' I said. But what sort of mother could cut her little girl's nails right back so savagely? How could I be sure?

'Will you promise you won't tell? If you don't keep your promise I'll drop down dead and die!'

'I promise! But you won't drop down dead and die, Mary. Don't say that, it's horrible. Your mum's horrible.'

'No, she's not. She's the loveliest nicest kindest mummy in the whole world,' said Mary.

She'd used these exact words before. She'd obviously been taught to say it.

I didn't know what to do when I went back to my own house. I wanted to cry when I thought of Mary being hurt. I knew I should tell someone, but I'd promised. I knew it was silly, but I could see myself telling Mum and then Mary keeling over and dying right in front of me.

'You look a bit doleful, Dixie,' said Uncle Bruce, when I went into the kitchen. 'What's up? You can tell your Uncle Bruce, can't you?'

'No, I can't,' I said, sighing.

I heard someone moving around in the living room. 'That's Mum!' I said.

I went running in to see her. Mum was hanging onto a pile of cardboard boxes, her face grey. Sundance was clutched tight in her other arm.

'Mum?'

'I'm OK, Dixie,' she mumbled.

'You're not. I think you'd better lie down again.'

'No, no. Look, I've got to go upstairs to the bathroom, sort myself out. Will you help me, lovie?'

'OK, Mum. Here, lean on me. Why don't you let me take Sundance?'

'No, I've got him,' said Mum.

He was awake now, his eyes wide open. They were a beautiful clear blue, though the lashes were black, like his soft tufty hair. He had lovely little arched eyebrows too, each tiny hair perfect. It seemed astonishing that he'd been forming in Mum's tummy all this time, all the delicate differences – soft skin, shiny eyes, downy hair.

'Don't go all moony on me, Dixie! I'm in a bad way, bleeding,' Mum said impatiently.

'Oh Mum! You've got to go to the hospital!'

'No, love, it's natural. It happens after you have a baby. I'll be all right.'

'Uncle Bruce could take you, just to make sure.'

'No! I'm not going back to that hospital. I'll be fine. I just need a bath. Now, let me lean on you.'

Mum shuffled along, Sundance still clutched tight. Halfway up the stairs Martine heard us and came running.

'Come on, Mum. I'll help you,' she said, dropping her brush and pail. 'I've just cleaned the bathroom.'

'Thanks, darling,' Mum said weakly. She leaned against the wall. 'Oh God, everything's spinning.'

'Look, I'll help you into the bath, come on,' said Martine. 'Dixie, take the baby.'

'No! No, I must keep him,' said Mum, swaying.

'Yeah, right, and you're going to drop him on his head any minute, so how daft is that!' said Martine. 'Dixie, take him!'

I hooked little Sundance out of Mum's arms. She staggered into the bathroom with Martine. I heard them murmuring together, the bath running.

I looked down at my little brother. He was surprisingly heavy for such a tiny baby. He was warm and wriggly . . . and very very wet. He'd wee'd right through his nappy and his little blue sleeping suit. Even his shawl had started to get soggy.

He started snuffling, mewing softly like a kitten.

'It's uncomfy, isn't it?' I whispered. 'I'm going to get you sorted out, little brother.'

I carried him very carefully downstairs, checking every step as I went. I could feel Sundance tensing inside his shawl. 'Don't worry, darling,' I whispered. 'I'm your big sister Dixie. I'll look after you.'

I carried him into the crowded living room and put him down very gently on Mum's mattress. I spread a towel under him, just in case, and found the pack of nappies and a box of tissues and some baby cream.

'There!' I said, proud of myself. 'OK, little boy, we'll soon have you clean and dry and happy.'

I unravelled the shawl carefully, as if I was unwrapping a very special present. Sundance kicked his damp legs happily. I caught hold of his dear little feet.

'I think you really are going to be a footballer,' I said. I unpopped his sleeping suit and peeled his little legs free.

'There! That's good, isn't it? Oh, you're so cute,' I crooned. 'Now, we've just got to get your gungy wet nappy off. Hold still a minute, there's a good boy.'

I tugged the plastic ties undone and cautiously pulled the nappy away from his bottom.

Then I stared.

I looked for Sundance's little willy.

He didn't have one.

He wasn't a baby boy.

He was quite unmistakably a little girl.

11

I didn't know what to do. I kept blinking at Sundance's little bare bottom, hoping it would rearrange itself in front of my eyes.

Sundance was a boy. Mum had known right from the start. She'd consulted her star charts, read the tarot, dangled rings above her stomach, gazed into her crystal ball. Jude had scoffed – but then Mum went to the hospital for her scan and they confirmed it. She was definitely having a baby boy.

Mum had bought a pair of little blue booties that very day. She'd stuck them on the ends of her fingers and made them dance up and down her tummy. She'd had a little baby boy. She'd *said* so. She'd called him her little son.

Perhaps the hospital had made a terrible mistake and mixed up the babies. Maybe my little brother Sundance had been whisked away by the wrong mother, leaving this dark little changeling girl by mistake.

'Who are you?' I whispered to the baby.

She didn't know. She kicked her tiny legs, her little feet arching, her toes so weeny, each tipped by the tiniest slither of nail. Her bottom looked very bare indeed as she lay there, flat on her back.

I got her a clean nappy and covered her up with it. I thought about finding her another sleeping suit as the legs were damp, but then Mum would know for sure that I'd undressed her.

I bundled her back into the damp leggings and wrapped the shawl round her. She didn't seem to mind. I looked at the wet nappy, not knowing what to do with it. I couldn't let Mum find it.

I gazed around the crowded room desperately. Rochelle's fancy white dressing table with the little gilt handles was right in front of me. She'd seen it at a car boot sale and nagged Mum rotten until she bought it for her. I opened the top drawer quickly and shoved the sopping nappy inside. Then I picked the baby up and held her against my thudding heart.

I didn't know what to do. I wished Jude hadn't sloped off. I heard Bruce whistling in the kitchen and wondered about telling him, but it seemed too extraordinary, too personal, too strange. I was already starting to wonder if I could possibly have been mistaken. I didn't know much about babies after all. I'd never seen a baby boy naked. Maybe they had very tiny willies at that age and I'd simply not noticed it. I wanted to undress the baby all over again to have another look but I could hear Martine murmuring above my head and I wasn't sure how long they were going to be.

I sat cross-legged on the mattress, holding the baby in my arms. 'Are you my *sister*?'

She looked at me with her strange blue eyes as if she understood, but couldn't tell me one way or the other. Then Mum and Martine came back, Mum a little pinker now and wearing her rose-red silky nightie and black embroidered kimono, trying to look pretty. Her hair was wet and tied back in a ponytail. She usually looked very young when she tied her hair back – schoolgirly, like our sister instead of our mum. But today she looked like an old lady.

She looked at me anxiously. 'Is Sundance asleep?'

'Nearly.'

'I'll feed him in a little while, get him changed, and then we can both have a nap,' said Mum. 'Give him here, Dixie. You two girls run along. Thank you, Martine. I feel a new woman now.'

We settled Mum down on the mattress and then went out into the hall together. Martine was shaking.

'I had to bath her,' she said. 'She's in such a *state*. Her tummy's all saggy and flabby still. I thought they just snapped back into place. And her boobs are all swollen. They look awful. *She* looks awful.'

'No she doesn't,' I said, because it seemed so mean to agree.

Martine was holding her own flat stomach, shaking her head. 'It's so *stupid*. Why does it have to be so messy and painful? Why can't we be like kangaroos and have babies the size of baked beans that just crawl up into a pocket in our stomachs?'

We both thought about it – and shuddered.

'Yuck,' I said.

'Yes, OK, *bad* idea,' said Martine, giggling, though she looked as if she might start crying instead.

I swallowed. 'Martine. Martine, I've got to tell you something,' I said.

'Not now, Dixie. I need to phone Tony.'

'But it's *important*. It's about the baby.'

'Yeah, well, tell me later, Dixie,' said Martine, running up the stairs, dialling as she went.

I was about to trail after her when there was a knock at the door. I went rushing to open it, hoping it was Jude.

It was Rochelle, jumping up and down in her suede heels, sparkling like a real diamond.

'Guess what, guess what, guess what!' she said.

'*You'll* never guess,' I said. 'Rochelle, come here.' I seized her by the arm and marched her past the living room, making *ssh!* gestures.

'Ah. Yes. Better not tell Mum. You won't tell, Dixie, will you?' Rochelle whispered urgently.

'Tell what?'

'I've got a boyfriend!' said Rochelle, and she twirled around, shaking her head wildly so that her long blonde curls flew up in a glorious golden halo.

'You what? Yeah, like you've stared at some boy and he's waved at you,' I said.

'No, really. I've got a date. Tonight. A *real* date, outside McDonald's. We'll maybe go for a drink later.'

'In a *pub*? As if they'd let you in – you're only twelve!'

'I'm nearly thirteen. He thinks I'm a bit older anyway.'

'How old is he?'

'Sixteen,' said Rochelle proudly.

'You're mad! You can't go out with a sixteen-year-old.' I stood still, halfway up the stairs. 'It's not that guy who had the fight with Jude?'

'Not the big fat one! No, the really cool guy with the

scarf and the earring. He likes me, Dixie, he really does. He says I'm much prettier than any of the other girls on the Planet Estate. He thinks that's why Jude made such a fool of herself. He says she must be jealous of me, seeing as I'm the pretty one.'

'Stop showing off!' I said.

'Look, *I* didn't say I was pretty. Ryan did.'

'That's his name?'

'Yes, isn't it great? Ryan and Rochelle. We sound like a couple already. And if you count up the letters in our names and play Love, Like, Hate, Adore, then we both come out Adore – how about that!'

'You can't adore him, you don't even *know* him yet.'

'Well, I'm going to get to know him properly tonight, aren't I?'

'You're not *really* going on a date with him?'

'I am, I am, I am! Has Brucie Weirdo got the washing machine working? I need to wash my best jeans.'

'Mum will go mad if she finds out.'

'Well, she won't find out, will she? Unless you tell her. And you're not going to tell, are you, Dixie?' Rochelle caught hold of me, her hands digging into my shoulders like big bird claws. 'You're not to tell Martine either. You're especially not going to tell Jude. Because if you do I'm going to take that stupid stuffed budgie and tear its head off, OK?'

Rochelle gave me a little shake to show she really meant it. I knew she'd probably tear *my* head off my shoulders too.

She went singing into the living room to find her boxes of clothes. I heard Mum mumbling something crossly, but Rochelle took no notice. She came out nudging a box across the bare floorboards, holding something wrapped in newspaper in one hand. Her arm stuck out stiffly, her face screwed up in disgust.

'Yuck! Dirty nappy alert. What am I going to *do* with it? Here, Dixie.' Rochelle tried to pass it on to me. I put my hands behind my back and dodged, running to Bruce in the kitchen.

If Mum had changed Sundance then she must have *seen* she wasn't a boy. What was she playing at? She was acting like a crazy person.

'You OK, Dixie?' said Bruce. 'Was that Roxanne having a go at you? What was she saying?'

'Oh, nothing much.'

'What is it? Are you *sure* you can't tell your Uncle Bruce. Spit it out, sweetheart.'

I couldn't spit out all the things that were troubling me or he'd be dripping from head to foot. I decided on a minimalist spit.

'Uncle Bruce, what do you do with dirty nappies?' I remembered there was still one hidden in Rochelle's dressing-table drawer. I decided it served her right. 'Shall I throw this down the toilet?'

Bruce stopped tapping pipes and stared at me. 'You must never ever throw them down the toilet, Dixie,' he said firmly. 'I've got enough to do sorting out this house without you blocking up the toilets.'

'So what *do* you do with them?'

'*I* don't know. It's not a problem I'm used to. Ask your sisters.'

'They're all busy,' I said.

Then I heard another knock at the door. 'Jude!' I said joyfully.

I flew to the front door. Then I stopped and stared. Jude had blood all over her face.

'Jude, what's *happened*? Mum! Martine! Uncle Bruce!'

'Shut *up*, Dixie,' said Jude, clapping her hand over my mouth.

'What have you done? You're bleeding!'

'I'm OK. I've just had a little nosebleed, that's all. Quit flapping, I'm fine.' She wiped her nose angrily on the edge of her T-shirt.

'No you're not.' I peered at her furious face. 'It's not just a nosebleed. Did someone hit you?'

'No! I fell over. Stupid of me. Now shut up about it.'

'I won't shut up! You didn't fall over, someone *knocked* you over. Oh Jude, was it that Ryan?'

'Who?'

'The boy Rochelle's nuts about. Oh gosh, I've told! But if he's beaten you up—'

'*No one's* beaten me up. Especially not that idiot with the earring. I could flatten him with one finger.' Jude sniffed contemptuously. Bubbles of blood came out of her nose. I gave a little squeal.

'Are you all right, Dixie?' Bruce called from the kitchen. 'What's the matter?'

'Nothing! You mind your own business,' Jude said fiercely. 'I'm going to wash the blood off.'

'You can't, Rochelle's in the bathroom.'

'Well, she'll have to get *out* of the bathroom because *I* need it,' Jude said thickly.

Bruce came out into the hall. 'Ouch,' he said, looking at Jude. 'Come into the kitchen. We'll put a wet towel on your nose – that'll stop it. Come on, Jade.'

'It's bloody *Jude*,' said Jude.

'Yes, you are bloody, Jude. You're bleeding like a stuck pig and making a mess of your shirt. Come here,' said Bruce. He took hold of her by the wrist and pulled.

I thought she'd sock him straight in his sticky-out teeth. She can't stand anyone pulling her, not even me. She did struggle for a few seconds, but then she gave in and let him steer her into the kitchen. She was shivering now and he patted her gently on the shoulder. He patted me too.

'Cheer up, chickie,' he said to me. 'We'll soon get your sister cleaned up.'

He didn't waste time asking how she'd got a bloody nose. He just fished an old towel out of the kitchen cardboard box, soaked it under the tap and held it firmly against her nose.

'There we are. Put your head back a bit.' He looked down at her right hand. The knuckles were bleeding. 'I think you need something on those knuckles too.'

'Do you think we need to take Jude to hospital, Uncle Bruce?'

'You Diamonds are turning my van into an ambulance service! No, she'll be fine, nothing to fuss about, like she said. We'll have a proper squint at that sore nose once it's stopped bleeding but I don't think she's broken it. I've got a little first aid kit in the van. I'll rustle up some arnica to stop the bruising and a spot of antiseptic for those knuckles. I'm a one-man casualty department.'

He went off to get them while Jude hid her head in the towel.

'Isn't Uncle Bruce magic?' I said.

'Bruce is not our blooming uncle,' Jude mumbled from

underneath the towel. She sounded as if she might be crying, though Jude never cries.

'Does it hurt ever so badly?'

'No, I'm fine, I *said*,' Jude insisted.

When Bruce came back she let him mop up the last of the blood and then gently feel along her nose. He cleaned her hand too. She winced when he rubbed antiseptic into the split knuckles but she didn't complain.

'You're a brave girl,' said Bruce.

'Rubbish,' said Jude. She was still shivering.

'Make us all a cup of tea, Dixie,' said Bruce. 'We'll give Jude lots of sugar for the shock. And me lots of sugar because I'm greedy.'

'I'm not *in* shock,' said Jude.

'You can't help but be in shock when you get beaten up,' said Bruce.

'I *haven't* been beaten up,' said Jude. 'No one ever beats me up. I can look after myself.'

'Yeah?' said Bruce. 'Mmm.'

'Look, all right, these boys had a go at me, but they took me by surprise. I didn't even see them coming. I was going up these steps and they kind of ambushed me. I didn't even know it was happening. They just laid into me. I did hit one of them. He went sprawling.'

'I should say so,' said Bruce, looking at her knuckles.

'I think he just tripped though. But he looked like he'd hurt himself.'

'Never mind him. You're the one that's hurt. A gang of yobs picking on one small girl! I thought I'd made it clear to that thick bunch to lay off all you Diamond girls.'

'We don't need you to fight our battles,' Jude said automatically. She paused. 'But thanks. No, this was a new gang, a different one.'

'Did they just start hitting you for nothing, Jude?'

'Well, they made out I was on their territory. They call themselves the Mercury Top Floor Boys – I mean, how sad is that? I laughed and said they were all plonkers and they couldn't stop me going wherever I wanted . . . only they did.'

'Oh Jude, promise you won't ever go there again!' I begged.

'I'll go where I want. We live on Mercury too,' Jude said defiantly.

'You'd better learn to defend yourself then,' said Bruce.

Jude jerked away from him. 'I can fight! I can take on anyone!'

'Jude's famous for fighting,' I said.

'Yes, I can see you could be handy with your fists, girl, but you need to use your whole body.' Bruce stood up straight in his baggy T-shirt and saggy trackies. 'OK, I know I'm not Mr Big Shot Muscleman, but I know what I'm saying.'

'Which is?'

'When you're in a fight situation and you can't back down—'

'I *never* back down.'

'You don't have to meet force with force. You block it. Go on, try to hit me.'

'I don't think that's a good idea, Uncle Bruce,' I said quickly.

'Give it a go, Jade,' said Bruce.

'*Jude!*' said Jude, swinging a punch at him.

Bruce brought his arm up, hand open, and blocked Jude's punch easily.

'Oh,' said Jude, trying not to look impressed. 'Kung fu! I suppose you watch all those Bruce Lee films. Your namesake, eh?'

'I actually took his name,' Bruce said, blushing. 'The greatest guy with the greatest philosophy on life.'

'Yeah, well, I'm not into all that great-guy stuff, thanks,' said Jude, jumping up.

'I practise Wing Chun kung fu – and Wing Chun was a woman,' said Bruce.

'You're kidding!'

'Truly. And because it's the only system devised by a woman it's especially suited to them. And weedy blokes like me. It depends on technique, not power. You're like a coiled spring.'

'Show me,' said Jude, giggling.

'Well, you can't just pick it up in an afternoon, girl. I've been going to classes for years, and I've read stuff, seen lots of videos. It's a whole way of life. Still, I can show you the basic movements.'

Bruce stood in the middle of the kitchen and demonstrated. He should have looked ridiculous, straddling his little legs and waving his skinny arms around in his *Simpsons* T-shirt, but somehow he looked pretty good. He didn't hitch his glasses up and down or grin nervously, hiding his teeth. His face was pure concentration, totally dignified.

'Wow,' said Jude.

I peered at her anxiously, but she wasn't sending him up, she was serious. She tried to copy what Bruce was doing.

'No, no, no. You start like this,' Bruce said. 'OK, the Horse Stance is the basic position. Stand with your legs together. Let your arms dangle by your side, nice and relaxed. Breathe easily. Well, it's meant to be through the nose but yours is a bit sore and stuffed up right now. Just do your best. Empty your mind. Let go of all your thoughts.'

Jude stood obediently, her feet together, arms dangling. I tried to do it too, but I couldn't empty my mind. My thoughts buzzed back and forth like bees. Sundance lay kicking in the middle of my mind, baring her little girl's bottom.

'I changed Sundance's nappy,' I blurted out.

'Yes, yes, well done, Dixie, but shush now, we're concentrating.'

'Dixie doesn't know how to concentrate,' said Jude.

She was wrong. I was concentrating so fiercely on Sundance I couldn't think about anything else, especially this Horse Stance.

I watched them sliding their heels and standing pointy-kneed. Bruce told Jude to imagine trapping a goat between her knees. She didn't giggle. She did her best to copy him. I saw a big brown billy goat between Bruce's knees; a little white woolly kid goat trapped between Jude's. I could smell their strange goaty stink, hear their indignant bleats. They seemed so real, but I knew they weren't there, I was just imagining them.

I clutched Bluebell, stroking her beak for comfort. She fluttered free, fanning her wings to cool my hot face. No. I was *imagining* her circling my head in a whirl of sky-blue. Maybe I was imagining Sundance's lack of little willy . . .

There was only one way to find out. I left Bruce and Jude in their weird Horse Stances and tiptoed into the living room. Mum was lying on the mattress, her dark hair tousled on the pillow. Her eyes were closed.

Sundance was lying beside her, wrapped in the blue blanket. I crept nearer, holding my breath. I got right up to the mattress. Mum still didn't stir. Sundance was sleeping too. I leaned over, hands outstretched. It would only take two seconds to unpop the little legs of the sleeping suit and open up the nappy. I flexed my fingers, willing them to work nimbly.

I grabbed the blue blanket.

'Leave your little brother alone!'

I nearly fell right on top of Sundance and smothered him. Mum propped herself up on her elbows, glaring at me.

'I told you to leave him be, Dixie!' she hissed.

'I'm sorry, Mum.'

'So you should be! Now push off and leave us in peace.'

'Yes, Mum,' I said.

I started crying as I backed out of the room, bumping into all the furniture.

'Oh for Gawd's sake, stop that,' said Mum. '*I* should be the one who's howling. I'm lying here like a beached whale, still all fat and flabby. I've ended up in a rubbish house at the back of beyond with five kids to care for. What am I going to do, eh? What have *you* got to cry about, Dixie Daydream?'

'Nothing,' I said, sobbing harder.

Sundance snuffled and started crying too.

'There! Now you've woken your little brother and he'll want another flipping feed.'

Mum sighed deeply and started unbuttoning her top. She picked Sundance up, still wrapped in the blanket like a swiss roll. She cradled him, his little downy head against her big white breast.

'Who's my greedy little darling?' Mum whispered. 'That's my boy. My thirsty little lad. You'll be a one for the beer when you're older.' Mum looked at me. 'Off you go then, Dixie. I feel all self-conscious with you staring at me like that. Dry your eyes, darling. There's nothing to cry about. You've got a lovely little brother, the most gorgeous boy in all the world.'

'No he's not,' I sobbed.

Mum frowned at me. 'Yes he is! For God's sake, Dixie, you're ten years old. You're surely not *jealous* of your little brother?'

'But he's not my real brother, Mum.'

'*Now* what are you on about?' Mum was so indignant her breasts bounced and Sundance came unlatched. 'Of course he's your real brother. Like Martine and Jude and Rochelle are your real sisters. Never mind about the dads. I'm your mum. I'm his mum. Simple.'

'I *know*, Mum.'

'You're driving me bonkers, Dixie! You know *what?*' Mum asked, trying to start Sundance feeding again. 'Come on, little darling, more drinkies. Don't let your silly sister put you off. We need to build you up, my lad, you're such a tiny little boy.'

I knelt down beside Mum. 'He's not a little boy, Mum. He's a little girl.'

'You what?' said Mum.

'You heard me, Mum. I know. I've seen him. I mean her. Sundance is a girl.'

'Don't be so stupid!' said Mum. 'Look at him. He's a boy. Of course he's a little boy.'

'I don't know why you're *saying* all this, Mum. Let's look at Sundance then. We'll soon see.'

'Get your hands off him!' Mum shouted. She held Sundance so tight he got frightened, and started crying.

'Are you OK in there? Can I get you anything?' Bruce called outside the door. 'Dixie, come in the kitchen with Jude and me and leave your mum alone.'

'In a minute, Uncle Bruce. I'm *helping* Mum.'

We heard him go back to the kitchen. Mum clutched Sundance, rocking backwards and forwards.

'You're a beautiful boy, aren't you, darling? Stupid stupid Dixie! How could you possibly not be a boy, little Sundance?'

'Take the nappy off, Mum.'

'You leave him be!'

'Look, Mum!' I said, scrabbling at Sundance's legs, trying to get hold of the nappy.

'Stop that! I don't want to look. I won't!' said Mum.

'Don't be mad, Mum. You can't pretend Sundance is a boy!'

'I can!'

'But what are you going to do – hide her bum from everyone for ever? That's just crazy. What about the baby clinic? Are you going to dress her in boys' clothes all the time? What about when she starts nursery? They'll take her to the boys' toilets in her little trousers and then what's she going to do? She won't be able to wee standing up.'

'All right, all right, give it a *rest*, Dixie. I know I can't keep her a boy for ever. I just want a few days, that's all. That's not too much to ask, is it? I wanted a boy so much. Every single symbol and sign showed I was having a boy – it was in all the charts, all the readings. I was so *sure*. I wouldn't ever swap you girls, I love you to bits, but you *know* how much I've always wanted a boy.'

'What about the scan, Mum? You said they told you the baby was a boy.'

'They did, they did. Well. I was sure they would have done. I so needed the baby to be a boy I didn't want them to cast any doubts. They're all such know-alls at these hospitals. That's why I came home just now, as soon as I could nip out without them noticing. I didn't want them telling me what to do, talking about my little girl, my baby daughter. I've *got* my daughters. I want a son!' She cradled Sundance, her hand cupped round her small head.

'She's not a son.'

'Let me pretend for a bit, Dixie. Just for a little while, to make me happy. I can't bear it that I got it all wrong. You're my daydream pretender girl. You know what it's like. Not like the others. Don't tell your sisters!'

'But—'

'You can't tell them, Dixie. They'll think I've gone nuts.'

'*I* think you've gone nuts.'

'Martine's upset enough as it is, going on about her blooming Tony. Jude's even stroppier than usual. Rochelle's acting extra flighty. They can't handle this the way you and I can. Just give me a few days, Dixie. Please. Don't tell on me.'

'All right then, Mum. I won't tell.'

Mum burst into tears. 'Oh darling. Thank you. Thank you so much. You promise, now?'

I found Bruce's hankie and mopped Mum's eyes. 'I promise,' I said. 'But it's just for a little bit. We'll have to tell *quite* soon. But you can pretend for now if it makes you happy.'

'You're such a good girl to me, Dixie,' Mum said, eyes brimming again. She held Sundance up and made the baby's soft cheek brush mine.

'He's giving you a kiss. He loves you so much already,' Mum whispered. 'You're his favourite big sister.'

12

Mum stayed stuck on her mattress with Sundance, as if they were marooned on a desert island. Martine and Jude and Rochelle came visiting but she sent them away, saying she was tired and wanted to rest. She didn't notice Martine had been crying. She didn't notice Jude had a sore nose. She didn't even notice Rochelle was all dressed up in her best (damp) jeans and silver sparkly top.

I was the only one Mum wanted. She let me make her a cup of tea, she let me help her to the loo, she let me fetch Sundance's clean nappies. She even let me stay while she changed her, though she kept her back to me, bending over Sundance, blocking her blatant little-girl bottom from my view.

'I'll give him a little feed now,' said Mum. 'You go off and play for a bit, Dixie. You've been such a good girl.'

I felt too grown up and important to *play*. It was so lovely to feel I was the chosen one, Mum's favourite. Sundance liked me too. I was good with babies. Maybe

I'd be a nursery nurse when I was grown up. No, I'd have my *own* nursery, and all the babies would have little white rocking cots with red and green and yellow and purple blankets so no one would know whether they were boys or girls. They'd have mobiles hanging above each cot, little birds flying round and round, and the babies would reach up with their little fat fists to try to catch them.

I'd feed them and change them and they'd all have a bath together in a special big shallow baby bath and then I'd cuddle them all in a huge white towel and tickle their tummies and play piggies with their tiny toes. I'd be Nurse Dixie and every single baby would love me and stop crying the minute I picked them up.

I thought about Mary. I wanted to stop her crying too. She didn't know how to play properly and have fun. She seemed worried about spoiling that scary baby doll. I thought about my old Barbies. They'd nearly all torn their clothes and they had skinhead haircuts and permanent gel pen tattoos. Maybe Mary could have a good game with them. It wouldn't matter in the slightest if they got spoilt.

I rummaged in my box and seized a handful of them. Rochelle was in the kitchen, trying to brush her red suede shoes.

'Got fed up playing real babies?' she said. 'Now we're back to normal and little braindead Dixie's playing dollies.'

'*I'm* not going to be playing with them,' I said haughtily. 'I thought my friend Mary might like them. I'm going to show *her* how to play.'

'Who do you think you are, Mary blooming Poppins?'

said Rochelle. 'And actually, they're not *your* Barbies, they're mine, and you haven't half ruined them! What's happened to their *hair*? Have you cut it all off?'

'You shut up, or I'll cut *your* hair off,' I said, and then I rushed out the back door quick before she could get me.

I hitched myself up on the wall, the Barbies clutched in one hand like a weird bouquet. Mary wasn't on the swing. The baby doll wasn't there in its buggy. The garden was empty.

I sat on the wall, swinging my legs. I waited. Then I got fed up with waiting. I decided it would be fun to arrange the Barbies in a little circle just inside Mary's gate, with their right arms all raised as if they were waving to her. She'd have a little laugh when she found them.

I jumped over my wall, crossed the alley, carefully opened the stiff latch and crept inside. I squatted down by the gate and propped each Barbie up against it, their hands up. They looked much dirtier in Mary's garden, their haircuts more brutal. I'd tipped all their breasts with red felt pen and now I wished I hadn't. I licked my finger and tried rubbing their chests hard to get it off.

'What are you up to, eh?'

I was so startled I fell backwards on my bottom. I looked up, scarlet in the face. A man was staring down at me. He had huge scary scissors in his hand. I gave a little squeal.

'Hey, hey, it's all right. Don't be frightened!' He saw me looking at the awful scissors and dropped them on the grass. 'It's all right, they're just my pruning shears. My little girl doesn't like them either.'

'You're Mary's dad?' I said.

'You know my Mary?'

I nodded, but I didn't say she was my friend. I didn't want to get her into trouble. But he was smiling at me now. He bent down and helped pull me up. The Barbies trembled and then fainted simultaneously.

'Are these your dollies? Why were you putting them in my garden? What are they, Pretty Maids all in a row?'

'I thought Mary might like to play with them,' I whispered.

'What a nice thought,' he said, though he looked at the Barbies a bit doubtfully.

'Can I see her?'

'Well, I think she's finishing her tea right now,' he said. 'She's a bit of a picky eater, our Mary. She's in trouble with her mum for not eating her crusts. Do you eat your crusts?'

I nodded, though I was fibbing.

He took a deep breath. 'Well, why don't you come in and show Mary a good example, eh?'

I gathered up the swooning Barbies and trotted along beside him, up the green striped lawn to the patio. He paused at their back door.

'Wipe your feet, dear. My wife's a bit particular. Very very houseproud.' He took his own gardening shoes off and walked indoors in his fluffy socks. I followed him on tiptoe.

I couldn't believe their house. Their kitchen looked like it was still in a showroom, brand new and pin-neat, every pan in place and shining like a little sun. The kitchen table was scrubbed clean and totally bare. They didn't eat in there.

They had a special dining room where they had their tea. It was rose-pink with dark gleaming furniture. The dining-room table had a fancy white cloth on it, its scalloped edges stiff with embroidery. It was still set for tea time, with special rosy plates and cups and saucers. There was a big plate containing a few sandwiches, another plate of chocolate biscuits and a third plate with a big iced sponge cake topped with cherries. There were a couple of slices missing, so I could see the thick jam and buttercream. My mouth started watering.

Mary was sitting up very straight, a plate of four crusts in front of her. They were in a square, like a frame without a picture. Mary's mother was standing beside her, arms folded, her mouth in a straight line. They both looked astonished to see me.

'Not you again!' said Mary's mother.

'I invited her in, love,' said Mary's dad. 'She's brought a little present for our Mary, isn't that nice of her?'

Mary's mother looked at my Barbies as if they were cockroaches. 'Yes, very nice, but Mary has her own dolls, dear,' she said. 'She doesn't want yours.'

There was a cabinet of dolls right behind her. They were dressed like old-fashioned little girls in pink and lilac and lemon smocked dresses, with flouncy petticoats and white socks and tiny black patent shoes. They all had pink cheeks and dimples and were smiling widely, showing off their little pearly teeth. Some had glossy ringlets and ribbons, some had short curls and heart-shaped hairslides, some had very neat nylon plaits.

'Are *they* Mary's dolls?' I asked, awed.

'Good heavens, no. They're *my* dolls, my Dimpled

Darlings special collection. They're collector's items,' said Mary's mother.

I couldn't help thinking she'd like to keep Mary in a cabinet too, squeaky clean and dusted, dimples permanently in place. Mary was blinking at me, nibbling her lip.

'I've come to tea!' I said, trying to reassure her.

Mary's mother frowned. 'Not today, dear. Off you run now. And take your dollies with you.'

'I asked her, love,' said Mary's dad. 'I thought it might help our Mary learn to eat up her crusts. Sit yourself down then. What's your name?'

'Dixie.'

'Wait a minute . . . Dixie,' said Mary's mum. She said my name as if it was a rude word. She thrust a glossy magazine on the pink and white striped seat of the dining chair, as if she thought my bottom would sully it. The magazine felt cold and uncomfy and it crackled whenever I moved. I fidgeted from buttock to buttock, not sure whether I should help myself to a sandwich or not. At home you just grabbed, but everything was so different in Mary's house.

Mary's mother offered me the plate, making it like a little ritual. I took two sandwiches, one in each hand, so she wouldn't have to go through the whole rigmarole again. She frowned at me, so I guessed this was a mistake. I ate the sandwiches quickly, taking alternate bites. One was cream cheese and cucumber, the other some sort of fishy stuff with green leafy bits. They weren't very nice.

'Oh, yummy,' I said politely. 'Look, Mary, I'm eating my crusts all up.'

They were quite hard crusts, with a burnt taste. I

could see how they'd stick in your throat and stop you swallowing. I chewed hard but the crusts took ages to turn into mush. My teeth were all gummed up with them. I'd simply spit them out at home but this obviously wasn't an option.

'The crusts are extra yummy, Mary,' I mumbled through my mouthful.

Mary looked at me forlornly. I felt like I was betraying her.

'Don't worry, I never ate crusts when I was your age though,' I said.

'Are you going to eat your crusts now, Mary?' said her dad.

Mary nodded, but when she tried poking a crust into her mouth I saw her shudder and retch. The crust slid out of her mouth, slippery and revolting.

'Dear, dear, Mary,' said her mother. She said it softly, but it sounded like a threat.

'Would you like a slice of cake now, Dixie?' said Mary's dad.

'Oooh yes. Please!' I said. I glanced at Mary. 'Can she have cake now too?'

'Yes, of course she can have some cake. In a minute. When she's eaten up those crusts,' said Mary's mum.

I ate a slice of cake. It was lovely, but I couldn't enjoy it. I wolfed it down to get rid of it, and choked, spraying crumbs everywhere. I felt myself going red again. 'Can I have a drink of water?' I gasped.

I didn't really need it. I thought if Mary's mum went to get it I'd have a chance to grab Mary's crusts off her plate and gobble them up for her. But Mary's dad went to get it. Mary's mum stood over Mary like a jailer.

'You'd better run along now, dear. Perhaps you'd like to take a slice of sponge for your sister?' She smiled graciously.

'Dixie's got three sisters,' Mary whispered.

Four, I thought.

Mary's mother made me up a paper napkin parcel of cake. 'Four slices,' she said.

'It's home-made,' said Mary's father proudly. 'Not many women find time to bake their own cakes nowadays.'

Mary's mother simpered and smoothed her blonde curls. She seemed so pretty and so sweet but she couldn't fool me.

I stood up to go. I swallowed hard. 'Mary's not going to get smacked for not eating her crusts, is she?' I said.

Mary's mother frowned. Her dad looked shocked.

'We don't ever smack our Mary,' he said.

'Whatever gave you that idea?' said Mary's mother.

I looked at Mary helplessly but kept my mouth shut.

Mary's dad ushered me out the dining room, back down the hall, through the spotless kitchen to the back garden.

'Mary can be a bit stubborn at times, I'm told. "Mary Mary, quite contrary," like the nursery rhyme. Oh, you forgot your dollies. I think it's best you take them home, dear.'

I ran back to the dining room where I'd dropped them. Mary and her mum were still at the table. Mary's mum was pinching Mary's nose so that her mouth fell open. She rammed the crusts right down her throat, so hard that Mary's head jerked backwards.

I gasped in terror. Mary's mum straightened up. She smiled at me.

'There!' she said. 'Mary's eaten up all her crusts like a good girl.'

Mary sat still, tears streaming down her face, her cheeks bulging with crusts. I went to run for Mary's dad. He was standing behind me.

'Well done, Mary,' he said.

I didn't know if he'd seen or not. I knew there was no point in telling.

I grabbed my Barbies and then ran back to my own house. I threw the cake under a bush in the garden. I kept shaking my head, trying to pretend it hadn't happened. I didn't know what to do.

I went running to Mum.

'Here's my little helper,' said Mum. 'Are you hungry, sweetheart? Your best pal Bruce has gone off to get us all pizzas.'

'Mum . . .'

'What?'

'Why are some mums so horrid?'

'Do what, love? You mean me?'

'No!'

'Some of those nosy interfering cows back at Bletchworth used to say I wasn't a good mum. One of them even called in the social workers when you were little, thinking I wasn't feeding you proper. Blooming cheek! I didn't half give her an earful.'

Sundance started whimpering in Mum's arms.

'What's up with you, darling? More milky? There's nothing wrong with *your* appetite, is there? You'd feed all the time, wouldn't you, my son? What a little greedy guts! Still, that's boys for you.'

I backed away from Mum. I hated her going on like that. Mums weren't *supposed* to pretend.

'Are you feeling OK, Dixie?' said Bruce, when I only

nibbled at the edge of the giant pizza he'd bought for tea.

'I'm fine,' I lied.

Martine wasn't hungry either. She only ate half a slice of pizza, picking out button mushrooms and slices of tomato and peppers and arranging them on her plate: two mushroom eyes, a blobby pepper nose, a grinning tomato mouth, making a weird baby face. It was the sort of game *I* usually played.

'Stop playing with your food and *eat* the flipping thing,' I said in Mum's voice.

Martine didn't laugh.

Rochelle didn't eat much either, because she was hoping Ryan would treat her at McDonald's.

'You girls are so picky,' said Bruce.

'I'm not,' said Jude. She wolfed slice after slice, scarcely swallowing.

'Well, you've been working hard,' said Bruce.

Jude grinned at him. 'Do you think I'm any good at Wing Chun?'

'You know you are. You're a natural,' said Bruce.

He thrust his clenched fist towards her chest and she immediately blocked it. They both laughed.

'You shouldn't encourage her,' said Martine. 'She'll only get in more fights, and the boys round here are really scary. They probably carry knives.'

'They're not all scary. Some are pretty cool looking,' said Rochelle.

Jude frowned at her. 'You're such a fool, Rochelle. Why are you all tarted up, eh? Where are you going?'

'Just because you like to dress like a scruff doesn't mean we all have to do the same. I felt like putting on my decent clothes, OK?'

'You look a sight. You've got half a vat of make-up smeared all over your face.'

'Take a look in the mirror if you want a *real* fright,' said Rochelle. 'I'm off.'

'You're not going out, Rochelle. Martine, stop her,' said Jude.

Martine wasn't paying attention. She was texting Tony, her finger going stab stab stab at the buttons on her phone. Jude yelled at her. Martine sighed.

'*You* stop her, Jude. I've got other stuff to think about.'

'You're the eldest.'

'I'm not going to be here much longer. Then *you'll* be the eldest. See how *you* like it.' Martine marched off upstairs, still texting.

'OK, I'm in charge now,' said Jude. 'You're not allowed out the house, Rochelle, do you hear me?'

'I hear you. I can hardly *help* hearing you, you're bellowing right in my ear,' said Rochelle. 'But I don't have to do what you say.'

'She's talking sense, Roxanne,' said Bruce. 'You can't go off by yourself. You're not old enough.'

Rochelle stood up, tossing back her golden curls. 'Number one – my name is *Rochelle*. Number two – I'm a teenager, very nearly, and can do what I please. Number three – *you* certainly can't boss me about, Mr Weirdo Guy.' She flounced out of the room.

'I'll tell Mum,' Jude called.

'And I'll tell Mum you've been fighting,' Rochelle yelled.

She slammed right out of the front door, banging it hard. There was a second of silence. Then we heard the baby start wailing.

'*Shall* we tell Mum?' I asked.

'I think so,' said Jude.

'I *know* so,' said Bruce. 'I'll tell her, and then I'd better go after Miss Fancy Pants, though she certainly won't thank me for it.'

He knocked on the living-room door and then tried to go in. Mum was starting to change Sundance. She told Bruce to go away. She used short, sharp words.

Bruce looked very put out when he came back. 'Your mum was very rude to me,' he said.

'She's not herself,' I said quickly.

'I'm only trying to help,' said Bruce. 'Roxanne – Rochelle – whatever – shouldn't be strutting round an estate like this all by herself. Look what happened to Jude, and she's older and got a lot more sense.'

Jude looked pleased at this. 'Let's go after her in your van, Bruce.'

I went with them. We drove up and down Mercury Street. Our end was the worst, with many of the houses boarded up. Some of the houses at the other end had curtains at the windows and neat grass at the front. Several even had flowers and little white picket fences.

'Maybe it's not too bad round here after all,' said Bruce.

Then he drove through the tower-block entrance. We looked up at the stained concrete and rusted railings, up and up and up, to the very top.

'I wonder if you can get out on the roof?' said Jude.

'I've just said you were a girl with common sense,' said Bruce. 'How could you have such a crazy idea?'

'I went up on the roof heaps of times in our old flats,' said Jude. 'It was my territory.'

Some boys went rattling past on skateboards, bashing on the van and making rude signs at us.

'It looks like it's their territory, Jude, like it or lump it. You try going up those stairs again and they'll likely toss you right over the balcony.'

'Wait till I get the hang of this Wing Chun,' Jude muttered. 'I'll go anywhere I want and no one will dare lift a finger.'

'Dream on, girl,' said Bruce. 'There's a limit, even with martial arts. It's fine in the movies – Bruce Lee can take on any number of opponents and *chop-chop-chop-kick* they all go flying. Their weapons hurtle up into the air and circle back and they get sliced to ribbons with their own swords. But it's fantasy, Jude. A little game of Let's Pretend.'

I was playing my own game of Let's Pretend. I played Bruce was our real uncle and he was taking us out for a drive in his van and we were going to Disneyland, a brand-new one conveniently situated down the road and round the corner. We'd hurtle up Space Mountain and whiz round the Indiana Jones ride and all the other stuff the kids at my old school showed off about. I'd maybe get a little bit scared. Uncle Bruce would sit me on his knee and tell me he'd look after me, and I didn't have to worry about anything any more. I didn't have to worry about my new friend Mary, I didn't have to worry about my mum, I didn't have to worry about any of my sisters – not even my brand-new baby sister in her blue boys' outfits.

When we were done with all the rides we'd go and have tea in McDonald's, and Uncle Bruce wouldn't nag me about eating meat; he'd buy me a portion of french fries and I'd share them chip for chip with Bluebell.

I thought of Bluebell without her head. I could see the stuffing, the sad dead body.

I couldn't tell.

But what if something bad really happened to Rochelle?

'I don't think Rochelle's round here,' I said. 'I have a feeling she might just be in McDonald's.'

'You have a *feeling*?' said Jude. 'Oh, Dixie, you're impossible. Why didn't you *say*?'

'You hate telltales.'

'Yeah, but that's only if you tell tales on *me*,' said Jude. 'You must always always always snitch on Rochelle because she's so stupid she'll get up to anything. So why McDonald's? Is she meeting someone there? Dixie, *tell*!'

'She said she'd tear Bluebell's head off if I did,' I said, clutching Bluebell tight in both hands. I could feel her small bird-heart beating under her feathers. She gave tiny cheeps of terror.

'I won't let her, don't worry, Dixie,' said Bruce.

'She *is* meeting someone?'

I wriggled my shoulders. 'Maybe.'

'But she doesn't know anyone here.' Then Jude clapped her hand over her mouth. 'Oh God. Not the guy with the earring, the one I beat up?'

Jude didn't beat up any of them the way I remembered it, but maybe she liked pretending too. I nodded.

'I can't believe she could be such an idiot! And you're an idiot too, Dixie, keeping quiet about it.'

'Hey, hey, that's unfair! It's not Dixie's fault,' said Bruce.

He drove out of the Mercury block, passing Neptune and Mars and Saturn and Venus and Jupiter, all as towering and terrifying. He headed towards the town.

'It's quite a walk. Rochelle was wearing her wibble-wobble heels. Maybe she won't have got there yet,' said

Jude. She reached over and took hold of my hand. 'Sorry, Dix. Of course it's not your fault.'

'Do you think he might hit her, like the boys hit you, Jude?'

'No,' said Jude, though she didn't sound sure.

'Might he do worse things?' I whispered.

'Stop it,' said Bruce. 'You're just frightening yourselves. He's not going to do anything untoward in McDonald's, for goodness' sake.'

'But he could take her off anywhere afterwards,' said Jude. 'Can't we go any quicker?'

'It's not going to help if I get done for speeding,' said Bruce, but he put his foot down on the accelerator.

We drove round the streets in the town centre, Jude staring at one side, me the other, straining to see the familiar golden M.

'There it is!' I cried.

Bruce parked the van on a double yellow line while Jude and I went running inside. There was no sign of Rochelle. I chewed on my fingers, panicking. Jude spotted a sign to the seating upstairs. She went rushing up and up, past the toilets and into the big room above. I went charging after her.

We saw Rochelle sitting in the corner, side by side with Ryan. Their heads were close. They were gazing into each other's eyes. Rochelle had her favourite McFlurry ice cream but her spoon was poised in mid-air. She was obviously so entranced she was forgetting all about eating. Ryan didn't look at all like he wanted to hit her or hurt her. He was gazing at her as if she was a princess with a jewelled crown on top of her long fair hair. Rochelle and Ryan seemed to shine in their own little spotlight, as if the McDonald's yellow arch was giving out its own golden glow.

I stopped still. I felt we should tiptoe away. Jude hesitated too, but then she marched over to them.

'Leave my sister alone!' she yelled, though Ryan wasn't even touching Rochelle.

'Oh God, it's not you again,' said Ryan. 'What your *problem*?'

'Take no notice of her. She's just my crazy sister,' said Rochelle. She spotted me hovering in the background. 'And there's my *other* crazy sister who's going to be very very sorry she's told on me.'

'Come home at once, Rochelle,' Jude shouted, a little too loudly. Everyone upstairs in McDonald's was starting to stare at us.

'We haven't *got* a home any more,' said Rochelle. 'I don't want to go back to that messy dump, thanks very much.'

'You're coming home *now*,' said Jude, tugging at Rochelle's arm.

'Leave her be!' said Ryan.

'Don't take any notice of her. I suppose she just can't help being jealous,' said Rochelle smugly.

'How *dare* you!' said Jude, tugging harder.

Rochelle tried to pull free. Jude hung on grimly. Rochelle's arm got a little bit twisted. She started shrieking loudly.

'Don't you dare try to push me about!' said Jude, letting go of Rochelle. She squared up to Ryan. She did her best to position herself feet apart, knock-kneed, all set to trap her goat. 'So you want a fight, do you? Come on, then!'

'I don't want to fight you. I don't fight girls. Especially not Rochelle's sisters,' said Ryan.

Rochelle fluttered her eyelashes at him adoringly. Jude was left hovering above them, at a loss.

'Just go home, Jude. I'm fine. Ryan's going to see me home. I won't be late. There's no need to get so worked up. You're just making a complete fool of yourself,' said Rochelle.

'Jude, please, let's go back to Uncle Bruce,' I begged.

'Yes, both of you bog off back to creepy Uncle Weirdo,' said Rochelle.

'He's *not* creepy Uncle Weirdo!' I shouted. 'Don't you dare call him that!'

Rochelle dared say worse things.

I flew at her, beating her chest and pulling her long golden hair. Rochelle yelled her head off.

'Oi, that's enough! Out of here!' yelled the McDonald's security guy.

He seized me in one big hand, Jude in the other, and dragged us both across the room and down the stairs.

Bruce came rushing in the entrance, looking anxious. 'What are you doing with these girls? Don't drag them like that!' he said to the McDonald's man.

'You should look after your kids properly. Sisters, are they? Fancy attacking that pretty little girl upstairs!'

'Oh Jude!' said Bruce, shaking his head at her.

'It's the little one who's the real spitfire,' said the McDonald's man. 'Going at it hell for leather!'

'*Dixie?*' said Bruce.

Then he saw a traffic warden coming along the road. 'Uh-oh! Quick, or I'll get a ticket. Are you going to let the girls go now?'

'Well, I don't know about that. I could call the cops.'

'No, wait!' It was Rochelle, running up to us. 'Look,

they're crazy, both of them, and I hate them to bits, but they're my sisters, so you won't actually arrest them, will you?'

'Oh for pity's sake – look, just go home with your dad, all of you.'

'He's not our *dad*!' said Rochelle.

'I'm jolly glad I'm not!' said Bruce. 'Come on, get in the van quick. You too, Rochelle.'

She argued bitterly, not wanting to leave Ryan.

Jude slammed into the van too, still furious. 'Fat lot of use learning Wing Chun defence when stupid guys won't try to hit you,' she muttered.

'Just as well he didn't take a swing at you. You're a natural, picking things up a treat, but you've got to train for months and months, girl, I told you that. Maybe we can find a proper club round here. Perhaps you'd better join too, Dixie! Were you *really* fighting?'

'I only fought a little bit,' I said. 'You know you said you were glad you're not our dad? Well, what about being our uncle?'

'I'll always want to be your uncle, Dixie, even if you get into more fights than Lennox Lewis,' said Bruce, chuckling. 'Just don't take a swing at me, that's all I ask.'

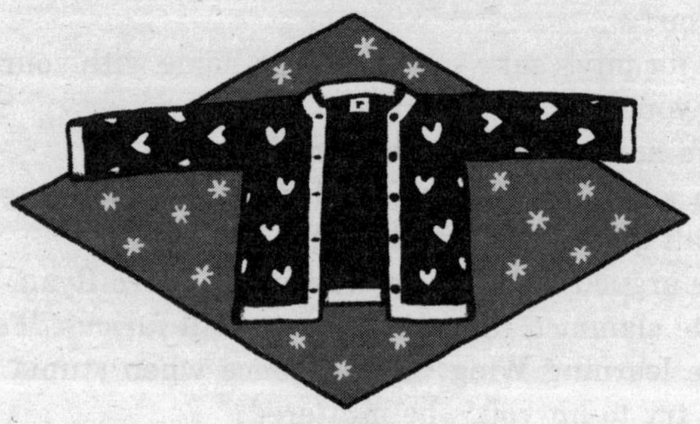

13

When we got back to Mercury Street I shut my eyes tight. I wished so hard I thought my head would burst. I wished that all the houses were whole and neat and newly painted with flowery gardens. I wished our house was the brightest and the best, with fairy lights hanging in the windows, roses rambling round our door, and a fountain in the front garden with a little marble mermaid spouting water into a turquoise pool.

I wished our house was beautiful inside, with satin curtains and velvet sofas and Persian rugs. I wished we'd find Mum dancing around in her slinky skirt and stilettos, all bouncy and bubbly, the way she used to be. I wished we'd find Sundance kicking his little legs on his blue changing mat, nappy off to show his little willy. I wished that my dad was there on a visit. He had a brand-new beautiful cardigan for me, a black one that wouldn't show the dirt, embroidered all over with little red hearts to prove how much he loved me. He'd put it on me and hug me and promise he was going to come and see me every single day for the rest of my life.

I wished Bluebell was real and flying freely round and round the garden. I wished Mary could come and play in our garden too, and run around roaring with laughter, her hair tumbling over her shoulders, free of those tight little plaits. I thought of that little blue vein throbbing in her forehead. I knew I should do something.

'Are you asleep, Dixie?' Bruce asked, patting me on the shoulder. 'Come on, lovey, out the van. We're home.'

'Do you believe wishes can ever come true, Uncle Bruce?'

'I'd give anything to make your wishes come true, little 'un, but I'm not magic.'

However, Bruce had worked quite a lot of magic in the house already. It smelled clean and fresh with all his lovely white lilies and roses and freesias. Mum had stuck them here and there in the living room, but she'd not given any further thought to getting it straight. She was lying back on the mattress with Sundance, furniture and cardboard boxes still crammed tightly in a ring around her.

Rochelle and Jude came crowding in, both of them complaining at the tops of their voices. Mum shut her eyes as if she was wishing too.

'*Mum!* Aren't you even listening? Jude just *totally* embarrassed me. She behaved like an idiot with Ryan, and then Dixie started *attacking* me.'

'This Ryan is years older than Rochelle. She thinks she's absolutely it because she's got a boyfriend. She doesn't have a clue. She'll end up a teenage mum if she's not careful. Tell her, Mum.'

457

'Shut up, Jude,' said Martine, coming into the room too. 'What have you done to your nose? Have you been fighting again? Mum, look at her!'

'Mum, should you tell on someone even if they beg you not to and say they'd get into trouble?' I asked.

'You should never ever tell. And you're in big big trouble, you and your stupid bird,' said Rochelle, snatching up my sleeve.

'Mum! She's got Bluebell!'

'I'll get her back,' Jude yelled, making a grab at Rochelle.

'Stop shouting, you two, you'll wake the baby. Here, Mum, you need to lie down properly. I'll mind the baby for you,' said Martine.

'No!' Mum opened her eyes, blinking in the sudden brightness. 'You leave him be. He's fine with me. Look, will you all please push off. You're doing my head in, all of you. I just want to be left in peace.'

'Don't worry, Sue, I'll get them sorted,' said Bruce.

'*I'll* sort them. I'm the oldest,' said Martine. 'I don't know what's up with you, Mum. You went on and on at me to come to this dump because you said you couldn't manage without me and yet now you won't let me do a blessed thing for the baby.'

'You can get some of this furniture shifted and try to make the place halfway decent. I can't stand lying with all this rubbish all around me,' said Mum.

'I'm not lifting all that stuff. It's much too heavy. I'll hurt myself,' said Martine.

'Ooh, precious,' Jude mocked. '*I'll* move it, Mum.'

'Who do you think you are, Jude? Ms Supergirl? You think you're it, don't you, charging round everywhere, throwing your weight about. You might have been looked up to back at Bletchworth but everyone just laughs at you here,' said Rochelle.

'Shut up, Rochelle,' I said, grabbing Bluebell back. 'Take no notice, Jude. I'll help with the furniture.'

'You're not shifting anything, Dixie, you're far too small. You'll be the one who'll hurt herself,' Bruce said from the doorway. 'Come on, girls, stop plaguing your mum. She's still not well. Maybe we can try a bit of teamwork and get the furniture shifted all together.'

'Can I be on your team, Uncle Bruce?' I begged.

'I'm going to be the boss, little 'un, getting you all organized. It's about time too. You girls all need taking in hand.'

'Excuse me?' said Mum. 'You're the boss of *my* daughters? They need taking in hand, do they? And whose hand would that be, eh? *Yours?* What a badword cheek!' She struggled up off the mattress and went striding over to him, hands on her hips, her big bosoms bouncing.

'Now look, Sue, I didn't mean anything,' Bruce said nervously. 'It was just a figure of speech. I just meant we needed to sort it out, moving the furniture, seeing as I daren't do anything daft with my back.'

'You and your bogging back,' said Mum. 'I reckon you just say that as an excuse because you're bone idle, like all men. You're fit enough to play silly beggars with my girls, teaching them this daft kung fu fiddlesticks. As if they need any encouragement fighting! You want to teach our Jude how *not* to fight, you daft pillock.'

Bruce rocked backwards on his feet, blinking behind his glasses.

'Don't get upset, Uncle Bruce. Mum doesn't really mean it, she's just in a strop,' I said, taking his hand.

'I am not in a strop, you lippy little madam!' Mum shouted. 'Stop snuggling up to him, Dixie. He's not your uncle, he's practically a stranger.'

Bruce let go my hand. 'I *was* a stranger – and I'd have been very happy to keep it that way too. I was just helping out with the van at first, that was the deal. For a bit of spare cash, although the only cash that's been spent so far has been my own. But I kind of got sucked into all this kerfuffle and so I tried to do the decent thing and help you and your girls. *I* didn't start the uncle thing, it was all little Dixie's idea. I was tickled pink as she's a great little kid. Still, I can see it's upsetting you, so we'll stop it now. Blow my bad back, I'll do my best to get your furniture upstairs and then I'll be off. For good.'

'No!' I wailed, clinging to him.

'Stop that nonsense, Dixie, you're showing me up,' Mum snapped. 'You're just being silly now.'

I looked Mum straight in the eyes. 'You're being silly too, Mum,' I said. I looked over at little Sundance abandoned on the mattress.

Mum looked too. She suddenly shut up. 'My baby,' she whispered, and went back to the mattress. She cradled Sundance, kissing the tufty hair.

Martine and Jude and Rochelle shook their heads in disbelief. Mum was usually incapable of shutting up when she went off on one of her rants. She always yelled herself hoarse and then she'd burst into noisy tears and give us all a hug and say she was a bad-tempered old bag and the worst mum in the world and we'd all be better off in care. Then we'd hug her back and tell her she was the *best* mum in the world and we didn't want to live with anyone else but her even if she *was* a bad-tempered old bag.

'Please please please don't go, Uncle Bruce,' I said.

'I *have* to go back home, Dixie. I've got to be up at crack of dawn to get to the flower market. But don't worry, dear, I'll keep in touch, if it's OK with your mum.'

'And you'll still be my uncle?' I asked.

Bruce glanced at Mum. She was rocking the baby, not bothering with either of us any more.

'If you want,' he whispered.

'I don't want you to be my soppy old uncle, but I need you to be my Wing Chun instructor,' said Jude.

'You're on,' said Bruce. 'Come on then, let's get some of this blessed furniture upstairs. It looks like it's just you and me doing the heaving and hauling.'

'I *would* help, but I can't,' said Martine. Her hands were cupped over her tummy.

'You got a stomach ache then?' said Jude.

'Yeah,' Martine said quickly.

'Yeah, me too,' said Rochelle.

'Rubbish!' I said.

'Fat lot you know about it, Dixie,' said Rochelle.

'Well OK, I'll help,' I said. 'I can, I can, I'm much stronger than I look, Uncle Bruce.' I took off my cardie and flexed my arms to show him.

'You've got muscles like little peanuts, sweetheart,' said Bruce. He rolled his own sleeves up in a businesslike fashion. He couldn't help flexing his own muscles proudly. It looked like he had an orange inside each skinny arm.

'Wow, Mr Body Builder!' said Jude. 'That's not from Wing Chun, is it?'

'I did use to go down the gym a lot too,' said Bruce.

'Get you, Freda Flowershop,' said Rochelle. 'Hey, Martine, can I borrow your mobile a sec? I want to text someone.'

'Not that creep in McDonald's!' said Jude.

'No, you can't have my mobile, *I* need it,' said Martine. 'What creep?'

'Get out of the way, all of you,' said Jude. 'Why *can't* you help, Martine? I know it's not your time of the month, so don't use that as an excuse.'

'Will you just shut up, Jude! I've got a stomach bug, if you must know. I feel sick.'

'Rubbish!' said Jude.

'It's not rubbish, Jude, I heard her being sick this morning,' I said. I was trying to be helpful but Martine looked horrified.

'Shut *up*, Dixie. Can't you ever keep your mouth shut?' she hissed.

'Yeah, she's the biggest telltale-tit ever,' said Rochelle.

'I *can* keep secrets! I can keep the most *amazing* secrets, so you two just shut up yourselves. Just you wait till you find out *my* secret!'

'Dixie!' Mum was shouting from the living room. 'Come in here! I need you. *Now!*'

'I'll help you, Mum,' said Martine, pushing me out the way.

'No, Martine, I want Dixie.'

'Oh, all right, then, suit yourself,' said Martine huffily, flouncing off.

'*Please* lend us your mobile, Martine,' said Rochelle,

running after her. 'Hey, Jude, do my stuff first, eh? I want to get my room sorted. But be careful, don't bash it all about. Watch my dressing table, won't you?'

'You watch it or we'll bash you all about, Roxanne,' said Bruce. 'Don't go giving us your orders. We're not the removal men. We're doing this as a favour, aren't we, Jude?'

'Spot on, Bruce,' said Jude.

She dragged Rochelle's bed out of Mum's room, tipping it on its side. She looked as if she'd like to tip Rochelle right over too.

'Dixie!' Mum said urgently. 'Come in here. Come nearer!'

I squatted beside her on the mattress.

'Now look, stop hinting stuff! Your sisters aren't idiots even though they act like it most of the time. You and me have a pact, kiddo. You swore you wouldn't breathe a word.'

'Only for a few days, Mum.'

'A few weeks?'

'That's not going to work, Mum. Imagine pushing Sundance down the shops in a buggy and people stopping you and doing all that coo-coo ga-ga Is-it-a-boy-or-a-girl? stuff. You can't say he's a little boy and then a few weeks later start putting her in a little pink dress.'

'I won't speak to anyone. They're a load of nutters and no-hopers round here anyway.' Mum paused. 'Maybe that's me. Ms Nutter No-Hope, who can't provide for her kids or find one single decent guy to be their dad. I knew we couldn't stay in Bletchworth for all sorts of reasons but why did I ever think this dump was the answer? I've just landed us in a worse mess. I got it all wrong – all the charts, the cards, the crystal ball. I got my baby wrong wrong wrong. I so wanted a boy, Dixie. I need my little baby boy. Don't take him away from me, please, darling. Let me keep him for a bit longer.'

Mum started crying. Sundance started wailing too, threshing sadly in her blue blanket. She smelled as if her nappy needed changing, but Jude and Bruce would be in and out all the time, shifting the furniture upstairs.

'Let me take Sundance upstairs to the bathroom and I'll change her— *him*,' I said. 'Don't cry, Mum. I won't breathe another word about our secret, I promise. Sundance can stay a boy for a bit if it'll really make you happy.'

I picked Sundance up and carried her carefully out of the room. Jude and Bruce were halfway up the stairs with Rochelle's bed. Bruce was sweating, his glasses misting up.

'You be careful, Uncle Bruce,' I said anxiously.

'I'll be OK – if I take it – slowly,' he panted.

Jude hauled, Bruce pushed, and they got the bed to the top of the stairs.

'I want it under the window,' said Rochelle. 'No, hang on, maybe it would be better against the wall.'

'*You* shove it wherever you want it, Lady Muck,' said Jude. 'Come on, Bruce, mate. Are you all right?'

'Sure,' said Bruce, though he was leaning against the wall, trying to catch his breath.

'Leave Rochelle's stuff. You go and have a sit down, Uncle Bruce. You look done in,' I said.

He just chuckled at me and walked stiffly downstairs.

I took Sundance into the bathroom and gingerly unpeeled her. She wasn't just wet. It was far worse than I'd imagined. I didn't know what to do.

'Please hurry up and get toilet trained,' I said to my little sister, rolling my cardie sleeves right up.

I tore off a wad of loo roll, seized her by the ankles and started dabbing at her. I dabbed and dabbed and dabbed. I wondered if it would be better to give her a bath. I didn't know *how* you bathed a baby. She was so little. I was scared I might drop her if she was all slippery with soap. Her head was too wobbly and she wriggled too much.

I managed the best I could, and then squidged the dirty nappy into a plastic carrier bag.

'There now, little Sundance. All clean and dry. Try to stay that way, eh? You're a lovely little baby but I wish you didn't have a bottom.'

It would be so easy if Sundance was like a little doll with smooth plastic instead of rude bits. Then she'd never need to be changed and no one would ever find out she was a little girl. Mum could play she was her special boy and no one would know any different. If no one had bottoms we could choose which sex we wanted to be all the time we were growing up. I could have been a boy, then I could always be Mum's favourite. Jude would be a boy too, even though she didn't seem to like them. Rochelle *loved* boys but I couldn't imagine her as anything else but the girliest girl. Martine was very girly too, even when she dressed up in Tony's big T-shirts or his black leather jacket.

I heard Jude and Bruce struggling back up the stairs.

I picked Sundance up and took her to watch from the landing. They were hauling Rochelle's unwieldy dressing table, both of them cursing as the drawers rattled and slid about.

'We should have taken the drawers out first,' Bruce gasped. 'I'm not thinking straight. Here, if we prop it against the wall can you balance it for a moment? Then I can edge up beside you and deal with the drawers.'

'What's she got *in* here? Something stinks!' said Jude.

As if in answer, the bottom drawer shot out. Sundance's first dirty nappy flew threw the air. It landed on poor Bruce's head.

He dodged sideways, shaking his head, still trying to hang onto the dressing table. Then he yelled. It was a horrible, high-pitched scream.

'Uncle Bruce!' I went hurtling down the stairs, clutching Sundance to my chest.

'Here, Bruce, I've got the poxy dressing table safe,' said Jude, heaving it away from him.

Bruce crouched on the stairs, back bent over.

'Uncle Bruce, are you all right?' I called.

'You can straighten up now, Bruce,' said Jude.

Bruce wasn't all right. He couldn't straighten up.

'I've done my back in,' he groaned.

'Was that my dressing table? Watch it, Jude, don't budge it against the wall like that, it'll get scratched,' Rochelle shouted.

She shut up when she got to the stairs and saw Bruce.

'Did someone fall?' Martine called, coming to check.

'Oh my God! Sundance? Dixie, have you dropped him?' Mum yelled. She came rushing out into the hall, her long black hair flying. Her big bosoms were nearly flopping right out of her nightie as she ran.

'Sundance is fine, Mum. I've got him. It's Uncle Bruce. He's hurt himself – and it's all my fault!' I said, starting to cry.

'Not – your fault – Dixie,' Bruce mumbled, still bent double.

'It was, it was! I stuffed the nappy in Rochelle's dressing table.'

'You did *what*?' said Rochelle. 'How *could* you, Dixie! How totally disgustingly mean of you!'

'Shut up, Rochelle, and help me get your bogging dressing table upstairs before I drop it,' said Jude.

'Are you all right, Bruce, mate?' said Mum. 'Maybe you'd better take it easy now.'

Bruce tried to shake his head totally free of the horrible nappy. He screamed again. 'Don't think – I've got – much choice,' he gasped. 'Can't move!'

'What? Of course you can move,' said Mum. 'Here, we'll get you up again. Martine, squeeze past Jude and Rochelle and help haul him up.'

'I can't *haul*,' said Martine.

'I will, I will! Take my hand, Uncle Bruce.' I flipped the last bit of nappy from his hair and held both his hands. 'Try now.'

'OK, little 'un. Give me a second – to get my breath. Then we'll see – if you can get – silly old uncle – back on his feet.'

I waited. We all waited. Bruce strained until the sweat stood out on his forehead but he couldn't stand up. He could barely move.

Jude and Martine sat on the steps above him. Mum

and I paced below him in the hall. Rochelle clattered about upstairs, dragging her furniture around in her room.

'Can't you come and help me, Jude? I've decided to have my bed over here.'

'Bog off, Rochelle. If you'd only lent a hand getting your stuff upstairs poor Bruce wouldn't be crippled up right this minute,' said Jude.

'Don't say crippled, it sounds too bloody permanent,' Mum said. She walked over to Bruce. 'What are we going to do with you, mate? Are you going to stay stuck here on the stairs for ever like a blooming carpet?'

'It's not – by choice,' Bruce mumbled.

'Come on then, stir yourself,' said Mum. 'Help me pull him, girls.'

'Don't, Mum, you'll hurt him.'

'Dixie, he can't stay here for ever. Right, Bruce, get a grip.'

We shoved, Bruce screamed. We hauled, Bruce hollered. We couldn't get him upright, but we did get him halfway there, his bottom in the air. Very very slowly, he managed to clamber down like a toddler. When he got to the hallway at long last he stayed in a crouch.

'Straighten up,' said Mum.

'I would if I could. I can't!' said Bruce.

'Oh Gawd, what are we going to do with you *now*?' said Mum.

'Should we get a doctor?' I said.

'We don't want any doctors snooping round here,' Mum said quickly. 'Anyway, we haven't *got* a doctor. I doubt anyone decent would dare come out to the Planet Estate. All the druggies would be after them.'

'I don't – need doctor,' said Bruce, teeth gritted. 'They can't – do anything. Just need – to rest – flat on back – till it's better.'

'How, long will that take then?' said Mum. 'A couple of hours?'

'A couple – of days – sometimes longer,' Bruce gasped.

'Oh! Well, looks like we've got an overnight guest, girls,' said Mum.

'No! No, I can't! Got to get home – sort the shop. If I can – make it to my van.'

Bruce tried his best but he couldn't even hobble as far as the front door. He jarred his back so badly that tears started trickling down his cheeks.

'Oh, *poor* Uncle Bruce. Look, you need to lie down *now*,' I said, steering him into the living room.

'Not in there, Dixie! That's my room now,' said Mum.

'It's the *only* room,' said Jude. 'He'll *have* to go in there, Mum.'

We pulled and prodded him in and out the furniture and then very gently pushed him down onto the big mattress.

'No! No, that's *my* mattress!' Mum protested. 'You can't settle down there! Get off it, Bruce.'

But Bruce was on it now, lying flat on his back like a dead man, trying not to move a muscle.

'Oh, thanks very much, mate!' said Mum.

'I did warn you – about my back,' Bruce whispered.

'OK, OK. I'm sorry,' said Mum. 'Well, as you've commandeered my mattress I suppose my boy and I will have to relocate upstairs.'

Mum summoned Jude and Martine and Rochelle and told them to take her stuff up to the bedroom.

'Look, Mum, I've done my fair share of lifting. *My* back hurts too,' said Jude.

'I told you, Mum, I can't lift things, I truly can't,' said Martine.

'I'm going out anyway,' said Rochelle.

'Oh no you're not,' said Mum. 'Well, thanks a bunch, girls. You're a dead helpful lot. Well, to hell with you. I need a bed if Bruce here is going to be stuck on mine. Rochelle's is upstairs already so I'll take that.'

'You can't, Mum! Where will *I* sleep?'

'You'll have to share with Martine.'

'That's not fair, Mum. I can't squash up with her. Let Dixie share, she's the littlest. Look, please please please let me go out, just for a bit. I want to see Ryan and explain that my sisters are idiots.'

'You're the idiot, having anything to do with that creep,' said Jude.

There was a big argument between Mum and Rochelle and Jude and Martine. I went and sat next to Bruce on the mattress, Sundance in my arms. Bruce had his eyes shut.

'Have you gone to sleep, Uncle Bruce?' I whispered.

'Chance would be a fine thing, with my back giving me merry hell and all that argy-bargy going on in the hall. Do they go on like this all the time, Dixie?'

'Yep.'

'It's driving me bonkers. Doesn't it get on your nerves?'

'I pretend stuff, like I have my own planet and Bluebell and I live there all by ourselves. You can come visiting on Planet Dixie if you like.'

'That's very nice of you,' said Bruce. He tried to look up at me and whimpered in pain.

Sundance was whimpering too, her little feet tangled up in her shawl.

'Here, darling, let's set you free,' I said, unwrapping her. I tickled her tummy and she waved her arms and legs around in her little blue sleeping suit. 'Hey, look, Sundance can whiz off to Planet Dixie too – she's already wearing a little baby spacesuit.'

'She?' said Bruce.

'I mean he,' I said, blushing.

'I'm like a blooming great baby now,' said Bruce, sighing.

I did wonder what on earth he was going to do about going to the loo. I thought hard about milk bottles and vases, though I knew Bruce would find this horribly embarrassing.

He solved the problem by rolling off the mattress and creeping, doubled over, to the downstairs toilet. He couldn't manage to straighten up at all, and he couldn't bear to sit either. He had to eat lying flat on his back, taking very tiny mouthfuls so he wouldn't choke. I tucked tissues all round his neck and found him a straw when he tried to drink his tea.

'You're a grand little nurse, Dixie,' said Bruce.

'Yeah, I'm good at it, aren't I!' I said, pleased with myself.

I was still number one nursemaid to Sundance. Mum got settled into Rochelle's bed upstairs but Sundance didn't seem to like the change of scenery and yelled.

'I'll see if I can calm him down,' I said grandly, going upstairs. 'Shall I take him, Mum?'

'Yes, love, walk him round for a bit, see if he'll nod off then.'

Jude and Rochelle and Martine were all watching.

'It's not fair, Mum – why do you keep choosing *Dixie*?' said Rochelle. 'He's my brother too. I want a go at holding him.'

'You're not taking one step with Sundance, not in those silly heels,' said Mum.

'*I'll* hold him for a bit,' said Jude, surprisingly. 'Look, I've got trainers on, so I'm not going to trip.'

'No way, Jude,' said Mum. 'You were always a shocker with your toys. You tugged your teddy's ears off and scalped your poor Barbie.'

'It was *my* Barbie,' said Rochelle.

'Whatever. We'll let the baby get a bit bigger before you tote him around. I want him to stay all in one piece.'

'Look, *I'm* the one who's only here because I'm supposed to be looking after the blooming baby,' said Martine bitterly.

'I need you to look after *me*, darling,' said Mum. 'How about making me another cup of tea, eh? And you'd better get the other beds upstairs somehow. Or at least the mattresses. You girls can't sleep downstairs with old Brucie Bad Back.' She sighed. 'Pity he's turned out such a liability.'

'That's not fair, Mum,' I said, walking Sundance up and down. She was settling already, her little warm head lolling in the crook of my neck. I patted her proudly. 'You *knew* Uncle Bruce had a bad back and yet you still made him shift the stuff.'

'Oh put another record on, Dixie. OK, maybe I'm not being fair to him. Who says we've got to be fair? *Life* isn't fair.' She sighed, then slipped right down under the duvet, pulling it over her head.

'But Mum—'

'Mum!'

'Mum?'

'*Mum!*'

'Will you all just go *away*. I'm sick of the lot of you. I just want to be left in peace. So push off!'

14

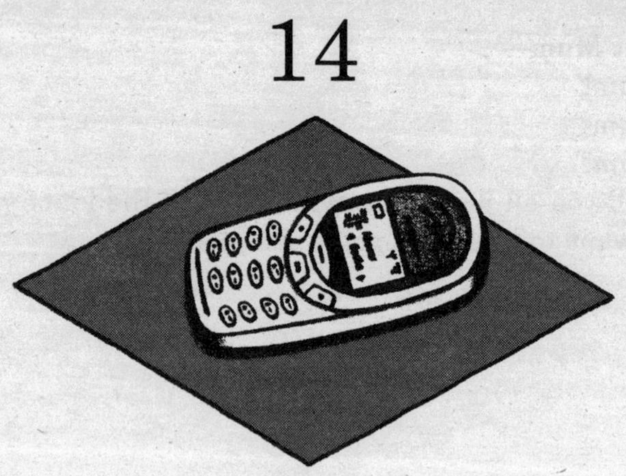

I ended up having to share a bed with Jude. It was fun at first, but I kept cuddling up too close and Jude pushed me away.

'You're like one of those little toy monkeys, Dixie. It's like you've got sticker pads on your palms and you just want to cling. I feel like I'm suffocating.'

'Bluebell will peck you if you're mean to me,' I said.

'Then I'll throw her out the bed,' said Jude, turning over and taking most of the duvet with her.

It was just as well I'm a clingy girl. I had to cling on grimly to the edge of the bed or I'd have tipped off onto the floor.

I woke up when dawn was breaking. I hate the dark because you can't see what might be creeping up on you, but it's magical when everything starts to turn silvery, as if it's been sprinkled with fairy dust. You couldn't see the bare walls and the ugly floorboards properly. Our rickety bed and the cardboard boxes could be mistaken for ornate painted chests and the finest fairytale four-poster.

I lay quietly making it up inside my head until I heard Sundance start crying. She was like a little car engine. She coughed and spluttered, stopped, started again, and then suddenly revved up into full-throttle roar.

I slid out of bed and went to find her. She was lying beside Mum, wailing away. Mum groaned, burrowing down under the duvet.

'Mum? Mum, Sundance is hungry.'

'I'm getting too old for this lark,' Mum moaned. 'I'm going to put him on a bottle soon, then you can feed him for me, Miss Earlybird.'

'I'll feed him now if you like,' I said, stuffing Mum's pillow up my nightie to make a really big chest.

'Oh Dixie, what are you like?' said Mum, grabbing the pillow back and putting it behind her head. 'Here, give me little guzzleguts.'

She took Sundance in her arms and started feeding her. I giggled at the slurping sound in the quiet house.

'She *is* a guzzleguts, isn't she, Mum?'

'*He*,' said Mum. 'Your little brother Sundance.'

'But Mum—'

'Not now, Dixie. Don't make me go all tense or we'll give Sundance hiccups. You go downstairs and make me a cup of tea, eh?'

I crept down the bare stairs, imagining rich red carpet and gilt banisters. I breathed in deeply downstairs. Bruce's lilies made everywhere smell like a beautiful garden. I felt my head and found my freesia still tangled up in my hair. I imagined Bruce coming every day and giving us all garlands of roses and carnation crowns and us stringing lilies across each room like great white paperchains.

I went to the living-room door and knocked politely. 'Uncle Bruce? Uncle Bruce, are you in there?' I whispered.

'I'm in here all right, Dixie,' he mumbled. 'Looks like I'm stuck here for the foreseeable future. My back's giving me bloody hell.'

'That's so great! I mean, I'm sorry your back's hurting, but I'm so glad you can stay. Would you like a cup of tea?'

'Yes please, little angel.'

I made two cups. I crept into the living room with Bruce's. He didn't have his glasses on. He looked a bit lost without them so I found them next to the mattress and gently edged them back onto his head. He gave his little nose a twitch and they settled into place.

He grunted whenever he lifted his head for a sip of tea. When he'd finished half the cup he lay right back and sighed deeply.

'Is it very painful, Uncle Bruce?'

'I'll live,' he said. 'Just about. Now, you'd better leave me be for a bit because I shall have to go to the toilet soon and I haven't got any trousers on. Oh Gawd, what am I going to do, stuck without pyjamas and toothbrush and shaving kit and underpants—'

'You've managed without pyjamas, you can borrow my toothbrush, Mum and Martine have both got razors – but I don't think we can help you with underpants!'

I went upstairs to give Mum her tea. She'd finished feeding Sundance and changed her too. We'd got a system going with plastic bags for used nappies now.

'I suppose I'd better get myself washed up now,' said Mum, yawning. 'I'll grab the bathroom first before all you girls go barging in and use up all the hot water.'

But before she could swing her legs out of bed someone stumbled across the landing and into the bathroom. We heard her being sick, though she was running the bath taps to mask the noise.

'Oh God,' said Mum. 'That's Martine.'

'She's got this stomach bug thing, remember? She was sick yesterday too.'

'I think I know why she's being sick. It's got damn all to do with stomach bugs!' said Mum.

'Are you cross, Mum?'

'Yes, I'm blooming mad at her, Dixie. I told her and told her to be careful. Why wouldn't she *listen*?' Mum thumped her pillow. Sundance wailed, startled.

'You quieten him, Dixie. I've got a few words to say to Martine.' Mum went storming into the bathroom.

I head Martine gasp as the door banged. Mum started shouting. Martine shouted back. It sounded like the start of an all-out Diamond big barney. Jude and Rochelle groaned sleepily.

'Dixie? Are you all right?' Bruce called from downstairs. 'What's all the shouting?'

I went down. He was crouched in the hall, duvet wrapped round him for modesty so he looked like a giant caterpillar.

'What's going on?' he groaned.

'Mum's mad at Martine.' I paused. I wasn't *that* thick. 'I think she's going to have a baby.'

Bruce blinked. 'But she's only just this minute had one!'

'Not *Mum*! Martine.'

'She's just a kid!' Bruce looked truly shocked. 'She's still at school! What a terrible waste. Fancy mucking up her life before she's even got started.'

'I'm not mucking up my life!' Martine shouted, banging out the bathroom. She stood at the top of the stairs, thin and shivering in her skimpy nightie, her hair sticking up all over the place. She didn't look like my bossy big sister Martine without her fancy hairdo and her make-up and her tight jeans and pointy boots. She looked younger than Jude, younger than Rochelle, almost as young as me.

'How dare you say I'm mucking up my life! You don't know anything about Tony and me. We're in love. I bet you've never been in love in your whole life. You're such a sad-looking old git no one would ever want you anyway. You're pathetic. You've got so little going for you in your own life you latch onto us like a leech, sucking up to my stupid little sister.'

'You shut up, Martine Diamond, or I'll smack you right in the gob!' I yelled, charging up the stairs. 'It was *me* latched onto Uncle Bruce. And *I'm* not stupid. You're the stupid one, getting pregnant.'

'Martine's going to have a *baby*?' said Rochelle, rushing out onto the landing.

'Oh, this is great! That's you and your big mouth, Mum. Now the whole family knows my business!' Martine said furiously.

'It's *my* business now,' said Mum. 'I'm the poor Joe Soap who's going to have to look after you *and* your baby, even though it's hard enough managing my own kids.'

'That's a big laugh,' said Martine. 'You can't manage yourself, let alone us. Look at us, stuck in this hideous house on the worst estate in England. The girls are running wild. Jude's getting into fights, Rochelle's going round with hoodies, Dixie's filthy dirty and running about barefoot. Oh yeah, well done, Mum. You really know how to bring up a family.'

'Give it a rest, Martine,' said Jude, coming to join us. She went to Mum and put her arm round her. 'Take no notice. She doesn't mean it, she's just upset.'

'I mean every word of it. It's true, and we all know it,' said Martine. 'How dare you lecture me, Mum. Look at you and all the guys in your life. Oh, pardon me – all the guys *no longer* in your life, like all our dads.'

'Shut your mouth, Martine,' said Jude.

'How can she see *my* dad when he's dead?' said Rochelle.

'She still sees *my* dad. Sometimes,' I said.

'What about the baby's dad? You can't fool me with that artist fairy tale. What was he, a one-night stand? I bet you don't even know his name! No wonder everyone calls you a slag back at Bletchworth,' said Martine.

We all gasped. It was the word we never said, not even to each other. We all looked at Mum. We expected her to fly at Martine. But she just stood there, looking stunned. Tears started falling down her cheeks.

Martine put her hand over her mouth, as if she wished she hadn't said it. She looked like she was starting to cry too. If only they'd been left alone they'd have both sobbed and then said sorry and they'd have a big hug and the barney would be over.

Bruce didn't understand. 'Don't you dare call your mother a slag, Martine!' he called from the bottom of the stairs. 'That's a terrible thing to say. Look, you've made her cry. Aren't you sorry?'

'No, I'm not bogging sorry!' Martine shouted. 'She *is* a slag. And she's made me cry heaps and heaps, but she's never said sorry to *me*. Well, I'm out of here now.'

'Don't go, Martine,' said Mum. 'We'll work things out. I'll look after you.'

'I don't *need* looking after. I'm going back to Bletchworth to live with Tony and his folks. I should have stayed there, like I planned. You made such a fuss about needing me to help with the baby but you won't even let me near him. You're bonkers enough to let daft little Dixie carry him round and change him but you won't let me. Every time I come near you tell me to clear off. So that's exactly what I'm going to do.' She went off to get dressed, and then started rushing round grabbing all her things and stuffing them into carrier bags.

'Mum!' I grabbed hold of her shoulder. Her old kimono split a little at the seam, but she didn't seem to notice. 'Mum, tell Martine about Sundance. Then she'll understand and she'll stay.'

Mum shook her head. She took Sundance in her arms and looked at her helplessly. 'My little boy,' she whispered.

'She's *not!*'

'Did they really all call me a slag back at Bletchworth?' Mum said.

'No! No, of course not. Martine was just being horrible. Don't take any notice of her, Mum. *I* don't care that she called me daft. Maybe we don't *care* that she's going.'

'She's not *really* going, she's just showing off,' said Mum. 'How could she get all the way back to Bletchworth by herself?'

There was a sudden bang down in the hall, like the front door slamming.

'She can't have gone yet! She hasn't got all her stuff. She didn't even say goodbye!' I said.

'She's just trying to scare us. She'll be back in ten minutes,' said Mum.

We waited.

Martine didn't come back.

'I'm going to go looking for her, Mum,' said Jude, stepping into her jeans and shoving on her trainers.

She was gone nearly an hour. She came back on her own.

'I've looked everywhere,' Jude said, almost in tears. 'She could have caught a bus, she could have gone anywhere – I didn't know where to look first. Then I thought about a railway station and I couldn't find it for ages; it's way over the other side of the town. She wasn't there though. I asked if they'd seen her, I asked heaps of people, describing her, but everyone just shrugged. I truly tried, Mum.'

'I know, Jude. Don't fret, darling. Maybe she's just gone round the shops, calming herself down. She'll be back soon, you'll see.'

Mum kept trying to phone Martine's mobile, but it was switched off. Mum left messages. Jude and Rochelle and I left messages. I decided to send a special secret text to Martine telling her why I was the only one Mum let care for Sundance. I was so slow at texting that I'd only got as far as 'I didn't want to tell tales but' when Mum said she wanted to try phoning again so I had to get the text cleared sharpish before she saw it.

We forgot to have breakfast. Bruce lay patiently on the mattress in the living room, but when I went to visit him I could hear his stomach rumbling. He made his own phone call to the lady who worked in his shop. She was called Iris, which seemed a perfect name for a lady who worked with flowers. I didn't like the sound of her all the same.

'Is she pretty, Uncle Bruce?'

'Mmm, I don't know. I suppose so. Though she's no spring chicken.'

'So she's more like a tough old bird?' I said hopefully.

'No, no, she's very genteel.'

'What does that mean? Posh?'

'She's got nice manners. Very ladylike. She's very kind too – she didn't make a fuss when she had to stay late on Saturday and she's going to open the shop for me today. She's being very helpful, my Iris.'

'Is she yours? You said you didn't have a girlfriend!'

'She's not my girlfriend, sweetheart,' said Bruce. 'She wouldn't look twice at a man like me!' He chuckled at the idea and then winced in pain. 'I think I'm going to have to ask Jude to go out to a chemist. Do they let kids buy painkillers? And we're all going to need a spot of lunch – and tea, come to that. Do you think your mum's up to cooking yet?'

'Mum doesn't really cook much. We play parties sometimes and she fixes us little sandwiches and cream buns and ice cream but mostly we just go down the chippy.'

'Then I suppose that's what we'll have to do today. When I can stand up properly I can maybe fix us something.'

'Can you cook then, Uncle Bruce?'

'Nothing too fancy, like, just good plain roasts and curries. I do a very tasty macaroni cheese – your mum might like that.'

'You're a very good catch, Uncle Bruce. Iris is mad not to look at you twice. So, you've never been married?'

'Nope. I don't think I'm the marrying kind, Dixie.'

'Do you think Martine will marry Tony?'

'Maybe,' Bruce said, but he sounded doubtful.

'I'd really love to be a bridesmaid in one of those long sticky-out frocks – pink or peach or lilac. No, *blue*, and then I could carry Bluebell and she'd match. I could have a proper bridesmaid's posy and she could carry a weeny raffia basket of flowers in her beak.'

'Very fetching,' said Bruce.

'Martine will be safe, won't she?'

'Of course she will,' said Bruce.

I knew he couldn't really know but I needed him to tell me even so. Mum had stopped reassuring me. She was starting to panic, phoning and phoning, while she paced around the house in her nightie and kimono.

'Shall we sort out the furniture now you're up, Mum?' said Jude. 'We could get all the boxes unpacked too.'

Mum shook her head distractedly. 'I don't want to make a home here. I hate it. We all hate it. And it's all my fault,' she said, tears brimming. 'It's a filthy dump.'

'It might be a dump but it's not filthy any more,' Bruce muttered. 'I cleaned it up, didn't I?'

'Look at all this scribbling on the walls,' Mum said despairingly.

'A quick coat of paint would soon sort it out,' said Bruce. 'You could get on to the council again. Or if you get no joy you could buy a few cans of paint and get the girls to help you. *I'd* do it if my back was up to it. A spot of white would brighten it up no end.'

'It would still be a dump if you painted it sky-blue pink,'

Mum said. 'If only I'd stayed put. It seemed so clear in the charts. I could see great changes, new opportunities; exciting challenges – but I got it all wrong. I should have stayed in Bletchworth. Even though they all called me a slag. Well. Maybe they're right.'

'You're not a slag, Mum,' said Rochelle.

'Definitely not,' said Jude. 'I'll punch anyone who says you are.'

'Of course you're not,' I said. I paused. 'What exactly *is* a slag?'

'Oh Dixie, you kill me, you really do,' said Mum, shaking her head. 'You girls are just trying to be sweet to me. I don't know why. I'm a terrible mum.'

'*I* don't want to be sweet to you,' said Bruce. 'I'm pretty damn annoyed with you, seeing as I've worked my bottom off for you and your girls and you've barely said thank you. Here I am, stuck on my back like a stag beetle, barely able to move, knowing I've got a flower shop without any flowers when the business is rapidly going down the pan as it is. But I'll tell you one thing. You're not *my* definition of a slag. A slag is a rude, rough woman, Dixie, who's got a bad mouth and rushes round drinking and chatting up all the men, and doesn't give a stuff about her children. Well, I've heard you sounding off, Sue, so I know you swear, and maybe you like a drink and going out clubbing. You've had quite a few boyfriends in your time. Maybe you don't always act like a little lady – though how should I know? But I do know one thing. Slags don't make good mums and you're a lovely mum to your kids.'

Mum blinked at Bruce, looking astonished. Then she pulled her kimono straight and tucked her hair behind her ears. 'Thank you,' she said. 'Thank you for saying that, Bruce. And thank you for all you've done for us. We couldn't have managed without you.'

I wanted this to be like a movie. I wanted Mum and Bruce to look at each other and realize their love. Then they'd fall into each other's arms. Well, Bruce would have to stay put with his bad back but Mum could fall down on top of him. They'd have a long romantic film-star kiss while music played and us girls sang and Bluebell flew over their heads like a little lovebird.

Mum went off to change Sundance, wiping her runny nose with the back of her hand. Bruce shifted uncomfortably on the mattress, groaning and grunting. They weren't really *acting* like movie stars just yet. Maybe I had to give them time.

Jude went out to get aspirins and fish and chips. I went with her because I was scared she might get into a fight. Rochelle came too, on the lookout for Ryan.

We didn't see any boys, or any girls either.

'They're all at school, lucky things,' said Rochelle.

Jude and I looked at her as if she'd gone totally mad.

'Well, it's boring just hanging out at home. I don't want to get behind. Mum should have sorted stuff out, got us enrolled at new schools so we could start today,' she said.

'Oh, like she's really had the time, seeing as she had a baby on Sunday and her eldest daughter ran away from home today,' said Jude.

'Yeah, well, that's not *my* fault, is it? Maybe I'll go and find the school myself. It's in Neptune Street, Ryan said.'

'So that's why you want to go to school! Only remember, you're one of the silly little twerps in Year Eight. He's one of the macho retards in Year Eleven. I bet he won't even look at you in school,' said Jude. 'Well, *I'm* not going near any school. I don't see why we can't simply stay off till the summer holidays and start again in September.'

That seemed like the best idea in the world to me.

15

'You really need me to look after Sundance, don't you, Mum?' I said.

'That's right, darling,' Mum muttered.

'So I can't go to school now, can I?'

'That's right, darling.' Mum repeated.

I knew she wasn't really listening. She was clutching her mobile the way I frequently clutched Bluebell. Still, she'd as good as promised I needn't go to school. I relaxed a little.

Mum stayed strung up all afternoon, phoning Martine's mobile every fifteen minutes. Then she tried a change of tactics. She found out Tony's mum's number and rang her. Her hand was shaking as she dialled the number. She took a deep breath when Tony's mum answered.

'I'm sorry to trouble you, Mrs Wingate,' Mum said very politely, though she was pulling a hideous face as she said it. 'It's Sue here, Sue Diamond.'

She paused. Tony's mum was saying stuff. She didn't

sound as if she was making an effort to be at all polite back.

'Yeah, well, OK, I know we don't see eye to eye on a lot of things,' Mum said, struggling to keep her temper. 'But the thing is, I believe my Martine is coming to see your Tony today. Is she at your place right now? Can I speak to her? *Please?* She's not? You swear that's true? Oh God. Well, will you get her to ring me on my mobile the moment you hear from her?' Mum clicked the phone off and started to cry.

'Where *is* she? What if she's lost somewhere? I'm not even sure how much money she had on her. What if she's mad enough to hitch a lift back home? What if something's happened to her?'

Bruce heard Mum crying and shouted up to her. 'Look, Sue, I'll see if I can get my back strapped up in some way. Then we can go out in the van looking for her.'

He did his best, struggling off the mattress on all fours, but whenever he tried to straighten up he got stuck, hissing with the pain.

'Get back on that mattress, you silly beggar. You couldn't drive for five seconds and you know it,' said Mum. She paused. 'Thanks for the offer though. You're a real mate, Bruce.'

She started pacing up and down again, yawning and sighing and rolling her head around, her fluffy mules going *shuffle-slap* on the bare floorboards. Sundance wailed in my arms, wanting another feed. Mum didn't seem to hear her, though her nightie top got damp. She clutched the mobile, checking it again and again for texts, leaving her own messages.

'Please please phone me, Martine. I'm so scared

something's happened to you. *Phone me!'* Mum begged.

Then the mobile rang and Mum jumped, as if an electric current had sizzled up her arm. 'Martine?' she gasped.

Jude and Rochelle came running. Bruce shuffled back off his mattress to the foot of the stairs. Even Sundance stopped wailing.

'She's with you, Mrs Wingate? Oh, thank God! She met your Tony and walked back from school with him? Right, right, of course. Well, can I speak to her?' Mum paused. 'What do you mean? Of course I need to talk to her! Stop telling me how to behave with my own daughter! I *know* she's in a state. I wonder if *you* know the full story! Now just you let her come to the phone. Please! Oh for God's sake, you interfering old bag, butt out of things and let me speak to Martine!'

Mum stopped. She shook her head. 'She's hung up on me,' she said.

She dialled again. And again and again. 'Now she's not even answering.'

Mum tried Martine's mobile but it was still switched off. '*Why* won't they let her talk to me?' she wept.

'Maybe Martine just doesn't want to talk right now,' said Jude.

'At least you know she's safe, Mum,' said Rochelle. She had her jacket on now and her best suede heels. She slipped out of the room – and a second later I heard the front door slam. Jude looked up, but she just sighed and shook her head.

I hoped Rochelle wasn't going to find this Neptune school. I busied myself with Sundance, trying to show Mum she couldn't possibly manage without me. Sundance kept fussing. She didn't want me rocking her or patting her on the back or whispering into her tiny pink ears. She wanted to be fed.

'Give him here, Dixie,' Mum said wearily.

'I think you really should put him on a bottle, Mum, and then I could feed him all by myself. You wouldn't have to bother,' I suggested.

'Maybe,' said Mum. It was clear she wasn't listening.

'Martine will come back soon, Mum, you'll see,' I said. 'And then when her baby's born I could look after him too. I could be like a childminder to both of them. I could feed them and bath them and take them for walks in a double buggy and—'

'For God's sake, stop nattering, Dixie, you're driving me daft,' Mum said. 'Go and play and leave me in peace.'

I marched out of her room. 'I was only trying to *help*,' I said to Jude.

'I know, babe.' Jude was putting her own hoodie jacket on.

'Are you going out too?' I asked.

'Oh yeah, I've got a hot date in McDonald's with a guy with a diamond earring – *not!*' said Jude.

'You're not going to get in any more fights, are you?'

'Don't worry, I'm fully trained in all the martial arts by our chum Kung Fu Brucie,' said Jude.

'Less of the cheek, girl,' Bruce called from his mattress. 'I might be an old crock with a dodgy back but I could take you on any day of the week. You stay here and look after your little sister, do you hear me?'

'Yes, Bruce, I hear you,' said Jude, but she went straight out the front door.

'Don't you girls *ever* do as you're told?' Bruce asked.

I thought about it. 'Jude doesn't. Or Rochelle. Or Martine. But *I* do. Sometimes,' I said. 'Can I get you anything, Uncle Bruce? Cup of tea?'

'No thanks, Dixie. It's such a struggle to get to the flipping toilet I'd better severely limit my liquid intake, sweetheart. But you could turn the telly on for me if you like. I got it working before I did my back in.'

'You've got *everything* working, Uncle Bruce.'

'Except myself! That's a good little lass.'

'Any special channel?'

'Afternoon telly's all a bit rubbish,' said Bruce, as I flicked through the channels. 'Hang on, is that woman doing flower arranging? I'd better watch it. Iris hasn't got much clue – she just dumps each bunch in a vase, willy-nilly. I can't say I'm much cop at it either. It was always Mum's department until she got poorly. She'd got her Interflora and all sorts.'

'My mum's ace at arranging flowers,' I said.

We both looked at the flowers Bruce had brought us. The roses were arranged in the rosy china milk jug and sugar bowl, the freesias were clustered in the coffee pot, and the tall lilies were in water in the metal wastepaper bin.

'Well, she's certainly unconventional in her approach,' said Bruce.

'We haven't got any vases, see. People don't usually give us flowers.'

'I'll send you flowers when I'm on my feet again, Dixie. Flowers every week, eh? That'll make your boyfriends jealous.'

'Boyfriends!' I said, giggling.

'We could maybe start taming that jungle out the back too, plant your own flowers, eh?'

'But could we keep some of it like a jungle so I can play there?' I said.

I left Bruce to his flower-arranging programme and went out into the back garden. I felt for Bluebell. She was a bit bent over and squashed from staying shoved up my cardie sleeve for so long. I groomed her carefully, tickling her under her beak until her head stopped lolling and she started cheeping cheerily.

It was windy out in the garden. The long grass rippled like green waves. I played that I was sailing a ship in a storm, and Bluebell was a seagull flying ahead, showing me the way across the seven seas. After a year and a day's long sailing I sighted dry land at last. The seagull circled my ship three times in farewell and then flew away back to sea . . . and I stuffed Bluebell back up my sleeve because I'd got to the Great Wall of China at the end.

I leaped up and hauled myself up onto the top of the rough bricks. I sat there, peering over the alleyway into Mary's back garden. She wasn't on the swing today. She was just standing still in the garden, head bent, sucking her thumb.

'Hey, Mary!'

She smiled when she saw me, put her finger to her lips and peered round cautiously. Then she ran towards her gate.

I jumped down from the wall and ran to meet her. She was in her school clothes: a little grey pinafore skirt and a dazzlingly white shirt. She had matching bright white socks and big brown shiny sandals.

'Are you all right, Mary? Did you choke on those horrid crusts?'

'I was a bit sick.'

'No wonder! Your mum's so horrid to you. I hate her.'

'Ssh!' Mary whispered, looking shocked.

'Where's your mum now?'

'She's doing this big spring clean. I've got to play by myself until tea time.'

'I'll come and play with you.'

'She might hear us! She says you're not to come again. She says you're . . . dirty and rough.'

'I *am* dirty, sort of, but I'm not a *bit* rough,' I said. 'Everyone says I'm much too soft.'

'I'm sorry,' said Mary anxiously.

'No, it's OK. I wouldn't mind being rough. Anyway, how about you coming to play in *my* garden?'

'Mummy wouldn't let me.'

'She won't find out! Come on. I'll help you over the wall.'

'But I'll get all dirty.'

'No you won't. Look.' I stuck Bluebell in my teeth and shrugged off my cardigan. 'I'll drape it over the top and then you won't even touch the wall. Come on, Mary.'

'What if Mummy comes to see what I'm doing?'

'You can always pretend you were playing Hide and Seek. And if you're gone a long time your mum will get really worried and think something's happened to you. Then she'll be so pleased to see you safe she'll give you a big hug and forget to be cross.'

Mary looked at me pityingly. 'Mummy doesn't ever forget to be cross,' she said.

'Well. OK. Maybe you'd better not then. I don't want to get you into trouble.'

Mary thought about it. 'I'm already in trouble,' she said. 'I'll come, Dixie. I so want to see your house and what your bedroom's like.'

'I haven't really got a *proper* bedroom yet,' I warned her. 'Maybe we can pretend one?'

Mary looked baffled, but nodded happily. She carefully unlatched her gate. The spring was stiff and she scraped her hand, but she didn't flinch. Her little fingers were still red-raw at the tips.

'Why are you in trouble, Mary?'

'Mummy checked my bedroom when I was at school and she said it was an untidy disgrace. She said I didn't deserve to have such lovely toys if I couldn't look after them. She found my teddy under my bed and now she's thrown him away because she says he's all dirty and I'd catch germs off him.'

'She won't have *really* thrown him away.'

'She did! She put him in the dustbin and she tipped tea bags and milk and potato peel all over him so he's all spoilt now,' said Mary, sniffling.

'I think your mum should be shoved in the dustbin, she's so mean to you,' I said. 'Why didn't you tell your dad?'

'He's not home till I'm in bed. And when I've tried to tell him stuff Mummy says I'm telling silly stories to get attention. Mummy always twists things round. She'll say I threw my teddy away myself.'

'Still, maybe your dad will get you a new teddy?' I said, helping Mary up onto the wall. 'That's it, sit on my cardie. It's easy-peasy. Hang on, I'll climb up too. Let me get down the other side first, then you can jump into my arms.'

I swung myself up and over quickly. Mary clung fear-
fully to my cardigan on top of the wall.

'It looks a long way down,' she said.

'That's just because you're so little. It's all right, I
promise you. You just have to give a little jump and I'll
catch you.'

'I can't! I'll fall. Oh Dixie, I'm stuck.'

'No, you're not. Don't cry. Just jump. Look, Bluebell
will help you.'

I stood on tiptoe and held her out to Mary. She grabbed
her and clutched her against her chest.

'There! That's it, hold her tight. Now, all you have to
do is jump into the air and Bluebell will flap her wings
and you'll both fly straight into my arms. Just try it!'

Mary tried. She jumped into the air, clutching
Bluebell, and I caught them both. They knocked me over
onto my bottom but the grass was so thick it was like
a cushion and we rolled around in a giggly heap until
Mary started fussing about her clothes getting dirty.

She stood up, carefully brushing herself down. I helped
her pull little bits of grass out of her hair. She smiled
up at me.

'You're so kind to me, Dixie. I wish you were my sister.'

'I wish you were my sister too, Mary. I'd swap you
with Rochelle any day of the week! Yes, you come and
be a Diamond girl with us.'

'I wish I could,' said Mary. 'But I can't, can I?'

'Don't you worry, Mary,' I made Bluebell say. 'Any time
you want to come and play with Dixie just hold me tight
and I'll fly you there quick as a wink.'

She flew round and round her head while Mary
laughed and tried to catch her. When Mary started to

grab a little desperately I made Bluebell slow right down and give her an affectionate peck on her nose.

'She's tickling!' said Mary. 'The grass is tickling too!'

'Well, we're in the jungle, aren't we, so what do you expect? Let's look for animals, eh?'

Mary looked nervous, but nodded.

'Look over there, behind that bush!' I whispered. 'See the lions? What about that big fierce one with the mane? Let's hope he stays asleep! Watch out if he wakes up, he might be hungry.'

Mary peered at the old doormat I was pointing at. 'You can't have a real lion in your garden,' she said, but she gripped my hand tightly.

'I've got a whole *pride* of lions! There's a mother lion, see – she's with her little cubs. Look, they're having a pretend fight. Aren't they cute?' I pointed at an upended shopping trolley.

Mary blinked several times, waiting for the lions to materialize.

'What's that trumpeting sound? Oh, elephants! See their great flappy ears? Shall we give them a bun?' I showed her a broken umbrella caught in a tree. I reached up to feed the 'elephants' and Mary copied me, though she looked baffled.

'Is this a jungle, Dixie, or is it a garden?'

'Well, it's a jungle now. But maybe when his back gets better my Uncle Bruce will turn it into a real garden. Do you want to come and meet him?'

'I've got an uncle. And an auntie. They took me to Alton Towers and we went on scary rides and I screamed and screamed. It was my best day ever but I ate too much ice cream and I was sick in my bed,' said Mary.

'I bet that annoyed your mum,' I said.

I led Mary through the back door. She stared all round the kitchen, looking astonished.

'Where are all your units?' she asked.

'We haven't got any. Come on through.' I knocked at the living-room door politely. 'Hey, Uncle Bruce, can we come in? I've brought my friend Mary to meet you.'

'That's nice, dear. Of course you can come in. It's your house, sweetheart, not mine.'

I led Mary in and out the furniture towards the mattress. She peered around, looking dazed. She jumped when she saw Bruce flat out on the mattress.

'How do you do, Mary?' said Bruce. 'Please excuse my looking such a sight. I'm a bit of an old crock at the moment as I've done my back in.'

I squatted at the edge of Bruce's mattress. Mary huddled up beside me. Bruce tried hard but she wouldn't say a word to him.

'You're not very chatty, are you, Mary?' said Bruce.

'Never mind. I chat enough for both of us, Uncle Bruce,' I said. 'Do you want me to change channels on the television for you? We're going to play now.'

'Yes, I think I'll watch a spot of *Richard and Judy*,' said Uncle Bruce. 'I feel terrible hogging your mum's mattress and your mum's telly. Ask her if she'd like the television upstairs. I'm sure Jude could carry it up for her.'

I took Mary out into the hall. 'He's lovely, isn't he, my Uncle Bruce?'

'Is that a living room or a bedroom?' Mary asked.

'Well, it's kind of an everything room at the moment. We're not sorted out yet because Mum's just had the baby. I'll show you Sundance. I'm allowed to look after her.' I clapped my hand over my mouth, hoping Mum hadn't heard.

'I thought Sundance was a baby boy,' said Mary.

'He is. Well. For the moment.' I put my mouth very close to Mary's ear. 'But he might turn into a girl soon.'

Mary nodded. She seemed to be getting used to extraordinary things.

'We'll take a peep,' I said.

But as we went upstairs I could hear Mum talking in her bedroom. She was leaving another phone message for Martine. It sounded as if she was crying.

'She's a bit upset just now,' I whispered to Mary. 'We'll leave her in peace, eh? Come on, we'll go in my bedroom.'

Mary looked at the bare floorboards and the cardboard boxes. She walked round them warily as if she thought they might be jungle animals too. She sat on the very edge of the bed, dangling her legs. 'This is your bedroom, Dixie?'

'I know it's not very clean and tidy. I bet your bedroom's ever so pretty. But my Uncle Bruce is going to paint it for me when his back is better. And perhaps we'll get some new furniture. Jude and I want bunk beds. This bed's all rickety because we used to play trampolines.'

'Trampolines?'

'Yeah, haven't you ever played it?'

I jumped up on the bed and bounced up and down. Mary stared at me, shocked.

'Won't your mum mind you jumping on the furniture?'

'Well, the springs are mostly bust now, so it doesn't really matter,' I said. 'Come on, you have a bounce too.'

I pulled Mary up, holding her by her wrists because

I didn't want to rub her sore fingers. I gave a big bounce. Mary squealed, nearly wobbling over, but then she steadied herself.

'Shouldn't I take my shoes off?'

'Never mind! Come on, bounce!'

I leaped up and down wildly. Mary gave teeny little bobs, still squealing.

'Are you OK? We'll stop if you like.'

'No, it's *lovely*!' Mary gasped.

We bounced until we were both bright red in the face. One of Mary's plaits started unravelling.

'Oh, my hair!' she said, stopping still, nearly toppling both of us. She grabbed at her trailing ribbon, looking terrified.

'I'll do it up for you. I'm good at hairdressing,' I said.

I did my best. I couldn't get the plait *exactly* even and the ribbon didn't look quite right either, but I hoped it would do. Mary seemed worried about it so I showed her all the things in my cardboard box to distract her. She fingered my old animals politely, but their missing limbs obviously alarmed her. She stroked the cover of my fairy story book but didn't open it. She liked my fibre-tip pen set though, unbuttoning the plastic wallet and rearranging them into rainbow order.

'I used to have a big set of pens but I kept going over the lines in my colouring books and spoilt them.'

'You can colour in my fairy story book if you like,' I said.

'You can't colour in *story* books!'

'Of course you can. Look, here's the little mermaid story. You can colour the mermaid if you like. I'll do all the fish.'

We rested the fairy story book on the bed and knelt in front of it. Mary took the yellow pen and started colouring the mermaid's hair very carefully, curl by curl. She was concentrating so fiercely her tongue stuck out. I leaned over and coloured one fish purple with red lips and a bright pink tail, another one jade-green with royal-blue stripes and a third ruby-red with emerald eyes and golden fins.

'Fish aren't really that colour. They're grey,' said Mary.

'Yes, but grey's *boring*. And these are fairy fish so they can be any colour they want. "Bubble bubble, we want to be *bright*, please, Dixie," they're saying. And your mermaid's asking, "What colour tail am I getting, Mary? Orange? Purple? Navy blue?"'

'You're getting a green tail, little mermaid,' said Mary. 'And if you don't behave I shall smack it very very hard and lock you up in your bedroom, young lady.'

I looked at Mary. 'Your little mermaid lives in an underwater palace. If she gets locked up she just swims straight out the window, see?'

Mary finished her mermaid, I finished my fish, and we used both blue fibre tips to colour in the sea, Mary one side of the page, me the other. Mary's hand relaxed a little and she scribbled freely, her arm moving up and down. Then she stopped and saw her sleeve. She gave a little moan.

'Look!' she whispered.

There was a faint blue smudge on her white cuff.

'That's nothing. Don't worry, it'll come out in the wash.'

Mary kept looking at her sleeve. She tried licking the blue but it just spread a little.

'Your mum won't notice,' I said.

'She will,' said Mary. 'She'll smack me and put me to bed. And I haven't got my teddy any more. I can't sleep without him.'

I thought hard about it as I took Mary back through the jungle garden and helped her up and over the wall.

'Can I hold Bluebell to make me fly?'

'Yep! Tell you what, you can take her with you and cuddle up with her tonight. She'll sing you to sleep, you'll see.'

'You're giving me *Bluebell*?'

'I'm not giving her to you, I'm just lending her for tonight, OK? But hide her from your mum! I don't want Bluebell chucked in the dustbin too.'

Mary clutched Bluebell tightly. We slipped across the alleyway. I helped Mary struggle with the gate latch. I was scared her mother would suddenly come running and pounce on her, but the garden stayed empty.

Mary sat on her swing. She made Bluebell wave her wing at me. Then she quickly stuffed her right down the neck of her school blouse, out of sight.

<h1 style="text-align:center">16</h1>

My cardie sleeve felt horribly empty without Bluebell inside, pecking companionably at my wrist. I wasn't sure Mary would be able to hide her. I kept thinking of her mother hurling her into the dustbin. I saw her buried under smelly rubbish, unable to flap her wings and fly away. I saw the dustbin men arriving in the morning and emptying her into their terrible stinking lorry. I thought of her being driven away to the rotting wilderness of the tip. I knew I'd never find her again.

I wanted to tell Mum. She was huddled up with Sundance and didn't want to be bothered.

'But Mum, I'm *miserable*,' I whined.

'So am I, Dixie, so that makes two of us,' said Mum, pulling away from me.

'Can you just tell me what time dustmen come in the mornings?'

'Can I *what*?'

'Mum, I've done something silly,' I said.

'Well, go and tell Jude, Dixie. Or your blooming Uncle

Bruce. Leave me in peace now, for pity's sake.'

I trailed away, holding my fist in a bird shape, trying to make my fingernail feel like a beak. Mum started whispering to Sundance when I was out the room. I hovered outside the door, listening.

'We won't take any notice, will we, darling? We just need to be together, you and me, my beautiful boy. Yes, you're a smashing little chap. Look at your big blue eyes! My, you're going to turn all the girls' heads, but you'll still have time for your old mum, won't you, sweetheart? You won't run away, you won't get into trouble. You'll stay my special blue-eyed boy, my Sundance.'

'You're *mad*, Mum,' I said loudly, and stomped downstairs.

I said it because I felt lonely and left out. Then I started to worry that it was true. Mum wasn't just pretending. She was trying to make it real. What if she never admitted to anyone that Sundance was a girl? Would Sundance have to have short hair and clump around in trousers and Timberlands for the rest of her life?

I went looking for Jude, but she was still out. So was Rochelle.

'Where have those girls got to?' said Bruce. 'I want to send one of them out for our supper. What do you fancy, Dixie?'

'I'm not really hungry, Uncle Bruce,' I said. 'Maybe some chips?'

'Chips! You need feeding up with some proper nosh.'

'I *like* chips. Mum always lets me have chips.' I paused. 'Uncle Bruce . . . do you think my mum is a little bit nuts?'

'Yes,' said Bruce. 'You're all nuts. I've never met a family like you Diamonds. You're all barmy, the lot of you.'

'Are you joking, Uncle Bruce?'

'Maybe,' he said.

There was a knock at the door.

'Let's hope it's Jude,' said Bruce. 'I'm not sure Princess Roxy-Poxy will deign to go down to the chip shop for us. Call out before opening the door, Dixie.'

'Who's there?' I called.

'It's your loveliest sister,' Rochelle trilled back.

'*Not!*' I said.

Rochelle was actually *acting* like a lovely sister. She'd bought a big bag of chips out of her own pocket money. She thrust them at me. 'Share them round, Dixie. Don't worry about me, I've already eaten.'

'With Ryan?'

'Yep! I met him from school.' Rochelle clasped her hands and twirled round theatrically. 'I was a bit worried about it. I didn't want him to think I was being too pushy. I thought I'd just saunter past. I decided if he was with all his mates I'd just give a little wave and walk on. He *was* with a great big bunch of them, those hoodie guys, though they look so different in their school uniform. Even the huge fat guy just looked like Mr Blobby in his school blazer. Anyway, Ryan came right over the moment he saw me. The other guys hung around for a bit, saying stuff. Some of the other boys from their school went by and wolf-whistled. It was dead embarrassing!' Rochelle boasted, dancing round the hall. 'I told Ryan I thought I'd be going to his school so he took me inside and I met the headteacher. He seems OK, and so I got our names down to go to the school, Jude and me. There didn't seem much point mentioning Martine as she's not going to be here.'

'You didn't mention me, did you?' I said.

'Well, I did say I had this younger sister still at primary and they said you'll have to be registered separately. Mum will have to take you.'

'Don't tell her,' I said quickly, starting to tuck into the chips.

Rochelle wasn't even listening. She was too busy telling about Ryan.

'He understands *totally* what it's like for me, Dixie. He's part of this big family too, nearly all boys, and his mum can't really cope. Two of his big brothers have got kids already, one's inside and another is a junkie, but he isn't getting into any of that. He's clever, Dixie. He's got it all sorted; he's going to keep his nose clean. He's going to work hard and get good grades in all his exams. He doesn't seem to mind that *I'm* clever too – he doesn't see it as a threat. He likes it that I can't seem to help getting a lot of attention.'

Rochelle was showing off so much I felt like throwing her chips at her. She whirled round and round, swinging her hips.

'No wonder you get lots of attention from those boys. It's because that skirt's so short your knickers show,' I said.

'Ryan says he really likes the way I dress. He loves it that I wear girly clothes. He says I've got a figure to be proud of. Ryan says he's never been that interested in having a girlfriend before, he says nearly all the girls on the estate act like slags, but I'm different. Ryan says he's getting a bit fed up trailing round with that gang of right losers. He's growing out of that stage. Ryan says . . . Ryan says . . . Ryan says . . .'

My head was buzzing with Ryan this, Ryan that. I went to offer Bruce some chips. Rochelle carried on telling the empty hall what Ryan said.

Bruce raised his eyebrows at me. 'I wish her Ryan would keep his mouth shut,' he whispered. 'Do you think we could press her mute button, Dixie?'

We both chuckled, though poor Bruce jarred his back and groaned.

We heard other voices as well as Rochelle's. Boys' voices, out in the street. Lots of shouting. Then we heard Jude shouting too.

'Oh no,' I said, hurtling out the room.

'No, Dixie! Don't you get involved! Look, I'll come – if I can just roll off the blooming mattress.'

I couldn't wait for him. I flung open the front door. I stopped dead, my mouth open.

It was the same gang, Ryan's mates, the Hoodies and Big Fat Guy, but Ryan wasn't with them. Jude was in the middle of them, holding up her fists, looking like she was about to swing a punch at Big Fat Guy, but she seemed to be stuck in slow motion. Then Big Fat Guy brought his arm up – s-l-o-w-l-y – and blocked Jude's punch.

'Yeah!' said Jude.

'Cool!' said Big Fat Guy.

They both laughed. The Hoodies laughed too and Jude slapped all their hands in high-five acknowledgement. She did an elaborate high-*ten* with the Big Fat Guy.

'See you around, cool dude Jude,' he said.

Jude came bounding into the house, grinning all over

her face. 'Shut your mouth, Dixie, or you'll catch a fly,' she said.

'I – am – gobsmacked!' I gasped. 'You haven't gone and got yourself a boyfriend too, have you, Jude?'

'No way!' said Jude. 'Are you totally off your trolley, little Dixie?'

'You're the girl slapping palms with that great big berk and all his gang. I thought you all hated each other.'

'Yeah, but their Neptune gang hate the Top Floor guys in Mercury even more. They heard I'd been in a fight with them, and that I'd punched their leader so hard he was knocked unconscious.'

'You didn't say you'd done that!' I stared at Jude. She grew upwards and outwards before my eyes, muscles bulging, fists encased in boxing gloves.

Jude put her head close. 'Don't tell, Dixie, but they've got it all wrong! I did swing a punch at the Top Floor guy but I don't think it hurt him one bit. He lunged forward to get me, I dodged and ran like hell, he ran after me down the stairs and tripped. *That's* how he hurt himself. But the Neptune guys all think I took on the hardest kid on the whole of the Planet Estate, so they kind of look up to me now. They wanted to know my fighting secrets so I waffled on a bit about Wing Chun. They think I'm an expert now, so I'll have to get old Bruce to teach me loads more.'

'Then you'll have to be very kind and considerate to old Bruce,' he called from the living room. 'And right this minute you can come and take supper orders. Maybe we'd better eat Chinese, seeing as you're so interested in oriental martial arts.'

'Your wish is my command, Wise Master,' said Jude.

She was in such a good mood that she didn't moan when I cuddled up really close that night.

'What's up, Dixie? You're a bit mopey. And how come I'm not being pecked to death tonight? Where's the bird?'

'I've lent Bluebell to Mary, to help her get to sleep.'

'That's very sweet of you, but duff move. Now *you're* lying wide awake – and so am I!' said Jude. 'You need old Bluebell more than Mary. She's probably got heaps more toys than you have.'

'Yes, but her mum takes them away. She's so mean to her. I'm not supposed to tell – Mary begged me not to, but I can't help it, I feel I'll burst if I don't. Her mum's so cruel and horrible.'

'Are you sure? I thought she seemed quite nice. She's too posh but she can't help that. So what does she do that's so horrible?'

'She threw Mary's teddy away. She said it was dirty.'

'Dixie, *lots* of mums do that. Most mums would have made you chuck Bluebell out *years* ago – *and* that awful old cardigan.'

'It's *not* awful! It's beautiful. And it still fits perfectly.'

'Yeah, yeah, whatever!'

'Mary's mum has done other stuff too. She forced her to eat her crusts and she cut her nails right back so they hurt.'

'Lots of kids have to eat up all their food and have their nails cut. It's no big deal.'

'Mary's mum says she's dirty when she's clean as clean.'

'That's not really being cruel, though. It's not like she's beating her or starving her or locking her up in a cupboard.'

'She does smack her.'

'Mum used to smack me when I was little, when I got into fights. It didn't stop me though. She doesn't smack me now because she knows I could smack her back, harder!'

'You wouldn't though, would you? Jude . . . I'm worried about Mum too.'

'You're a right old worrypot, Dixie. Look, there's only one thing you've got to worry about right this minute. If you don't curl up and go straight to sleep and let me have a decent kip too I'm going to tip you right out of this bed, OK? So night-night.'

I curled up and kept very still, pretending to be asleep. Jude started breathing heavily, her arms and legs twitching as if she was fighting in her dreams. I didn't go to sleep for a long long time. Then I woke early, listening anxiously for the sound of dustcarts.

Sundance woke early too and kept fussing, not feeding properly.

'Please try, little darling,' Mum kept whispering.

'Maybe he's not hungry, Mum?' I suggested.

'No, he's starving, poor little mite. It's all my fault. I'm all tense with worrying about Martine. I've lost her, Dixie.'

'No you haven't, Mum.'

'She's not coming back. She obviously hates me. I don't blame her. I'm a useless mum. I can't look after any of you. I can't even feed my own baby.'

I didn't know what to do. Mum wouldn't stop crying. Sundance cried too, and I couldn't quieten her.

'God, what a racket!' said Rochelle. 'I'm out of here. I'm going to the school over on Neptune to see if they'll let me sit in on some lessons.' She was all dressed up in her shortest skirt and highest heels.

'What *kind* of lessons?' said Jude. 'How to be a mini-hooker? You can't wear that to school! Put your Bletchworth uniform on.'

'But I'm seeing Ryan. I can't let him see me in that old uniform, I look like a silly little kid.'

'Rochelle, guess what: you *are* a silly little kid,' I said.

'Shut up, you silly little squirt. It's a waste of time *you* going to school, you're so braindead you just get to sit by yourself and do colouring. But you'll come with me, won't you, Jude?'

'What? I've got better things to do than try to blag my way into a new school!' she said. 'You're crazy, Rochelle.'

Jude wanted to spend the day with Bruce, having intensive Wing Chun instruction. Bruce's back was a little better, so he could just about hobble around downstairs, though he was still happiest flat out on the mattress. Jude stood by his head, barely able to move for furniture, adopting the front fighting stance and practising an arrow punch.

I joined in for a bit but it was so boring doing it over and over fifty times that I wandered off by myself.

I trekked through the jungle, heaved myself up onto the wall and stared at Mary's empty garden. I couldn't see a sign of any dustbins. They must be kept round the front of the house.

I jumped down off the wall and walked along the alleyway to the end, wishing I had Jude with me. I made it along Mary's street and stood outside her house for several minutes, wondering if I dared creep up the crazy paving and search for their dustbin.

I had my hand on the front gate when I saw Mary's mother spraying the living-room window and then wiping away at it vigorously, even though the glass was already sparkling. I ducked down and ran bent over until I was sure I was out of sight. I didn't feel safe until I was in my own back garden. I didn't know why I felt so frightened. Jude had made me wonder if she was really as scary as Mary made out. Even if she *was*, she couldn't smack *me* or make *me* eat crusts or cut *my* nails or throw out anything of *mine*. She wouldn't really throw Bluebell into the bin too, would she? It seemed so awful she could do all these things to Mary, just because she was her daughter.

I decided I should get Bruce to teach little Mary Wing Chun too. Then every time her mum made a move Mary could block it. If her mum got really mad Mary could spring into action and whirl her way over her head. Then Mary and Bluebell and I could whiz off to Planet Dixie where no one could pick on us.

I so so so hoped Bluebell was safe and sound. I kept automatically reaching for her up my sleeve. I did a lot of colouring in my fairy story book to keep my hands busy but it still seemed endless hours until lunch time, and then the whole afternoon stretched out for ever.

I was waiting on the wall, watching out for Mary, from three o'clock onwards. I knew I was much too early to see Mary but I couldn't help it. I fidgeted so much on the rough bricks that I rubbed my legs raw. I heard a clock chime quarter past, half past, quarter to four, then four.

Mary *must* be home from school by now. Why didn't she come out in the garden to see me? She knew I'd be wanting to see her. Couldn't she get away from her mother? Had she taken Bluebell to school with her, hidden in her school bag? Or had she tried to hide her in her bedroom? I thought of her mum shaking the duvet, pounding the pillows, opening every drawer and cupboard.

I was starting to think I'd never ever see Bluebell again.

'Fly home to me!' I whispered, and I looked up. There was Mary at the upstairs window, her palms on the glass. She was standing right up on the windowsill in her bare feet. I saw a flash of dusty blue in one of her hands.

I jumped down off the wall, rushed across the alleyway and climbed right over her gate. I crept across the velvety grass, nearer and nearer.

Mary stayed spread-eagled against the glass, wearing a long white gown. She was mouthing something. I couldn't see her lips clearly enough to work out what she was saying. I shook my head. She tried again and again.

I got as near as I dared, almost up to the house, craning my neck up at Mary. It looked as if she was crying. I realized the long white gown was her nightie. She was obviously in trouble again and had been sent to bed.

She waved Bluebell to show me she was safe. She held her to the glass, as if willing her to fly straight through. 'It's OK!' I mouthed. 'You keep her for a bit.'

Mary tried to reply. I still didn't understand, but I nodded my head to encourage her. Mary still looked very anxious but she smiled bravely. She started fiddling with the catch on her window. I stared up at her, wondering if she was going to try to throw Bluebell down to me.

'Don't, Mary! Careful! No, it's too dangerous!' I called.

Mary jerked the window right open. She leaned forward and put one foot out of the window, right onto the ledge. She was still clutching Bluebell in one hand.

Then I remembered my own words.

All you have to do is jump into the air and Bluebell will flap her wings and you'll both fly into my arms.

'No! No, Mary, don't!' I screamed.

It was too late.

Mary leaped into the air, her white nightie billowing. For a split second I thought she might really fly. Then she tumbled downwards.

I ran to catch her, my arms out.

Then she fell on me with hammer-blow force and the ground opened up and swallowed both of us.

17

I could smell lilies, lots and lots of lilies, so overwhelming they were sickly sweet. I felt their soft velvety petals stroking my cheeks. My head throbbed, my legs felt weirdly heavy and my whole body ached. I tried to roll over but I couldn't move. I was held rigidly in some sort of container, trapped.

I opened my eyes and there was Dad leaning over me. My dad, who never came to see me. My dad, the embalmer.

I was lying in a bed of flowers and I couldn't move, as if I was in a coffin.

My whole family were gathered all around me. Mum, Martine holding little Sundance, Jude, Rochelle and Uncle Bruce. They were all gazing down at me, and everyone was crying.

'Am I *dead*?' I whispered.

'Oh Dixie, what are you *like*?' Mum said. She was laughing shakily but tears were pouring down her cheeks.

'What's happened?' I said.

'You've been in an accident, lovey. Don't you remember?' said Mum. 'You're in hospital now.'

'What did I do?'

'You went round to Mary's house,' said Jude.

Then I remembered. I saw Mary flying through the air like a little white angel. 'Mary!' I said, and I started sobbing.

'Hush now, darling, it's all right. Don't cry so. You've been such a good brave little girl,' Mum said, rubbing her face against mine.

'I'm bad, I'm terrible, it's all my fault,' I wept. 'I told Mary to jump off the wall and then she tried to jump right out the window and I couldn't stop her. Where is she? Is Mary all right? Oh please, tell me, is *Mary* dead?'

'Ssh, ssh, Mary's fine. There's barely a scratch on her, I promise you,' said Mum. 'Look, my darling, here's Bluebell. Mary said you had to have her back.' Mum tucked Bluebell in beside me, her beak nuzzling my neck.

'Where is Mary? Is she really really all right? Can I see her?'

'Well, her dad's taken her home now, pet,' said Mum.

'Her mum will be so cross with her!'

'No, no. I had a long talk with her dad. Don't you worry about Mary now. She's going to be staying with her auntie and uncle while her mum's in hospital.'

'Did her mum get hurt too?'

'No, but she's . . . she's not very well.'

'She's gone off her head and now she's in the loony ward. *I* think they should lock her up and throw away the key,' said Rochelle.

'Now, we shouldn't judge. Mary's dad said she's always

been bothered with her nerves, right from when Mary was born. It started off as post-natal depression.'

'That's just a fancy excuse. *As if!*'

'That's *enough*, Rochelle. It can make you do all sorts,' said Mum. 'You don't know the half of it.'

'I know she was being horrible to Mary. Why didn't you *tell*, Dixie?' said Rochelle.

'She did tell. She told me. And I just told her to shut up and go to sleep,' said Jude. 'It's *my* fault.'

'It's not anybody's fault. Don't be so silly, girls,' said Mum. 'And Dixie, you must feel very very proud. You saved little Mary's life running forward like that.'

'I caught her?'

'Yes, you did, you mad little darling. You took the full force of her weight. You were knocked unconscious.'

'Yeah, you've been in a coma, Dixie, and we were all starting to think you'd never come round and you'd stay a total vegetable,' said Rochelle. 'I felt so bad because I've always made out you were braindead anyway—'

'Rochelle!' said Martine.

'Yeah, but I vowed I'd look after you and nurse you and do everything for you if you really *were* braindead,' said Rochelle.

'I'm glad I'm not,' I said.

I tried to wriggle up on my pillows to look at everyone properly but my legs wouldn't budge. 'I can't move!' I said. I suddenly panicked. 'Can't I walk? Will I have to have a wheelchair?'

'No, darling, you're not paralysed – feel,' said Mum. 'Wiggle your toes! That's my girl. You can't move your legs because they're strung up in plaster, see?'

Mum slid her arm behind my head and helped me

peer at my new weird white legs, my pink toes sticking out of each end.

'They feel so *heavy*,' I said.

'Still, think how hard you'll be able to stamp on Rochelle if she gets on your nerves,' said Jude.

'How long have I got to keep the plaster on?'

'We're not quite sure yet, darling. Both your legs are quite badly broken. But you'll mend, sweetheart, and you'll be running around all over the place before long, you'll see. I'm going to stay with you while you're in hospital, with little Sundance. I'm going to have a mattress in a side ward – it's all arranged. I'm getting used to camping on blooming mattresses! But by the time you come home, Dixie, we're going to have your own bed all sorted, and we'll paint up your bedroom and make it as pretty as a picture. You'll help me, won't you, guys?'

'Of *course* we will,' said Bruce.

'If I can manage it,' said my dad.

'And I'm going to come visiting, Dixie. I'm going to be able to feed *you* little treats and help *you* drink out of a straw now,' said Bruce.

'Is your back better now, Uncle Bruce?'

'Yes, little 'un, it's on the mend now.'

'So are you going back to your own house now?'

'Well, I'm dashing backwards and forwards in the van. I'll have to see to the shop some of the time, but I'll come every weekend and I'll bring you lots more flowers. The nurses thought you were a little film star with all my lilies.'

'I'll come and see you too, little Dixie,' said my dad. 'But maybe not *every* weekend. I could bring my other daughters too. Would you like to meet your sisters?'

'I think she's got more than enough sisters as it is,' said Mum.

'How come *you're* here, Martine?' I asked.

'I came the minute I heard about you, Dixie – don't be daft,' said Martine.

'Is Tony here too?'

'No. We've had a row, him and me – *and* his mum. I got sick of them saying stuff, badmouthing us Diamonds. Bogging cheek! I'm not going back to Bletchworth. I'm staying with you lot.'

'My Ryan's here,' said Rochelle proudly. 'He's outside because hospitals give him the heebie-jeebies, but I could call him if you like. He wants to say hello.'

'No more visitors, please!' said a big friendly nurse, bustling up beside my bed. She put a thermometer in my mouth. 'Hello, my lovely. So you've woken up, have you! I think you might get a bit over-excited with all this crowd round your bed. How about just the immediate family staying?'

'We're all immediate family,' said Mum. 'I'm her mum.'

'I'm her dad.'

'I'm her uncle.'

'Her *favourite* uncle,' said Jude. 'And I'm her sister.'

'I'm her big sister,' said Martine.

'Well, I'm her sister too,' said Rochelle.

'Goodness, what a lot of sisters,' said the nurse. She looked at Sundance's blue sleeping suit and shawl. She winked at Mum. 'I bet you were glad when you had their little baby brother!'

Mum took a deep breath. 'Not a bit of it,' she said. 'Girls are just as good as boys. *Better*. And the little one isn't a boy at all. I just fancied dressing her in blue because I got a bit bored with all that pink.'

'Mum?' said Jude.

'Oh God, now Mum's gone nuts,' said Rochelle.

'Mum, Sundance is a *boy*,' said Martine.

'Well, I think my little babe's nappy needs changing, so have a quick peep and see if I'm right,' said Mum.

Poor Sundance had everyone peering at her little pink bottom.

'*Why* did you pretend she was a boy, then?' said Jude.

'I told you, she's gone loopy,' Rochelle hissed. 'And Sundance is an even weirder name for a girl.'

'Shut *up*, Rochelle,' said Martine. 'Mum, you said all along you were having a boy. It was all in the stars about your boy.'

'Maybe it's Sundance's *dad* who's the boy,' Bruce muttered.

'You're a much cannier bloke than you look, Bruce,' said Mum. 'I hadn't thought of that! Maybe I *have* got psychic powers after all.'

'I don't get it, Mum,' said Jude.

'I don't get it either, do you, mate?' said my dad to Bruce.

'Sue's a woman who's full of surprises,' said Bruce.

'If that's a nice way of saying I'm off my trolley then I'd have to agree with you,' said Mum. 'I *did* go a bit loopy, Rochelle. I couldn't even tell *you*, Martine. I suppose I didn't dare, because I knew you wouldn't keep it quiet like our Dixie.'

'Dixie *knew*?' said Martine and Jude and Rochelle.

I spat out the thermometer triumphantly. 'I knew right from the start, didn't I, Mum?' I said. 'Mum isn't bonkers. She just pretended a bit, that's all. Because she wanted Sundance to be a boy so much.'

'That's right, my darling. I just wanted to stay in my own private little dream world. But I couldn't. All you girls needed me. It's a drama every day in our blooming household – Rochelle getting a boyfriend, Jude getting into fights, our Martine getting pregnant. Then little Dixie damn near died and I was shocked back into my senses. About bogging time and all!'

'Well, Mum, maybe *my* baby will be a boy. Your first grandson, eh?' said Martine.

'We'll love it whether it's a boy or a girl,' said Mum. 'But let's hope it's another girl. Then we'll all be Diamond girls together.'

ABOUT THE AUTHOR

JACQUELINE WILSON is one of Britain's most outstanding writers for young readers. She is the most borrowed author from British libraries and has sold over 20 million books in this country. As a child, she always wanted to be a writer and wrote her first 'novel' when she was nine, filling countless exercise books as she grew up. She started work at a publishing company and then went on to work as a journalist on *Jackie* magazine (which was named after her) before turning to writing fiction full-time.

Jacqueline has been honoured with many of the UK's top awards for children's books, including the Guardian Children's Fiction Award, the Smarties Prize, the Red House Book Award and the Children's Book of the Year. She was awarded an OBE in 2002 and is the Children's Laureate for 2005-2007.

ABOUT THE ILLUSTRATOR

NICK SHARRATT knew from an early age that
he wanted to use his drawing skills as his career,
so he went to Manchester Polytechnic to do an
Art Foundation course. He followed this up with
a BA (Hons) in Graphic Design at St Martin's
School of Art in London from 1981-1984.

Since graduating, Nick has been working full-time
as an illustrator for children's books, publishers and
a wide range of magazines. His brilliant illustrations
have brought to life many books, most notably
the titles by Jacqueline Wilson.

Nick also writes books as well as illustrating them.

JACKY DAYDREAM

Jacqueline Wilson -
The Story of Her Childhood

Illustrated by Nick Sharratt

Everybody knows Tracy Beaker, Jacqueline Wilson's best-loved character. But what do they know about the little girl who grew up to become Jacqueline Wilson?

How she played with paper doll like April in *Dustbin Baby*.

How she dealt with an unpredictable father like Prue in *Love Lessons*.

How she chose new toys in Hamleys like Dolphin in *The Illustrated Mum*.

How she sat entrance exams like Ruby in *Double Act*.

But most of all how she loved reading and writing stories. Losing herself in a new world was the best possible way she could think of spending her time. From the very first story she wrote, *Meet the Maggots*, it was clear that this little girl had a very vivid imagination.

Now her fans can discover a little more about Jacky herself in this utterly captivating, charming and poignant memoir.

'Literary superstar' INDEPENDENT

'A brilliant writer of wit and subtlety whose stories are never patronising and are often complex and multi-layered' THE TIMES

DOUBLEDAY
978 0 385 61015 5

LOVE LESSONS

Jacqueline Wilson

*For one mad, magical moment I thought
he was going to kiss me . . .*

Fifteen-year-old Prue and her sister, Grace, have
been educated at home by their controlling, ultra-strict
father all their lives. When Dad is suddenly rushed
to hospital, unable to move or speak, Prue at last
discovers what it's like to have a little freedom.

Sent to school for the first time in years, Prue
finds it unexpectedly difficult to settle in. The only
person she can talk to is her kindly and handsome
young art teacher, Rax. When she starts babysitting for
Rax's children, Prue finds herself longing for the ten
minutes they have alone together as he drives her home.
But she can't act on her secret feelings, can she?

For teenage readers, an absorbing portrait of a forbidden
relationship from bestselling author Jacqueline Wilson.

ISBN: 978 0 385 60836 7

GIRLS IN LOVE
Jacqueline Wilson

REASONS TO READ MY BOOK,
NUMBERS 1 TO 9

1. It's about three girls in Year Nine
2. You can learn all sorts of secrets about me (I'm Ellie)
3. Ditto my best friend Nadine
4. Ditto my equally best friend Magda
5. You can see if your nine all-time heroes/heroines
match up with mine
6. You can squirm at my most embarrassing moments
7. You can have lots of laughs (mostly at me!)
8. You might even cry a bit, too
9. PLUS, you get to find out a lot more about BOYS!

The first of Jacqueline Wilson's fantastic,
best-selling GIRLS books – now with a new
introduction by Jacqueline herself!

ISBN: 978 0 552 55733 7

DUSTBIN BABY
Jacqueline Wilson

April Showers.
That's my nickname now. It's better than April Fool.
It's much, much better than Dustbin Baby.

April started out in life as a dustbin baby,
unceremoniously abandoned in a rubbish bin
on 1st April. Now she's turned fourteen,
April is determined to find out where she came from.
If only she could remember her birth mother
or, maybe, even find her . . .

It's not going to be easy but can April
discover who she really is?

This unforgettable story for older readers now includes
an extra-special new introduction by Jacqueline.

ISBN: 978 0 552 55611 8

THE ILLUSTRATED MUM
Jacqueline Wilson

*Star used to love Marigold, love me, love our life together.
We three were the colourful ones, like the glowing pictures
inked all over Marigold . . .*

Covered from head to foot with glorious tattoos,
Marigold is the brightest, most beautiful mother
in the world. That's what Dolphin thinks (she just
wishes her beautiful mum wouldn't stay out
partying all night or go weird now and then).

Her older sister, Star, isn't so sure any more.
She loves Marigold too, but sometimes she just
can't help wishing she were more normal . . .

This powerful and memorable tale for older readers now
includes a special new introduction from Jacqueline Wilson.

**WINNER OF THE GUARDIAN
CHILDREN'S FICTION AWARD**

ISBN: 978 0 440 86781 4